THE

TESTIMONY OF THE ROCKS

SPHENOPTERIS AFFINIS.
A Fern of the Lower Coal Measures
(*Restored.*)

Hugh Miller

THE

TESTIMONY OF THE ROCKS;

OR,

GEOLOGY IN ITS BEARINGS

ON THE

TWO THEOLOGIES, NATURAL AND REVEALED.

BY

HUGH MILLER,

AUTHOR OF "THE OLD RED SANDSTONE,"
"FOOTPRINTS OF THE CREATOR," ETC. ETC.

"Thou shalt be in league with the stones of the field"—JOB

MMI

Originally published
MDCCCLVII
IN EDINBURGH:
THOMAS CONSTABLE & CO.; SHEPHERD & ELLIOT.
LONDON: HAMILTON, ADAMS & CO.

This edition published in MMI
by St Matthew Publishing Ltd,
24 Geldart Street, Cambridge CB1 2LX UK
Tel: +44 (0)1223 504871 Fax: +44 (0)1223 512304
Email: PF.SMP@dial.pipex.com

ISBN 1901546 1 1 X

The text is based on the first edition published in 1857. Not having access to the
original diagrams and sketches meant that the plates have been reproduced from
the printed versions of 1881 & 1857. The quality of these was somewhat variable.
In some instances, where the scale was indicated (for example "nat. size."),
reproductions are not entirely accurate to scale. Where this has occurred a '~' is
added. Figs. 1., 4. & 53. have been redrawn.

Front cover: view of Cromarty from a watercolour by Peter Foster 1936
Back top left: Hugh Miller from a engraving by Bell based on a
photograph by Tunny.
Back bottom right: Hugh Miller's Cottage owned by the National Trust for
Scotland, used with permission.

Printed and bound by Printcorp.
18, Kuprevitcha Street, Minsk, Belarus, 220141.
Or. 0179. Qty 2 000 cps.
Tel: +375 172 64 75 13

CONTENTS.

Editor's PREFACE

'Those who do not learn from history are doomed to repeat it.'

Hugh Miller was an extraordinary man. Brought up in humble circumstances, he was the son of a sea captain who was drowned at sea when Hugh was only five. He struggled to gain a living as a stonemason, working his apprenticeship among the bothy teams of the day. It was an exceedingly tough life which might have broken many a man. His own account in *My Schools and Schoolmasters* paints a vivid picture of the poverty and exploitation of this time.

But it was his commitment to the Christian faith and his passion for geology which brought him fame (but hardly fortune)—a fame he neither sought nor much enjoyed. He was converted while working in Edinburgh and later became the first and most famous editor of the Free Church paper, *The Witness*. At the same time his reputation as a geologist was growing. His discoveries and meticulous studies of the fossils of the old Red Sandstone were pioneering achievements, and he is remembered with awe to this day by those who study in this field.

As an evangelical Christian, he was keenly aware of the debates about geology and the Bible and he entered the fray armed with a deep knowledge of both. What makes him stand out, from a Christian perspective, was his clear grasp of the essential question: does the Bible provide revealed science or are its purposes otherwise directed? Lecture Tenth, *The Discoverable and the Revealed*, provides his answer to that important question. Lecture Eleventh, *The geology of the anti-geologists*, was his reply to those critics who had sniped at him for many years. What is really startling is the nature of their attacks on geology. Their arguments are still being reproduced (in very thin disguise) in some modern religious books—particularly (but not exclusively) those from the United States. Hugh Miller's answers still have clarity and truth for today's debate.

Miller's style, once one becomes acclimatised to the rhetorical prose (in its proper sense), is clear, sparkling and at times humorous—he is a natural writer as his many other books show. One word which he uses could, in today's climate, be miscontrued: the word 'occult'. He uses it in its simple sense of hidden and is not suggesting any sinister implication.

In this edition I have published the text of the lectures, including Miller's own footnotes, as they were in the edition of 1857 (though in some lectures I have numbered the notes and listed them at the end of the lecture). I have not added any footnotes of my own.

Lastly it must be said that Miller was also a man of his time (as we are of ours). He inevitably accepted some of the views of his own day (expressed in Lecture Sixth) which we would regard as erroneous and inappropriate.

Revd. Philip Foster
Cambridge MMI

INTRODUCTION

Dr. Michael A. Taylor

In 1830, while still an obscure stonemason, Hugh Miller discovered the fossils of strange and then unknown fishes in the Old Red Sandstone near Cromarty. These (and other finds beginning to emerge from the Old Red elsewhere) were some of the oldest vertebrate fossils then known (we'd now say of Devonian age, around 380 million years old). Miller's finds came to the notice of the geological community and were studied by Louis Agassiz, the foremost authority on fossil fishes. Even after his move to Edinburgh, Miller continued to build up his palæontological collection, both from the Edinburgh area, and from finds on his annual holiday exploring the fossil sites of Scotland. His collection, now in the National Museums of Scotland, comprises a major contribution to the nation's geological heritage, as do the sites he discovered.

Miller made his biggest contributions to geology in two ways: by his fossil finds and his studies of them, but also, and in my view ultimately more importantly, as one of the élite Victorian natural history authors, the David Attenboroughs and Stephen Jay Goulds of that pre-television era. The foundation of Miller's success was that he was a good and lively writer on exciting new finds, and on the pleasures of searching for fossils in beautiful countryside, and for this he continues to be dearly loved, especially by geologists. This might seem surprising to a new reader, as yet unattuned to the Victorian tempo of Miller's prose, which is in fact brilliantly successful when spoken: Miller's writing evokes lamplit evenings reading aloud around the fire. But there was more to his success. He was deeply imbued with Protestantism and more specifically Calvinism, and had impeccable moral credentials as the editor of the Free Church newspaper, *The Witness*. He thus helped to reassure Scots Presbyterians and, more widely, Protestants in the English-speaking world that the practice of geology was not merely compatible with a devout Christian life but positively beneficial in a way that perfectly met the spirit of the time.

Miller presented geology as an improving recreation. A long-standing Protestant tradition espoused natural theology—the study of the Lord through his works: the beauty and also the creatively functional design of flowers, insects, fossils and so on. This encouraged many men of the cloth on both sides of the Border to take up natural history as a recreation. Together with the real physical and mental labour involved, it also confirmed the serious collecting of fossils as a constructive recreation rather than an example of the idle accumulation and dilettante timewasting deeply repugnant to the Calvinist Protestant psyche. A healthy outdoor activity, geology could be done cheaply, so it was highly relevant to Miller's warmly espoused aim of the broadest education for the most people, especially the ordinary working classes.

Miller tackled the question of evolution, the great issue of the time which drew journalists to the honeypot of controversy. Fellow Edinburgh journalist Robert Chambers published the anonymous and controversially pro-evolutionary *Vestiges of the Natural History of Creation* in 1844, and Miller himself wrote *Footprints of the Creator* in response in 1849. Although no biblical literalist in the modern sense, Miller saw evolutionary theories, in their blurring of the line between irresponsible beast and responsible human, as a direct attack on Christian revelation, notably the creation of humanity, the Fall and Redemption. These theories threatened to decoy individuals from their hope of salvation, and to undermine the Christian foundations of society whose own hope, Miller and his ilk believed, lay in the Godly Commonwealth of the Scots Reformers. In this, Miller was perhaps less self-serving than those upper-class élite geologists who saw evolution as a French revolutionary concept threatening the overturn of society through its attack on the Established Churches.

Although no political radical, still less a socialist, Miller did condemn the abuse of power and property, as when he bitterly lacerated the landowners in the controversies over rural poverty and the Highland clearances. His apparent racism in the sixth lecture is, as Philip Foster points out in the Preface, partly because he was a man of his time. But the conceptual background was quite different. His acceptance that, for example, certain Irish peasants were hereditarily degenerate may reflect the genetic theories of his age which espoused the inheritance of acquired characteristics within the limits of each species. Although now known to be wrong, this is an understandable conclusion—it is commonplace that undernourished and badly housed parents give rise to physically, emotionally and mentally stunted children, indeed an 'inheritance' if not a genetic one. And if the Irish, and the Gaelic Highlanders, were degraded, Miller was in no doubt that the blame often lay in their landlords' outrageous abuse of these rational beings responsible before their Maker.

It is critical to appreciate that *Testimony*, technical as it may seem today, was written for a general audience. Miller was, effectively, reviewing current science. Generally, he is not to be credited with originating the information, any more than the typical modern presenter did the scientific research for the facts presented in a TV documentary. Miller was, however, apt to bring in his own finds and assessments where relevant, in his engagingly autobiographical style (another element in his success).

Miller could be described as the last of the 'scriptural geologists' for mixing science and religion in his books. By the 1850s, such mixtures had no place in formal scientific debate. It would have been inconceivable for the Geological Society of London, for instance, to debate the possible mechanism of Noah's Flood, however geologically reasonable by the standards of the time. Certainly, also, *Testimony* resembles a collection of sermons, though this simply reflects its genesis in lecture scripts. But to criticise Miller for mixing science and religion in much of his writing (ignoring for the moment the actual conclusions reached) would, I think, misunderstand the target audience, which was the general public.

Miller was therefore a competent journalist writing for a public hungry for news of the latest discoveries. The public wanted, and still want, to know not only the newest scientific facts but also their wider ethical, philosophical and religious implications, and how they fitted into their understanding of life and the universe. Given that Calvinist Presbyterianism was the foundation of the world view of the vast majority of mid-19th century Scots, Miller's well-known personal religious commitment, if anything, lent strength and authority to his writing. *Testimony* is as much part of the mid-19th century as, say, the Darwinian evolutionist Thomas Henry Huxley's own essays—some revealingly called *Lay Sermons*—were of the later 19th century, and Stephen Jay Gould's *Wonderful Life* or Richard Dawkins' *The Selfish Gene* are of our time.

In *Testimony* and elsewhere, Miller rightly enough rejected Lamarckian evolution because the fossil record did not show the simple progress which Lamarck and Chambers imputed to it—and there wasn't any other kind of evolution. But after Miller died (in 1856) everything changed with the publication of Charles Darwin's *Origin of Species* in 1859. Darwin provided credible and cogent scientific evidence for evolution forcing many, sometimes unwillingly, to accept it. He also described a mechanism for evolution in natural selection, which is not inherently progressive: Miller's scientific objection therefore fell.

However, until misunderstandings of genetics and of the age of the earth were cleared up at the start of the 20th century, there were persisting doubts about natural selection as the mechanism of evolution. No doubt this is one reason why the clergy, including Free Churchmen and Presbyterians, often had little problem accepting evolution, contrary to popular image. Given the range of views prevalent amongst scientists, some crediting a kind of Lamarckian mechanism while accepting Darwin's evidence for evolution itself, the average cleric could quite easily find a comfortable position (especially if the subtler implications were not always understood). But whatever its detailed mechanism, the clergy increasingly accepted that evolution was the proximate method by which Creation played out its story, one subtly more worthy of the divine wisdom and power than one requiring the creation of every species individually. As Miller's favourite poet Cowper said,

> God moves in a mysterious way
> His wonders to perform ...

So, if Miller had lived a little longer, how would he have reacted to the *Origin of Species* (1859), and to the other books which Darwin was to write, notably on the origin of humanity? At the very least, he would have attacked the crucial problems with all the energy and intellectual criticism he could bring to bear. Miller was always one to think for himself, and to accept compelling evidence from the natural world: after all, this was the essence of natural theology for him. I think that he would have appreciated the strength of Darwin's evidence for evolution. As for its mechanism, he would undoubtedly have grasped the implications of Darwin's replacement of divinely creative design by natural selection as the origin of biological adaptation, and the *Origin's* tactfully brief assertion that 'Light will be thrown on the origin of man'. Miller, so taken with the aesthetic beauty of living things, would also have noted Darwin's devastatingly effective later analyses of sexual selection, to explain the beauty of birds, and the interrelationships of plants and their pollinating insects, with its insight into the beauty of flowers. But what conclusions Miller would have reached, we cannot know.

A note on the science and terminology of *Testimony of the Rocks*

Geology, palæontology and biology have advanced greatly since 1857. This is, in one sense, plainly irrelevant when considering Miller's point of view, and his analysis of the basic problems of religion and science. No attempt has therefore been made to bring *Testimony* up to date—indeed, part of its fascination lies in its insight into the then current understanding of geology. Nevertheless, some pitfalls may trap the unwary modern reader.

Firstly come the sometimes different readings based on the then available evidence. For instance, Miller refers to the Old Red Sandstone as a marine deposit whereas it is now interpreted as a freshwater lake deposit. Plate tectonics have moved England from a more tropical climate to a cooler one, hence fossils of tropical plants near London. Coelacanths are still living; cetiosaurs were terrestrial dinosaurs not marine reptiles; and so on. Notably, *Testimony* catches a transition in thought about the confusing and complex landscape phenomena which we now ascribe to the huge icecaps of the Ice Ages and the resulting fluctuations in sea levels. Although the new idea of small local mountain glaciers was increasingly accepted, larger scale phenomena were still attributed to the older theory of major inundations by the sea (and Miller is wrong in stating that raised beaches run all around the shores of Great Britain and Ireland: they only occur in certain areas, notably including Edinburgh and his Cromarty birthplace). But these 'errors' simply reflect the state of 1850s science, and are no reflection on Miller. One point that might nevertheless cause real confusion is Miller's apparent allusion to the 'impression of a human hand' from Triassic rocks (p. 171). Miller is not suggesting that it actually *is* a pre-Adamite hand print; it was the *Chirotherium* footprint, famous for its resemblance to a hand print. We now know it was made by a reptile.

Secondly, terminology has changed. For instance, Miller's 'reptiles' are, for instance, what we call amphibians and reptiles; his 'Lias' rocks are, as with us, of early Jurassic age, but Miller apparently uses 'Oolitic' to denote rocks of middle and later Jurassic age, and his 'Silurian' roughly corresponds to our modern Silurian, Ordovician and Cambrian periods together; and so on. What we call 'evolution' was apt to be called 'development', a word we now use for ontogeny, or the embryonic development of an egg into an individual; this last was sometimes confusingly called evolution!

Finally, one or two of Miller's scientific concepts are so obsolete that they simply do not translate across to any modern concept, such as his apparent racism which I have already discussed. When he makes approving mention of 'relations', 'gradations', and even 'missing links', he is talking not about evolution, but its complete opposite, the emphatically static Great Chain of Being, in what must have been one of its last mainstream public airings in science-writing before Darwin. This traditional way of ordering the diversity and plenitude of divine creation arranged inanimate objects at the bottom, moving to simpler living things, then more complex ones, and finally humanity, with God at the apex.

Department of Geology and Zoology,
National Museums of Scotland.
Edinburgh MMI

To

JAMES MILLER, ESQ. F.R.S.E.,

PROFESSOR OF SURGERY IN THE UNIVERSITY OF EDINBURGH.

MY DEAR SIR,

This volume is chiefly taken up in answering, to the best of its author's knowledge and ability, the various questions which the old theology of Scotland has been asking for the last few years of the newest of the sciences. Will you pardon me the liberty I take in dedicating it to you? In compliance with the peculiar demand of the time, that what a man knows of science or of art he should freely communicate to his neighbours, we took the field nearly together as popular lecturers, and have at least so far resembled each other in our measure of success, that the same class of censors have been severe upon both. For while you have been condemned as a physiologist for asserting that the human framework, when fairly wrought during the week, is greatly the better for the rest of the Sabbath, I have been described by the same pen as one of the wretched class of persons who teach, that geology, rightly understood, does not conflict with revelation. Besides, I owe it to your kindness that, when set aside by the indisposition which renders it doubtful whether I shall ever again address a popular audience, you enabled me creditably to fulfil one of my engagements by reading for me in public two of the following discourses, and by doing them an amount of justice on that occasion which could never have been done them by their author. Further, your kind attentions and advice during the crisis of my illness were certainly every way suited to remind me of those so gratefully acknowledged by the wit of the last century, when he bethought him of

"kind Arbuthnot's aid,

Who knew his art, but not his trade."

And so, though the old style of dedication has been long out of fashion, I avail myself of the opportunity it affords me of expressing my entire concurrence in your physiological views, my heartfelt gratitude for your good services and friendship, and my sincere respect for the disinterested part you have taken in the important work of elevating and informing your humbler countryfolk,—while at the same time maintaining professionally, with Simpson and with Goodsir, the reputation of that school of anatomy and medicine for which the Scottish capital has been long so famous.

I am,

MY DEAR SIR,

With sincere respect and regard,

Yours affectionately,

HUGH MILLER.

TO THE READER

OF the twelve following Lectures, four (the First, Second, Fifth, and Sixth) were delivered before the members of the Edinburgh Philosophical Institution (1852 and 1855). One (the Third) was read at Exeter Hall before the Young Men's Christian Association (1854), and the substance of two of the others (the Eleventh and Twelfth) at Glasgow, before the Geological Section of the British Association (1855). Of the five others,—written mainly to complete and impart a character of unity to the volume of which they form a part,—only three (the Fourth, Seventh, and Eighth) were addressed *viva voce* to popular audiences. The Third Lecture was published both in this country and America, and translated into some of the Continental languages. The rest now appear in print for the first time. Though their writer has had certainly no reason to complain of the measure of favour with which the read or spoken ones have been received, they are perhaps all better adapted for perusal in the closet than for delivery in the public hall or lecture-room; while the two concluding Lectures are mayhap suited to interest only geologists who, having already acquainted themselves with the generally-ascertained facts of their science, are curious to cultivate a further knowledge with such new facts as in the course of discovery are from time to time added to the common fund. In such of the following Lectures as deal with but the established geologic phenomena, and owe whatever little merit they may possess to the inferences drawn from these, or to the conclusions based upon them, most of the figured illustrations, though not all, will be recognised as familiar: in the two concluding Lectures, on the contrary, they will be found to be almost entirely new. They are contributions, representative of the patient gleanings of years, to the geologic records of Scotland; and exhibit, in a more or less perfect state, no inconsiderable portion of all the forms yet detected in the rocks of her earlier Palæozoic and Secondary floras.

It will be seen that I adopt, in my Third and Fourth Lectures, that scheme of reconciliation between the Geologic and Mosaic Records which accepts the six days of creation as vastly extended periods; and I have been reminded by a somewhat captious critic that I once held a very different view, and twitted with what he terms inconsistency. I certainly did once believe with Chalmers and with Buckland that the six days were simply natural days of twenty-four hours each,—that they had compressed the entire work of the existing creation,—and that the latest of the geologic ages was separated by a great chaotic gap from our own. My labours at the time as a practical geologist had been very much restricted to the Palæozoic and Secondary rocks, more especially to the Old Red and Carboniferous Systems of the one division, and the Oolitic System of the other; and the long extinct organisms which I found in them certainly did not conflict with the view of Chalmers. All I found necessary at the time to the work of reconciliation was some scheme that would permit me to assign to the earth a high antiquity, and to regard it as the scene of many succeeding creations. During the last nine years, however, I have spent a few weeks every autumn in exploring the later formations, and acquainting myself with their peculiar organisms. I have traced them upwards from the raised beaches and old coast lines of the human period, to the brick clays, Clyde beds, and drift and boulder deposits of the Pleistocene era, and again from these, with the help of museums and collections, up through the mammaliferous crag of England, to its Red and its Coral crags. And the conclusion at which I have been compelled to arrive is, that for many long ages ere man was ushered into being, not a few of his humbler contemporaries of the fields and woods enjoyed life in their present haunts, and that for thousands of years anterior to even *their* appearance, many of the existing molluscs lived in our seas. That *day* during which the present creation came into being, and in which God, when he had made "the beast of the earth after his kind, and the cattle after their kind," at length terminated the work by moulding a creature in His own image, to whom he gave dominion over them all, was not a brief period of a few hours' duration, but extended over mayhap millenniums of centuries. No blank chaotic gap of death and darkness separated the creation to which man belongs from that of the old extinct elephant, hippopotamus, and hyæna; for familiar animals such as the red deer, the roe, the fox, the wildcat, and the badger, lived throughout the period which connected their times with our own; and so I have been compelled to hold, that the days of creation were not natural, but prophetic days, and stretched far back into the bygone eternity. After in some degree committing myself to the other side, I have yielded to evidence which I found it impossible to resist; and such in this matter has been my *inconsistency*,—an inconsistency of which the world has furnished examples in all the sciences, and will, I trust, in its onward progress, continue to furnish many more.

NOTE

Few readers of this volume, it is presumed, need to be informed that its lamented author spent a part of the last day of his life in correcting the proofs of its concluding pages. Nothing remained but to give their proper place and name to some of the woodcuts. This has been done by Professor Fleming, to whom Mrs Miller takes the present opportunity of tendering her grateful acknowledgment for this and other offices of kindness so willingly and effectively rendered to the family of his departed friend.

March 1857.

LECTURE FIRST.

THE PALÆONTOLOGICAL HISTORY OF PLANTS.

PALÆONTOLOGY, or the science of ancient organisms, deals, as its subject, with all the plants and animals of all the geologic periods. It bears nearly the same sort of relation to the *physical* history of the past that biography does to the civil and political history of the past. For just as a complete biographic system would include every name known to the historian, a complete palæontologic system would include every fossil known to the geologist. It enumerates and describes all the organic existences of all the extinct creations,—all the existences, too, of the present creation that occur in the fossil or semi-fossil form; and, thus co-extensive in space with the earth's surface,—nay, greatly more than co-extensive with the earth's surface,—for in the vast hieroglyphic record which our globe composes, page lies beneath page, and inscription covers over inscription,—co-extensive, too, in time with every period in the terrestrial history since being first began upon our planet,—it presents to the student a theme so vast and multifarious, that it might seem but the result, on his part, of a proper modesty, conscious of the limited range of his powers, and of the brief and fleeting term of his life, were he to despair of being ever able effectually to grapple with it. "But," to borrow from one of the most ingenious of our Scottish metaphysicians, "in this, as in other instances in which nature has given us difficulties with which to cope, she has not left us to be wholly overcome." "If," says Dr Thomas Brown, in his remarks on the classifying principle,—"if she has placed us in a labyrinth, she has at the same time furnished us with a clue which may guide us, not, indeed, through all its dark and intricate windings, but through those broad paths which conduct us into day. The single power by which we discover resemblance or relation in general is a sufficient aid to us in the perplexity or confusion of our first attempts at arrangement. It begins by converting thousands, and more than thousands, into one; and, reducing in the same manner the numbers thus formed, it arrives at last at the few distinctive characters of those great comprehensive tribes on which it ceases to operate, because there is nothing left to oppress the memory or the understanding."

But is this all? Can the palæontologist but say that that classifying principle which in every other department of science yields such assistance to the memory is also of use in his, or but urge that it enables him to sort and arrange his facts, and that, by converting one idea into the type and examplar of many resembling ones, it imparts to him an ability of carrying not inadequate conceptions of the mighty whole in his mind? If this were all, you might well ask, Why obtrude upon us, in connection with *your* special science, a common semi-metaphysical idea, equally applicable to all the sciences,—in especial, for example, to that botany which is the science of existing plants, and to that zoology which is the science of existing animals? Nay, I reply, but it is not all. I refer to this classifying principle because, while it exists in relation to all other sciences as a principle—to use the words of the metaphysician just quoted—"given to us by nature,"—as a principle of *the mind within,*—it exists in palæontological science as a principle of nature itself,—as a principle palpably *external to the mind.* It is a marvellous fact, whose full meaning we can as yet but imperfectly comprehend, that myriads of ages ere there existed a human mind, well nigh the same principles of classification now developed by man's intellect in our better treatises of zoology and botany were developed on this earth by the successive geologic periods; and that the by-past productions of our planet, animal and vegetable, were chrono-logically arranged in its history, according to the same laws of thought which impart regularity and order to the works of the later naturalists and phytologists.

I need scarce say how slow and interrupted in both provinces the course of arrangement has been, or how often succeeding writers have had to undo what their predecessors had done, only to have their own classifications set aside by *their* successors in turn. At length, however, when the work appears to be wellnigh completed, a new science has arisen, which presents us with a very wonderful means of testing it. Cowley, in his too eulogistic ode to Hobbes,—smit by the singular ingenuity of the philosophic infidel, and unable to look through his sophisms to the consequences which they involved,—could say, in addressing him, that

"only God could know
Whether the fair idea he did show
Agreed entirely with God's own or no,"

and he then not very wisely added,—

"This I dare boldly tell,—
'Tis so like truth, 'twill serve our turn as well."

We now know, however, that no mere resemblance to truth will for any considerable length of time serve its turn. It is because the resemblances have, like those of Hobbes, been mere resemblances, that so much time and labour have had to be wasted by the pioneers of science in their removal; and, now that a wonderful opportunity has occurred of comparing, in this matter of classification, the human with the Divine idea,—the idea embodied by the zoologists and botanists in their respective systems, with the idea embodied by the Creator of all in geologic history,—we cannot perhaps do better, in entering upon our subject, than to glance briefly at the great features in which God's order of classification, as developed in Palæontology, agrees with the order in which man has at length learned to range the living productions, plant and animal, by which he is surrounded, and of which he himself forms the most remarkable portion. In an age in which a class of writers not without their influence in the world of letters would fain repudiate every argument derived from *design*, and denounce all who hold with Paley and Chalmers as anthropomorphists, that labour to create for themselves a god of their own type and form, it may be not altogether unprofitable to contemplate the wonderful parallelism which exists between the Divine and human systems of classification, and—remembering that the geologists who have discovered the one had no hand in assisting the naturalists and phytologists who framed the other—soberly to inquire whether we have not a new argument in the fact for an identity in constitution and quality of the Divine and human minds,—not a mere fanciful identity, the result of a disposition on the part of man to imagine to himself a God bearing his own likeness, but an identity real and actual, and the result of that creative act by which God formed man in his own image.

The study of plants and animals seems to have been a favourite one with thoughtful men in every age of the world. According to the Psalmist, these great "works of the Lord are sought out of all them that have pleasure therein." The Book of Job, probably the oldest writing in existence, is full of vivid descriptions of the wild denizens of the flood and desert; and it is expressly recorded of the wise old king, that he "spake of trees, from the cedar tree that is in Lebanon, even unto the hyssop that springeth out of the wall; and also of beasts, and of fowl, and of creeping things, and of fishes." Solomon was a zoologist and botanist; and there is palpable classification in the manner in which his studies are described. It is a law of the human mind, as has been already said, that wherever a large stock of facts are acquired, the classifying principle steps in to arrange them. "Even the rudest wanderer in the fields," says Dr Brown, "finds that the profusion of blossoms around him—in the greater number of which he is able himself to discover many striking resemblances—may be reduced to some order of arrangement." But for many centuries this arranging faculty laboured to but little purpose. As specimens of the strange classification that continued to obtain down till comparatively modern times, let us select that of two works which, from the literary celebrity of their authors, still possess a classical standing in letters,—Cowley's "Treatise on Plants," and Goldsmith's "History of the Earth and Animated Nature." The plants we find arranged by the poet on the simple but very inadequate principle of size and show. Herbs are placed first, as lowest and least conspicuous in the scale; then flowers; and finally trees. Among the herbs, at least two of the ferns—the true maidenhair and the spleenwort—are assigned places among plants of such high standing as sage, mint, and rosemary; among the flowers, monocotyledons such as the iris, the tulip, and the lily, appear among dicotyledons such as the rose, the violet, the sunflower, and the auricula; and among trees we find the palms placed between the plum and the olive; and the yew, the fir, and the juniper, flanked on the one side by the box and the holly, and on the other by the oak. Such, in treating of plants, was the classification adopted by one of the most learned of English poets in the year 1657.

Nor was Goldsmith, who wrote more than a century later, much more fortunate in dealing with the animal kingdom. Buffon had already published his great work; and even he could bethink him of no better mode of dividing his animals than into wild and tame. And in Goldsmith, who adopted, in treating of the mammals, a similar principle, we find the fishes and molluscs placed in advance of the sauroid, ophidian, and batrachian reptiles,—the whale united in close relationship to the sharks and rays,—animals of the tortoise kind classed among animals of the lobster kind, and both among shell fish, such as the snail, the nautilus, and the oyster. And yet Goldsmith was engaged on his work little more than eighty years ago. In fine, the true principles of classification in the animal kingdom are of well nigh as recent development as geologic science itself, and not greatly more ancient in even the *vegetable* kingdom. It would, of course, be wholly out of place to attempt giving a minute history here of the progress of arrangement in either department; but it can scarce be held that the natural system of plants was other than very incomplete previous to 1789, when Jussieu first enunciated his scheme of classification; nor did it receive its later improvements until so late as 1846, when, after the publication in succession of the schemes of De Candolle and Endlicher, Lindley communicated his finished system to the world. And there certainly existed no even tolerably perfect system of zoology until 1816, when the "Animal Kingdom" of Cuvier appeared. Later naturalists, such as Agassiz in his own special department, the history of fishes, and Professor Owen in the invertebrate divisions, have improved on the classification of even the great Frenchman; but for purposes of comparison between the scheme developed in geologic history and that at length elaborated by the human mind, the system of Cuvier will be found, for at least our present purpose; sufficiently complete. And in tracing through time the course of the vegetable kingdom, let us adopt, as our standard to measure it by, the system of Lindley.

Commencing at the bottom of the scale, we find the Thallogens, or flowerless plants which lack proper stems and leaves,—a class which includes all the algæ. Next succeed the Acrogens, or flowerless plants that possess both stems and leaves, such as the ferns and their allies. Next, omitting an inconspicuous class, represented by but a few parasitical plants incapable of preservation as fossils, come the Endogens,—monocotyledonous flowering plants, that include the palms, the liliaceæ, and several other families, all characterized by the parallel venation of their leaves. Next, omitting another inconspicuous tribe, there follows a very important class,—the Gymnogens,—polycotyledonous trees, represented by the coniferæ and cycadaceæ. And last of all come the dicotyledonous Exogens,—a class to which all our fruit, and what are known as our "forest trees," belong, with a vastly preponderating majority of the herbs and flowers that impart fertility and beauty to our gardens and meadows. This last class, though but one, now occupies much greater space in the vegetable kingdom than all the others united.

Such is the arrangement of Lindley, or rather an arrangement the slow growth of ages, to which this distinguished botanist has given the last finishing touches. And let us now mark how closely it resembles the geologic arrangement as developed in the successive stages of the earth's history.

The most ancient period of whose organisms any trace remains in the rock seems to have been, prevailingly at least, a period of Thallogens. We must of course take into account the fact, that it has yielded no land plants, and that the sea is everywhere now, as of old, the great habitat of the algæ,—one of the four great orders into which the Thallogens are divided. There appear no traces of a terrestrial vegetation until we reach the uppermost beds of the Upper Silurian System. But, account for the fact as we may, it is at least worthy of notice that, alike in the systems of our botanists

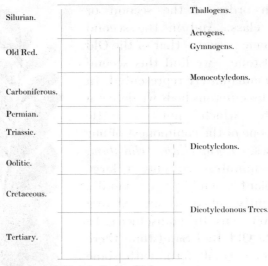

Fig. 1.*

Silurian.

Thallogens.

Acrogens.

Old Red.

Gymnogens.

Monocotyledons.

Carboniferous.

Permian.

Triassic.

Dicotyledons.

Oolitic.

Cretaceous.

Dicotyledonous Trees.

Tertiary.

Geologic [Thal. Ac. Gy. Mon. Dic.] arrangement.
Lindley's [Thal. Ac. Mon. Gy. Dic.] arrangement.

THE GENEALOGY OF PLANTS.

and in the chronological arrangements of our geologists, the first or introductory class which occurs in the ascending order is this humble thallogenic class. There is some trace in the Lower Silurians of Scotland of a vegetable structure which may have belonged to one of the humbler Endogens, of which at least a single genus, the *Zosteraceæ*, still exists in salt water; but the trace is faint and doubtful; and, even were it established, it would form merely a solitary exception to the general evidence that the first-known period of vegetable existence was a period of Thallogens. The terrestrial remains of the Upper Silurians of England, the oldest yet known, consist chiefly of spore-like bodies, which belonged,

* The horizontal lines in this diagram indicate the divisions of the various geologic systems; the vertical lines, the sweep of the various classes or sub-classes of plants across the geologic scale, with, so far as has yet been ascertained, the place of their first appearance in creation; while the double line of type below shows in what degree the order of their occurrence agrees with the arrangement of the botanist. The single point

says Dr Hooker, to Lycopod- iaceæ,—an order of the second or acrogenic class. And in the second great geologic period,—that of the Old Red Sandstone,—we find this second class not inadequately represented. In its lowest fossiliferous beds we detect a Lycopodite which not a little resembles one of the commonest of our club-mosses,—*Lycopodium clavatum*, —with a minute fern and a large striated plant resembling a calamite, and evidently allied to an existing genus of Acrogens, the equisetaceæ. In the Middle Old Red Sandstone there also occurs a small fern, with some trace of a larger; and one of its best preserved vegetable organisms is a lepidodendron,—an extinct ally of the Lycopodiums; while in the upper beds of the system, especially as developed in the south of Ireland, the noble fern known as *Cyclopteris Hibernicus* is very abundant. This fern has been detected also in the Upper Old Red of our own country, mingled with

Fig. 2.

CYCLOPTERIS HIBERNICUS.
(~Nat. Size.)

of difference indicated by the diagram between the order of occurrence and that of arrangement, viz. the transposition of the gymnogenous and monocotyledonous classes, must be regarded as purely provisional. It is definitely ascertained that the Lower Old Red Sandstone has its coniferous wood, but not yet definitely ascertained that it has its true monocotyledonous plants; though indications are not awanting that the latter were introduced upon the scene at least as early as the pines or araucarians; and the chance discovery of some fossil in a sufficiently good state of keeping to determine the point may of course at once re-transpose the transposition, and bring into complete correspondence the geologic and botanic arrangements.

fragments of contemporary calamites. With, however, these earliest plants of the land yet known there occurs a true wood, which belonged, as shown by its structure, to a gymnospermous or polycotyledonous tree, and which we find associated with remains of Coccosteus and Diplacanthus.

Fig. 3.

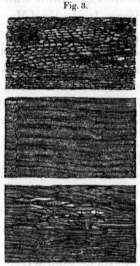

CONIFER OF THE LOWER OLD RED SANDSTONE.
Cromarty.
(Mag. Forty diameters.)

And here let me remark, that the facts of palæontological science compel us to blend, in some degree, with the classification of our modern botanists, that of the botanists of an earlier time. In a passage already quoted Solomon is said to have discoursed of plants, "from the cedar tree that is in Lebanon, to the hyssop that springeth out of the wall,"—from the great tree to the minute herb; and Cowley rose, in his metrical treatise, as has been shown, from descriptions of herbs and flowers to descriptions of fruit and forest trees. And as in every age in which there existed a terrestrial vegetation there seem to have been "trees" as certainly as "herbs," the palæontological botanist finds that he has in consequence to range his classes, not in one series, but in two,—the Gymnogens, or cone-bearing trees, in a line nearly parallel with the Acrogens, or flowerless, spore-bearing herbs. But the arrangement is in no degree the less striking from the circumstance that it is ranged, not in one, but in two lines. It is, however, an untoward arrangement for the purposes of the Lamarckian, whose peculiar hypothesis would imperatively demand, not a double but a single column, in which the ferns and club-mosses would stand far in advance, in point of time, of the Coniferæ. In the Coal Measures, so remarkable for the great luxuriance of their flora, both the Gymnogens and Acrogens are largely developed, with a very puzzling intermediate class, that, while they attained to the size of trees, like the former, retained in a remarkable degree, as in the Lepidodendra and the Calamites, the peculiar features of the latter. And with these there appear, though more sparingly, the Endogens,—monocotyledonous plants, represented by a few palm-like trees (Palmacites), a few date-like fruits (Trigonocarpum), and a few grass-like herbs (Poacites). In the great Secondary division, the true dicotyledonous plants first appear, but, so far as is yet known, no dicotyledonous wood. In the earlier formations of the division a degree of doubt attaches to even the few leaves of this class hitherto detected; but in the Lower Cretaceous strata they become at once unequivocal in their character, and comparatively abundant, both as individuals and species; and in the Tertiary deposits they greatly outnumber all the humbler classes, and appear not only as herbs, but also as great trees. Not, however, until shortly before the introduction of man do some of their highest orders, such as the Rosaceæ, come upon the scene, as plants of that great garden,—including the fields of the agriculturist,—which it has been part of man's set task upon earth to keep and to dress. And such seems to be the order of classification in the vegetable kingdom, as developed in creation, and determined by the geologic periods.

The parallelism which exists between the course of creation as exhibited in the animal kingdom, and the classification of the greatest zoologist of modern times, is perhaps still more remarkable. Cuvier divides all animals into vertebrate and invertebrate; the invertebrates consisting, according to his arrangement, of three great divisions,—mollusca, articulata, and radiata and the vertebrates, of four great classes,—the mammals, the birds, the reptiles, and the fishes. From the lowest zone at which organic remains occur, up till the higher beds of the Lower Silurian System, all the animal remains yet found belong to the invertebrate divisions. The numerous tables of stone which compose the leaves of this first and earliest of the geologic volumes correspond in their contents with that concluding volume of Cuvier's great work in which he deals with the mollusca, articulata, and radiata; with, however, this difference, that the three great divisions, instead of occurring in a continuous series, are ranged, like the terrestrial herbs and trees, in parallel columns. The chain of animal being on its first appearance is, if I may so express myself, a threefold chain;—a fact nicely correspondent with the further fact, that we cannot in the present creation range *serially*, as either higher or lower in the scale, at least two of these divisions,—the mollusca and articulata. In one of the higher beds of the Upper Silurian System,—a bed which borders on the base of the Old Red Sandstone,—the vertebrates make their earliest appearance in their fourth or ichthyic class; and we find ourselves in that volume of the geologic record which corresponds to Cuvier's volume on the fishes. In the many-folded pages of the Old Red Sandstone, till we reach the highest and last, there occur the remains of no other vertebrates than those of this fourth class; but in its uppermost deposits there appear traces of the third or reptilian class; and in passing upwards still, through the Carboniferous, Permian, and Triassic Systems, we find reptiles continuing the master existences of the time. The geologic volume in which these great formations are included corresponds to the Cuvierian one devoted to the Reptilia. Early in the Oolitic System, birds, Cuvier's second class of the vertebrata, make their first appearance, though their remains, like those of birds in the present time, are rare and infrequent; and, for at least the earlier periods of their existence, we know that they were,—that they haunted for food the waters of the period, and waded in their shallows,—only from marks similar to those by which Crusoe became first aware of the visits paid to his island by his savage neighbours,—their footprints, left impressed on the sands over which they stalked of

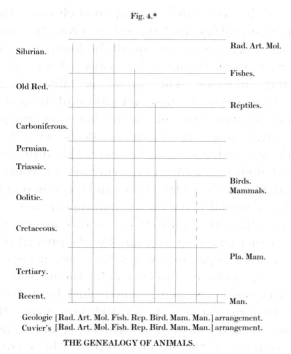

Fig. 4.*

Geologic [Rad. Art. Mol. Fish. Rep. Bird. Mam. Man.] arrangement.
Cuvier's [Rad. Art. Mol. Fish. Rep. Bird. Mam. Man.] arrangement.

THE GENEALOGY OF ANIMALS.

* The horizontal lines of the diagram here indicate, as in fig.1, the divisions of the several geologic systems; the vertical lines represent the leading divisions and classes of animals, and, as shown by the formations in which their earliest known remains occur, the probable period of their first appearance in creation; while the double line of text below exhibits the complete correspondence which obtains between their occurrence in nature and the Cuvierian arrangement. The line representative of the radiata ought perhaps to have been elevated a little higher than either of its two neighbours.

old. This early Oolitic volume corresponds in its contents to the section devoted by Cuvier, in his great work, to his second class, the birds. And in the Stonesfield slate,—a deposit interposed between the "Inferior" and "Great Oolites," we detect the earliest indications of his first or mammaliferous class, apparently represented, however, by but one order,—the Marsupiata, or pouched animals, to whose special place in the scale I shall afterwards have occasion to refer. Not until we reach the times of the Tertiary division do the mammals in their higher orders appear. The great Tertiary volume corresponds to those volumes of Cuvier which treat of the placental animals that suckle their young. And finally,—last-born of creation,—man appears upon the scene, in his several races and varieties: the sublime arch of animal-being at length receives its keystone; and the finished work stands up complete, from foundation to pinnacle, at once an admirably adjusted occupant of space, and a wonderful monument of Divine arrangement and classification, as it exists in time. Save at two special points, to which I shall afterwards advert, the particular arrangement unfolded by geologic history is exactly that which the greatest and most philosophic of the naturalists had, just previous to its discovery, originated and adopted as most conformable to nature: the arrangements of geologic history as exhibited in time, if, commencing at the earliest ages, we pursue it downwards, is exactly that of the "Animal Kingdom" of Cuvier read backwards.

Let us then, in grappling with the vast multiplicity of our subject, attempt reducing and simplifying it by means of the classifying principle; not simply, however,—again to recur to the remark of the metaphysician,—as an internal principle given us by nature, but as an external principle *exemplified* by nature. Let us take the organisms of the old geologic periods in the order in which they occur in time; secure, as has been shown, that if our chronology be correct, our classification will, as a consequence, be good. It will be for the natural theologians of the coming age to show the bearing of this wonderful fact on the progress of man towards the just and the solid, and on the being and character of man's Creator,—to establish, on the one hand, against the undue depreciators of intellect and its results, that in certain departments of mind, such as that which deals with the arrangement and development of the scheme of organic being, human thought is not profitlessly revolving in an idle circle, but progressing Godwards, and gradually unlocking the order of creation. And, on the other hand, it will be equally his proper business to demand of the Pantheist how,—seeing that only *persons* (such as the Cuviers and

Lindleys) could have wrought out for themselves the real arrangement of this scheme,—how, I say, or on what principle, it is to be held that it was a scheme originated and established at the beginning, not by a *personal*, but by an *im*personal God. But our present business is with the *fact* of the parallel arrangements, Divine and human,—not with the inferences legitimately deducible from it.

Beginning with the plants, let us, however, remark, that they do not precede in the order of their appearance the humbler animals. No more ancient organism than the *Oldhamia* of the Lowest Irish Silurians, a plant-like zoophyte somewhat resembling our modern sertularia, has yet been detected by the geologist;

Fig. 5.

OLDHAMIA ANTIQUA;—the oldest known Zoophyte.

Wrae Head, Ireland.

though only a few months ago the researches of **Mr** Salter in the ancient rocks of the Longmynd, Shropshire, previously deemed unfossiliferous, have given to it what seem to be contemporary vegetable organisms, in a few ill-preserved fucoids. So far as is yet known, plants and animals appear together. The long upward march of the animal kingdom takes its departure at its starting-point from a thick forest of algæ. In Bohemia, in Norway, in Sweden, in the British Islands, in North America, wherever, in fine, what appears to be the lowest, or at least one of the lowest, zones of life has yet been detected, the rocks are found to be darkened by the remains of algæ, so abundantly developed in some cases, that they compose, as in the ancient Lower Silurians of Dumfriesshire, impure beds of anthracite several feet in thickness. Apparently from the original looseness of their texture, the individual plants are but indifferently preserved; nor can we expect that organisms so ancient should exhibit any *very* close resemblance to the plants which darken the half-tide rocks and skerries of our coasts at the present time. We do detect, however, in some of these primordial fossils, at least a noticeable likeness to families familiar to the modern algæologist. The cord-like plant, *Chorda filum*, known to our children as "dead men's ropes," from its proving fatal at times to the too adventurous swimmer who gets entangled in its thick wreaths, had a Lower Silurian representative, known to the Palæontologist as the *Palæochorda*, or ancient chorda, which existed apparently in two species,—a

Fig. 6.

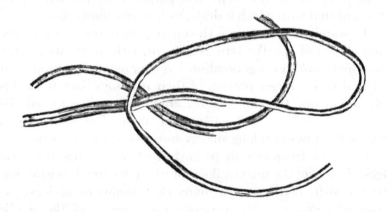

PALÆOCHORDA MINOR.

(three-quarters nat. Size.)

larger and smaller. The still better known *Chondrus crispus*, the Irish-moss or carrageen of our cookery books, has likewise its apparent though more distant representative in *Chondritis*, a Lower Silurian alga, of which there seems to exist at least three species. The fucoids, or kelp-weeds, appear to have had also their

representatives in such plants as *Fucoides gracilis* of the Lower
Silurians of the Malverns; in short, the Thallogens of the first ages
of vegetable life seem to have resembled, in the group, and in at
least their more prominent features, the algæ of the existing time.
And with the first indications of land we pass direct from the
Thallogens to the Acrogens,—from the sea-weeds to the fern-allies.
The Lycopodiaceæ, or clubmosses, bear in the axils of their leaves
minute circular cases, which form the receptacles of their
sporelike-seeds. And when, high in the Upper Silurian System, and
just when preparing to quit it for the Lower Old Red Sandstone,
we detect our earliest terrestrial organisms, we find that they are
composed exclusively of those little spore-receptacles. The number
of land plants gradually increases as we ascend into the overlying
system. Still, however, the flora of even the Old Red is but meagre
and poor; and you will perhaps permit me to lighten this part of
my subject, which threatens too palpably to partake of the
poverty of that with which it deals, by a simple illustration.

We stand, at low ebb, on the outer edge of one of those iron-
bound shores of the Western Highlands, rich in forests of algæ,
from which, not yet a generation bygone, our Celtic proprietors
used to derive a larger portion of their revenues than from their
fields and moors. Rock and skerry are brown with sea-weed. The
long cylindrical lines of *Chorda filum*, many feet in length, lie
aslant in the tide-way; long shaggy bunches of *Fucus serratus* and
Fucus nodosus droop heavily from the rock sides; while the flatter
ledges, that form the uneven floor on which we tread, bristle thick
with the stiff, cartilaginous, many-cleft fronds of at least two
species of chondrus,—the common carrageen, and the smaller
species, *C.Norvegicus.* Now, in the thickly-spread fucoids of this
Highland shore we have a not *very* inadequate representation of
the first or thallogenic vegetation,—that of the great Silurian
period, as exhibited in the rocks, from the base to nearly the top of
the system. And should we add to the rocky tract, rich in fucoids, a
submarine meadow of pale shell-sand, covered by a deep green
swathe of zostera, with its jointed saccharine roots and slim
flowers, unfurnished with petals, we would render it perhaps more
adequately representative still.

We cross the beach, and enter on a bare brown moor, comparatively fertile, however, in the clubmosses. One of the largest and finest of the species, *Lycopodium clavatum*, with its long scaly stems and upright spikes of lighter green,—altogether a graceful though flowerless plant, which the herd-boy learns to select from among its fellows, and to bind round his cap,—goes trailing on the drier spots for many feet over the soil; while at the edge of trickling runnel or marshy hollow, a smaller and less hardy species, *Lycopodium inundatum*, takes its place. The marshes themselves bristle thick with the deep green horse-tail, *Equisetum fluviatile*, with its fluted stem and verticillate series of linear

Fig. 7. Fig. 8.

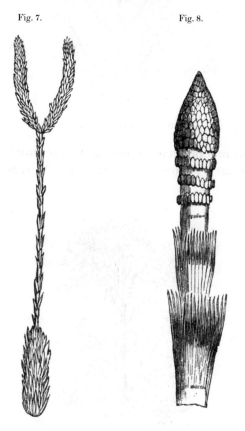

LYCOPODIUM CLAVATUM   EQUISETUM FLUVIATILE

branches. Two other species of the same genus, *Equisetum sylvaticum* and *Equisetum arvense*, flourish on the drier parts of the moor, blent with two species of minute ferns, the moon wort and the adder's-tongue,—ferns that, like the magnificent royal fern (*Osmunda regalis*), though on a much humbler scale, bear their

Fig. 9.

OSMUNDA REGALIS. (*Royal Fern.*)

seed-cases on independent stems, and were much sought after of old for imaginary virtues, which the modern schools of medicine

Fig. 10.

PINUS SYLVESTUS. (*Scotch Fir.*)

refuse to recognise. Higher up the moor, ferns of ampler size occur, and what seem to be rushes, which bear atop conglobate panicles on their smooth leafless stems; but at its lower edge little else appears than the higher Acrogens,—ferns and their allies. There occurs, however, just beyond the first group of club-mosses,—a remarkable exception in a solitary pine,—the advanced guard of one of the ancient forests of the country, which may be seen far in the back-ground, clothing with its shaggy covering of deep green the lower hill-slopes. And as we found in the Thallogens of that littoral zone over which we have just passed, representatives of the marine flora of the Silurian System, from the first appearance of organisms in its nether beds, to its bone-bed of the Upper Ludlow rocks, in which the Lycopodites first appear, so in the Acrogens of that moor, with its solitary coniferous tree, we may recognise an equally striking representative of the terrestrial flora which existed during the deposition of these Ludlow rocks, and of the various formations of the Old Red Sandstone, Lower, Middle, and Upper.

In the upper beds of the Upper Silurian, as has been already remarked, Lycopodites are the only terrestrial plants yet found. In the Lower Old Red Sandstone we find added to these, with Thallogens that bear at least the same *general* character as in the system beneath, minute ferns, and a greatly larger plant, allied to the horsetails. The Old Red flora seems to have been prevailingly an acrogenic flora; and yet with almost its first beginnings,—contemporary with at least the earlier fossils of the system in Scotland, we find a true polycotyledonous tree, not lower in the scale than the araucarites of the Coal Measures,—which in structure it greatly resembles,—or than the pines or cedars of our own times (see fig. 3). In the Middle Old Red Sandstone there occurs, with plants representative apparently of the ferns and their allies, a somewhat equivocal and doubtful organism, which may have been the panicle or compound fruit of some aquatic rush; while in the Upper Old Red, just ere the gorgeous flora of the Coal Measures began to be, there existed in considerable abundance a stately fern, the *Cyclopteris Hibernicus* (see fig. 2), of mayhap not smaller proportions than our monarch of

Fig. 11.

CALAMITE?
Of the Lower Old Red Sandstone.
Shetland.
(~One eighth nat. size)

LYCOPODITE?
Of the Lower Old Red Sandstone.
Thurso.
(Mag. ~Two diameters.)

the British ferns, *Osmunda regalis,* associated with a peculiar lepidodendron, and what seems to be a lepidostrobus,—possibly the fructiferous spike or cone of the latter, mingled with carbonaceous stems, which, in the simplicity of their texture, and their abundance, give evidence of a low but not scanty vegetation. Ere passing to the luxuriant carboniferous flora, I shall make but one other remark. The existing plants whence we derive our analogies in dealing with the vegetation of this early period contribute but little, if at all, to the support of animal life. The ferns and their allies remain untouched by the grazing animals. Our native club-mosses, though once used in medicine, are

Fig. 13.

FERN? of the Lower Old Red Sandstone.
Orkney.
(~Nat. size)

positively deleterious; the horsetails, though harmless, so abound
in silex, which wraps them round with a cuticle of stone, that they
are rarely cropped by cattle; while the thickets of fern which cover
our hill-sides, and seem so temptingly rich and green in their
season, scarce support the existence of a single creature, and
remain untouched in stem and leaf, from their first appearance in
spring, until they droop and wither under the frosts of early
winter. Even the insects that infest the herbaria of the botanist
almost never injure his ferns. Nor are our resin-producing conifers,
though they nourish a few beetles, favourites with the herbivorous
tribes in a much greater degree. Judging from all we yet know, the
earliest terrestrial flora may have covered the dry land with its
mantle of cheerful green, and served its general purposes, chemical
and others, in the well-balanced economy of nature; but the herb-
eating animals would have fared but ill even where it throve most
luxuriantly; and it seems to harmonize with the fact of its non-
edible character, that up to the present time we know not that a
single herbivorous animal lived among its shades. From all that
appears, it may be inferred that it had not to serve the purposes of
the floras of the passing time, in which, according to the poet,

"The world's bread depends on the shooting of a seed."

The flora of the Coal Measures was the richest and most luxuriant, in at least individual productions, with which the fossil botanist has formed any acquaintance. Never before or since did our planet bear so rank a vegetation as that of which the numerous coal seams and inflammable shales of the carboniferous period form but a portion of the remains,—the portion spared, in the first instance, by dissipation and decay, and in the second by the denuding agencies. Almost all our coal,—the stored up fuel of a world,—forms but a comparatively small part of the produce of this wonderful flora. Amid much that was so strange and antique of type in its productions as to set the analogies of the botanist at fault, there occurred one solitary order, not a few of whose species closely resembled their cogeners of the present time. I refer, of course, to its ferns. And these seem to have formed no small proportion of the entire flora of the period. Francis estimates the recent dorsiferous ferns of Great Britain at thirty-five species, and the species of all the other genera at six more,—forty-one species in all; and as the flowering plants of the country do not fall short of fourteen hundred species, the ferns bear to them the rather small proportion of about one to thirty-five; whereas of the British Coal Measure flora, in which we do not yet reckon quite three hundred species of plants, about a hundred and twenty were ferns. Three-sevenths of the entire carboniferous flora of Britain belonged to this familiar class; and for about fifty species more we can discover no nearer analogies than those which connect them with the fern allies. And if with the British Coal Measures we include those also of the Continent and America, we shall find the proportion in favour of the ferns still greater. The number of carboniferous plants hitherto described amounts, says M. Ad. Brogniart, to about five hundred, and of these, two hundred and fifty,—one-half of the whole,—were ferns.

Rising in the scale from the lower to the higher vegetable forms of the system,—from its ferns to its trees,—we find great conifers,—so great that they must have raised their heads more than a hundred feet over the soil; and such was their abundance in this neighbourhood, that one can scarce examine a fragment of coal beside one's household fire that is not charged with their

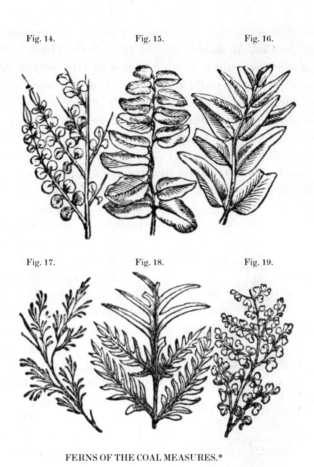

FERNS OF THE COAL MEASURES.*

* Fig. 14, Neuropteris Loshii. Fig. 15, Neuropteris gigantea.
Fig. 16, Neuropteris acuminata. Fig. 17 Sphenopteris affinus.
Fig.18, Pecopteris heterophylla. Fig. 19, Sphenopteris dilata.

carbonized remains. Though marked by certain peculiarities of structure, they bore, as is shown by the fossil trunks of Granton and Craigleith, the familiar outlines of true coniferous trees; and would mayhap have differed no more in appearance from their successors of the same order that now live in our forests, than these differ from the conifers of New Zealand or of New South Wales.

We have thus, in the numerous ferns and numerous coniferous trees of the Coal Measures, known objects by which to conceive of some of the more prominent features of the flora of which they composed so large a part. We have not inadequate conceptions of at once the giants of its forests and the green swathe of its plains and hill-sides,—of its mighty trees and its dwarf *underwood,*—of its cedars of Lebanon, so to speak, and its hyssop of the wall. But of an intermediate class we have no existing representatives; and in this class the fossil botanist finds puzzles and enigmas with which hitherto at least he has been able to deal with only indifferent

Fig. 20.

ALTINGIA EXCELSA.
Norfolk Island Pine. (Young specimen.)

success. There is a view, however, sufficiently simple, which may be found somewhat to lessen, if not altogether remove, the difficulty. Nature does not dwell willingly in mediocrity; and so in all ages she as certainly produced trees, or plants of tree-like proportions and bulk, as she did minute shrubs and herbs. In not a few of the existing orders and families, such as the Rosaceæ, the Leguminosæ, the Myrtaceæ, and many others, we have plants of all sizes, from the creeping herb, half-hidden in the sward, to the stately tree. The wild dwarf strawberry and minute stone-bramble are of the same order as our finer orchard-trees,—apple, pear, and plum,—or as those noble hawthorn, mountain-ash, and wild cherry trees, that impart such beauty to our lawns and woods; and the minute spring-vetch and everlasting pea are denizens of the same great family as the tall locust and rosewood trees, and the gorgeous laburnum. Did there exist no other plants than the Rosaceæ or the Leguminosæ, we would possess, notwithstanding, herbs, shrubs, and trees, just as

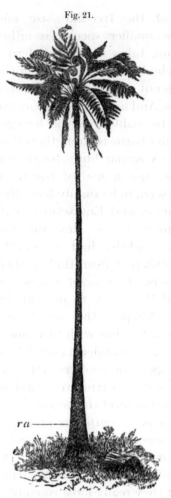

Fig. 21.

we do now. And in plants of a greatly humbler order we have instances of similar variety in point of size. The humblest grass in our meadows belongs to the same natural order as the tall bamboo, that, shooting up its panicles amid the jungles of India to the height of sixty feet, looks down upon all the second-class trees of the country. Again, the minute forked spleenwort of Arthur Seat, which rarely exceeds three inches in length, is of the same family as those tree-ferns of New Zealand and Tasmania that rise to an elevation of from twenty to thirty feet. And we know how in the ferns provision is made for

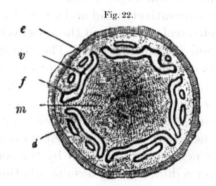

Fig. 22.

EAST INDIA TREE FERN.*
(*Asophila perrotetiana.*)

SECTION OF THE STEM OF TREE-FERN.†
(*Cyathea.*)

* Fig. 21, *ra*, Rachis, greatly thickened towards its base by numerous aerial roots, shot downwards to the soil, and which closely cover the stem.

† Fig. 22, *m*, Cellular tissue of the centre of rachis; *d*, similar tissue of the circumference; *f*, *v*, darkly-coloured woody fibres of great strength, the "internal buttresses" of the illustration; *e* the outer cortical portion formed by the bases of the leaves.

the attainment and maintenance of the tree-like size and character. The rachis, which in the smaller species is either subterranean or runs along the ground, takes in the tree-fern a different direction, and, rising erect, climbs slowly upward in the character of a trunk or stem, and sends out atop, year after year, a higher and yet higher coronal of fronds. And in order to impart the necessary strength to this trunk, and to enable it to war for ages with the elements, its mass of soft cellular tissue is strengthened all round by internal buttresses of dense vascular fibre, tough and elastic as the strongest woods. Now, not a few of the more anomalous forms of the Coal Measures seem to be simply fern allies of the types Lycopodiaceæ, Marsileaceæ, and Equisetum, that, escaping from the mediocrity of mere herbs, shot up into trees,—some of them very great trees,—and that had of necessity to be furnished with a tissue widely different from that of their minuter contemporaries and successors. It was of course an absolute mechanical necessity, that if they were to present, by being tall and large, a wide front to the tempest, they should also be comparatively solid and strong to resist it; but with this simple mechanical requirement there seems to have mingled a principle of a more occult character. The Gymnogens or conifers were the highest vegetable existences of the period,—its true trees; and all the tree-like fern allies were strengthened to meet the necessities of their increased size, on, if I may so speak, a *coniferous* principle. Tissue resembling that of their contemporary conifers imparted the necessary rigidity to their framework; nay, so strangely were they pervaded throughout by the coniferous characteristics, that it seems difficult to determine whether they really most resembled the acrogenous or gymnogenous families. The Lepido-dendra,—great plants of the club-moss type, that rose from fifty to seventy feet in height—had well nigh as many points of resemblance to the coniferæ as to the Lycopodites. The Calamites,—reed-like, jointed plants, that more nearly resemble the Equisetaceæ than aught else which now exists, but which attained, in the larger specimens, to the height of ordinary trees,—also manifest very decidedly, in their internal structure, some of the characteristics of the conifers. It has been remarked by

Fig. 23.

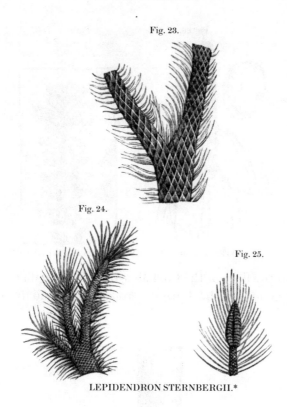

Fig. 24.

Fig. 25.

LEPIDENDRON STERNBERGII.*

* Fig. 23, Branching stem, with bark and leaves.
Fig. 24, Extremity of branch. Fig. 25, Extremity of another
branch, with indication of cone-like receptacle of spores or seed.

Lindley and Hutton of even Sphenophyllum,—a genus of plants
with verticillate leaves, of which at least six species occur in our
Coal Measures, and which Brogniart refers to one of the humblest
families of the fern allies,—that it seems at least as nearly related
to the Coniferæ as to its lowlier representatives the Marsileaceæ.
And it is this union of traits, pertaining to what are now widely
separated orders, that imparts to not a few of the vegetables of the
Coal Measures their singularly anomalous character.

Let me attempt introducing you more intimately to one of
those plants which present scarce any analogy with existing forms,
and which must have imparted so strange a character and

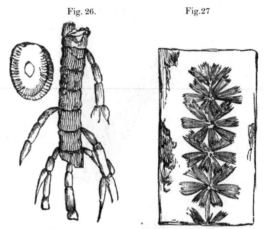

Fig. 26.

Fig.27

CALAMITES MOUGEOTII.   SPHENOPHYLLUM DENTATUM.

appearance to the flora of the Coal Measures. The Sigillaria formed a numerous genus of the Carboniferous period: no fewer than

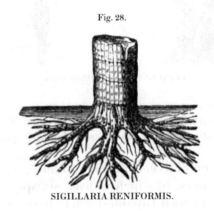

Fig. 28.

SIGILLARIA RENIFORMIS.

twenty-two different species have been enumerated in the British coal-fields alone; and such was their individual abundance, that there are great seams of coal which seem to be almost entirely composed of their remains. At least the ancient soil on which these seams rest, and on which their materials appear to have been elaborated from the elements, is in many instances as thickly traversed by their underground stems as the soil occupied by our densest forests is traversed by the tangled roots of the trees by

Fig. 29..

SIGILLARIA RENIFORMIS.
(~Nat. Size.)

which it is covered; and we often find associated with them in these cases the remains of no other plant. The Sigillaria were remarkable for their beautifully sculptured stems, various in their pattern, according to their species. All were fluted vertically, somewhat like columns of the Grecian Doric; and each flute or channel had its line of sculpture running adown its centre. In one species (*S. flexuosa*) the sculpture consists of round knobs, surrounded by single rings, like the heads of the bolts of the ship-carpenter; in another (*S. reniformis*) the knobs are double, and of an oval form, somewhat resembling pairs of kidneys,—a resemblance to which the species owes its name. In another species (*S. catenulata*) what seems a minute chain of distinctly formed elliptical links drops down the middle of each flute; in yet another (*S. oculata*) the carvings are of an oval form, and, bearing each a round impression in its centre, they somewhat resemble rows of staring gogle eyes; while the carvings in yet another species (*S. pachyderma*) consist chiefly of crescent-shaped depressions. The roots, or rather underground stems, of this curious genus attracted notice, from their singularity, long ere their connection with the carved and fluted stems had been determined; and have been often described as the "stigmaria" of the fossil botanist. They, too, have their curious carvings, consisting of deeply marked stigmata, quincuncially arranged, with each a little ring at its bottom, and, in at least one rare species, surrounded by a sculptured star. Unlike true roots,

Fig. 30.

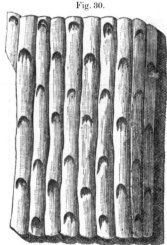

SIGILLARIA PACHYDERMA.
(One-fourth nat. Size.)

Fig. 31.

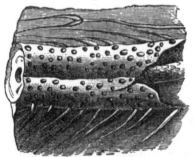

STIGMARIA FICOIDES.
(One-fourth nat. Size.)

they terminate abruptly: each rootlet which they sent forth was
jointed to the little ring or dimpled knob at the bottom of the
stigmata; and the appearance of the whole, as it radiated from the
central mass, whence the carved trunk proceeded, somewhat
resembled that of an enormous coach-wheel divested of the rim.
Unfortunately we cannot yet complete our description of this
strange plant. A specimen, traced for about forty feet across a
shale bed, was found to bifurcate atop into two great branches,—a
characteristic in which, with several others, it differed from most

of the tree ferns,—a class of plants to
which Adolphe Brogniart is inclined to
deem it related; but no specimen has yet
shown the nature of its foliage. I am,
however, not a little disposed to believe
with Brogniart that it may have borne as
leaves some of the supposed ferns of the
Coal Measures; nowhere, at least, have I
found these lie so thickly, layer above
layer, as around the stems of Sigillaria;
and the fact that, even in our own times,
plants widely differing from the tree
ferns,—such, for instance, as one of the
Cycadeæ,—should bear leaves scarce distinguishable from fern
fronds, may well reconcile us to an appparent anomaly in the case
of an ancient plant such as Sigillaria, whose entire constitution, so
far as it has been ascertained, appears to have been anomalous.
The sculpturesque character of this richly fretted genus was shared
by not a few of its contemporaries. The Ulodendra, with their
rectilinear rows of circular scars, and their stems covered with leaf-
like carvings, rivalled in effect the ornately relieved torus of a

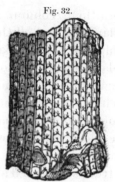

Fig. 32.

FAVULARIA TESSELLATA
(~One-fifth nat. size.)

Fig. 33.

LEPIDENDRON OBOVATUM.
(Nat. size.)

Corinthian column: Favularia, Knorria, Halonia, many of the
Calamites, and all the Lepidodendra, exhibited the most delicate
sculpturing. In walking among the ruins of this ancient flora, the
Palæontologist almost feels as if he had got among the broken
fragments of Italian palaces, erected long ages ago, when the
architecture of Rome was most ornate, and every moulding was
roughened with ornament; and in attempting to call up in fancy
the old Carboniferous forests, he has to dwell on this peculiar
feature as one of the most prominent, and to see, in the multitude
of trunks darkened above by clouds of foliage that rise upon him in
the prospect, the slim columns of an elder Alhambra, roughened
with arabesque tracery and exquisite filagree work.

In the Oolitic flora we find a few peculiar features introduced.
The Cycadeæ,—a family of plants allied to the ferns on the one

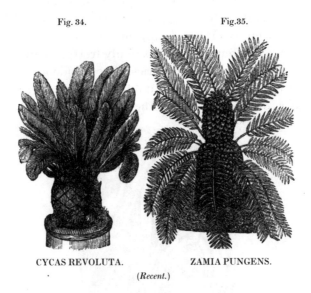

Fig. 34.   Fig. 35.

CYCAS REVOLUTA.   ZAMIA PUNGENS.
(*Recent.*)

hand, and to the conifers on the other, and which in their general
aspect not a little resemble stunted palms,—appear in this flora for
the first time. Its coniferous genera, too, receive great accessions to
their numbers, and begin to resemble, more closely than at an
earlier period, the genera which still continue to exist. The
cypresses, the yews, the thujas, the dammaras, all make their

Fig. 36.

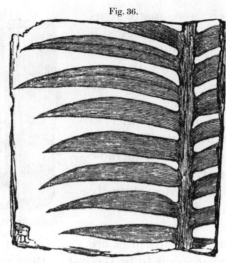

ZAMIA FENEONIS.
(*Portland Oolite*)

earliest appearance in the flora of the Oolite.

Among our existing woods there seem to be but two conifers (that attain to the dignity of trees) indigenous to Britain,—the common yew, **Taxus baccata**, and the common Scotch fir, **Pinus sylvestris**; and yet we know that the latter alone formed, during the last few centuries, great woods, that darkened for many miles together the now barren moors and bare hill-sides of the Highlands of Scotland,—moors and hill-sides that, though long since divested of their last tree, are still known by their old name of *forests*. In the times of the Oolite, on the other hand, Britain had from fourteen to twenty different species of conifers; and its great forests, of whose existence we have direct evidence in the very abundant lignites of the system, must have possessed a richness and variety which our ancient fir-woods of the historic or human period could not have possessed. With the Conifers and

Fig. 37.

MANTELLIA NIDIFORMIS.
(Portland Dirt-bed.)

the Cycadeæ there were many ferns associated,—so many, that they still composed nearly two-fifths of the entire flora; and associated with these, though in reduced proportions, we find the fern-allies. The reduction, however, of these last is rather in species than in individuals. The Brora Coal, one of the most considerable Oolitic seams in Europe, seems to have been formed almost exclusively of an equisetum,—*E. columnare.* In this flora the more equivocal productions of the Coal Measures are

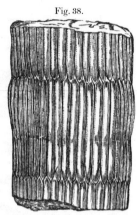

Fig. 38.

EQUISETUM COLUMNARE.
(~Nat. Size.)

represented by what seems to be the last of the Calamites; but it contains no Lepidodendra,—no Ulodendra,—no Sigillaria,—no Favularia,—no Knorria or Halonia. Those monsters of the vegetable world that united to the forms of its humbler productions the bulk of trees, had, with the solitary exception of the Calamites, passed into extinction; and ere the close of the system they too had disappeared. The forms borne by most of the Oolitic plants were comparatively familiar forms. With the Acrogens and Gymnogens we find the first indication of the Liliaceæ, or lily-like plants,—of plants, too, allied to the Pandanaceæ or screw-pines, the fruits of which are sometimes preserved in a wonderfully perfect state of keeping in the Inferior Oolite, together with Carpolithes,—palm-like fruits, very ornately sculptured,—and the remains of at least one other monocotyledon, that bears the somewhat general name of an Endogenite. With these there occur a few disputed leaves, which I must persist in regarding as dicotyledonous. But they formed, whatever their true character, a very inconspicuous feature in the Oolitic flora; and not until the overlying Cretaceous System is ushered in do we find leaves in any considerable quantity decidedly of this high family; nor until we enter into the earlier Tertiaries do we succeed in detecting a true dicotyledonous tree. On such an amount of observation is this order of succession determined,—though the

Fig. 39.   Fig. 40.

CARPOLITHES CONICA.   CARPOLITHES BUCKLANDII.*
(Reduced ~one-third.)

* No true fossil palms have yet been detected in the great Oolitic and Wealden Systems, though they certainly occur in the Carboniferous and Permian rocks, and are comparatively common in the earlier and middle Tertiary formations. Much cannot be founded on merely negative evidence; but it would be certainly a curious circumstance should it be found that this graceful family, first ushered into being some time in the later Palæozoic periods, was withdrawn from creation during the Middle ages of the earth's history, to be again introduced in greatly more than the earlier proportions during the Tertiary and recent periods.

Fig. 41.

ACER TRILOBATUM.*
(*Miocene of Œningen.*)

* Leaf of a tree allied to the maple.

evidence is, of course, mainly negative,—that when, some eight or ten years ago, Dr John Wilson, the learned Free Church missionary to the Parsees of India, submitted to me specimens of fossil-woods which he had picked up in the Egyptian Desert, in order that I might if possible determine their age, I told him, ere yet the optical lapidary had prepared them for examination, that if they exhibited the coniferous structure, they might belong to any geologic period from the times of the Lower old Red Sandstone downwards; but that if they manifested in their tissue the dicotyledonous character, they could not be older than the times of the Tertiary. On submitting them in thin slices to the microscope, they were found to exhibit the peculiar dicotyledonous structure as strongly as the oak or chestnut; and Lieutenant Newbold's researches in the deposit in which they occur has since demonstrated, on stratigraphical evidence, that not only does it belong to the great Tertiary division, but also to one of the comparatively modern formations of the Tertiary.

Fig. 42.

ULMUS BRONNII.*
(*Miocene of Bohemia.*)

* Leaf of a tree allied to the elm.

The earlier flora of this Tertiary division presents an aspect widely different from that of any of the previous ones. The ferns and their allies sink into their existing proportions; nor do the coniferæ, previously so abundant, occupy any longer a prominent place. On the other hand, the dicotyledonous herbs and trees, previously so inconspicuous in creation, are largely developed. Trees of those Amentiferous orders to which the oak, the hazel, the beech, and the plane belong, were perhaps not less abundant in the Eocene woods than in those of the present time: they were mingled with trees of the Laurel, the Leguminous, and the Anonaceous or custard-apple families, with many others; and deep forests, in the latitude of London (in which the intertropical forms must now be protected, as in the Crystal Palace, with coverings of glass, and warmed by artificial heat), abounded in graceful palms. Mr Bowerbank found in the London Clay of the island of Sheppey alone the fruits of no fewer than thirteen different species of this picturesque family, which lends so peculiar a feature to the landscapes in which it occurs; and ascertained that the undergrowth beneath was composed, in large proportion, of creeping plants of the gourd and melon order. From the middle or

Fig. 43.

PALMACITES LAMANONIS
(*A Palm of the Miocene of Aix.*)

Miocene flora of the Tertiary division,—of which we seem to
possess in Britain only the small but interesting fragment detected
by his Grace the Duke of Argyll among the trap-beds of
Mull,—most of the more exotic forms seem to have been excluded.
The palms, however, still survive in no fewer than thirty-one
different species; and we find in great abundance, in the place of
the other exotics, remains of the plane and buckthorn
families,—part of a group of plants that in their general aspect, as
shown in the Tertiary deposits of the Continent, not a little
resembled the vegetation of the United States at the present day.
The nearer we approach to existing times, the more familiar in
form and outline do the herbs and trees become. We detect, as has
been shown, at least one existing *order* in the ferns of the Coal
Measures; we detect at least existing *genera* among the Coniferæ,
Equisetaceæ, and Cycadaceæ of the Oolite; the acacias, gourds,
and laurels of the Eocene flora, and the planes, willows, and
buckthorns of the Miocene, though we fail to identify their species
with aught that now lives, still more strongly remind us of the
recent productions of our forests or conservatories; and, on
entering, in our downward course, the Pleistocene period, we at
length find ourselves among familiar *species*. On old terrestrial
surfaces, that date before the times of the glacial period, and
underlie the boulder clay, the remains of forests of oak, birch,
hazel, and fir have been detected,—all of the familiar species
indigenous to the country, and which still flourish in our native
woods. And it was held by the late Professor Edward Forbes, that
the most ancient of his live existing British floras,—that which
occurs in the south-west of Ireland, and corresponds with the flora
of the north-west of Spain and the Pyrenees,—had been
introduced into the country as early, perhaps, as the times of the
Miocene. Be this, however, as it may, there can rest no doubt on
the great antiquity of the prevailing trees of our indigenous forests.

The oak, the birch, the hazel, the Scotch fir, all lived, I repeat,
in what is now Britain, ere the last great depression of the land.
The gigantic northern elephant and rhinoceros, extinct for untold
ages, forced their way through their tangled branches; and the
British tiger and hyæna harboured in their thickets. Cuvier framed

an argument for the fixity of species on the fact that the birds and
beasts embalmed in the catacombs were identical in every respect
with the animals of the same kinds that live now. But what, it has
been asked, was a brief period of three thousand years, compared
with the geologic ages? or how could any such argument be
founded on a basis so little extended? It is, however, to no such
narrow basis we can refer in the case of these woods. All human
history is comprised in the nearer corner of the immense period
which they measure out: and yet, from their first appearance in
creation till now they have not altered a single fibre. And such, on
this point, is the invariable testimony of Palæontologic
science,—testimony so invariable, that no great Palæontologist
was ever yet an asserter of the development hypothesis. With the
existing trees of our indigenous woods it is probable that in even
these early times a considerable portion of the herbs of our recent
flora would have been associated, though their remains, less fitted
for preservation, have failed to leave distinct trace behind them.
We at least know generally, that with each succeeding period there
appeared a more extensively useful and various vegetation than
that which had gone before. I have already referred to the sombre,
unproductive character of the earliest terrestrial flora with which
we are acquainted. It was a flora unfitted, apparently, for the
support of either graminivorous bird or herbivorous quadruped.
The singularly profuse vegetation of the Coal Measures was, with
all its wild luxuriance, of a resembling cast. So far as appears,
neither flock nor herd could have lived on its greenest and richest
plains. Nor does even the flora of the Oolite seem to have been in
the least suited for the purposes of the shepherd or herdsman. Not
until we enter on the Tertiary periods do we find floras amid which
man might have profitably laboured as a dresser of gardens, a tiller
of fields, or a keeper of flocks and herds. Nay, there are whole
orders and families of plants of the very first importance to man
which do not appear until late in even the Tertiary ages. Some
degree of doubt must always attach to merely negative evidence;
but Agassiz, a geologist whose statements must be received with
respect by every student of the science, finds reason to conclude
that the order of the Rosaceæ,—an order more important to the

gardener than almost any other, and to which the apple, the pear, the quince, the cherry, the plum, the peach, the apricot, the victorine, the almond, the raspberry, the strawberry, and the various brambleberries belong, together with all the roses and the potentillas,—was introduced only a short time previous to the appearance of man. And the true grasses,—a still more important order, which, as the corn-bearing plants of the agriculturist, feed at the present time at least two thirds of the human species, and in their humbler varieties form the staple food of the *grazing* animals,—scarce appear in the fossil state at all. They are peculiarly plants of the human period.

Let me instance one other family of which the fossil botanist has not yet succeeded in finding any trace in even the Tertiary deposits, and which appears to have been specially created for the gratification of human sense. Unlike the Rosaceæ, it exhibits no rich blow of colour, or tempting show of luscious fruit;—it does not appeal very directly to either the sense of taste or of sight: but it is richly odoriferous; and, though deemed somewhat out of place in the garden for the last century and more, it enters largely into the composition of some of our most fashionable perfumes. I refer to the *Labiate* family,—a family to which the lavenders, the mints, the thymes, and the hyssops belong, with basil, rosemary, and marjorum,—all plants of "gray renown," as Shenstone happily remarks in his description of the herbal of his "Schoolmistress,"

> "Herbs too she knew, and well of each could speak,
>   That in her garden sipp'd the silvery dew,
>   Where no vain flower disclos'd a gaudy streak,
>   But herbs for use and physic not a few,
>   Of gray renown, within those borders grew.
>   The tufted basil, pun-provoking thyme,
>   And fragrant balm, and sage of sober hue.

> * * * * * * * * * * * * *
> "And marjorum sweet in shepherd's posie found,
>   And lavender, whose spikes of azure-bloom
>   Shall be erewhile in arid bundles bound,
>   To lurk amid her labours of the loom,

And crown her kerchiefs clean with meikle rare perfume.

"And here trim rosemary, that whilom crown'd
  The daintiest garden of the proudest peer,
  Ere, driven from its envied site, it found
  A sacred shelter for its branches here,
  Where, edged with gold, its glittering skirts appear,
  With horehound gray, and mint of softer green."

All the plants here enumerated belong to the labiate family; which, though unfashionable even in Shenstone's days, have still their products favourably received in the very best society. The rosemary, whose banishment from the gardens of the great he specially records, enters largely into the composition of eau de Cologne. Of the lavenders, one species (*Lavendula vera*) yields the well-known lavender oil, and another (*L. latifolio*) the spike oil. The peppermint (*Mentha viridus*) furnishes the essence so popular under that name among our confectioners; and one of the most valued perfumes of the East (next to the famous *Attar*, a product of the Rosaceæ) is the oil of the *Patchouly* plant, another of the labiates. Let me indulge, ere quitting this part of the subject, in a single remark. There have been classes of religionists, not wholly absent from our own country, and well known on the Continent, who have deemed it a merit to deny themselves every pleasure of sense, however innocent and delicate. The excellent but mistaken Pascal refused to look upon a lovely landscape; and the Port Royalist nuns remarked, somewhat simply for their side of the argument, that they seemed as if warring with Providence, seeing that the favours which He was abundantly showering upon them, they, in obedience to the stern law of their lives, were continually rejecting. But it is better, surely, to be on the side of Providence against Pascal and the nuns, than on the side of Pascal and the nuns against Providence. The great Creator, who has provided so wisely and abundantly for all his creatures, knows what is best for us, infinitely better than we do ourselves; and there is neither sense nor merit, surely, in churlishly refusing to partake of that ample entertainment, sprinkled with delicate perfumes, garnished with

roses, and crowned with the most delicious fruit, which we now
know was not only specially prepared for us, but also got ready, as
nearly as we can judge, for the appointed hour of our appearance
at the feast. This we also know, that when the Divine Man came
into the world,—unlike the Port Royalists, he did not refuse the
temperate use of any of these luxuries, not even of that "ointment
of spikenard, very precious" (a product of the labiate family), with
which Mary anointed his feet.

Though it may at first seem a little out of place, let us
anticipate here, for the sake of the illustration which it affords, one
of the sections of the other great division of our subject,—that
which treats of the fossil animals. Let us run briefly over the
geologic history of insects, in order that we may mark the peculiar
light which it casts on the character of the ancient floras. No
insects have yet been detected in the Silurian or Old Red
Sandstone Systems. They first appear amid the hard, dry,
flowerless vegetation of the Coal Measures, and in genera suited to
its character. Among these the scorpions take a prominent
place,—carnivorous arachnidæ of ill repute, that live under stones
and fallen trunks, and seize fast with their nippers upon the
creatures on which they prey,—crustaceans usually, such as the
wood-louse, or insects, such as the earth-beetles and their grubs.
With the scorpions there occur cockroaches of types not at all
unlike the existing ones, and that, judging from their appearance,
must have been foul feeders, to which scarce anything could have
come amiss as food. Books, manuscripts, leather, ink, oil, meat,
even the bodies of the dead, are devoured indiscriminately by the
recent *Blatta gigantea* of the warmer parts of the globe,—one of the
most disagreeable pests of the European settler,—or of war-vessels
on foreign stations. I have among my books an age-embrowned
copy of Ramsay's "Tea-Table Miscellany," that had been carried
into foreign parts by a musical relation, after it had seen hard
service at home, and had become smoke-dried and black; and yet
even it, though but little tempting, as might be thought, was not
safe from the cockroaches; for, finding it left open one day, they
ate out in half an hour half its table of contents, consisting of
several leaves. Assuredly, if the ancient *Blattæ* were as little nice in

Fig. 44.

CYCLOPHTHALMUS BUCKLANDI.
(A Fossil Scorpion of the Coal Measures of Bohemia)

their eating as the devourers of the "Tea Table Miscellany," they would not have lacked food amid even the unproductive flora and meagre fauna of the Coal Measures. With these ancient cockroaches a few locusts and beetles have been found associated, together with a small *Tinea*,—a creature allied to the common clothes-moth; and a *Phasmia*,—a creature related to the spectre insects. But the group is an inconsiderable one; for insects seem to have occupied no very conspicuous place in the carboniferous fauna. The beetles appear to have been of the wood and seed devouring kinds, and would probably have found their food among the conifers; the *Phasmidæ* and grasshoppers would have lived on the tender shoots of the less rigid plants their contemporaries; the *Tinea* probably on ligneous or cottony fibre. Not a single insect has the system yet produced of the now numerous kinds that seek their food among flowers. In the Oolitic ages, however, insects become greatly more numerous,—so numerous that they seem to have formed almost exclusively the food of the earliest mammals, and apparently also of some of the flying reptiles of the time. The magnificent dragon flies, the carnivorous tyrants of their race, were abundant; and we now know, that while they were, as their

Fig. 45.

FOSSIL DRAGON-FLY
Solenhofen.

name indicates, dragons to the weaker insects, they themselves were devoured by dragons as truly such as were ever yet feigned by romancer of the middle ages. Ants were also common, with crickets, grasshoppers, bugs both of the land and water, beetles, two-winged flies, and, in species distinct from the preceding carboniferous ones, the disgusting cockroaches. And for the first time amid the remains of a flora that seems to have had its few flowers,—though flowers could have formed no conspicuous feature in even an Oolitic landscape,—we detect, in a few broken fragments of the wings of butterflies, decided trace of the flowersucking insects. Not, however, until we enter into the great Tertiary division do these become numerous. The first bee makes its appearance in the amber of the Eocene, locked up hermetically in its gem-like tomb,—an embalmed corpse in a crystal coffin,—along with fragments of flower-bearing herbs and trees. The first of the Bombycidæ too—insects that may be seen suspended over flowers by the scarce visible vibrations of their wings, and sucking the honied juices by means of their long slender trunks,—also appear in the amber, associated with moths, butterflies, and a few caterpillars. Bees and butterflies are present in increased proportions in the latter Tertiary deposits; but not until that terminal creation to which we ourselves belong was ushered on the scene did they receive their fullest development. There is exquisite poetry in Wordsworth's reference to "the soft murmur of the vagrant bee,"—

> "A slender sound, yet hoary Time
>   Doth to the soul exalt it with the chime
>   Of all his years; a company
>   Of ages coming, ages gone,
>   Nations from before them sweeping."

And yet, mayhap, the naked scientific facts of the history of this busy insect are scarcely less poetic than the pleasing imagination of the poet regarding it. They tell that man's world, with all its griefs and troubles, is more emphatically a world of flowers than any of the creations that preceded it; and that as one great family—the grasses—were called into existence, in order, apparently, that he might enter in favouring circumstances upon his two earliest avocations, and be in good hope a keeper of herds and a tiller of the ground; and as another family of plants—the Rosaceæ—was created in order that the gardens which it would be also one of his vocations to keep and to dress should have their trees "good for food and pleasant to the taste;" so flowers in general were profusely produced just ere he appeared, to minister to that sense of beauty which distinguishes him from all the lower creatures, and to which he owes not a few of his most exquisite enjoyments. The poet accepted the bee as a sign of high significance: the geologist also accepts her as a sign. Her entombed remains testify to the gradual fitting up of our earth as a place of habitation for a creature destined to seek delight for the mind and the eye as certainly as for the grosser senses, and in especial marks the introduction of the stately forest trees, and the arrival of the delicious flowers. And,

> "Thus in their stations lifting toward the sky

The foliaged head in cloud-like majesty,
The shadow-casting race of trees survive:
Thus in the train of spring arrive
Sweet flowers: what living eye hath viewed
Their myriads? endlessly renewed
Wherever strikes the sun's glad ray,
Where'er the subtile waters stray,
Wherever sportive zephyrs bend
Their course, or genial showers descend."

LECTURE SECOND.

THE PALÆONTOLOGICAL HISTORY OF ANIMALS.

AMID the unceasing change and endless variety of nature there occur certain great radical ideas, that, while they form, if I may so express myself, the groundwork of the change,—the basis of the variety,—admit in themselves of no change or variety whatever. They constitute the aye-enduring tissue on which the ever-changing patterns of creation are inscribed: the patterns are ever varying; the tissue which exhibits them for ever remains the same. In the animal kingdom, for instance, the prominent ideas have always been uniform. However much the faunas of the various geologic periods may have differed from each other, or from the fauna which now exists, in their general aspect and character, they were all, if I may so speak, equally underlaid by the great leading ideas which still constitute the master types of animal life. And these leading ideas are four in number. *First*, there is the *star-like* type of life,—life embodied in a form that, as in the corals, the sea-anemones, the sea-urchins, and the star-fishes, radiates outwards from a centre; *second*, there is the *articulated* type of life,—life embodied in a form composed, as in the worms, crustaceans, and insects, of a series of rings united by their edges, but more or less moveable on each other; *third*, there is the bilateral or *molluscan* type of life,—life embodied in a form in which there is a duality of corresponding parts, ranged, as in the cuttle-fishes, the clams, and the snails, on the sides of a central axis or plane; and *fourth*, there is the *vertebrate* type of life,—life embodied in a form in which an internal skeleton is built up into two cavities placed the one over the other; the upper for the reception of the nervous centres, cerebral and spinal,—the lower for the lodgment of the respiratory, circulatory, and digestive organs. Such have been the four central ideas of the faunas of every succeeding creation, except perhaps the earliest of all, that of the Lower Silurian System, in which, so far as is yet known, only three of the number existed,—the radiated, articulated, and molluscan ideas or types. That Omnipotent Creator, infinite in his resources,—who, in at least the details of his workings, seems never yet to have repeated himself, but, as Lyell well expresses it, breaks, when the parents of a species have been moulded, the dye in which they were cast,—manifests himself, in these four great ideas, as the unchanging and unchangeable One. They serve to bind together the present with all the past; and determine the unity of the authorship of a wonderfully complicated design, executed on a groundwork broad as time, and whose scope and bearing are deep as eternity.

Fig. 46.

CYATHAXONIA DALMANI.

The fauna of the Silurian System bears in all its three great types the stamp of a fashion peculiarly antique, and which, save in a few of the mollusca, has long since become obsolete. Its radiate animals are chiefly corals, simple or compound, whose inhabitants may have somewhat resembled the sea-anemones; with zoophytes, akin mayhap to the sea-pens, though the relationship must have been a remote one; and numerous crinoids, or stone lilies, some of which consisted of but a sculptured calyx without petals, while others threw off a series of long flexible arms, that divided and subdivided like the branches of a tree, and were thickly fringed by hair-like fibres. There is great variety and beauty among these Silurian crinoids; and, from the ornate sculpture of their groined and ribbed *capitals* and slender *columns*, the Gothic architect might borrow not a few striking ideas.

Fig. 47.

GLYPTOCRINUS
DECADACTYLUS.
(*Hudson River Group,
Lower Silurian.*)

The difference between the older and newer fashions, as exemplified in the cup-shaped corals, may be indicated in a single sentence. The ancient corals were stars of four rays, or of multiples of four; the modern corals are stars of six rays, or of multiples of six. But though, at a certain definite period—that during which the great Palæozoic division ended and the Secondary division began—nature, in forming this class of creatures, discarded the number four, and adopted instead the number six, the great leading idea of the star itself was equally retained in corals of the modern as in those of the more ancient type.

The articulata of the Silurian period bore a still more peculiar character. They consisted mainly of the Trilobites,—a family in whose nicely-jointed shells the armourer of the middle ages might have found almost all the contrivances of his craft anticipated, with not a few besides which he had failed to discover; and which, after receiving so immense a development during the middle and later times of the Silurian period, that whole rocks were formed almost exclusively. of their remains, gradually died out in the times of the Old Red Sandstone, and disappeared for ever from

Fig. 48.

CALYMENE BLUMENBACHII

creation after the Carboniferous Limestone had been deposited. The Palæontologist knows no more unique family than that of the Trilobites, or a family more unlike any which now exists, or a family which marks with more certainty the early rocks in which they occur. And yet, though formed in a fashion that perished myriads of ages ago, how admirably does it not exhibit the articulated type of being, and illustrate that unity of design which,

amid endless diversity, pervades all nature! The mollusca of the
Silurians ranged from the high cephalopoda, represented in our
existing seas by the nautili and the cuttlefishes, to the low
brachipods, some of whose cogeners may still be detected in the
terebratulæ of our Highland lochs and bays, and some in the

Fig. 49.   Fig. 50.   Fig 51.

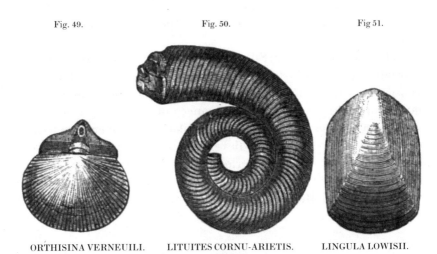

ORTHISINA VERNEUILI.   LITUITES CORNU-ARIETIS.   LINGULA LOWISII.

lingulæ of the southern hemisphere. The cephalopods of the system
are all of an obsolete type, that disappeared myriads of ages
ago,—a remark which, with the exceptions just intimated, and
perhaps one or two others, applies equally to its brachipods; but of
at least two of its intermediate families,—the gasteropoda and
lamellibranchiata,—several of the forms resemble those of recent
shells of the temperate latitudes. In its general aspect, however,
the Silurian fauna, antiquely fashioned, as I have said, as became
its place in the primæval ages of existence, was unlike any other
which the world ever saw; and the absence of the vertebrata, or at
least the inconspicuous place which they occupied if they were at
all present, must have imparted to the whole, as a group, a humble
and mediocre character. It seems to have been for many ages
together a creation of molluscs, corals, and crustacea. At length, in
an upper bed of the system, immediately under the base of the Old
Red Sandstone, the remains of the earliest known fishes appear,

blent with what also appears for the first time,—the fragmentary remains of a terrestrial vegetation. The rocks beneath this ancient bone-bed have yielded, as I have already said, no trace of any plant higher than the Thallogens, or at least not higher than the Zosteraceæ,—plants whose proper habitat is the sea; but, through an apparently simultaneous advance of the two kingdoms, animal and vegetable,—though of course the simultaneousness may be but merely apparent,—the first land-plants and the first vertebrates appear together in the same deposit.

What, let us inquire, is the character of these ancient fishes, that first complete the scale of animated nature in its four master ideas, by adding the vertebrate to the invertebrate divisions? So far as is yet known, they all consist of one well-marked order,—that placoidal order of Agassiz that to an internal framework of cartilage adds an external armature, consisting of plates, spines, and shagreen points of solid bone. Either of the two kinds of dog-fishes on our coasts,—the spiked or spotted,—may be accepted as not inadequate representatives of this order as it now exists. The Port-Jackson shark, however,—a creature that to the dorsal spines and shagreen-covered skin of the common dog-fish adds a mouth terminal at the snout, not placed beneath, as in most other sharks, and a palate covered with a dense pavement of crushing teeth,—better illustrates the order as it first appeared in creation than any of our British placoids.

Fig. 52.

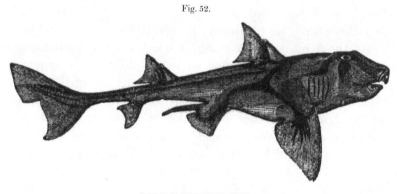

PORT-JACKSON SHARK.
(*Cestracion Phillippi.*)

And here let me adduce another and very remarkable instance of the correspondence which obtains between the sequence in which certain classes of organisms were first ushered into being, and the order of classification adopted, after many revisions, by the higher naturalists. Cuvier, with not a few of the ichthyologists who preceded him, arranged the fishes into two distinct series,—the Cartilaginous and Osseous; and these last he mainly divided into the hard or spiny-finned fishes, and the soft or joint-finned fishes. He placed the sturgeon in his Cartilaginous series; while in his soft-finned order he found a place for the Polypterus of the Nile and the Lepidosteus of the Ohio and St Lawrence. But the arrangement, though it seemed at the time one of the best and most natural possible, failed to meet any corresponding arrangement in the course of geologic history. The place assigned to the class of fishes as a whole corresponded to their place in the palæontological scale;—first of the vertebrate division in the order of their appearance, they bordered, as in the "Animal Kingdom" of the naturalist, on the invertebrate divisions. But it was not until the new classification of Agassiz had ranged them after a different fashion that the correspondence became complete in all its parts. First he erected the fishes that to an internal cartilaginous skeleton unite an external armature of plates and points of bone, into his Placoid order; next, gathering together a mere handful of individuals from among the various orders and families over which they had been scattered,—the sturgeons from among the cartilaginous fishes, and the lepidosteus and polypterus from among the Clupia or herrings,—he erected into a small ganoid order all the fishes that are covered, whatever the consistency of their skeleton, by a continuous or nearly continuous armour of enamelled bone, or by great bony plates that lock into each other at their edges. Out of the remaining fishes,—those covered with scales of a horny substance, and which now comprise nearly nine-tenths of the whole class,—he erected two orders more,—a Ctenoid order, consisting of fishes whose scales, like those of the perch, are pectinated at their lower edges like the teeth of a comb, and a Cycloid order, composed of fishes whose scales, like those of the salmon, are defined all around by a simple continuous margin; and

Fig. 53.*

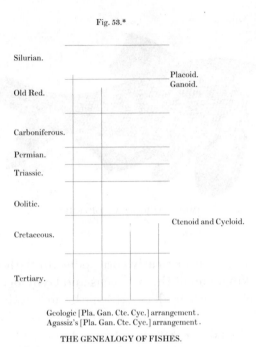

Silurian.

Placoid.
Ganoid.

Old Red.

Carboniferous.

Permian.

Triassic.

Oolitic.

Ctenoid and Cycloid.

Cretaceous.

Tertiary.

Geologic [Pla. Gan. Cte. Cyc.] arrangement.
Agassiz's [Pla. Gan. Cte. Cyc.] arrangement.

THE GENEALOGY OF FISHES.

* Here, as in the former diagrams (figs. 1 and 4), the horizontal lines represent the divisions of the great geologic systems; while the vertical lines indicate the sweep of the several orders of fishes across the scale, and the periods, so far as has yet been determined, of their first occurrence in creation.

no sooner was the division effected than it was found to cast a singularly clear light on the early history of the class. The earliest fishes—first-born of their family—seem to have been all placoids. The Silurian System has not yet afforded trace of any other vertebral animal. With the Old Red Sandstone the ganoids were ushered upon the scene in amazing abundance; and for untold ages, comprising mayhap millions of years, the entire ichthyic class consisted, so far as is yet known, of but these two orders. During the times of the Old Red Sandstone, of the Carboniferous, of the Permian, of the Triassic, and of the Oolitic Systems, all fishes, though apparently as numerous individually as they are now, were comprised in the ganoidal and placoidal orders. The period of these

Fig. 54.

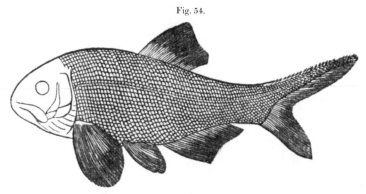

AMBLYPTERUS MACROPTERUS.
From the Coal at Saarbruck.
(A Ganoid of the Carboniferous System.)

orders seems to have been nearly correspondent with the reign, in the vegetable kingdom, of the Acrogens and Gymnogens, with the intermediate classes, their allies. At length, during the ages of the Chalk, the Cycloids and Ctenoids were ushered in, and were gradually developed in creation until the human period, in which they seem to have reached their culminating point, and now many

Fig. 55.

LEBIAS CEPHALOTES.
Cycloids of Aix. (*Miocene.*)

times exceed in number and importance all other fishes. We do not see a sturgeon (our British representative of the ganoids) once in a

Fig. 56.

PLATAX ALTISSIMUS.
A Ctenoid of Monte-Bolca. (*Eocene.*)

twelvemonth; and though the skate and dog-fish (our representatives of the placoids) are greatly less rare, their number bears but a small proportion to that of the fishes belonging to the two prevailing orders, of which thousands of boat-loads are landed on our coasts every day.

The all but entire disappearance of the ganoids from creation is surely a curious and not unsuggestive circumstance. In the human family there are races that have long since reached their culminating point, and are now either fast disappearing or have already disappeared. The Aztecs of Central America, or the Copts of the valley of the Nile, are but the inconsiderable fragments of once mighty nations, memorials of whose greatness live in the vast sepulchral mounds of the far West, or in the temples of Thebes or Luxor, or the pyramids of Gizah. But in the rivers of these very countries,—in the Polypterus of the Nile, or the Lepidosteus of the Mississippi,—we are presented with the few surviving fragments of a dynasty compared with which that of Egypt or of Central America occupied but an exceedingly small portion of either space or time. The dynasty of the ganoids was at one time co-extensive with every river, lake, and sea, and endured during the unreckoned *eons* which extended from the times of the Lower Old Red Sandstone until those of the Chalk. I may here mention, that as there are orders of plants, such as the Rosaceæ and the Grasses, that scarce preceded man in their appearance, so there are families of fishes that seem peculiarly to belong to the human period. Of these, there is a family very familiar on our coasts, and which, though it furnishes none of our higher ichthyic luxuries, is remarkable for the numbers of the human family which it provides with a wholesome and palatable food. The delicate Salmonidæ and the Pleuronectidæ,—families to which the salmon and turbot belong,—were ushered into being as early as the times of the Chalk; but the Gadidæ or cod family,—that family to which the cod proper, the haddock, the dorse, the whiting, the coal-fish, the pollock, the hake, the torsk, and the ling belong, with many other useful and wholesome species,—did not precede man by at least any period of time appreciable to the geologist. No trace of the family has yet been detected in even the Tertiary rocks.

Of the ganoids of the second age of vertebrate existence,—that of the Old Red Sandstone,—some were remarkable for the strangeness of their forms, and some for constituting links of connection which no longer exist in nature, between the ganoid and placoid orders. The Acanth family, which

ceased with the Coal Measures, was characterized, especially in its
Old Red species, by a combination of traits common to both
orders; and among the extremer forms, in which Palæontologists
for a time failed to detect that of the fish at all, we reckon those of
the genera Coccosteus, Pterichthys, and Cephalaspis. The more
aberrant genera, however, even while they consisted each of
several species, were comparatively shortlived. The Coccosteus
and Cephalaspis were restricted to but one formation a-piece;
while the Pterichthys, which appears for the first time in the lower
deposits of the Old Red Sandstone, becomes extinct at its close. On
the other hand, some of the genera that exemplified the general
type of their class were extremely longlived. The Celacanths were
reproduced in many various species, from the times of the Lower

Fig. 57.

PTERICHTHYS OBLONGUS.
(~One-half nat. Size.)

Old Red Sandstone to those of the Chalk; and the Cestracions, which appear in the Upper Ludlow Rocks as the oldest of fishes, continue in at least one species to exist still. It would almost seem as if some such law influenced the destiny of genera in this ichthyic class as that which we find so often exemplified in our own species. The dwarf, or giant, or deformed person, is seldom a long liver; all the more remarkable instances of longevity have been furnished by individuals cast in the ordinary mould and proportions of the species. Not a few of these primordial ganoids were, however, of the highest rank and standing ever exemplified by their class; and we find Agassiz boldly assigning a reason for their superiority to their successors, important for the fact which it embodies, and worthy, as coming from him, of our most respectful attention. "It is plain," we find him saying, "that before the class of reptiles was introduced upon our globe, the fishes, being then the only representatives of the type of vertebrata, were invested with the characters of a higher order, embodying, as it were, a prospective view of a higher development in another class, which was introduced as a distinct type only at a later period; and from that time the reptilian character, which had been so prominent in the oldest fishes, was gradually reduced, till in more recent periods, and in the present creation, the fishes lost all this herpetological relationship, and were at last endowed with characters which contrast as much, when compared with those of reptiles, as they agreed closely in the beginning. Lepidosteus alone reminds us in our time of these old-fashioned characters of the class of fishes as it was in former days."

The ancient fishes seem to have received their fullest development during the Carboniferous period. Their number was very great: some of them attained to an enormous size, and, though the true reptile had already appeared, they continued to retain till the close of the System the high reptilian character and organization. Nothing, however, so impresses the observer as the formidable character of the offensive weapons with which they were furnished, and the amazing strength of their defensive armature. I need scarce say, that the Palæontologist finds no trace in nature of that golden age of the world, of which the poets delighted to sing, when all creatures lived together in unbroken peace, and war and bloodshed were unknown. Ever since animal life began upon our planet, there existed, in all the departments of being, carnivorous classes, who could not live but by the death of their neighbours, and who were armed, in consequence, for their destruction, like the butcher with his axe and knife, and the angler with his hook and spear. But there were certain periods in the history of the past during which these weapons assumed a more formidable aspect than at others; and never were they more formidable than in the times of the Coal Measures. The teeth of the Rhizodus—a ganoidal fish of our coalfields—were more sharp and trenchant than those of the crocodile of the Nile, and in the larger specimens fully four times the bulk and size of the teeth of the hugest reptile of this species that now lives. The dorsal spine of its contemporary the Gyracanthus, a great placoid, much exceeded in size that of any existing fish; it was a mighty spear-head, ornately carved like that of a New Zealand chief, but in a style that, when he first saw a specimen in my collection, greatly excited the admiration of Mr Ruskin. But one of the most remarkable weapons of the period was the sting of the Pleuracanthus, another great placoid of the age of gigantic fishes. It was sharp and polished as a stiletto, but, from its rounded form and dense structure, of great strength; and along two of its sides, from the taper point to within a few inches of the base, there ran a thickly-set row of barbs,

Fig. 58.

PLEURACANTHUS
LÆVISSIMUS.
(*Coal Measures.*)
(~Half nat. size.)

hooked downwards, like the thorns that bristle on the young
shoots of the wild rose, and which must have rendered it a weapon
not merely of destruction, but also of torture. The defensive
armour of the period, especially that of its ganoids, seems to have
been as remarkable for its powers of resistance as the offensive
must have been for their potency in the assault; and it seems
probable that in the great strength of the bony and enamelled
armature of this order of fishes we have the secret of the extremely
formidable character of the teeth, spines, and stings that co-
existed along with it. Such of the fishes of the present time as live
on crustacea and the shelled molluscs,—such as the Wrasse or
rock-fish family, and at least one of the Goby family, the sea-
wolf,—have an apparatus of crushing teeth greatly more solid and
strong than the teeth of such of their contemporaries as are either
herbivorous or feed on the weaker families of their own class. A
similar remark applies to the ancient sharks, as contrasted with
those of later times. So long as the strongly armed ganoidal order
prevailed in nature, the sharks were furnished with massive
crushing teeth; but when the ganoids waned in creation, and the
soft-scaled cycloid and ctenoid orders took and amply filled the
place which they had left vacant, the well-known modern form of

Fig. 59.

Fig. 60.

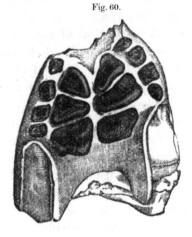

CARCHARIAS PRODUCTUS.
Cutting Tooth. (*Miocene.*)

PLACODUS GIGAS.
Crushing Teeth. (*Trias.*)

sharks' teeth was introduced,—a form much rather suited for cutting soft bodies than for crushing hard ones. In fine, the offensive weapons of the times of the Coal Measures seem very formidable, just as those personal weapons of the middle ages seem so that were borne at a time when every soldier took the field cased in armour of proof. The slim scimitar or slender rapier would have availed but little against massive iron helmets or mail coats of tempered steel. And so the warriors of the period armed themselves with ponderous maces, battleaxes as massive as hammers, and double-handed swords of great weight and strength.

Before passing onwards to other and higher classes and orders, as they occurred in creation, permit me to make the formidable armour of the earlier fishes, offensive and defensive, the subject of a single remark. We are told by Goethe, in his autobiography, that he had attained his sixth year when the terrible earthquake at Lisbon took place,—"an event," he says, "which greatly disturbed" his "peace of mind for the first time." He could not reconcile a catastrophe so suddenly destructive to thousands with the ideas which he had already formed for himself of a Providence all-powerful and all-benevolent. But he afterwards learned, he tells us, to recognise in such events the *"God of the Old Testament."* I know not in what spirit the remark was made; but this I know, that it is the God of the Old Testament whom we see exhibited in all nature and all providence; and that it is at once wisdom and duty in his rational creatures, however darkly they may perceive or imperfectly they may comprehend, to hold in implicit faith that the Adorable Monarch of all the past and of all the future is a King who "can do no wrong." This early exhibition of tooth, and spine, and sting,—of weapons constructed alike to cut and to pierce,—to unite two of the most indispensable requirements of the modern armourer,—a keen edge to a strong back,—nay, stranger still, the examples furnished in this primæval time, of weapons formed not only to kill, but also to torture,—must be altogether at variance with the preconceived opinions of those who hold that until man appeared in creation, and darkened its sympathetic face with the stain of moral guilt, the reign of violence and outrage did not begin, and that there was no death among the inferior creatures.

and no suffering. But preconceived opinion, whether it hold fast, with Lactantius and the old Schoolmen, to the belief that there can be no antipodes, or assert, with Caccini and Bellarmine, that our globe hangs lazily in the midst of the heavens, while the sun moves round it, must yield ultimately to scientific truth. And it is a truth as certain as the existence of a southern hemisphere, or the motion of the earth round both its own axis and the great solar centre, that, untold ages ere man had sinned or suffered, the animal creation exhibited exactly its present state of war,—that the strong, armed with formidable weapons, exquisitely constructed to kill, preyed upon the weak; and that the weak, sheathed, many of them, in defensive armour equally admirable in its mechanism, and ever increasing and multiplying upon the earth far beyond the requirements of the mere maintenance of their races, were enabled to escape, as species, the assaults of the tyrant tribes, and to exist unthinned for unreckoned ages. It has been weakly and impiously urged,—as if it were merely with the geologist that men had to settle this matter,—that such an economy of warfare and suffering,—of warring and of being warred upon,—would be, in the words of the infant Goethe, unworthy of an all-powerful and all-benevolent Providence, and in effect a libel on his government and character. But that grave charge we leave the objectors to settle with the great Creator himself. Be it theirs, not ours, according to the poet, to

> "Snatch from his hand the balance and the rod,
> Rejudge his justice, be the god of God."

Be it enough for the geologist rightly to interpret the record of creation,—to declare the truth as he finds it,—to demonstrate, from evidence no clear intellect ever yet resisted, that He, the Creator, from whom even the young lions seek their food, and who giveth to all the beasts, great and small, their meat in due season, ever wrought as He now works in his animal kingdom,—that He gave to the primæval fishes their spines and their stings,—to the primæval reptiles their trenchant teeth and their strong armour of bone,—to the primæval mammals their great tusks and their sharp claws,—that He of old divided all his creatures, as now, into animals of prey and the animals preyed upon,—that from the beginning of things he inseparably established among his non-responsible existences the twin laws of generation and of death,—nay, further, passing from the established truths of *Geologic* to one of the best established truths of *Theologic* science,—God's eternal justice and truth,—let us assert, that in the Divine government the matter of fact always determines the question of right, and that whatever has been done by Him who rendereth no account to man of his matters, He had in all ages, and in all places, an unchallengeable right to do.

The oldest known reptiles appear just a little before the close of the Old Red Sandstone, just as the oldest known fishes appeared just a little before the close of the Silurian System. What seems to be the Upper Old Red of our own country, though there still hangs a shade of doubt on the subject, has furnished the remains of a small reptile, equally akin, it would appear, to the lizards and the batrachians; and what seems to be the Upper Old Red of the United States has exhibited the foot-tracks of a larger animal of the same class, which not a little resemble those which would be impressed on recent sand or clay by the alligator of the Mississippi, did not the alligator of the Mississippi efface its own foot-prints (a consequence of the shortness of its legs) by the trail of its abdomen. In the Coal Measures, the reptiles hitherto found,—and it is still little more than ten years since the first was detected,—are all allied, though not without a cross of the higher crocodilian or lacertian nature, to the batrachian order,—that lowest order of the reptiles to which the frogs, newts, and salamanders belong. These reptiles of the carboniferous era, though only a few twelvemonths ago we little suspected the fact, seem to have been not very rare in our own neighbourhood. My attention was called some time since by Mr Henry Cadell—an intelligent practical geologist,—to certain appearances in one of the Duke of Buccleuch's coal pits near Dalkeith, which he regarded as the tracks of air-breathing quadrupeds; and, after examining a specimen, containing four foot-prints, which he had brought above ground, and which not a little excited my curiosity, we visited the pit together. And there, in a side working about half a mile from the pit-mouth, and about four hundred feet under the surface, I found the roof of the coal, which rose at a high angle, traversed by so many foot-tracks, upwards, downwards, and athwart, that it cost me some little care to trace the individual lines. At least one of the number, however,—consisting of eleven foot-prints of the right and as many of the left foot,—I was able to trace from side to side of the working, a distance of four yards; and several of the others for shorter spaces. The prints, which were reverses or casts in a very coarse sandstone, were about thirteen inches apart across the creature's chest, and rather more than a foot apart from its fore to its hinder limbs. They were alternately larger and smaller,—the smaller (those of the fore feet) measuring about four inches in length, and the larger (those of the hinder feet) about six inches. The number of toes seemed to be alternately four and five; but from the circumstance that the original matrix on which the tracks had been impressed,—a micaceous clay resolved into a loose fissile sandstone,—had fallen away in the working of the pit, leaving but the boldly-relieved though ill-defined casts on the coarse sandstone, I could not definitely determine the point. Enough, however, remained to show that at that spot,—little more than a mile from where the Duke of Buccleuch's palace now stands,—large reptiles had congregated in considerable numbers shortly after the great eight feet coal-seam of the Dalkeith basin had been formed. In another part of the pit I found foot-tracks of apparently the same animal in equal abundance, but still less distinct in their state of keeping. But they bore testimony with the others to the comparative abundance of reptilian life at an early period, when the coal-bearing strata of the empire were little more than half-deposited. It was not, however, until the Permian and Triassic Systems had come to a close, and even the earlier ages of the Oolitic System had passed away, that the class received its fullest development in creation. And certainly very wonderful was the development which it then did receive. Reptiles became everywhere the lords and masters of this lower world. When any class of the air-breathing vertebrates is very largely developed, we find it taking possession of all the three old terrestrial elements,—earth, air, and water. The human period, for instance, like that which immediately preceded it, is peculiarly a period of mammals; and we find the class, *free*, if I may so express myself, of the three elements, disputing possession of the sea with the fishes, in its Cetaceans, its seals, and its sea-lions, and of the air with the birds, in its numerous genera of the bat family. Further, not until the great mammaliferous period is fairly ushered in do either the bats or the whales make their appearance in creation. Remains of Oolitic reptiles have been mistaken in more than one instance for those of Cetacea; but it is now generally held that the earliest known specimens of the family belong to the Tertiary ages, while those of the oldest bats occur in the Eocene of the Paris Basin, associated with the bones of dolphins, lamantines, and morses.

Fig. 61.

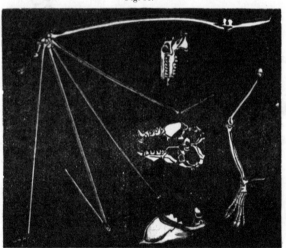

VESPERTILIO PARISIENSIS.
A Bat of the Eocene.

Now, in the times of the Oolite it was the reptilian class that possessed itself of all the elements. Its gigantic enaliosaurs, huge reptilian *whales* mounted on paddles, were the tyrants of the ocean, and must have reigned supreme over the already reduced class of fishes; its pterodactyles,—dragons as strange as were ever feigned by romancer of the middle ages, and that to the jaws and

Fig. 62.

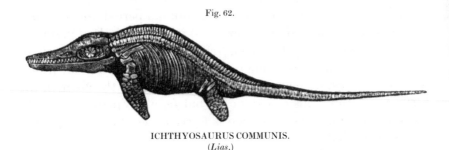

ICHTHYOSAURUS COMMUNIS.
(*Lias.*)

Fig. 63.

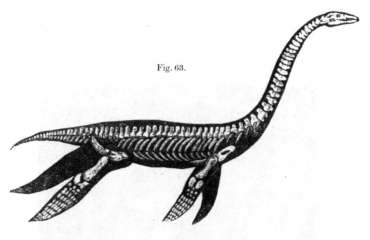

PLESIOSAURUS DOLICHODEIRUS.
(*Lias.*)

teeth of the crocodile added the wings of a bat and the body and
tail of an ordinary mammal, had the "power of the air," and,
pursuing the fleetest insects in their flight, captured and bore them

* Some of these *dragons* of the Secondary ages were of very considerable
size. The wings of a Pterodactyle of the Chalk, in the possession of Mr
Bowerbank, must have had a spread of about eighteen feet; those of a
recently-discovered Pterodactyle of the Greensand, a spread of not less
than twenty-seven feet. The *Lammer-geyer* of the Alps has an extent of
wing of but from ten to eleven feet; while that of the great Condor of the
Andes, the largest of flying birds, does not exceed twelve feet.

Fig. 64.

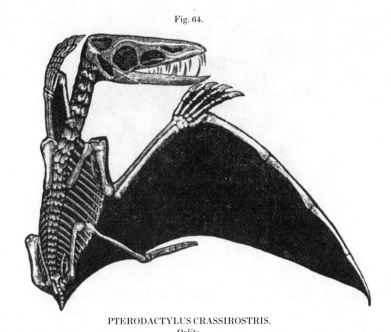

PTERODACTYLUS CRASSIROSTRIS.
Oolite.

down;* its lakes and rivers abounded in crocodiles and fresh-water tortoises of ancient type and fashion; and its woods and plains were the haunts of a strange reptilian fauna of what has been well termed "fearfully great lizards,"—some of which, such as the iguanodon, rivalled the largest elephant in height, and greatly more than rivalled him in length and bulk. Judging from what remains, it seems not improbable that the reptiles of this Oolitic period were quite as numerous individually, and consisted of well-nigh as many genera and species, as all the mammals of the present time. In the cretaceous ages, the class, though still the dominant one, is visibly reduced in its standing: it had reached its culminating point in the Oolite, and then began to decline; and with the first dawn of the Tertiary division we find it occupying, as now, a very subordinate place in creation. Curiously enough, it is not until its times of humiliation and decay that one of the most remarkable of its orders appears,—an order itself illustrative of extreme degradation, and which figures largely, in every scheme of

Fig. 65.

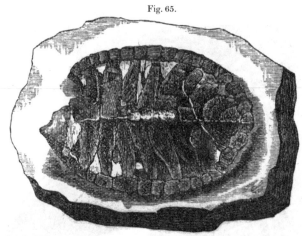

CHELONIA BENSTEDI.
(*Chalk.*)

mythology that borrowed through traditional channels from Divine revelation, as a meet representative of man's great enemy the Evil One. I of course refer to the ophidian or serpent family.

Fig. 66.

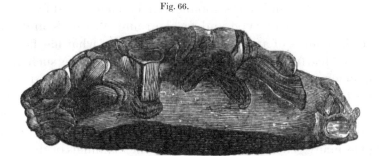

PALÆOPHIS TOLIAPICUS.
(*Ophidian of the Eocene.*)

The earliest ophidian remains known to the Palæontologist occur in that ancient deposit of the Tertiary division known as the London Clay, and must have belonged to serpents, some of them allied to the Pythons, some to the sea-snakes, which, judging from the corresponding parts of recent species, must have been from fourteen to twenty feet in length.

And here let us again pause for a moment, to remark how strangely these irascible, repulsive reptiles,—creatures lengthened out far beyond the proportions of the other members of their class by mere vegetative repetitions of the vertebræ,—condemned to derive, wormlike, their ability of progressive motion from the ringlike scutes of the abdomen,—venomous in many of their species,—formidable in others to even the noblest animals, from their fascinating powers and their great craft,—without fore or hinder limbs, without thoracic or pelvic arches,—the very types and exemplars (our highest naturalists being the judges) of the extreme of animal degradation,—let us, I say, remark how strangely their history has been mixed up with that of man and of religion in all the older mythologies, and in that Divine Revelation whence the older mythologies were derived. It was one of the most ancient of the Phœnician fables, that the great antagonist of the gods was a gigantic serpent, that had at one time been their subject, but revolted against them and became their enemy. It was a monstrous serpent that assailed and strove to destroy the *mother* of Apollo ere yet the birth of the god, but which, long after, *Apollo* in turn assaulted and slew. It was a great serpent that watched over the apples of the Hesperides, and that Hercules, ere he could possess himself of the fruit, had to combat and kill. It was a frightful serpent that guarded the golden fleece from Jason, and which the hero had to destroy in the first instance, and next to exterminate the strange brood of armed men that sprang up from its sown teeth. In short, the old mythologies are well-nigh as full of the serpent as those ancient Runic obelisks of our country whose endless knots and complicated fret-work are formed throughout of the interlacings of snakes. Let us, however, accept as representative of this innumerable class of legends, the classical story, rendered yet more classical by the profound and reverend comment given by Bacon in his "Wisdom of the Ancients." "Jupiter and the other gods," says the philosopher, in his simple version of the tradition, "conferred upon men a most acceptable and desirable boon,—the gift of perpetual youth. But men, foolishly overjoyed hereat, laid this present of the gods upon an ass, who, in returning back with it, being extremely thirsty, and coming to a fountain, the serpent who was guardian thereof would not suffer him to drink but upon condition of receiving the burden he carried, whatever it should be. The silly ass complied; and thus the perpetual renewal of youth was for a sup of water transferred from men to the race of serpents." "That this gift of perpetual youth should pass from men to serpents," continues Bacon, "seems added, by way of ornament and illustration, to the fable." And it certainly *has* much the appearance of an afterthought. But how very striking the resemblance borne by the story, as a whole, to that narrative in the opening page of human history which exhibits the first parents of the race as yielding up to the temptation of the serpent the gift of immortality; and further, how remarkable the fact, that the reptile selected as typical here of the great fallen spirit that kept not his first estate, should be at once the reptile of latest appearance in creation, and the one selected by philosophic naturalists as representative of a reversed process in the course of being,—of a downward, sinking career, from the vertebrate antetype towards greatly lower types in the invertebrate divisions! The fallen spirit is represented in revelation by what we are now taught to recognise in science as a *degraded* reptile.

Birds make their first appearance in a Red Sandstone deposit of the United States, in the valley of the Connecticut, which was at one time supposed to belong to the Triassic System, but which is now held to be at least not older than the times of the Lias. No fragments of the skeletons of birds have yet been discovered in formations older than the Chalk: the Connecticut remains are those of footprints exclusively; and yet they tell their extraordinary story, so far as it extends, with remarkable precision and distinctness. They were apparently all of the Grallæ or stilt order of birds,—an order to which the cranes, herons, and bustards belong, with the ostriches and cassowaries, and which is characterized by possessing but three toes on each foot (one species of ostrich has but two), or, if a fourth toe be present, so imperfectly is it developed in most of the cases, that it fails to reach the ground. And in almost all the footprints of the primæval birds of the Connecticut there are only three toes exhibited. Peculiar, ill

Fig. 67.

BIRD TRACKS OF THE CONNECTICUT.
(*Lias or Oolite.*)

understood laws regulate the phalangal divisions of the various animals. It is a law of the human kind, for instance, that the thumb should consist of but three phalanges; while the fingers, even the smallest, consist of four. And, in the same way, it is a law generally exemplified among birds, that of the three toes which correspond to the fingers, the inner toe should be composed of three phalanges, the middle or largest toe of four phalanges, and the outer toe, though but second in point of size, of five phalanges. Such is the law *now*, and such was equally the law, as shown by the American foot-prints, in the times of the Lias. Some of the impressions are of singular distinctness. Every claw and phalange has left its mark in the stone; while the trifid termination of the

Fig. 68.

FOSSIL FOOT-PRINT.
(*Connecticut.*)

tarso-metatarsal bone leaves three marks more,—fifteen in all,—the true ornithic number. In some of the specimens even the pressure of a metatarsal brush, still possessed by some birds, is distinctly traceable; nay, there are instances in which the impress of the dermoid papillæ has remained as sharply as if made in wax. But the immense size of some of these foot-prints served to militate for a time against belief in their ornithic origin. The impressions that are but secondary in point of size greatly exceed those of the hugest birds which now exist; while those of the largest class equal the prints of the bulkier quadrupeds. There are tridactyle footprints in the red sandstones of Connecticut that measure eighteen inches in length from the heel to the middle claw, nearly thirteen inches in breadth from the outer to the inner toe, and which indicate, from their distance apart in the straight line, a stride of about six feet in the creature that impressed them in these ancient sands,—measurements that might well startle zoologists who had derived their experience of the ornithic class from existing birds exclusively. Comparatively recent discoveries have, however, if not lessened, at least familiarized us to the wonder. In a deposit of New Zealand that dates little if at all in advance of the human period, there have been detected the remains of birds scarce inferior in size to those of America in the Liassic ages. The bones of the *Dinornus giganteus,* exhibited by the late Dr Mantell in Edinburgh in the autumn of 1850, greatly exceeded in bulk those of the largest horse. A thigh-bone sixteen inches in length measured nearly nine inches in circumference in the middle of the shaft: the head of a tibia measured twenty-one inches in circumference. It was estimated that a foot entire in all its parts, which formed an interesting portion of the exhibition, would, when it was furnished with nails, and covered by the integuments, have measured about fifteen inches in length; and it was calculated by a very competent authority, Professor Owen, that of the other bones of the leg to which it belonged, the tibia must have been about two feet nine inches, and the femur about fourteen and a half inches long. The larger thigh-bone referred to must have belonged, it was held, to a bird that stood from eleven to twelve feet high,—the extreme height of the great African elephant. Such were the monster birds of a comparatively recent period; and their remains serve to render credible the evidence furnished by the great foot-prints of their remote predecessors of the Lias. The huge feet of the greatest Dinornus whose bones have yet been found would have left impressions scarcely an inch shorter than those of the still huger birds of the Connecticut. Is it not truly wonderful, that in this late age of the world, in which the invention of the poets seems to content itself with humbler and lowlier flights than of old, we should thus find the facts of geology fully rivalling, in the strange and the *outré*, the wildest fancies of the romancers who flourished in the middle ages? I have already referred to flying dragons,—real existences of the Oolitic period,—that were quite as extraordinary of type, if not altogether so huge of bulk, as those with which the Seven Champions of Christendom used to do battle; and here are we introduced to birds of the Liassic ages that were scarce less gigantic than the roc of Sinbad the Sailor. They are fraught with strange meanings these foot-prints of the Connecticut. They tell of a time far removed into the by-past eternity, when great birds frequented by myriads the shores of a

nameless lake, to wade into its shallows in quest of mail-covered
fishes of the ancient type, or long-extinct molluscs; while reptiles
equally gigantic, and of still stranger proportions, haunted the
neighbouring swamps and savannahs; and when the same sun that
shone on the tall moving forms beside the waters, and threw their
long shadows across the red sands, lighted up the glades of deep
forests, all of whose fantastic productions,—tree, bush, and
herb,—have, even in their very species, long since passed away.
And of this scene of things only the foot-prints
remain,—"foot-prints on the sands of time," that tell us, among
other matters, whence the graceful American poet derived his
quiet but singularly effective and unmistakeably indigenous
figure:—

> "Lives of great men all remind us
>   We can make our lives sublime,
> *And, departing, leave behind us*
>   *Foot-prints on the sands of time,*
> Foot-prints that perhaps another,
>   Sailing o'er life's solemn main,
> A forlorn and shipwreck'd brother,
>   Seeing, shall take heart again."

With the Stonesfield slates,—a deposit which lies above what
is known as the Inferior Oolite,—the remains of mammaliferous
animals first appear. As, however, no other mammalian remains
occur until after the close of the great Secondary Division, and as
certain marked peculiarities attach to these Oolitic ones, it may be
well to inquire whether their place, so far in advance of their
fellows, may not be indicative of a radical difference of
character,—a difference considerable enough to suggest to the
zoologist an improvement in his scheme of classification. It has
been shown by Professor Owen,—our highest authority in
comparative anatomy,—that while one Stonesfield genus
unequivocally belonged to the marsupial order, another of its
genera bears also certain of the marsupial traits; and that the
group which they composed,—a very small one, and consisting

Fig. 69.

THYLACOTHERIUM PREVOSTI
(*Stonesfield Slate.*)

exclusively of minute insect-eating animals,—exhibits in its general aspect the characteristics of this pouched family. Even the genus of the group that least resembles them was pronounced by Cuvier to have its nearest affinities with the opossums. And let us mark how very much may be implied in this circumstance. In the "Animal Kingdom" of the great naturalist just named, the marsupiata, or pouched animals, are made to occupy the fourth place among the nine orders of the Mammalia; but should they not rather occupy a place intermediate between the placental mammals and the birds? and does not nature indicate their true position by the position which she assigns to them in the geologic scale? The birds are oviparous; and between the extrusion of the egg and the development of the perfect young bird they have to hatch it into life during a long period of incubation. The marsupiata are not oviparous, for their *eggs* want the enveloping shell or skin; but they, too, are extruded in an exceedingly rudimentary and fœtal state, and have to undergo in the pouch a greatly longer period of *incubation* than that demanded by nature for any bird whatever. The young kangaroo is extruded, after it has remained for little more than a month in the womb, as a fœtus scarcely an inch in length by somewhat less than half an inch in breadth: it is blind, exhibiting merely dark eyespots; its limbs are so rudimentary, that even the hinder legs, so largely developed in the genus when mature, exist as mere stumps; it is unable even to suck, but, holding permanently on by a minute dug, has the sustaining fluid occasionally pressed into its mouth by the mother.

And, undergoing a peculiar but not the less real process of incubation, the creature that had to remain for little more than a month in the womb,—strictly thirty-nine days,—has to remain in the mother's pouch, ere it is fully developed and able to provide for itself, for a period of eight months. It is found to increase in weight during this hatching process, from somewhat less than an ounce to somewhat more than eight pounds. Now, this surely is a process quite as nearly akin to the incubation of egg-bearing birds as to the ordinary nursing process of the placental mammals; and on the occult but apparently real principle, that the true arrangement of the animal kingdom is that which we find exemplified by the successive introduction of its various classes and orders in the course of geologic history, should we not anticipate a point of time for the introduction of the marsupiata, intermediate between the widely-distant points at which the egg-bearing birds and the true placental mammals appeared? Ranged at once chronologically, and by their mode of reproduction, the various classes of the vertebrata would run, did we accept the suggested reading, as follows:—First appear cold-blooded vertebrates (fishes), that propagate by eggs or spawn,—chiefly by the latter. Next appear cold-blooded vertebrates (reptiles), that propagate by eggs or spawn,—chiefly by the former. Then appear warm-blooded vertebrates (birds), that propagate by eggs exclusively. Then warm-blooded vertebrates come upon the stage, that produce *eggs* without shells, which have to be subjected for months to a species of extra placental incubation. And last of all the true placental mammals appear. And thus, tried by the test of perfect reproduction, the great vertebral division receives its full development in creation.

The placental mammals make their appearance, as I have said, in the earliest ages of the great Tertiary division, and exhibit in the group an aspect very unlike that which they at present bear. The Eocene ages were peculiarly the ages of the Palæo-theres,—strange animals of that pachydermatous or thick-skinned order to which the elephants, the tapirs, the hogs, and the horses belong. It had been remarked by naturalists, that there are fewer families of this order in living nature than of almost any other, and

Fig. 70.

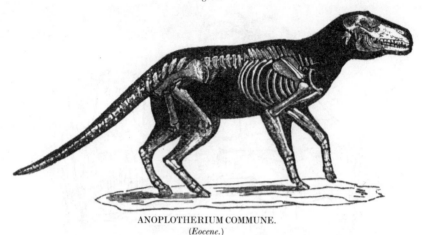

ANOPLOTHERIUM COMMUNE.
(*Eocene.*)

that, of the existing genera, not a few are widely separated in their
analogies from the others. But in the Palæotheres of the Eocene,
which ranged in size from a large horse to a hare, not a few of the
missing links have been found,—links connecting the tapirs to the
hogs, and the hogs to the Palæotheres proper; and there is at least
one species suggestive of an union of some of the more peculiar
traits of the tapirs and the horses. It was among these extinct
Pachydermata of the Paris basin that Cuvier effected his
wonderful restorations, and produced those figures in outline
which are now as familiar to the geologist as any of the forms of the
existing animals. The London Clay and the Eocene of the Isle of
Wight have also yielded numerous specimens of these pachyderms,
whose identity with the Continental ones has been established by
Owen; but they are more fragmentary, and their state of keeping
less perfect, than those furnished by the gypsum quarries of Velay
and Montmartre. In these the smaller animals occur often in a
state of preservation so peculiar and partial as to excite the
curiosity of even the untaught workmen. Only half the skeleton is
present. The limbs and ribs of the under side are found lying in
nearly their proper places; while of the limbs and ribs of the upper
side usually not a trace can be detected,—even the upper side of
the skull is often awanting. It would almost seem as if some pre-

Fig. 71.

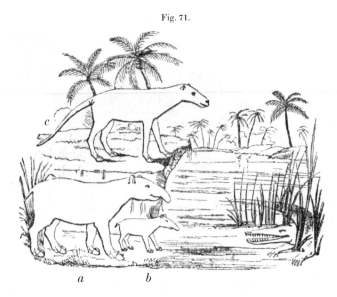

ANIMALS OF THE PARIS BASIN.*
(*Eocene.*)

* *a* Palæotherium magnum. *b*. Palæotherium minus.
c. Anoplotherium commune.

Adamite butcher had divided the carcasses longitudinally, and
carried away with him all the upper halves. The reading of the
enigma seems to be, that when the creatures lay down and died,
the gypsum in which their remains occur was soft enough to
permit their under sides to sink into it, and that then gradually
hardening, it kept the bones in their places; while the uncovered
upper sides, exposed to the disintegrating influences, either
mouldered away piecemeal, or were removed by accident. The
bones of the larger animals of the basin are usually found
detached; and ere they could be re-constructed into perfect
skeletons, they taxed the extraordinary powers of the greatest of
comparative anatomists. Rather more than twenty different
species of extinct mammals have been detected in the Paris
basin,—not a great number, it may be thought; and yet for so
limited a locality we may deem it not a very small one, when we

take into account the fact that all our native mammals of Britain and Ireland amount (according to Fleming), if we except the Cetaceæ and the seals, to but forty species.

In the Middle or Miocene Tertiary, pachyderms, though of a wholly different type from their predecessors, are still the prevailing forms. The Dinotherium, one of the greatest quadrupedal mammals that ever lived, seems to have formed a connecting link in this middle age between the Pachydermata and the Cetaceæ. Each ramus of the under jaw, which in the larger specimens are fully four feet in length, bore at the symphysis a great bent tusk turned downwards, which appears to have been employed as a pick-axe in uprooting the aquatic plants and liliaceous roots on which the creature seems to have lived. The head, which measured about three feet across,—a breadth sufficient, surely, to satisfy the demands of the most exacting phrenologist,—was provided with muscles of enormous strength, arranged so as to give potent effect to the operations of this strange tool. The hinder part of the skull not a little resembled that of the Cetaceæ; while, from the form of the nasal bones, the

Fig. 72.

DINOTHERIUM GIGANTEUM.
(*Miocene.*)

creature was evidently furnished with a trunk like the elephant. It seems not improbable, therefore, that this bulkiest of mammaliferous quadrupeds constituted, as I have said, a sort of uniting tie between creatures still associated in the human mind, from the circumstance of their massive proportions, as the greatest that swim the sea or walk the land,—the whale and the elephant. The mastodon, an elephantoid animal, also furnished, like the elephant, with tusks and trunk, but marked by certain peculiarities which constitute it a different genus, seems in Europe to have been contemporary with the Dinotherium; but in North America (the scene of its greatest numerical development) it appears to belong to a later age. In height it did not surpass the African elephant, but it considerably exceeded it in length,—a specimen which could not have stood above twelve feet high indicating a length of about twenty-five feet: it had what the elephants want,—tusks fixed in its lower jaw, which the males retained through life, but the females lost when young; its limbs were proportionally shorter, but more massive, and its abdomen more elongated and slim; its grinder teeth too, some of which have been known to weigh from seventeen to twenty pounds, had their cusps elevated into great mammæ-like protuberances, to which the creature owes its name, and wholly differ in their proportions and outline from the grinders of the elephant. The much greater remoteness of the mastodonic period in Europe than in America is a circumstance worthy of notice, as it is one of many facts that seem to indicate a general transposition of at least the later geologic ages on the opposite sides of the Atlantic. Groupes of corresponding character on the eastern and western shores of this great ocean were not contemporaneous in time. It has been repeatedly remarked, that the existing plants and trees of the United States, with not a few of its fishes and reptiles, bear in their forms and construction the marks of a much greater antiquity than those of Europe. The geologist who set himself to discover similar types on the eastern side of the Atlantic would have to seek for them among the deposits of the later Tertiaries. North America seems to be still passing through its later Tertiary ages; and it appears to be a consequence of this curious transposition, that while in Europe the mastodonic period is removed by two great geologic eras from the present time, it is removed from it in America by only one. Even in America, however, that period lies far beyond the reach of human tradition,—a fact borne out by the pseudo-traditions retailed by the aborigines regarding the mastodon. By none of at least the higher naturalists has there been a doubt entertained respecting its herbivorous character; and the discovery of late years of the stomach of an individual charged with decayed herbage and fragments of the succulent branches of trees, some of them of existing species, has demonstrated the solidity of the reasonings founded on its general structure and aspect. The pseudo-traditions, however, represent it in every instance as a carnivorous tyrant, that, had it not been itself destroyed, would have destroyed all the other animals its contemporaries. It is said by the red men of Virginia, "that a troop of these tremendous quadrupeds made fearful havoc for some time among the deer, the buffaloes, and all the other animals created for the use of the Indians, and spread desolation far and wide. At last *'the Mighty Man above'* seized his thunder and killed them all, with the exception of the largest of the males, who, presenting his head to the thunderbolts, shook them off as they fell; but, being wounded in the side, he betook himself to flight towards the great lakes, where he still resides at the present day."

Let me here remind you, in the passing, that that antiquity of type which characterizes the recent productions of North America is one of many wonders,—not absolutely geological in themselves, but which, save for the revelations of geology, would have for ever remained unnoted and unknown,—which have been pressed, during the last half-century, on the notice of naturalists. "It is a circumstance quite extraordinary and unexpected," says Agassiz, in his profoundly interesting work on Lake Superior, "that the fossil plants of the Tertiary beds of Oeningen resemble more closely the trees and shrubs which grow at present in the eastern parts of North America, than those of any other parts of the world; thus allowing us to express correctly the difference between the opposite coasts of Europe and America, by saying that the present eastern American flora, and, I may add, the fauna also, have a more ancient character than those of Europe. The plants, especially the trees and shrubs, growing in our days in the United States, are, as it were, old-fashioned; and the characteristic genera Lagomys, Chelydra, and the large Salamanders with permanent gills, that remind us of the fossils of Oeningen, are at least equally so;—they bear the marks of former ages." How strange a fact! Not only are we accustomed to speak of the eastern continents as the Old World, in contradistinction to the great continent of the west, but to speak also of the world before the Flood as the Old World, in contradistinction to that post-diluvian world which succeeded it. And yet equally, if we receive the term in either of its acceptations, is America an older world still,—an older world than that of the eastern continents,—an older world, in the fashion and type of its productions, than the world before the Flood. And when the immigrant settler takes axe amid the deep backwoods, to lay open for the first time what he deems a new country, the great trees that fall before him,—the brushwood which he lops away with a sweep of his tool,—the unfamiliar herbs which he tramples under foot,—the lazy fish-like reptile that scarce stirs out of his path as he descends to the neighbouring creek to drink,—the fierce alligator-like tortoise, with the large limbs and small carapace, that he sees watching among the reeds for fish and frogs, just as he reaches the water,—and the little hare-like rodent, without a tail, that he startles by the way,—all attest, by the antiqueness of the mould in which they are cast, how old a country the seemingly new one really is,—a country vastly older, in type at least, than that of the antediluvians and the patriarchs, and only to be compared with that which flourished on the eastern side of the Atlantic long ere the appearance of man, and the remains of whose perished productions we find locked up in the *loess* of the Rhine, or amid the lignites of Nassau. America is emphatically the *Old* World. If we accept, however, as sound the ingenious logic by which Colton labours to show, in not inelegant verse, that the *Moderns* are the true *Ancients*, we may continue to term it the New World still.

> "We that on these late days are thrown
> Must be the oldest Ancients known.

The *earliest* Modern earth has seen
Was Adam, in his apron green.
He lived when young Creation pealed
Her morning hymn o'er flood and field,
Till all her infant offspring came
To that great christening for a name.
And he that would the Ancients know
Must forward come, not backward go:
The learned lumber of the shelves
Shows nothing older than ourselves.
But who in older times than we
Shall live?—That infant on the knee,—
See sights to us were never shown,
And secrets know to us unknown."

The group of mammals which, in Europe at least, immediately preceded the human period seems to have been everywhere a remarkable one; and nowhere was it more so than in the British islands. Our present mammaliferous fauna is rather poor; but the contents of the later deposits show that we must regard it as but a mere fragment of a very noble one. Associated with species that still exist in the less cultivated parts of the country, such as the badger, the fox, the wild cat, the roe, and the red deer, we find the remains of great animals, whose cogeners must now be sought for in the intertropical regions. Britain during the times of the boulder clay, and for ages previous, had its native elephant, its two species of rhinoceros, its hippopotamus, its hyæna, its tiger, its three species of bears, its two species of beavers, its great elk, and its gigantic deer. Forms now found widely apart, and in very different climates, meet within the British area. During at least the earlier times of the group, the temperature of our island seems to have been very much what it is now. As I have already had occasion to remark, the British oak flourished on its plains and lower slopes, and the birch and Scotch fir on its hills. And yet under these familiar trees the lagomys or tailless hare, a form now mainly restricted to Siberia and the wilds of Northern America, and the reindeer, an animal whose proper habitat at the present time is Lapland, were associated with forms that are now only to be found

Fig. 73.

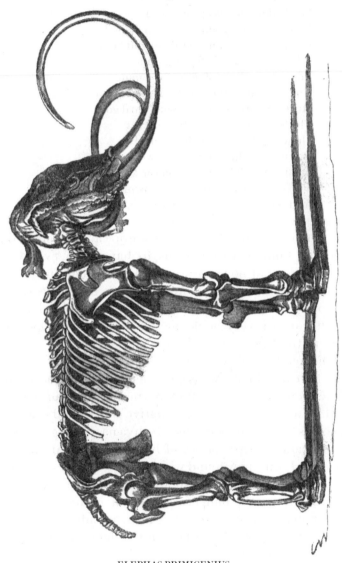

ELEPHAS PRIMIGENIUS.
(*Mammoth.*) Great British Elephant.

between the tropics, such as that of the hippopotamus and
rhinoceros. These last, however, unequivocally of extinct species,

Fig. 74.

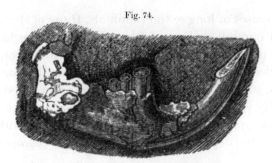

TROGONTHERIUM CUVIERI.
Gigantic Beaver. (*Pleistocene.*)

seem to have been adapted to live in a temperate climate; and we know from the famous Siberian specimen, that the British

Fig. 75.

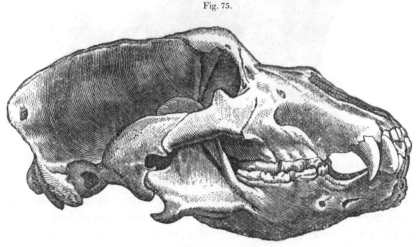

URSUS SPELÆUS.
Cave Bear. (*Pleistocene.*)

elephant, with its covering of long hair and closely felted wool, was fitted to sustain the rigours of a very severe one. It is surely a strange fact, but not less true than strange, that since hill and dale assumed in Britain their present configuration, and the oak and birch flourished in its woods, there were caves in England haunted for ages by families of hyænas,—that they dragged into their dens,

with the carcases of long extinct animals, those of the still familiar
denizens of our hill-sides, and feasted, now on the lagomys, and
now on the common hare,—that they now fastened on the beaver
or the reindeer, and now upon the roebuck or the goat. In one of
these caves, such of the bones as projected from the stiff soil have
been actually worn smooth in a narrow passage where the hyænas
used to come in contact with them in passing out and in; and for
several feet in depth the floor beneath is composed almost

Fig. 76.

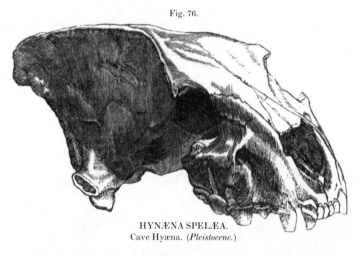

HYNÆNA SPELÆA.
Cave Hyæna. (*Pleistocene.*)

exclusively of gnawed fragments, that still exhibit the deeply
indented marks of formidable teeth. In the famous Kirkdale cave
alone, part of the skeletons of from two to three hundred hyænas
have been detected, mixed with portions of the osseous framework
of the cave-tiger, the cave-bear, the ox, the deer, the mammoth,
and the rhinoceros. That cave must have been a den of wild
creatures for many ages ere the times of the boulder clay, during
which period it was shut up from all access to the light and air by a
drift deposit, and lay covered over until again laid open by some
workmen little more than thirty years ago. Not only were many of
the wild animals of the country which still exist contemporary for
a time with its extinct bears, tigers, and elephants, but it seems at
least highly probable that several of our domesticated breeds

derived their origin from progenitors whose remains we find
entombed in the bone-caves and other deposits of the same age;
though of course the changes effected by domestication in almost
all the tame animals renders the question of their identity with the
indigenous breeds somewhat obscure. Cuvier was, however, unable
to detect any difference between the skeleton of a fossil horse
contemporary with the elephant, and that of our domestic breed; a
fossil goat of the same age cannot be distinguished from the
domesticated animal; and one of our two fossil oxen (*Bos
longifrons*) does not differ more from some of the existing breeds
than these have, in the course of time, been made, chiefly by
artificial means, to differ among themselves. But of one of our
domestic tribes no trace has yet been found in the rocks: like the
cod family among fishes, or the Rosaceæ among plants, it seems to
have preceded man by but a very brief period. And certainly, if
created specially for his use, though the pride of the herald might
prevent him from selecting it as in aught typical of the human
race, it would yet not be easy to instance a family of animals that
has ministered more extensively to his necessities. I refer to the
sheep,—that soft and harmless creature, that clothes civilized man
everywhere in the colder latitudes with its fleece,—that feeds him
with its flesh,—that gives its bowels to be spun into the catgut
with which he refits his musical instruments,—whose horns he has
learned to fashion into a thousand useful trinkets,—and whose
skin, converted into parchment, served to convey to later times
the thinking of the first full blow of the human intellect across the
dreary gulf of the middle ages.

At length the human period begins. A creature appears upon
the scene unlike all that had preceded him, and whose nature it
equally is to look back upon the events of the past—among other
matters, on that succession of beings upon the planet which he
inhabits with which we are this evening attempting to deal,—and
to anticipate at least one succession more, in that still future state
in which he himself is again to appear, in happier circumstances
than now, and in a worthier character. We possess another history
of the primæval age and subsequent chronology of the human
family than that which we find inscribed in the rocks. And it is well

that we do so. From various causes, the geologic evidence regarding the period of man's first appearance on earth is singularly obscure. That custom of "burying his dead out of his sight," which obtained, we know, in the patriarchal times, and was probably in use ever since man came first under the law of death, has had the effect of mingling his remains with those of creatures that were extinct for ages ere he began to be. The cavern, once a haunt of carnivorous animals, that in the first simple ages of his history had furnished him with a shelter when living, became his burying-place when dead; and thus his bones, and his first rude attempts in pottery and weapon-making, have been found associated with the remains of the cave-hyæna and cave-tiger, with the teeth of the ancient hippopotamus, and the tusks of the primæval elephant. The evidence on the point, too,—from the great paucity of human remains of a comparatively remote period, and from the circumstance that they are rarely seen by geologists in the stratum in which they occur,—is usually very imperfect in its details. Further, it is an evidence obnoxious to suspicion, from the fact that a keen controversy has arisen on the subject of man's antiquity, that such fragments of man himself or of his works as manifest great age have been pressed to serve as weapons in the fray,—that, occurring always in superficial and local deposits, their true era may be greatly antedated, under the; influence of prejudice, by men who have no design wilfully to deceive,—and that while, respecting the older formations, with their abundant organisms, the conclusions of any one geologist may be tested by all the others, the geologist who once in a lifetime picks up in a stratified sand or clay a stone arrow-head or a human bone, finds that the data on which he founds his conclusions may be received or rejected by his contemporaries, but not re-examined. It may be safely stated, however, that that ancient record in which man is represented as the last-born of creation is opposed by no geologic fact; and that if, according to Chalmers, "the Mosaic writings do not fix the antiquity of the globe," they at least *do* fix—making allowance, of course, for the varying estimates of the chronologer—"the antiquity of the human species." The great column of being, with its base set in the sea, and inscribed, like some old triumphal pillar, with many a strange form,—at once hieroglyphic and figure,—bears, as the ornately sculptured capital, which imparts beauty and finish to the whole, reasoning, responsible man. There is surely a very wonderful harmony manifested in the proportions of that nice sequence in which the invertebrates—the fishes, the reptiles, the birds, the marsupials, the placental mammals, and, last of all, man himself—are so exquisitely arranged. It reminds us of the fine figure employed by Dryden in his first Ode for St Cecilia's Day,—a figure which, viewed in the light cast on it by the modern science of Palæontology, stands out in bolder relief than that in which it could have appeared to the poet himself:—

> "From harmony, from heavenly harmony,
>   This universal frame began;
>   From harmony to harmony,
>   Through all the compass of the notes it ran,
>   The *diapason* closing full in man."

In the limits to which I have restricted myself, I have been able to do little more than simply to chronicle the successive eras in which the various classes and divisions of the organic kingdom,

Fig. 77.   Fig. 78.   Fig. 79.

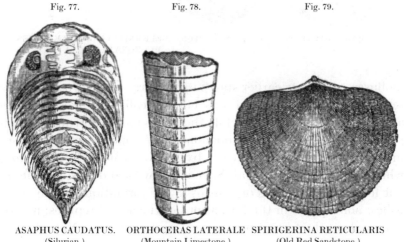

ASAPHUS CAUDATUS.   ORTHOCERAS LATERALE   SPIRIGERINA RETICULARIS
(Silurian.)   (Mountain Limestone.)   (Old Red Sandstone.)

vegetable and animal, make their appearance in creation. I have
produced merely a brief record of the various births, in their order,
of that great family whose father is God. And in pursuing such a
plan, much, of necessity, must have been omitted. I ought perhaps
to have told you, that very rarely, if ever, do the master-forms of
period constitute the prevailing or typical organisms of its
deposits. Of the three great divisions of which the geologic scale
consists,—Palæozoic, Secondary, and Tertiary,—the first, or
ichthyic period, is marked chiefly, not by its great fishes, but by
the peculiar character of its brachipodous and cephalopodous

Fig. 80.   Fig. 81.   Fig. 82.   Fig. 83.

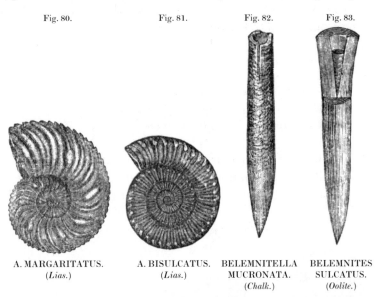

A. MARGARITATUS.   A. BISULCATUS.   BELEMNITELLA   BELEMNITES
    (*Lias.*)   (*Lias.*)   MUCRONATA.   SULCATUS.
                                            (*Chalk.*)   (*Oolite.*)

mollusca, and in its earlier stages by its three-lobed crustaceæ; the
second or reptilian period was emphatically the period of the
ammonite and belemnite; while the third and last, or mammalian
period, was that of gastropodous and conchiferous molluscs,
impressed, generically at least, by all the features of the group
which still exists in our seas. Save in a few local deposits, fishes do
not form the prevailing organisms in the formations of the age of
fishes; nor reptiles in the formations of the age of reptiles; nor yet
mammals in the formations of the age of mammals. Nay, it is not

Fig. 84.

Fig. 85.

MUREX ALVEOLATUS.

ASTARTE OMALII.

(*Red Crag.*)

improbable that the recent or human period may be marked most prominently in the future, when it comes to exist simply as a geologic system, by a still humbler organism than most of these molluscs. On almost all rocky shores a line of pale gray may be seen at low water, running for mile after mile along the belt that has been laid bare at the bases of the cliffs by the fall of the tide. It owes its pale colour to millions of millions of a small balanus (*B. balanoides*), produced in such amazing abundance in the littoral zone as to cover with a rough crust every minute portion of rock and every sedentary shell. Other species of the same genus (*B. crenatus* and *B. porcatus*) occupy the depths of the sea beyond; and their remains, washed ashore by the waves, and mingled with those of the littoral species, form often great accumulations of shell-sand. I have seen among the Hebrides a shell-sand accumulated along the beach to the depth of many feet, of which fully two-thirds was composed of the valves and compartments of balanidæ; and a similar sand on the east coast of Scotland, a little to the south of St Andrews, formed in still larger proportions of the fragments of a single species,—*Balanus crenatus*. Now, this genus, so amazingly abundant at the present time in

Fig. 86.

BALANUS CRASSUS.
(*Red Crag.*)

every existing sea, and whose accumulated remains bid fair to
exist as great limestone rocks in the future, had no existence in the
Palæozoic or Secondary ages. It first appears in the times of the
earlier Tertiary, in, however, only a single species; and, becoming
gradually of more and more importance as a group, it receives its
fullest numerical development in the present time. And thus the
remains of a sub-class of animals, low in their standing among the
articulata, may form one of the most prominent Palæontological
features of the human period. But enough for the present of
circumstance and detail.

Such, so far as the geologist has yet been able to read the
records of his science, has been the course of creation, from the first
beginnings of vitality upon our planet, until the appearance of
man. And very wonderful, surely, has that course been! How
strange a procession! Never yet on Egyptian obelisk or Assyrian
frieze,—where long lines of figures seem stalking across the granite,
each charged with symbol and mystery,—have our Layards or
Rawlinsons seen aught so extra-ordinary as that long procession of
being which, starting out of the blank depths of the bygone
eternity, is still defiling across the stage, and of which we ourselves
form some of the passing figures. Who shall declare the profound
meanings with which these geologic hieroglyphics are charged, or
indicate the ultimate goal at which the long procession is destined
to arrive?

The readings already given, the conclusions already deduced,
are as various as the hopes and fears, the habits of thought, and
the cast of intellect, of the several interpreters who have set
themselves,—some, alas! with but little preparation and very
imperfect knowledge,—to declare in their order the details of this
marvellous, dream-like vision, and, with the dream, the
"interpretation thereof." One class of interpreters may well remind
us of the dim-eyed old man,—the genius of unbelief so poetically
described by Coleridge,—who, sitting in his cold and dreary cave,
"talked much and vehemently concerning an infinite series of
causes and effects, which he explained to be a string of blind men,
the last of whom caught hold of the skirt of the one before him, he
of the next, and so on, till they were all out of sight, and that they

all walked infallibly straight, without making one false step, though all were alike blind." With these must I class those assertors of the development hypothesis who can see in the upward progress of being only the operation of an incomprehending and incomprehensible law, through which, in the course of unreckoned ages, the lower tribes and families have risen into the higher, and inferior into superior natures, and in virtue of which, in short, the animal creation has grown, in at least its nobler specimens, altogether unwittingly, without thought or care on its own part, and without intelligence on the part of the operating law, from irrational to rational, and risen in the scale from the mere promptings of instinct to the highest exercise of reason,—from apes and baboons to Bacons and Newtons. The blind lead the blind;—the unseeing law operates on the unperceiving creatures; and they go, not together into the ditch, but direct onwards, straight as an arrow, and higher and higher at every step.

Another class look with profound melancholy on that great city of the dead,—the burial-place of all that ever lived in the past,—which occupies with its everextending pavements of grave-stones, and its everlengthening streets of tombs and sepulchres, every region opened up by the geologist. They see the onward procession of being as if but tipped with life, and nought but inanimate carcases all behind,—dead individuals, dead species, dead genera, dead creations,—a universe of death; and ask whether the same annihilation which overtook in turn all the races of all the past, shall not one day overtake our own race also, and a time come when men and their works shall have no existence save as stone-pervaded fossils locked up in the rock for ever. Nowhere do we find the doubts and fears of this class more admirably portrayed than in the works of perhaps the most thoughtful and suggestive of living poets:—

> "Are God and Nature then at strife,
>   That Nature lends such evil dreams,
>   So careful of the type she seems,
> So careless of the single life?
> 'So careful of the type!' but no,

From scarped cliff and quarried stone,
　　She cries, 'a thousand types' are gone;
I care for nothing; all shall go:
Thou makest thine appeal to me;
　　I bring to life, I bring to death;
　　The spirit does but mean the breath.
I know no more.' And he,—shall he,
Man, her last work, who seem'd so fair,
　　Such splendid purpose in his eyes,
　　Who roll'd the psalm to wintry skies,
And built him fanes of fruitless prayer,—
Who trusted God was love indeed,
　　And love creation's final law,
　　Though Nature, red in tooth and claw,
With ravine shriek'd against his creed,—
Who loved, who suffered countless ills,
　　Who battled for the true, the just,—
　　Be blown about the desert dust,
Or seal'd within the iron hills?
No more? A monster then, a dream,
　　A discord. Dragons of the prime,
　　That tore each other in their slime,
Were mellow music, match'd with him.
O, life, as futile then as frail,—
　　O for thy voice to soothe and bless!
　　What hope of answer or redress,
Behind the veil, behind the veil!"

The sagacity of the poet here,—that strange sagacity which seems so nearly akin to the prophetic spirit,—suggests in this noble passage the true reading of the enigma. The appearance of man upon the scene of being constitutes a new era in creation; the operations of a new *instinct* come into play,—that *instinct* which anticipates a life after the grave, and reposes in implicit faith upon a God alike just and good, who is the pledged "rewarder of all who diligently seek Him." And in looking along the long line of being,—ever rising in the scale from higher to yet higher manifestations, or abroad on the lower animals, whom instinct never deceives,—can we hold that man, immeasurably higher in his place, and infinitely higher in his hopes and aspirations, than all that ever went before him, should be, notwithstanding, the one grand error in creation,—the one painful worker, in the midst of present trouble, for a state into which he is never to enter,—the befooled expectant of a happy future, which he is never to see? Assuredly no. He who keeps faith with all his humbler creatures,—who gives to even the bee and the dormouse the winter for which they prepare,—will to a certainty not break faith with man,—with man, alike the deputed lord of the present creation, and the chosen heir of all the future. We have been looking abroad on the old geologic burying-grounds, and deciphering the strange inscriptions on their tombs; but there are other burying-grounds, and other tombs,—solitary churchyards among the hills, where the dust of the martyrs lie, and tombs that rise over the ashes of the wise and good; nor are there awanting, on even the monuments of the perished races, frequent hieroglyphics, and symbols of high meaning, which darkly intimate to us, that while *their* burial-yards contain but the debris of the past, we are to regard the others as charged with the sown seed of the future.

LECTURE THIRD.

THE TWO RECORDS, MOSAIC AND GEOLOGICAL.

It is now exactly fifty years since a clergyman of the Scottish Church, engaged in lecturing at St Andrews, took occasion, in enumerating the various earths of the chemist, to allude to the science, then in its infancy, that specially deals with the rocks and soils which these earths compose. "There is a prejudice," he remarked, "against the speculations of the geologist, which I am anxious to remove. It has been said that they nurture infidel propensities. It has been alleged that geology, by referring the origin of the globe to a higher antiquity than is assigned to it by the writings of Moses, undermines our faith in the inspiration of the Bible, and in all the animating prospects of the immortality which it unfolds. This is a false alarm. *The writings of Moses do not fix the antiquity of the globe.*"

The bold lecturer on this occasion,—for it needed no small courage in a divine of any Established Church to take up, at the beginning of the present century, a position so determined on the geologic side,—was at the time an obscure young man, characterized, in the small circle in which he moved, by the ardour of his temperament and the breadth and originality of his views, but not yet distinguished in the science or literature of his country, and of comparatively little weight in the theological field. He was marked, too, by what his soberer acquaintance deemed eccentricities of thought and conduct. When the opposite view was all but universal, he held and taught that free trade would be not only a general benefit to the people of this country, but would inflict permanent injury on no one class or portion of them; and further, at a time when the streets and lanes of all the great cities of the empire were lighted with oil burnt in lamps, he held that the time was not distant when a carburetted hydrogen gas would be substituted instead; and, on getting his snug parsonage-house repaired, he actually introduced into the walls a system of tubes and pipes for the passage into its various rooms of the gaseous fluid yet to be employed as the illuminating agent. Time and experience have since impressed their stamp on these supposed eccentricities, and shown them to be the sagacious forecastings of a man who saw farther and more clearly than his contemporaries; and fame has since blown his name very widely, as one of the most comprehensive and enlightened, and, withal, one of the most thoroughly earnest and sincere, of modern theologians. The bold lecturer of St Andrews was Dr Thomas Chalmers,—a divine whose writings are now known wherever the English language is spoken, and whose wonderful eloquence lives in memory as a vanished power, which even his extraordinary writings fail adequately to represent. And in the position which he took up at this early period with respect to geology and the Divine Record, we have yet another instance of the great sagacity of the man, and of his ability of correctly estimating the prevailing weight of the evidence with which, though but partially collected at the time, the geologist was preparing to establish the leading propositions of his science. Even in this late age, when the scientific standing of geology is all but universally recognised, and the vast periods of time which it demands fully conceded, neither geologist nor theologian could, in any new scheme of reconciliation, shape his first proposition more skilfully than it was shaped by Chalmers a full half-century ago. It has formed since that time the preliminary proposition of those ornaments of at once science and the English Church, the present venerable Archbishop of Canterbury, Dr Bird Sumner, with Doctors Buckland, Conybeare, and Professor Sedgwick; of eminent evangelistic Dissenters too, such as the late Dr Pye Smith, Dr John Harris, Dr Robert Vaughan, Dr James Hamilton, and the Rev. Mr Binney,—enlightened and distinguished men, who all came early to the conclusion, with the lecturer of St Andrews, that "the writings of Moses do not fix the antiquity of the globe."

In 1814, ten years after the date of the St Andrews lectures, Dr Chalmers produced his more elaborate scheme of reconciliation between the Divine and the Geologic Records, in a "Review of Cuvier's Theory of the Earth;" and that scheme, perfectly adequate to bring the Mosaic narrative into harmony with what

was known at the time of geologic history, has been very
extensively received and adopted. It may, indeed, still be regarded
as the most popular of the various existing schemes. It teaches,
and teaches truly, that between the first act of creation, which
evoked out of the previous nothing the *matter* of the heavens and
earth, and the first act of the first day's work recorded in Genesis,
periods of vast duration may have intervened; but further, it
insists that the days themselves were but natural days of twenty-
four hours each; and that, ere they began, the earth, though
mayhap in the previous period a fair residence of life, had become
void and formless, and the sun, moon, and stars, though mayhap
they had before given light, had been, at least in relation to our
planet, temporarily extinguished. In short, while it teaches that
the successive creations of the geologist may all have found ample
room in the period preceding that creation to which man belongs,
it teaches also that the record in Genesis bears reference to but the
existing creation, and that there lay between it and the preceding
ones a chaotic period of death and darkness. The scheme
propounded by the late Dr Pye Smith, and since adopted by
several writers, differs from that of Chalmers in but one
circumstance, though an important one. Dr Smith held, with the
great northern divine, that the Mosaic days were natural days;
that they were preceded by a chaotic period; and that the work
done in them related to but that last of the creations to which the
human species belong. Further, however, he held in addition, that
the chaos of darkness and confusion out of which that creation was
called was of but limited extent, and that outside its area, and
during the period of its existence, many of our present lands and
seas may have enjoyed the light of the sun, and been tenanted by
animals and occupied by plants, the descendants of which still
continue to exist. The treatise of Dr Pye Smith was published
exactly a quarter of a century posterior to the promulgation,
through the press, of the argument of Dr Chalmers; and this
important addition,—elaborated by its author between the years
1837 and 1839,—seems to have been made to suit the more
advanced state of geological science at the time. The scheme of
reconciliation perfectly adequate in 1814 was found in 1839 to be

no longer so; and this mainly through a peculiarity in the order in which geological fact has been evolved and accumulated in this country, and the great fossiliferous systems studied and wrought out; to which I must be permitted briefly to advert.

William Smith, the "Father of English Geology," as he has been well termed (a humble engineer and mineral surveyor, possessed of but the ordinary education of men of his class and profession), was born upon the English Oolite,—that system which, among the five prevailing divisions of the great Secondary class of rocks, holds exactly the middle place. The Triassic system and the Lias lie beneath it; the Cretaceous system and the Weald rest above. Smith, while yet a child, had his attention attracted by the Oolitic fossils; and it was observed, that while his youthful contemporaries had their garnered stores of marbles purchased at the toy-shop, he had collected instead, a hoard of spherical fossil terebratulæ, which served the purposes of the game equally well. The interest which he took in organic remains, and the deposits in which they occur, influenced him in the choice of a profession; and, when supporting himself in honest independence as a skilful mineral surveyor and engineer, he travelled over many thousand miles of country, taking as his starting point the city of Bath, which stands near what is termed the Great Oolite; and from that centre he carefully explored the various Secondary formations above and below. He ascertained that these always occur in a certain determinate order; that each contains fossils peculiar to itself; and that they run diagonally across the kingdom in nearly parallel lines from north-east to south-west. And, devoting every hour which he could snatch from his professional labours to the work, in about a quarter of a century, or rather more, he completed his great stratigraphical map of England. But, though a truly Herculean achievement, regarded as that of a single man unindebted to public support, and uncheered by even any very general sympathy in his labours, it was found to be chiefly valuable in its tracings of the Secondary deposits, and strictly exact in only that Oolitic centre from which his labours began. It was remarked at an early period, that he ought to have restricted his publication to the formations which lie between the Chalk and the Red Marl inclusive; or, in other words, to the great Secondary division. The Coal Measures had, however, been previously better known, from their economic importance, and the number of the workings opened among them, than the deposits of any other system; and ere the publication of the map of Smith, Cuvier and Brogniart had rendered famous all over the world the older Tertiary formations of the age of the London Clay. But both ends of the geological scale, comprising those ancient systems older than the Coal, and representative of periods in which, so far as is yet known, life, animal and vegetable, first began upon our planet, and those systems of comparatively modern date, representative of the periods which immediately preceded the human epoch, were equally unknown. The light fell strongly on only that middle portion of the series on which the labours of Smith had been mainly concentrated. The vast geologic bridge, which, like that in the exquisite allegory of Addison, strode across a "part of the great tide of eternity," "had a black cloud hanging at each end of it." And such was the state of geologic science when, in 1814, Dr Chalmers framed his scheme of reconciliation.

Since that time, however, a light not less strong than the one thrown by William Smith on the formations of the Lias and the Oolite has been cast on both the older and the newer fossiliferous systems. Two great gaps still remain to be filled up,—that which separates the Palæozoic from the Secondary division, and that which separates the Secondary from the Tertiary one. But they occur at neither end of the geological scale. Mainly through the labours of two distinguished geologists, who, finding the geologic school of their own country distracted by a fierce and fruitless controversy, attached themselves to the geologic school of England, and have since received the honour of knighthood in acknowledgment of their labours, both ends of the geologic scale have been completed. Sir Roderick Murchison addressed himself to the formations older than the Coal, more especially to the Upper and Lower Silurian systems, from the Ludlow rocks to the Llandeilo flags. The Old Red Sandstone too, a system which lies more immediately beneath the Coal, has also been explored, and its various deposits, with their peculiar organic remains, enumerated and described. And Sir Charles Lyell, setting himself to the other extremity of the scale, has wrought out the Tertiary formations, and separated them into the four great divisions which they are now recognised as forming. And of these, the very names indicate that certain proportions of their organisms still continue to exist. It is a great fact, now fully established in the course of geological discovery, that between the plants which in the present time cover the earth, and the animals which inhabit it, and the animals and plants of the later extinct creations, there occurred no break or blank, but that, on the contrary, many of the existing organisms were contemporary during the morning of their being with many of the extinct ones during the evening of theirs. We know further, that not a few of the shells which now live on our coasts, and several of even the wild animals which continue to survive amid our tracts of hill and forest, were in existence many ages ere the human age began. Instead of dating their beginning only a single natural day, or at most two natural days, in advance of man, they must have preceded him by many thousands of years. In fine, in consequence of that comparatively recent extension of geologic fact in the direction of the later systems and formations, through which we are led to know that the present creation was not cut off abruptly from the preceding one, but that, on the contrary, it dovetailed into it at a thousand different points, we are led also to know, that any scheme of reconciliation which would separate between the recent and the extinct existences by a chaotic gulf of death and darkness, is a scheme which no longer meets the necessities of the case. Though perfectly adequate forty years ago, it has been greatly outgrown by the progress of geological discovery, and is, as I have said, adequate no longer; and it becomes a not unimportant matter to determine the special scheme that would bring into completest harmony the course of creation, as now ascertained by the geologist, and that brief but sublime narrative of its progress which forms a meet introduction in Holy Writ to the history of the human family. The first question to which we must address ourselves in any such inquiry is of course a very obvious one,—*What are the facts scientifically determined which now demand a new scheme of reconciliation?*

There runs around the shores of Great Britain and Ireland a flat terrace of unequal breadth, backed by an escarpment of varied height and character, which is known to geologists as the old coast line. On this flat terrace most of the seaport towns of the empire are built. The subsoil which underlies its covering of vegetable mould consists usually of stratified sands and gravels, arranged after the same fashion as on the neighbouring beach, and interspersed in the same manner with sea-shells. The escarpment behind, when formed of materials of no great coherency, such as gravel or clay, exists as a sloping, grass-covered bank,—at one place running out into promontories that encroach upon the terrace beneath,—at another receding into picturesque, bay-like recesses; and where composed, as in many localities, of rock of an enduring quality, we find it worn, as if by the action of the surf,—in some parts relieved into insulated stacks, in others hollowed into deep caverns,—in short, presenting all the appearance of a precipitous coast line, subjected to the action of the waves. Now, no geologist can or does doubt that this escarpment was at one time the coast line of the island,—the line against which the waves broke at high water in some distant age, when either the sea stood from twenty to thirty feet higher along our shores than it does now, or the land sat from twenty to thirty feet lower. Nor can the geologist doubt, that along the flat terrace beneath, with its stratified beds of sand and gravel, and its accumulations of sea-shells, the tides must have risen and fallen twice every day, as they now rise and fall along the beach that at present girdles our country. But, in reference to at least human history, the age of the old coast line and terrace must be a very remote one. Though geologically recent, it lies far beyond the reach of any written record. It has been shown by Mr Smith of Jordanhill, one of our highest authorities on the subject, that the wall of Antoninus, erected by the Romans as a protection against the Northern Caledonians, was made to terminate at the Friths of Forth and Clyde, with relation, not to the level of the old coast line, but to that of the existing one. And so we must infer that, ere the year A.D. 140 (the year during which, according to our antiquaries, the greater part of the wall was erected) the old coast line had attained to its present elevation over the sea. Further, however, we know from the history of Diodorus the Sicilian, that at a period earlier by at least two hundred years, St Michael's Mount, in Cornwall, was connected with the mainland at low water, just as it is now, by a flat isthmus, across which, upon the falling of the tide, the ancient Cornish miners used to carry over their tin in carts. Had the relative levels of sea and land been those of the old coast line at the time, St Michael's Mount, instead of being accessible at low ebb, would have been separated from the shore by a strait from three to five fathoms in depth. It would not have been then as now, as described in the verse of Carew,—

"Both land and island twice a-day."

But even the incidental notice of Diodorus Siculus represents very inadequately the antiquity of the existing coast line. Some of its caves, hollowed in hard rock in the line of faults and shifts by the attrition of the surf, are more than a hundred feet in depth; and it must have required many centuries to excavate tough trap or rigid gneiss to a depth so considerable, by a process so slow. And yet, however long the sea may have stood against the present coast line, it must have stood for a considerably longer period against the ancient one. The latter presents generally marks of greater attrition than the modern line, and its wave-hollowed caves are of a depth considerably more profound. In determining, on an extensive tract of coast, the average profundity of both classes of caverns from a considerable number of each, I ascertained that the proportional average depth of the modern to the ancient is as two to three. For every two centuries, then, during which the waves have been scooping out the caves of the present coast line, they must have been engaged for three centuries in scooping out those of the old one. But we know *historically*, that for at least twenty centuries the sea has been toiling in these modern caves; and who shall dare affirm that it has not been toiling in them for at least ten centuries more? But if the sea has stood for but even two thousand six hundred years against the present coast line (and no geologist would dare fix his estimate lower), then must it have stood against the old line, ere it could have excavated caves one-third deeper, three thousand nine hundred years. And both periods united (six thousand five hundred years) more than exhaust the Hebrew chronology. Yet what a mere beginning of geologic history does not the epoch of the old coast line form! It is but a mere starting point from the recent period. Not a single shell seems to have become extinct during the last six thousand five hundred years! The shells which lie embedded in the subsoils beneath the old coast line are exactly those which still live in our seas.

Above this ancient line of coast we find, at various heights, beds of shells of vastly older date than those of the low-lying terrace, and many of which are no longer to be found living around our shores. I spent some time last autumn in exploring one of these beds, once a sea-bottom, but now raised two hundred and thirty feet over the sea, in which there occurred great numbers of shells now not British, though found in many parts of Britain at heights varying from two hundred to nearly fourteen hundred feet over the existing sea-level. But though no longer British shells, they are shells that still continue to live in high northern latitudes, as on the shores of Iceland and Spitzbergen; and the abundance in which they were developed on the submerged plains and hill-sides of what are now England and Scotland, during what is termed the Pleistocene period, shows of itself what a very protracted period

Fig. 87.

Fig. 88.

ASTARTE ARCTICA.

TELLINA PROXIMA.

that was. The prevailing tellina of the bed which I last explored,—a bed which occurs in some places six miles inland, in others elevated on the top of dizzy crags,—is a sub-arctic shell (*Tellina proxima*), of which only dead valves are now to be detected on our coasts, but which may be found living at the North Cape and in Greenland. The prevailing astarte, its contemporary, was *Astarte arctica*, now so rare as a British species, that many of our most sedulous collectors have never seen a native specimen, but which is comparatively common on the northern shores of Iceland, and on the eastern coasts of Norway, within the arctic circle. In this elevated Scottish bed of the Pleistocene period I laid these boreal shells open to the light by hundreds, on the spot evidently where the individuals had lived and died. Under the severe climatal conditions to which (probably from some change in the direction of the gulf-stream) what is now Northern Europe had been brought, this tellina and astarte had increased and multiplied until they became prevailing shells of the British area; and this increase must have been the slow work of ages, during which the plains and not a few of the table-lands of the country were submerged in a sub-arctic sea, and Great Britain existed as but a scattered archipelago of wintry islands. But in a still earlier period, of which there exists unequivocal evidence in the buried forests of Happisburgh and Cromer, the country had not only its head above water, as now, but seems to have possessed even more than its present breadth of surface. During this ancient time,—more remote by many centuries than not only the times of the old coast line, but than even those of the partial submergence of the island,—that northern mammoth lived in great abundance, of which the remains have been found by hundreds in England alone, together with the northern hippopotamus, and at least two northern species of rhinoceros. And though they have all ceased to exist, with their wild associates in the forests and jungles of the Pleistocene, the cave-hyæna, the cave-tiger, and the cave-bear, we know that the descendants of some of their feebler contemporaries, such as the badger, the fox, the wild cat, and the red-deer, still live amid our hills and brakes. The trees, too, under which they roamed, and whose remains we find buried in the same deposits as theirs, were of species that still hold their place as aboriginal trees of the country, or of at least the more northerly provinces of the continent. The common Scotch fir, the common birch, and a continental species of conifer of the far north, the Norwegian spruce (*Abies excelsa*), have been found underlying the Pleistocene drift, and rooted in the mammiferous crag; and for many ages must the old extinct elephant have roamed amid these familiar trees. From one limited tract of sea-bottom on the Norfolk coast the fishermen engaged in dredging oysters brought ashore, in the course of thirteen years (from 1820 to 1833), no fewer than two thousand elephants' grinders, besides great tusks and numerous portions of skeletons. It was calculated that these remains could not have belonged to fewer than five hundred individual mammoths of English growth; and, various in their states of keeping, and belonging to animals of which only a few at a time could have found sufficient food in a limited tract of country, the inference seems inevitable that they must have belonged, not to one or two, but to many succeeding generations. The

Fig. 89.

NORWEGIAN SPRUCE.
(Abies excelsa.)

further fact, that remains of this ancient elephant (*Elephas primigenius*) occur all round the globe in a broad belt, extending from the fortieth to near the seventieth degree of north latitude, leads to the same conclusion. It must have required many ages ere an animal that breeds so slowly as the elephant could have extended itself over an area so vast.

Many of the contemporaries of this northern mammoth, especially of its molluscan contemporaries, continue, as I have said, to live in their descendants. Of even a still more ancient period, represented by the Red Crag, seventy out of every hundred species of shells still exist; and of an older period still, represented by the Coraline Crag, there survive sixty out of every hundred. In the Red Crag, for instance, we find the first known ancestors of our common edible periwinkle and common edible mussel; and in the Coraline Crag, the first known ancestors of the common horsemussel, the common whelk, the common oyster, and the great pecten. There then occurs a break in the geologic deposits of Britain, which, however, in other parts of Europe we find so filled up as to render it evident that no corresponding break took place in the chain of existence; but that, on the contrary, from the present time up to the times represented by the earliest Eocene formations of the Tertiary division, day has succeeded day, and season has followed season, and that no chasm or hiatus—no age of general chaos, darkness, and death—has occurred, to break the line of succession, or check the course of life. All the evidence runs counter to the supposition that immediately before the appearance of man upon earth there existed a chaotic period which separated the previous from the present creation. Up till the commencement of the Eocene ages, if even then, there was no such chaotic period, in at least what is now Britain and the European continent; the persistency from a high antiquity of some of the existing races, of not only plants and shells, but of even some of the mammiferous animals, such as the badger, the goat, and the wild cat, prove there was not; and any scheme of reconciliation which takes such a period for granted must be deemed as unsuited to the present state of geologic knowledge as any scheme would have been forty years ago which took it for granted that the writings of Moses do "fix the antiquity of the globe."

The scheme of reconciliation adopted by the late Dr Pye Smith, though, save in one particular, identical, as I have said, with that of Dr Chalmers, is made, in virtue of its single point of difference, to steer clear of the difficulty. Both schemes exhibit the creation recorded in Genesis as an event which took place about six thousand years ago; both describe it as begun and completed in six natural days; and both represent it as cut off from a previously existing creation by a chaotic period of death and darkness. But while, according to the scheme of Chalmers, both the Biblical creation and the previous period of death are represented as co-extensive with the globe, they are represented, according to that of Dr Smith, as limited and local. They may have extended, it is said, over only a few provinces of Central Asia, in which, when all was life and light in other parts of the globe, there reigned for a time only death and darkness amid the welterings of a chaotic sea; which, at the Divine command, was penetrated by light, and occupied by dry land, and ultimately, ere the end of the creative week, became a centre in which certain plants and animals, and finally man himself, were created. And this scheme, by leaving to the geologist in this country and elsewhere, save mayhap in some unknown Asiatic district, his unbroken series, certainly does not conflict with the facts educed by geologic discovery. It virtually removes Scripture altogether out of the field. I must confess, however, that on this, and on some other accounts, it has failed to satisfy me. I have stumbled, too, at the conception of a merely local and limited chaos, in which the darkness would be so complete, that when first penetrated by the light, that penetration could be described as actually a *making* or creating of light; and that, while life obtained all around its precincts, could yet be thoroughly void of life. A local darkness so profound as to admit no ray of light seems to have fallen for a time on Egypt, as one of the ten plagues; but the event was evidently miraculous; and no student of natural science is entitled to have recourse, in order to extricate himself out of a difficulty, to supposititious, unrecorded miracle. Creation cannot take place without miracle; but it would be a strange reversal of all our previous conclusions on the subject, should we have to hold that the dead, dark blank out of which creation arose was miraculous also. And if, rejecting miracle, we cast ourselves on the purely natural, we find that the local darknesses dependent on known causes, of which we have any record in history, were always either very imperfect, like the darkness of your London fogs, or very temporary, like the darkness described by Pliny as occasioned by a cloud of volcanic ashes; and so, altogether inadequate to meet the demands of a hypothesis such as that of Dr Smith. And yet further, I am disposed, I must add, to look for a broader and more general meaning in that grand description of the creation of all things with which the divine record so appropriately opens, than I could recognise it as forming were I assured it referred to but one of many existing creations,—a creation restricted to mayhap a few hundred square miles of country, and to mayhap a few scores of animals and plants. What, then, is the scheme of reconciliation which I would venture to propound?

Let me first remark, in reply, that I come before you this evening, not as a philologist, but simply as a student of geological fact, who, believing his Bible, believes also that, though theologians have at various times striven hard to pledge it to false science, geographical, astronomical, and geological, it has been pledged by its Divine Author to no falsehood whatever. I occupy exactly the position now, with respect to geology, that the mere Christian geographer would have occupied with respect to geography in the days of those doctors of Salamanca who deemed it unscriptural to hold with Columbus that the world is round,—not flat; or exactly the position which the mere Christian astronomer would have occupied with respect to astronomy in the days of that Francis Turrettine who deemed it unscriptural to hold with Newton and Galileo, that it is the earth which moves in the heavens, and the sun which stands still. The mere geographer or astronomer might have been wholly unable to discuss with Turrettine or the doctors the niceties of Chaldaic punctuation, or the various meanings of the Hebrew verbs. But this much, notwithstanding, he would be perfectly qualified to say:—However great your skill as linguists, your reading of what you term the scriptural geography or scriptural astronomy must of necessity be a false reading, seeing that it commits Scripture to what, in my character as a geographer or astronomer, I know to be a monstrously false geography or astronomy. Premising, then, that I make no pretensions to even the slightest skill in philology, I remark further, that it has been held by accomplished philologists, that the days of the Mosaic creation may be regarded, without doing violence to the genius of the Hebrew language, as successive periods of great extent. And certainly, in looking at my English Bible, I find that the portion of time spoken of in the first chapter of Genesis as *six* days, is spoken of in the second chapter as *one* day. True, there are other philologers, such as the late Professor Moses Stuart, who take a different view; but then I find this same Professor Stuart striving hard to make the phraseology of Moses "fix the antiquity of the globe;" and so, as a mere geologist, I reject his philology, on exactly the same principle on which the mere geographer would reject, and be justified in rejecting, the philology of the doctors of Salamanca, or on which the mere astronomer would reject, and be justified in rejecting, the philology of Turrettine and the old Franciscans. I would, in any such case, at once, and without hesitation, cut the philological knot, by determining that that philology cannot be sound which would commit the Scriptures to a science that cannot be true. Waiving, however, the question as a philological one, and simply holding with Cuvier, Parkinson, and Silliman, that each of the *six* days of the Mosaic narrative in the first chapter were what is assuredly meant by the *day* referred to in the second,—not natural days, but lengthened periods,—I find myself called on, as a geologist, to account for but three of the six. Of the period during which light was created,—of the period during which a firmament was made to separate the waters from the waters,—or of the period during which the two great lights of the earth, with the other heavenly bodies, became visible from the earth's surface,—we need expect to find no record in the rocks. Let me, however, pause for a moment, to remark the peculiar character of the language in which we are first introduced, in the Mosaic narrative, to the heavenly bodies,—sun, moon, and stars. The moon, though absolutely one of the smallest lights of our system, is described as secondary and subordinate to only its greatest light, the sun. It is the apparent, then, not the actual, which we find in the passage,—what *seemed* to be, not what *was*; and as it was merely what appeared to be greatest that was described as greatest, on what grounds are we to hold that it may not also have been what *appeared* at the time to be made that has been described as made? The sun, moon, and stars may have been created long before, though it was not until this fourth period of creation that they became visible from the earth's surface.

The geologist, in his attempts to collate the Divine with the geologic record, has, I repeat, only three of the six periods of creation to account for,—the period of plants, the period of great sea-monsters and creeping things, and the period of cattle and beasts of the earth. He is called on to question his systems and formations regarding the remains of these three great periods, and of these only. And, the question once fairly stated, what, I ask, is the reply? All geologists agree in holding that the vast geological scale naturally divides into *three* great parts. There are many lesser divisions,—divisions into systems, formations, deposits, beds, strata; but the master divisions, in each of which we find a type of life so unlike that of the others, that even the unpractised eye can detect the difference, are simply three,—the Palæozoic or oldest fossiliferous division; the Secondary or middle fossiliferous division; and the Tertiary or latest fossiliferous division.

In the first or Palæozoic division we find corals, crustaceans, molluscs, fishes, and, in its later formations, a few reptiles. But none of these classes of organisms give its leading character to the Palæozoic; they do not constitute its prominent feature, or render it more remarkable as a scene of life than any of the divisions which followed. That which chiefly distinguished the Palæozoic from the Secondary and Tertiary periods was its gorgeous flora. It was emphatically the period of plants,—"of herbs yielding seed after their kind." In no other age did the world ever witness such a flora: the youth of the earth was peculiarly a green and umbrageous youth,—a youth of dusk and tangled forests, of huge pines and stately araucarians, of the reed-like calamite, the tall tree-fern, the sculptured sigillaria, and the hirsute lepidodendron. Wherever dry land, or shallow lake, or running stream appeared, from where Melville Island now spreads out its ice wastes under the star of the pole, to where the arid plains of Australia lie solitary beneath the bright cross of the south, a rank and luxuriant herbage cumbered every footbreadth of the dank and steaming soil; and even to distant planets our earth must have shone through the enveloping cloud with a green and delicate ray. Of this extraordinary age of plants we have our cheerful remembrancers and witnesses in the flames that roar in our chimneys when we pile up the winter fire,—in the brilliant gas that now casts its light on this great assemblage, and that lightens up the streets and lanes of this vast city,—in the glowing furnaces that smelt our metals, and give moving power to our ponderous engines,—in the long dusky trains that, with shriek and snort, speed dart-like athwart our landscapes,—and in the great cloud-enveloped vessels that darken the lower reaches of your noble river, and rush in foam over ocean and sea. The geologic evidence is so complete as to be patent to all, that the first great period of organized being was, as described in the Mosaic record, peculiarly a period of herbs and trees, "yielding seed after their kind."

The middle great period of the geologist—that of the Secondary division—possessed, like the earlier one, its herbs and plants, but they were of a greatly less luxuriant and conspicuous character than their predecessors, and no longer formed the prominent trait or feature of the creation to which they belonged. The period had also its corals, its crustaceans, its molluscs, its fishes, and in some one or two exceptional instances its dwarf mammals. But the grand existences of the age,—the existences in which it excelled every other creation, earlier or later,—were its huge creeping things,—its enormous monsters of the deep,—and, as shown by the impressions of their footprints stamped upon the rocks, its gigantic birds. It was peculiarly the age of egg-bearing animals, winged and wingless. Its wonderful *whales*, not, however, as now, of the mammalian, but of the reptilian class, —ichthyosaurs, plesiosaurs, and cetiosaurs,—must have tempested the deep; its creeping lizards and crocodiles; such as the teliosaurus, megalosaurus, and iguanodon,—creatures some of which more than rivalled the existing elephant in height, and greatly more than rivalled him in bulk,—must have crowded the plains or haunted by myriads the rivers of the period; and we know that the footprints of at least one of its many birds are of fully twice the size of those made by the horse or camel. We are thus prepared to demonstrate, that the second period of the geologist was peculiarly and characteristically a period of whale-like reptiles of the sea, of enormous creeping reptiles of the land, and of numerous birds, some of them of gigantic size; and, in meet accordance with the fact, we find that the second Mosaic period with which the geologist is called on to deal was a period in which God created the fowl that flieth above the earth, with moving [or creeping] creatures, both in the waters and on the land, and what our translation renders great whales, but that I find rendered in the margin, great sea-monsters.

The Tertiary period had also its prominent class of existences. Its flora seems to have been no more conspicuous than that of the present time; its reptiles occupy a very subordinate place; but its beasts of the field were by far the most wonderfully developed, both in size and numbers, that ever appeared upon earth. Its mammoths and its mastodons, its rhinoceri and its hippopotami, its enormous dinotherium and colossal megatherium, greatly more than equalled in bulk the hugest mammals of the present time, and vastly exceeded them in number. The remains of one of its elephants (*Elephas primigenius*) are still so abundant amid the frozen wastes of Siberia, that what have been not inappropriately termed "ivory quarries" have been wrought among their bones for more than a hundred years. Even in our own country, of which, as I have already shown, this elephant was for long ages a native, so abundant are the skeletons and tusks, that there is scarcely a local museum in the kingdom that has not its specimens, dug out of the Pleistocene deposits of the neighbourhood. And with this ancient elephant there were meetly associated in Britain, as on the northern continents generally all around the globe, many other mammals of corresponding magnitude. "Grand indeed," says an English naturalist, "was the fauna of the British islands in those early days. Tigers as large again as the biggest Asiatic species lurked in the ancient thickets; elephants of nearly twice the bulk of the largest individuals that now exist in Africa or Ceylon roamed in herds; at least two species of rhinoceros forced their way through the primæval forest; and the lakes and rivers were tenanted by hippopotami as bulky, and with as great tusks, as those of Africa." The massive cave-bear and large cave-hyæna belonged to the same formidable group, with at least two species of great oxen (*Bos longifrons* and *Bos primigenius*), with a horse of smaller size, and an elk (*Megaceros Hibernicus*) that stood ten feet four inches in height. Truly this Tertiary age—this third and last of the great geologic periods—was peculiarly the age of great "beasts of the earth after their kind, and of cattle after their kind."

Permit me at this stage, in addressing myself to a London audience, to refer to what has been well termed one of the great sights of London. An illustration drawn from what must be familiar to you all may impart to your conceptions respecting the facts on which I build, a degree of tangibility which otherwise they could not possess.

One of perhaps the most deeply interesting departments of your great British Museum—the wonder of the world—is that noble gallery, consisting of a suite of rooms, opening in line, the one beyond the other, which forms its rich store-house of organic remains. You must of course remember the order in which the organisms of that gallery are ranged. The visitor is first ushered into a spacious room devoted to fossil plants, chiefly of the Coal Measures. And if these organisms are in any degree less imposing in their aspect than those of the apartments which follow in the series, it is only because that, from the exceeding greatness of the Coal Measure plants, they can be exhibited in but bits and fragments. Within less than an hour's walk of the Scottish capital there are single trees of this ancient period deeply embedded in the sandstone strata, which, though existing as mere mutilated portions of their former selves, would yet fail to find accommodation in that great apartment. One of these fossil trees,—a, noble araucarian,—which occurs in what is known as the Granton quarry, is a mere fragment, for it wants both root and top, and yet what remains is sixty-one feet in length by six feet in diameter; and beside it there lies a smaller araucarian, also mutilated, for it wants top and branches, and *it* measures seventy feet in length by four feet in diameter. I saw lately in a quarry of the Coal Measures about two miles from my dwelling-house, near Edinburgh, the stem of a plant (*Lepidodendron Sternbergii*), allied

Fig. 90.

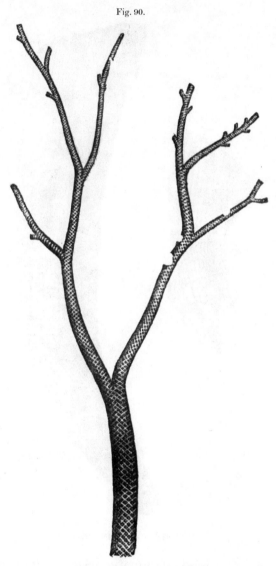

LEPIDODENDRON STERNBERGII.

to the dwarfish club-mosses of our moors, considerably thicker than the body of a man, and which, reckoning on the ordinary proportions of the plant, must have been at least seventy feet in

Fig. 91.

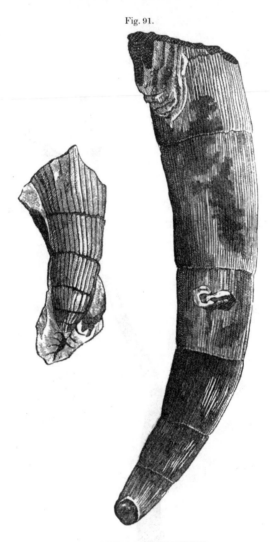

CALAMITES CANNÆFORMIS.

height. And of a kind of aquatic reed (calamites), that more resembles the diminutive mare's tail of our marshes than aught else that now lives, remains have been found in abundance in the same coal-field, more than a foot in diameter by thirty feet in length. Imposing, then, as are the vegetable remains of this portion of the National Museum, they would be greatly more imposing still did they more adequately represent the gigantic flora of the remote age to which they belong.

Passing onwards in the gallery from the great plants of the Palæozoic division to the animals of the Secondary one, the attention is at once arrested by the monstrous forms on the wall. Shapes that more than rival in strangeness the great dragons, and griffins, and "laithly worms," of mediæval legend, or, according to Milton, the "gorgons, hydras, and chimeras dire," of classical fable, frown on the passing visitor, and, though wrapped up in their dead and stony sleep of ages, seem not only the most strange, but also the most terrible, things on which his eye ever rested. Enormous jaws, bristling with pointed teeth, gape horrid in the stone, under staring eye-sockets a full foot in diameter. Necks that half-equal in length the entire body of the boa-constrictor stretch out from bodies mounted on fins like those of a fish, and furnished with tails somewhat resembling those of the mammals. Here we see a winged dragon, that, armed with sharp teeth and strong claws, had careered through the air on leathern wings like those of a bat; there an enormous crocodilian whale, that, mounted on many-jointed paddles, had traversed, in quest of prey, the green depths of the sea; yonder an herbivorous lizard, with a horn like that of the rhinoceros projecting from its snout, and that, when it browsed amid the dank meadows of the Wealden, must have stood about twelve feet high. All is enormous, monstrous, vast, amid the creeping and flying things and the great sea-monsters of this division of the gallery.

We pass on into the third and lower division, and an entirely different class of existences now catch the eye. The huge mastodon, with his enormous length of body, and his tusks projecting from both upper and under jaw, stands erect in the middle of the floor,—a giant skeleton. We see beside him the great bones of the megatherium,—thigh-bones eleven inches in diameter, and claw-armed toes more than two feet in length. There, too, ranged species beyond species, are the extinct elephants; and there the ponderous skull of the dinotherium, with the bent tusks in its lower jaw, that give to it the appearance of a

Fig. 92.

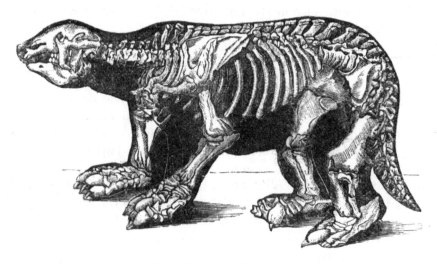

MEGATHERIUM CUVIERI.

great pickaxe, and that must have dug deeply of old amid the liliaceous roots and bulbs of the Tertiary lakes and rivers. There

Fig. 93.

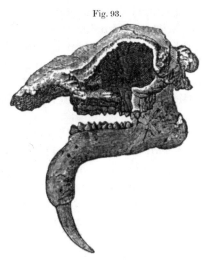

SKULL OF DINOTHERIUM GIGANTEUM.
(*Miocene.*)

also are the massive heads and spreading horn-cores of the *Bos primigenius*, and the large bones and broad plank-like horns of the great Irish elk. And there too, in the same apartment, but leaning against its farther wall,—last, as most recent, of all the objects of wonder in that great gallery,—is the famous human skeleton of Guadaloupe, standing out in bold relief from its slab of gray limestone. It occurs in the series, just as the series closes, a little beyond the mastodon and the mammoths; and, in its strange character as a fossil-man, attracts the attention scarce less powerfully than the great Palæozoic plants, the great Secondary reptiles, or the great Tertiary mammals.

I last passed through this wondrous gallery at the time when the attraction of the Great Exhibition had filled London with curious visitors from all parts of the empire; and a group of intelligent mechanics, fresh from some manufacturing town of the midland counties, were sauntering on through its chambers immediately before me. They stood amazed beneath the dragons of the Oolite and Lias; and, with more than the admiration and wonder of the disciples of old when contemplating the huge stones of the Temple, they turned to say, in almost the old words, "Lo! master, what manner of great beasts are these?" "These are," I replied, "the sea-monsters and creeping things of the second great period of organic existence." The reply seemed satisfactory, and we passed on together to the terminal apartments of the range appropriated to the Tertiary organisms. And there, before the enormous mammals, the mechanics again stood in wonder, and turned to inquire. Anticipating the query, I said, "And these are the huge beasts of the earth, and the cattle of the third great period of organic existence; and yonder, in the same apartment, you see, but at its farther end, is the famous fossil-man of Guadaloupe, locked up by the petrifactive agencies in a slab of limestone." The mechanics again seemed satisfied. And, of course, had I encountered them in the first chamber of the suite, and had they questioned me respecting the organisms with which *it* is occupied, I would have told them that they were the remains of the herbs and trees of the *first* great period of organic existence. But in the chamber of the mammals we parted, and I saw them no more.

There could not be a simpler incident. And yet, rightly apprehended, it reads its lesson. You have all visited the scene of it, and must all have been struck by the three salient points, if I may so speak, by which that noble gallery lays strongest hold of the memory, and most powerfully impresses the imagination,—by its gigantic plants of the first period (imperfectly as these are represented in the collection), by its strange misproportioned sea-monsters and creeping things of the second, and by its huge mammals of the third. Amid many thousand various objects, and a perplexing multiplicity of detail, which it would require the patient study of years even partially to classify and know, these are the great prominent features of the gallery, that involuntarily, on the part of the visitor, force themselves on his attention. They at once pressed themselves on the attention of the intelligent though unscientific mechanics, and, I doubt not, still dwell vividly in their recollections; and I now ask you, when you again visit the national museum, and verify the fact of the great prominence of these classes of objects, to bear in mind, that the gallery in which they occur represents, both in the order and character of its contents, the course of creation. I ask you to remember that, had there been human eyes on earth during the Palæozoic, Secondary, and Tertiary periods, they would have been filled in succession by the great plants, the great reptiles, and the great mammals, just as those of the mechanics were filled by them in the museum. As the sun and moon, when they first became visible in the heavens, would have seemed to human eyes—had there been human eyes to see—not only the greatest of the celestial lights, but peculiarly the prominent objects of the epoch in which they appeared, so would these plants, reptiles, and mammals have seemed in succession the prominent objects of the several epochs in which *they* appeared. And, asking the geologist to say whether my replies to the mechanics were not, with all their simplicity, true to geological fact, and the theologian to say whether the statements which they embodied were not, with all their geology, true to the scriptural narrative, I ask further whether (of course, making due allowance for the laxity of the terms botanic and zoological of a primitive language unadapted to the niceties of botanic or zoologic science) the Mosaic account of creation could be rendered more essentially true than we actually find it, to the history of creation geologically ascertained. If, taking the Mosaic days as equivalent to lengthened periods, we hold that, in giving their brief history, the inspired writer seized on but those salient points that, like the two great lights of the day and night, would have arrested most powerfully, during these periods, a human eye, we shall find the harmony of the two records complete. In your visit to the museum, I would yet further ask you to mark the place of the human skeleton in the great gallery. It stands—at least it stood only a few years ago—in the same apartment with the huge mammifers. And it is surely worthy of remark, that while in both the sacred and geologic records a strongly-defined line separates between the period of plants and the succeeding period of reptiles, and again between the period of reptiles and the succeeding period of mammals, no line in either record separates between this period of mammals and the human period. Man came into being as the last-born of creation, just ere the close of that sixth day—the third and terminal period of organic creation—to which the great mammals belong.

Let me yet further remark, that in each of these three great periods we find, with respect to the classes of existences, vegetable or animal, by which they were most prominently characterized, certain well-marked culminating points together, if I may so express myself,—twilight periods of morning dawn and evening decline. The plants of the earlier and terminal systems of the Palæozoic division are few and small: it was only during the protracted *eons* of the carboniferous period that they received their amazing development, unequalled in any previous or succeeding time.[1] In like manner, in the earlier or Triassic deposits of the Secondary division, the reptilian remains are comparatively inconsiderable; and they are almost equally so in its Cretaceous or later deposits. It was during those middle ages of the division represented by its Liassic, Oolitic, and Wealden formations, that the class existed in that abundance which rendered it so peculiarly, above every other age, an age of creeping things and great sea-monsters. And so also in the Tertiary, regarded as but an early portion of the human division, there was a period of increase and diminution,—a morning and evening of mammalian life. The mammals of its early Eocene ages were comparatively small in bulk and low in standing; in its concluding ages, too, immediately ere the appearance of man, or just as he had appeared, they exhibited, both in size and number, a reduced and less imposing aspect. It was chiefly in its middle and latter, or Miocene, Pliocene, and Pleistocene ages, that the myriads of its huger giants,—its dinotheria, mastodons, and mammoths,—cumbered the soil. I, of course, restrict my remarks to the three periods of organic life, and have not inquired whether aught analogous to these mornings and evenings of increase and diminution need be sought after in any of the others.

Such are a few of the geological facts which lead me to believe that the *days* of the Mosaic account were great periods, not natural days; and be it remembered, that between the scheme of lengthened periods and the scheme of a merely local chaos, which existed no one knows how, and of a merely local creation, which had its scene no one knows where, geological science leaves us now no choice whatever. It has been urged, however, that this scheme of periods is irreconcileable with that Divine "reason" for the institution of the Sabbath which He who appointed the day of old has, in his goodness, vouchsafed to man. I have failed to see any force in the objection. God the Creator, who wrought during six periods, rested during the seventh period; and as we have no evidence whatever that He recommenced his work of creation,—as, on the contrary, man seems to be the last formed of creatures,—God may be resting still. The presumption is strong that his Sabbath is an extended period, not a natural day, and that the work of Redemption is his Sabbath-day's work. And so I cannot see that it in the least interferes with the integrity of the reason rendered, to read it as follows:—Work during six periods, and rest on the seventh; for in six periods the Lord created the heavens and the earth, and on the seventh period *He* rested. The Divine periods may have been very great,—the human periods very small; just as a vast continent or the huge earth itself is very great, and a map or geographical globe very small. But if in the map or globe the proportions be faithfully maintained, and the scale, though a minute one, be true in all its parts and applications, we pronounce the map or globe, notwithstanding the smallness of its size, a faithful copy. Were man's Sabbaths to be kept as enjoined, and in the Divine proportions, it would scarcely interfere with the logic of the "reason annexed to the fourth commandment," though in this matter, as in all others in which man can be an imitator of God, the imitation should be a miniature one.

The work of Redemption may, I repeat, be the work of God's Sabbath-day. What, I ask, viewed as a whole, is the prominent characteristic of geologic history, or of that corresponding history of creation which forms the grandly-fashioned vestibule of the sacred volume? Of both alike the leading characteristic is progress. In both alike do we find an upward progress from dead matter to the humbler forms of vitality, and from thence to the higher. And after great cattle and beasts of the earth had, in due order, succeeded inanimate plants, sea-monsters, and moving creatures that had life, the moral agent, man, enters upon the scene. Previous to his appearance on earth, each succeeding elevation in the long upward march had been a result of creation. The creative fiat went forth, and dead matter came into existence. The creative fiat went forth, and plants, with the lower animal forms, came into existence. The creative fiat went forth, and the oviparous animals,—birds and reptiles,—came into existence. The creative fiat went forth, and the mammiferous animals,—cattle and beasts of the earth,—came into existence. And, finally, last in the series, the creative fiat went forth, and responsible, immortal man, came into existence. But has the course of progress come, in consequence, to a close? No. God's work of elevating, raising, heightening—of making the high in due progression succeed the low,—still goes on. But man's responsibility, his immortality, his God-implanted instincts respecting an eternal future, forbid that that work of elevation and progress should be, as in all the other instances, a work of creation. To create would be to supersede. God's work of elevation *now* is the work of fitting and preparing peccable, imperfect man for a perfect, impeccable future state. God's seventh day's work is the work of Redemption. And, read in this light, his reason vouchsafed to man for the institution of the Sabbath is found to yield a meaning of peculiar breadth and emphasis. God, it seems to say, rests on *his* Sabbath from his creative labours, in order that by his Sabbath-day's work He may save and elevate you. Rest ye also on your Sabbaths, that through your co-operation with Him in this great work ye may be elevated and saved. Made originally in the image of God, let God be your pattern and example. Engaged in your material and temporal employments, labour in the proportions in which he laboured; but, in order that you may enjoy an eternal future with Him, rest also in the proportions in which He rests.

One other remark ere I conclude. In the history of the earth which we inhabit, molluscs, fishes, reptiles, mammals, had each in succession their periods of vast duration; and then the human period began,—the period of a fellow-worker with God, created in God's own image. What is to be the next advance? Is there to be merely a repetition of the past?—an introduction a second time of man made in the image of God? No. The geologist, in those tables of stone which form his records, finds no example of dynasties once passed away again returning. There has been no repetition of the dynasty of the fish, of the reptile, of the mammal. The dynasty of the future is to have glorified man for its inhabitant; but it is to be the dynasty—"*the kingdom*"—not of glorified man made in the image of God, but of God himself in the form of man. In the doctrine of the two conjoined natures, human and Divine, and in the farther doctrine that the terminal dynasty is to be peculiarly the dynasty of **HIM** in whom the natures are united, we find that required progression beyond which progress cannot go. We find the point of elevation never to be exceeded meetly coincident with the final period never to be terminated,—the infinite in height harmoniously associated with the eternal in duration. Creation and the Creator meet at one point, and in one person. The long ascending line from dead matter to man has been a progress Godwards,—not an asymptotical progress, but destined from the beginning to furnish a point of union; and, occupying that point as true God and true man,—as Creator and created,—we recognise the adorable Monarch of all the future!

1. It will be seen that there is no attempt made in this lecture to represent the great Palæozoic division as characterized *throughout its entire extent* by a luxuriant flora. It is, on the contrary, expressly stated here, that the "plants of its earlier and terminal formations (*i.e.* those of

the Silurian, Old Red, and Permian Systems) were *few and small,"* and that "it was *only during the protracted eons of the carboniferous period that they received their amazing development, unequalled in any previous or succeeding time."* Being thus express in my limitation, I think I have just cause of complaint against any one who represents me as unfairly labouring, in this very composition, to make it be believed that the *whole* Palæozoic period was characterized by a gorgeous flora; and as thus sophistically generalizing in the first instance, in order to make a fallacious use of the generalization in the second, with the intention of misleading non-geologic readers. Such, however, as may be seen from the following extracts from the " Proceedings of the Academy of Natural Science at Philadelphia," is the charge preferred against me by a citizen of the United States.

"Mr William Parker Foulke asked the attention of the Society to a lecture by Mr Hugh Miller, recently republished in the United States under the title of 'The Two Records, Mosaic and Geological,' and made some remarks upon the importance of maintaining a careful scrutiny of the logic of the natural sciences. . . . . Mr Miller teaches that, in the attempt to reconcile the two 'records,' there are only three periods to be accounted for by the geologist, viz. 'the period of *plants*; the period of *great sea-monsters and creeping things*; and the period of *cattle and beasts of the earth;*' and that the first of these periods is represented by the rocks grouped under the term *Palæozoic*, and is distinguished from the *Secondary* and *Tertiary* chiefly by its gorgeous flora; and that the geological evidence is so complete as to be patent to all, that the first great period of organized being was, as described in the Mosaic record, peculiarly a period of herbs and trees, yielding seed after their kind. The general reader, not familiar with the details of geological arrangement, could not fail to infer from such a statement, used for such a purpose, that the Palæozoic rocks are regarded by geologists as forming one group representative of one period, which can properly be said to be distinguished as a *whole* by its gorgeous flora; and that it is properly so distinguished *for the argument in question*. It was familiar to the Academy, as well as to Mr Miller, that from the *carboniferous* rocks downward (backward in order of time), there have been discriminated a large number of periods, differing from one another in mineral and in organic remains; and that the proportion of the *carboniferous* era to the whole series is small, whether we regard the thickness of its deposits or its conjectural chronology. It is only of this *carboniferous* era, *the latest of this series*, that the author's remarks could be true; and even of this, if taken for the entire surface of the earth, it could not be truly asserted that 'the evidence is so complete as to be patent to all,' that the quantity of its vegetable products distinguish it from the earth's surface during the era in which we live. To confound by implication all the periods termed Palæozoic, so as to apply to them as a whole what could be true, if at all, only of the *carboniferous* period, is a fallacious use of a generalization, *made for a purpose*, and upon a principle not properly available for the writer's argument," &c. So far the "Proceedings" of the Academy.

This, surely, is very much the reverse of fair. I, however, refer the matter, without note or comment (so far at least as it involves the question whether Mr Foulke has not, in the face of the most express statement on my part, wholly misrepresented me), to the judgment of candid and intelligent readers on both sides the Atlantic.

I know not that I should recognise Mr Foulke as entitled, after such a display, to be dealt with simply as the member of a learned society who differs from me on a scientific question; nor does his reference to the "carboniferous era" as "the *latest* of the" Palæozoic "series," and his apparent unacquaintance with that Permian period, in reality the terminal one of the division during which the Palæozoic forms seem to have gradually died away, in order to give place to those of the Secondary division, inspire any very high respect for his acquirements as a geologist. Waiving, however, the legitimacy of his claim, I may be permitted to repeat, for the further information of the non-geological reader, that the *carboniferous* formations, *wherever they have yet been detected*, justify, in the amazing abundance of their carbonized vegetable organisms, the name which they bear. Mr Foulke, in three short sentences, uses the terms "carboniferous era," "carboniferous rocks," "carboniferous period," four several times; and these terms are derived from the predominating amount of carbon (elaborated of old by the plants of the period) which occurs in its several formations. The very language which he has to employ is of itself a confirmation of the statement which he challenges. For so "patent" is this *carboniferous* character of the system, that it has given to it its universally accepted designation,—the verbal sign by which it is represented wherever it is known. Mr Foulke states, that "if taken for the entire surface of the earth," it cannot be truly asserted that the carboniferous flora preponderated over that of the present time, or, at least, that its preponderance could not be regarded as "patent to all." The statement admits of so many different meanings, that I know not whether I shall succeed in replying to the special meaning intended by Mr Foulke. There are no doubt carboniferous deposits on the earth's surface still unknown to the geologist, the evidence of which on the point must be regarded, in consequence, not as "patent to all," but as *nil*. They are witnesses absent from court, whose testimony has not yet been tendered. But equally certain it is, I repeat, that wherever carboniferous formations *have* been discovered and examined, they have been found to bear the unique characteristic to which the system owes its name,—they have been found charged with the carbon, existing usually as great beds of coal, which was elaborated of old by its unrivalled flora from the elements. And as this evidence is certain and positive, no one would be entitled to set off against it, as of equal weight, the merely negative evidence of some one or two deposits of the carboniferous age that did not bear the carboniferous character, even were such known to exist; far less is any one entitled to set off against it the *possibly* negative evidence of deposits of the carboniferous age not yet discovered nor examined; for that would be simply to set off against good, positive evidence, what is no evidence at all. It would be to set off the *possible* evidence of the absent witnesses, not yet precognosced in the case, against the express declarations of the witnesses already examined, and strong on the positive side.

Surely an American, before appealing, in a question of this kind, to the bare possibility of the existence somewhere or other of barely negative evidence, ought to have bethought him of the very extraordinary positive evidence furnished by the carboniferous deposits of his own great country. The coal-fields of Britain and the European continent had been wrought for ages ere those of North America were known, and for ages more after it had been but ascertained that the New, like the Old World, has its Coal Measures; And during the latter period the *argument* of Mr Foulke might have been employed, just as now, and some member of a learned society might have urged that, though the coal-fields of Europe bore evidence to the former existence of a singularly luxuriant flora, beyond comparison more vast than the European one of the present day, the same could not be predicated of the American coal-fields, whose carbonized remains *might* be found representative of a flora which had been at least not more largely developed than that existing American flora to which the great western forests belong. Now, however, the time for any such argument has gone by: the American coal-fields have been carefully explored; and what is the result? The geologist has come to know, that even the mighty forests of America are inconsiderable, compared with its deposits of coal; nay, that all its forests gathered into one heap would fail to furnish the materials of a single coal-seam equal to that of Pittsburg; and that centuries after all its thick woods shall have disappeared before the axe, and it shall have come to present the comparatively bare, unwooded aspect of the long-civilized countries of Southern Europe, it will continue to derive the elements of its commercial greatness, and the cheerful blaze of its many millions of domestic hearths, from the unprecedentedly luxuriant flora of the old carboniferous ages. Truly, very wonderful are the coal-fields of Northern America! If geologists inferred, as they well might, that the extinct flora which had originated the European coal vastly outrivalled in luxuriance that of the existing time, what shall be said of that flora of the same age which originated the coal deposits of Nova Scotia and the United States,—deposits *twenty times as great* as all those of all Europe put together!

LECTURE FOURTH.

THE MOSAIC VISION OF CREATION.

THE history of creation is introduced into the "Paradise Lost" as a piece of narrative, and forms one of the two great episodes of the poem. Milton represents the common father of the race as "led on" by a desire to know

> "What within Eden or without was done
> Before his memory;"

and straightway Raphael, "the affable archangel," in compliance with the wish, enters into a description of the six days' work of the Divine Creator,—a description in which, as Addison well remarks, "the whole energy of our tongue is employed, and the several great scenes of creation rise up to view, one after another, in such a manner, that the reader seems present at this wonderful work, and to assist among the choirs of angels who are spectators of it." In the other great episode of the poem,—that in which the more prominent changes which were to happen in after time upon the earth are made to pass before Adam, he is represented as carried by Michael to the top of a great mountain, lofty as that on which in a long posterior age the Tempter placed our Saviour, and where the coming events are described as rising up in vision before him. In the earlier episode, as in those of the Odyssey and Æneid, in which heroes relate in the courts of princes the story of their adventures, there is but narrative and description; in the later, a series of magnificent pictures, that form and then dissolve before the spectator, and comprise, in their vivid tints and pregnant outlines, the future history of a world. And one of these two episodes,—that which relates to the creation of all things,—must have as certainly had a place in human history as in the master epic of England. Man would have for ever remained ignorant of many of those events related in the opening chapters of Scripture which took place ere there was a human eye to witness or a human memory to record, had he not been permitted, like Adam of old, to hold intercourse with the intelligences that had preceded him in creation, or with the great Creator himself, the Author of them all; and the question has been asked of late, both in our own country and on the Continent, What was the form and nature of the revelation by which the pre-Adamic history of the earth and heavens was originally conveyed to man? Was it conveyed, like the sublime story of Raphael, as a piece of narrative, dictated, mayhap, to the inspired penman, or miraculously borne in upon his mind? Or was it conveyed by a succession of sublime visions like that which Michael is represented as calling up before Adam, when, purging his "visual nerves with euphrasy and rue," he enabled him to see, in a series of scenes, the history of his offspring from the crime of Cain down to the destruction of the Old World by a flood? The passages in which the history of creation is recorded give no intimation whatever of their own history; and so we are left to balance the probabilities regarding the mode and form in which they were originally revealed, and to found our ultimate conclusions respecting them on evidence, not direct, but circumstantial.

The Continental writers on this curious subject may be regarded as not inadequately represented by Dr J. H. Kurtz, Professor of Theology at Dorpat,—one of the many ingenious biblical scholars of modern Germany. We find him stating the question, in his *Bibel und Astronomie* (second edition, 1849), with great precision and clearness, but in a manner, so far at least as the form of his thinking is concerned, strikingly characteristic of what may be termed the theological fashion of his country in the present day. "The source of all human history," he says, "is *eye-witness*, be it that of the reporter, or of another whose account has been handed down. Only what man has himself seen or experienced can be the subject of man's historical compositions. So that history, so far as man can write it, can begin with but the point at which he has entered into conscious existence, and end with the moment that constitutes the present time. Beyond these points, however, lies a great province of historic development, existing on the one

side as the *Past*, on the other side as the *Future*. For when man
begins to be an observer or actor of history, he himself, and the
whole circumstantials of his condition, have already come
historically into being. Nor does the flow of development stop with
what is his present. Millions of influences are spinning the thread
still on; but no one can tell what the compound result of all their
energies is to be. Both these sorts of history, then, lie beyond the
region of man's knowledge, which is shut up in space and time, and
can only call the present its own. It is God alone who, standing
beyond and above space and time, sees backwards and forwards
both the development which preceded the first *present* of men, and
that which will succeed this our latest *present*. Whatever the
difference of the two kinds of history may be, they hold the same
position in relation both to the principle of the human ignorance
and the principle of the human knowledge. The principle of the
ignorance is man's condition as a creature; the principle of the
knowledge is the Divine knowledge; and the medium between
ignorance and knowledge is objectively Divine revelation, and
subjectively prophetic vision by man, in which he beholds with the
eye of the mind what is shut and hid from the eye of his body."
From these premises Dr Kurtz goes on to argue that the pre-
Adamic history of the past being *theologically* in the same category
as the yet undeveloped history of the future, that record of its
leading events which occurs in the Mosaic narrative is simply
prophecy described backwards; and that, coming under the
prophetic law, it ought of consequence to be subjected to the
prophetic rule of exposition. There are some very ingenious
reasonings employed in fortifying this point; and, after quoting
from Eichhorn a passage to the effect that the opening chapter in
Genesis is much rather a creative picture than a creative history,
and from Ammon to the effect that the author of it evidently takes
the position of a beholder of creation, the learned German
concludes his general statement by remarking, that the scenes of
the chapter are prophetic tableaux, each containing a leading
phase of the drama of creation. "Before the eye of the seer," he
says, "scene after scene is unfolded, until at length, in the seven of
them, the course of creation, in its main *momenta*, has been fully

represented." The revelation has every characteristic of prophecy by vision,—prophecy by eyewitnessing; and may be perhaps best understood by regarding it simply as an exhibition of the actual phenomena of creation presented to the mental eye of the prophet under the ordinary laws of perspective, and truthfully described by him in the simple language of his time.

In our own country a similar view has been taken by the author of a singularly ingenious little work which issued about two years ago from the press of Mr Constable of Edinburgh, "The Mosaic Record in Harmony with the Geological."[1] The writer, however, exhibits, in dealing with his subject, the characteristic sobriety of the Anglo-Saxon mind; and while the leading features of his theory agree essentially with those of the Continental one, he does not press it so far. In canvassing the *form* of the revelation made to Moses in the opening of Genesis, he discusses the nature of the inspiration enjoyed by that great prophet; and thus retranslates literally from the Hebrew the passage in which the Divine being is himself introduced as speaking direct on the point in the controversy raised by Aaron and Miriam. "And He [the Lord] said, hear now my words: If he [Moses] were *your* prophet [subordinate, or at least not superior, to the prophetess and the high priest], I, Jehovah, in the vision to him would make myself known; in the dream would I speak to him. Not so *my* servant Moses [God's prophet, not theirs]: in all my house faithful is he. Mouth to mouth do I speak to him, and vision, but not in dark speeches; and likeness of Jehovah he beholds." (Num. xii.6-8.) Moses, then, was favoured with "visions without dark speeches."

Now, as implied in the passage thus retranslated, there is a grand distinction between symbolic and therefore *dark* visions, and visions not symbolic nor dark. Visions addressed, as the word indicates, to the eye may be obviously of a twofold character;—they may be either darker than words, or a great deal clearer than words. The vision, for instance, of future monarchies which Daniel saw symbolized under the form of monstrous animals had to be explained in words; the vision of Peter, which led to the general admission of the Gentiles into the Christian Church, had also virtually to be explained in words; they were both visions of the dark class; and revelation abounds in such. But there were also visions greatly clearer than words. Such, for instance, was the vision of the secret chamber of imagery, with its seventy men of the ancients of Israel given over to idolatry, which was seen by the prophet as he sat in his own house; and the vision of the worshippers of the sun in the inner court of the temple, witnessed from what was *naturally* the same impossible point of view; with the vision of the Jewish women in the western gate "weeping for Thammuz,"when, according to Milton's noble version,

> "The love tale
> Infected Sion's daughters with like heat,
> Whose wanton passions in the sacred porch
> Ezekiel saw, when, by the vision led,
> His eye surveyed the dark idolatries
> Of alienated Judah."

Here, then, were there visions of scenes actually taking place at the time, which, greatly clearer than any merely verbal description, substituted the seeing of the eye for the hearing of the ear. And visions of this latter kind were enjoyed, argues the writer of this ingenious treatise, by the prophet Moses.

One of the cases adduced may be best given in the author's own words. "Moses," he says, "received directions from God how to proceed in constructing the Tabernacle and its sacred furniture; and David also was instructed how the Temple of Solomon should be built. Let us hear Scripture regarding the nature of the directions given to these men:—

"According unto the *appearance* [literally sight, vision] which the Lord had showed unto Moses, so he made the *candlestick*."—(Num. viii.4.)

"The whole in *writing*, by the hand of Jehovah upon me, he taught; the whole works of the pattern."—(1 Chron. xxviii. 19.)

"There was thus a writing in the case of David; a sight or vision of the thing to be made in that of Moses."

So far the author of the Treatise. He might have added farther, that from the nature of things, the revelation to Moses in this instance *must* have been "sight or vision," if, indeed, what is not in the least likely, the peculiar architecture and style of ornament used in the Tabernacle was not a borrowed style, already employed in the service of idolatry. An old, long established architecture can be adequately described by speech or writing; a new, original architecture can be adequately described only by pattern or model, *i.e.* by sight or vision. Any intelligent cutter in stone or carver in wood could furnish to order, though the order were merely a verbal one, a Corinthian or Ionic capital; but no such mechanic, however skilful or ingenious, could furnish to order, if unprovided with a pattern or drawing, a *fac simile* of one of the ornately sculptured capitals of Gloucester Cathedral or York Minster. To ensure a *fac simile* in any such case, the originals, or representations of them, would require to be submitted to the eye,—not merely described to the ear. Nay, from the example given in the text—that of the golden candlestick,—we have an instance furnished in recent times of the utter inadequacy of mere description for the purposes of the sculptor or artist. Ever since copperplate engravings and illustrated Bibles became comparatively common, representations of the branched candlestick taken from the written description have been common also. The candlestick on the arch of Titus, though not deemed an exact representation of the original one described in the Pentateuch, is now regarded,—correctly, it cannot be doubted,—as at least the nearest approximation to it extant. Public attention was first drawn to this interesting piece of sculpture in comparatively modern times; and it was then found that all the previous representations taken from the written description were widely erroneous. They only served to show, not the true outlines of the golden candlestick, but merely that inadequacy of verbal description for artistic purposes which must have rendered *vision*, or, in other words, optical representation, imperative in the case of Moses. Some of our most sober-minded commentators take virtually the same view of this necessity of vision for ensuring the production of the true pattern of the Tabernacle. "The Lord," says Thomas Scott, "not only directed Moses by words how to build the Tabernacle and form its sacred furniture, but showed him a model exactly representing the form of every part, and the proportion of each to all the rest." There must have been clear optical vision in the case,—"vision without dark speeches." Such, too, was the character of other of the Mosaic visions besides that of the "pattern" seen in the Mount. The burning bush, for instance, was a vision addressed to the eye; and seemed to come so palpably under the ordinary optical laws, that the prophet *drew near* to examine the extraordinary phenomena which it exhibited.

The visual or optical character of *some* of the revelations made to Moses thus established, the writer goes on to inquire whether that special revelation which exhibits the generations of the heavens and earth in their order was not a visual revelation also. "Were the words that Moses wrote," he asks, "merely impressed upon his mind? Did he hold the pen, and another dictate? Or did he see in vision the scenes that he describes? The freshness and point of the narrative," he continues, "the freedom of the description, and the unlikelihood that Moses was an unthinking machine in the composition, all indicate that he saw in vision what he has here given us in writing. *He is describing from actual observation.*" The writer remarks in an earlier portion of his treatise, that all who have adopted the theory advocated in the previous lecture,—the "Two Records," which was, I may state, published in a separate form ere the appearance of his work, and which he does me the honour of largely quoting,—go upon the supposition that things during the Mosaic days are described as they would appear to the eye of one placed upon earth; and he argues that, as no man existed in those distant ages, a reason must be assigned for this *popular* view of creation which the record is rightly assumed to take. And certainly, if it was in reality a view described from actual vision, the fact would form of itself an adequate reason. What man had actually seen, though but in dream or picture, would of course be described *as seen by man;* like all human history, it would, to borrow from Kurtz, be founded on eye-witnessing; and the fact that the Mosaic record of creation is *apparently* thus founded, affords a strong presumption that it was in reality revealed, not by dictation, but by vision.

Nor, be it remembered, has the recognition of a purely *optical* character in the revelation been restricted to the assertion of any one theory of reconciliation: it was as certainly held by Chalmers and Dr Pye Smith as by Dr Kurtz and the author of this treatise; nay, it has been recognised by not a few of their opponents also. Granville Penn, for instance, does not scruple to avow his belief, in his elaborate "Estimate of the Mineral and Mosaic Geologies," that both sun and moon were created on the first day of creation, though they did not become "*optically* visible" until the fourth. "In truth, that the fourth day only rendered visible the sidereal creation of the first day, is manifested," he says, "by collating the transactions of the two days. On the first day, we are told generally, 'God divided the light, or day, and the darkness, or night;' but the physical agents which he employed for that division are not there declared. On the fourth day, we are told referentially, 'God commanded the lights [or luminaries] for dividing day and night, to give their light upon earth.' Here, then, it is evident from the retrospective implication of the latter description, that the lights or luminaries for dividing day and night, which were to give their light upon the earth for the first time on the fourth day, were the unexpressed physical agents by which God divided the day and night on the first day." Now, whatever may be thought of Mr Penn's argument here, there can be no doubt that it demonstrates at least his own belief in the purely optical character of the Mosaic account of the sidereal creation. It is an account, he held, not of what God wrought on the first day in the heavens, but of what a human eye would have seen on the fourth day from the earth. And Moses Stuart, in his philological assault on the geologists, is scarce less explicit in his avowal of a similar belief. "Every one sees," he says, "that to speak of the sun as rising and setting, is to describe, in common parlance, what appears *optically, i.e.* to our sensible view, as reality. But the history of creation is a different affair. In ONE RESPECT, indeed, there is a resemblance. *The historian everywhere speaks as an optical observer stationed on a point of our world, and surveying from this the heavens and the earth, and speaking of them as seen in this manner by his bodily eye.* The sun, and moon, and stars, are servants of the earth, lighted up to garnish and to cheer it, and to be the guardians of its times and seasons. Other uses he knows not for them: certainly of other uses he does not speak. The distances, magnitudes, orbicular motions, gravitating powers, and projectile forces of the planets and of the stars, are all out of the circle of his history, and probably beyond his knowledge. Inspiration does not make men *omniscient*. It does not teach them the scientific truths of astronomy, or chemistry, or botany, nor any science as such. Inspiration is concerned with teaching *religious* truths, and such facts or occurrences as are connected immediately with illustrating or with impressing them on the mind." Thus far Dr Stuart and Mr Penn,—men whose evidence on this special head must be sufficient to show that it is not merely geologists who have recognised an *optical*, or *visual* character in the Mosaic history of creation. And certainly the inference deduced from the admitted *fact, i.e.* the inference that the optical description must have been founded on a revelation addressed to the eye,—a revelation by vision,—does seem a fair and legitimate one. The revelation must have been either a revelation in words or ideas, or a revelation of scenes and events pictorially exhibited. Failing, however, to record its own history, it leaves the student equally at liberty, so far as *external* evidence is concerned, to take up either view; while, so far as *internal* evidence goes, the presumption seems all in favour of revelation by vision; for, while no reason can be assigned why, in a revelation by word or idea, appearances which took place ere there existed a human eye should be *optically* described, nothing can be more natural or obvious than that they should be so described had they been revealed by vision as a piece of *eye-witnessing*. It seems, then, at least eminently probable that such was the mode or form of the revelation in this case, and that he who saw by vision on the Mount the pattern of the Tabernacle and its sacred furniture, and in the Wilderness of Horeb the bush burning but not consumed,—types and symbols of the coming dispensation and of its Divine Author,—saw also by vision the *pattern* of those successive pre-Adamic creations, animal and vegetable, through which our world was fitted up as a place of human habitation. The *reason* why the drama of creation has been *optically* described *seems* to be, that it was in reality *visionally* revealed.

A further question still remains: *If* the revelation was by vision, that circumstance affords of itself a satisfactory reason why the description should be *optical*; and, on the other hand, since the description is decidedly *optical*, the presumption is of course strong that the revelation was by vision. But why, it may be asked, by vision? Can the presumption be yet further strengthened by showing that this visual mode or form was preferable to any other? Can there be a reason, in fine, assigned *for* the *reason*,—for that revelation by vision which accounts for the optical character of the description? The question is a difficult one; but I think there can. There seems to be a peculiar fitness in a revelation made by vision, for conveying an account of creation to various tribes, and peoples of various degrees of acquirement, and throughout a long course of ages in which the knowledge of the heavenly bodies or of the earth's history, *i.e.* the sciences of astronomy and geology, did not at first exist, but in which ultimately they came to be studied and known. We must recognise such a mode as equally fitted for the earlier and the more modern times,—for the ages anterior to the rise of science, and the ages posterior to its rise. The prophet, by describing what he had actually seen in language fitted to the ideas of his time, would shock no previously existing prejudice that had been founded on the apparent evidence of the senses; he could as safely describe the moon as the second great light of creation, as he could the sun as its first great light, and both, too, as equally subordinate to the planet which we inhabit. On the other hand, an enlightened age, when it had come to discover this key to the description, would find it *optically* true in all its details. But how differently would not a revelation have fared, in at least the earlier time, that was strictly scientific in its details,—a revelation, for instance, of the great truth demonstrated by Galileo, that the sun rests in the centre of the heavens, while the apparently immoveable earth sweeps with giddy velocity around it; or of the great truth demonstrated by Newton, that our ponderous planet is kept from falling off into empty space by the operation of the same law that impels a descending pebble towards the ground! A great miracle wrought in proof of the truth of the revelation might serve to enforce the belief of it on the generation to whom it had been given; but the generations that followed, to whom the miracle would exist as a piece of mere testimony, would credit, in preference, the apparently surer evidence of their senses, and become unbelievers. They would act, all unwittingly, on the principle of Hume's famous argument, and prefer to rest rather on their own *experience* of the great phenomena of nature, than on the doubtful testimony of their ancestors, reduced, in the lapse of ages, to a dim, attenuated tradition. Nor would a geological revelation have fared better, in at least those periods intermediate between the darker and more scientific ages, in which ingenious men, somewhat sceptical in their leanings, cultivate literature, and look down rather superciliously on the ignorance and barbarism of the past. What would sceptics such as Hobbes and Hume have said of an opening chapter in Genesis that would describe successive periods,—first of molluscs, star-lilies, and crustaceans, next of fishes, next of reptiles and birds, then of mammals, and finally of man; and that would minutely portray a period in which there were lizards bulkier than elephants, reptilian whales furnished with necks slim and long as the bodies of great snakes, and flying dragons, whose spread of wing greatly more than doubled that of the largest bird? The world would assuredly not receive such a revelation. Nor, further, have scientific facts or principles been revealed to man which he has been furnished with the ability of observing or discovering for himself. It is according to the economy of revelation, that the truths which it exhibits should be of a kind which, lying beyond the reach of his ken, he himself could never have elicited. From every view of the case, then, a prophetic exhibition of the pre-Adamic scenes and events by vision seems to be the one best suited for the opening chapters of a revelation vouchsafed for the accomplishment of moral, not scientific purposes, and at once destined to be contemporary with every stage of civilization, and to address itself to minds of every various calibre, and every different degree of enlightenment.

The statement of Dr Kurtz, that as vision of pre-Adamic history comes under the same laws as vision of history still future, it ought therefore to be read by the same rules, craves reflection. "Since the source of knowledge for both kinds of history," we find him saying, "and not only the source, but the means, and manner, and way of coming to know, is the same, viz. the *eye-witness* of the prophet's mental eye, it follows that the historical representation which he who thus comes to know, *projects* [or portrays] in virtue of this eye-witnessing of his, holds the same relation to the reality in both the cases we speak of, and must be subjected to the same laws of exposition. We thus get this very important rule of interpretation, viz. that the representations of pre-human events, which rest upon revelation, are to be handled from the same point of view, and expounded by the same laws, as the prophecies and representations of future times and events, which also rest upon revelation. This, then, is the only proper point of view for scientific exposition of the Mosaic history of creation; that is to say, if we acknowledge that it proceeded from Divine revelation, not from philosophic speculation or experimental investigation, or from the ideas of reflecting men." There is certainly food for thought in this striking and original view; and there is at least one simple rule of prophetic exposition which may be applied to the pre-Adamic history, in accordance with the principle which it suggests. After all that a scientific theology has done for the right interpretation of prophecy, we find the prediction always best read by the light of its accomplishment. The event which it foretold forms its true key; and when this key is wanting, all is uncertainty. The past is comparatively clear. The hieroglyphic forms which crowd the anterior portions of the prophetic tablet are found wonderfully to harmonize (men such as the profound Newton being the judges) with those great historic events, already become matter of history, which they foreshadowed and symbolized; but, on the other hand, the hieroglyphics which occupy the tablet's posterior portion,—the hieroglyphics that symbolize events still future,—are invincibly difficult and inexplicable. I have read several works on prophecy produced in the last age, in which the writers were bold enough to quit the clue with which history furnishes the student of fulfilled prophecy, and, with the prophecies yet unfulfilled as their guide, to plunge into a troubled sea of speculation regarding the history of the future. And I have found that in every instance they were deplorably at fault regarding even the events that were nearest at hand at the time. History is thus the surest interpreter of the revealed prophecies which referred to events *posterior* to the times of the prophet. In what shall we find the surest interpretation of the revealed *prophecies* that referred to events *anterior* to his time? In what light, or on what principle, shall we most correctly read the prophetic drama of creation? In the light, I reply, of scientific discovery,—on the principle that the clear and certain must be accepted, when attainable, as the proper exponents of the doubtful and obscure. What fully developed history is to the prophecy which of old looked forwards, fully developed science is to the prophecy which of old looked backwards. Scarce any one will question whether that portion of the creation drama which deals with the heavenly bodies ought to be read in the light of established astronomic discovery or no; for, save by perhaps a few of Father Cullen's monks, who can still hold that the sun moves round the earth, and is only six feet in diameter, all theologians have now received the astronomic doctrines, and know that they rest upon a basis at least as certain as any of the historic events symbolized in fulfilled prophecy. And were we to challenge for the established geologic doctrines a similar place and position with respect to those portions of the drama which deal with the two great kingdoms of nature, plant and animal, we might safely do so in the belief that the claim will be one day as universally recognised as the astronomic one is now.

On this principle there may, of course, be portions of the *prophetic* pre-Adamic past of as doubtful interpretation at the present time, from the imperfect development of physical science, as is any portion of the prophetic future from the imperfect development of historic events. The science necessary to the interpretation of the one may be as certainly still to discover as the events necessary to the interpretation of the other may be still to take place. Three centuries have not yet passed since astronomic science was sufficiently developed to form a true key to the various notices of the heavenly bodies which occur in Scripture; among the others, to the notice of their final appearance on the *fourth* day of creation. Little more than half a century has yet passed since geologic science was sufficiently developed to influence the interpretation given of the three *other* days' work. And respecting the work of at least the first and second days, more especially that of the second, we can still but vaguely guess. The science necessary to the right understanding of these portions of the prophetic record has still, it would seem, to be developed, if, indeed, it be destined at all to exist; and at present we can indulge in but doubtful surmises regarding them. What may be termed the three *geologic* days,—the third, fifth, and sixth,—may be held to have extended over those Carboniferous periods during which the great plants were created,—over those Oolitic and Cretaceous periods during which the great sea-monsters and birds were created,—and over those Tertiary periods during which the great terrestrial mammals were created. For the intervening or fourth day we have that wide space represented by the Permian and Triassic periods, which, less conspicuous in their floras than the period that went immediately before, and less conspicuous in their faunas than the periods that came immediately after, were marked by the decline, and ultimate extinction, of the Palæozoic forms, and the first partially developed beginnings of the Secondary ones. And for the first and second days there remain the great Azoic period, during which the immensely developed gneisses, mica schists, and primary clay slates, were deposited, and the two extended periods represented by the Silurian and Old Red Sandstone systems. These, taken together, exhaust the geologic scale, and may be named in their order as, *first*, the Azoic day or period; *second*, the Silurian and Old Red Sandstone day or period; *third*, the Carboniferous day or period; *fourth*, the Permian and Triassic day or period; *fifth*, the Oolitic and Cretaceous day or period; and *sixth*, the Tertiary day or period. Let us attempt conceiving how they might have appeared pictorially, if revealed in a series of visions to Moses, as the successive scenes of a great air-drawn panorama.

During the Azoic period, ere life appears to have begun on our planet, the temperature of the earth's crust seems to have been so high, that the strata, at first deposited apparently in water, passed into a semi-fluid state, became strangely waved and contorted, and assumed in its composition a highly crystalline character.

Such is peculiarly the case with the fundamental or gneiss deposits of the period. In the overlying mica schist there is still much of contortion and disturbance; whereas the clay-slate, which lies over all, gives evidence, in its more mechanical texture, and the regularity of its strata, that a gradual refrigeration of the general mass had been taking place, and that the close of the Azoic period was comparatively quiet and cool. Let us suppose that during the earlier part of this period of excessive heat the waters of the ocean had stood at the boiling point even at the surface, and much higher in the profounder depths, and further, that the half-molten crust of the earth, stretched out over a molten abyss, was so thin that it could not support, save for a short time, after some convulsion, even a small island above the sea-level. What, in such circumstances, would be the aspect of the scene, optically exhibited from some point in space elevated a few hundred yards over the sea? It would be simply a blank, in which the intensest glow of fire would fail to be seen at a few yards distance. An inconsiderable escape of steam from the safety-valve of a railway engine forms so thick a screen, that, as it lingers for a moment, in the passing, opposite the carriage windows, the passengers fail to discern through it the landscape beyond. A continuous stratum of steam, then, that attained to the height of even our present atmosphere, would wrap up the earth in a darkness gross and palpable as that of Egypt of old,—a darkness through which even a single ray of light would fail to penetrate. And beneath this thick canopy the unseen deep would literally "boil as a pot," wildly tempested from below; while from time to time more deeply-seated convulsion would upheave sudden to the surface vast tracts of semi-molten rock, soon again to disappear, and from which waves of bulk enormous would roll outwards, to meet in wild conflict with the giant waves of other convulsions, or return to hiss and sputter against the intensely heated and fast foundering mass, whose violent upheaval had first elevated and sent them abroad. Such would be the probable state of things during the times of the earlier gneiss and mica-schist deposits,—times buried deep in that chaotic night or "evening" which must have continued to exist for mayhap many ages after that beginning of things in which God

created the heavens and the earth, and which preceded the first
day. To a human eye stationed within the cloud, all, as I have said,
must have been thick darkness: to eyes Divine, that could have
looked through the enveloping haze, the appearance would have
been that described by Milton, as seen by angel and archangel at
the beginning of creation, when from the gates of heaven they
looked down upon chaos:—

> "On heavenly ground they stood, and from the shore
> They viewed the vast immeasurable abyss,
> Outrageous as a sea, dark, wasteful, wild,
> Up from the bottom turned by furious *heat*
> And surging waves, as mountains to assault
> Heaven's height, and with the centre mix the pole."

At length, however, as the earth's surface gradually cooled
down, and the enveloping waters sunk to a lower
temperature,—let us suppose, during the latter times of the mica
schist, and the earlier times of the clay slate,—the steam
atmosphere would become less dense and thick, and at length the
rays of the sun would struggle through, at first doubtfully and
diffused, forming a faint twilight, but gradually strengthening as
the latter ages of the slate formation passed away, until, at the
close of the great primary period, day and night,—the one still dim
and gray, the other wrapped in a pall of thickest darkness,—would
succeed each other as now, as the earth revolved on its axis, and
the unseen luminary rose high over the cloud in the east, or sunk in
the west beneath the undefined and murky horizon.

And here again the *optical* appearance would be exactly that
described by Milton:—

> "'Let there be light,' said God, and forthwith light
> Ethereal, first of things, quintessence pure,
> Sprung from the deep, and from her native east
> To journey through the airy gloom began,
> Sphered in a radiant cloud, for yet the sun
> Was not: she in a cloudy tabernacle

Sojourned the while. God saw the light was good,
And light from darkness by the hemisphere
Divided: light the day, and darkness night,
He named. This was the first day, even and morn."

The second day's work has been interpreted variously, according to the generally received science of the times of the various commentators who have dealt with it. Even in Milton, though the great poet rejected the earlier idea of a solid firmament, we find prominence given to that of a vast hollow sphere of "circumfluous waters," which, by encircling the atmosphere, kept aloof the "fierce extremes of chaos." Later commentators, such as the late Drs Kitto and Pye Smith, hold that the Scriptural analogue of the *firmament* here—by the way, a Greek, not a Hebrew idea, first introduced into the Septuagint—was in reality simply the atmosphere with its clouds. "The historian" [Moses], says Dr Kitto, "speaks as things would have appeared to a spectator at the time of the creation. A portion of the heavy watery vapour had flown into the upper regions, and rested there in dense clouds, which still obscured the sun; while below, the whole earth was covered with water. Thus we see the propriety with which the firmament is said to have divided the waters from the waters." It is certainly probable that in a vision of creation the atmospheric phenomena of the second great act of the creation drama might have stood out with much greater prominence to the prophetic eye placed in the circumstances of a natural one, than any of its other appearances. The invertebrate life of the Silurian period, or even the ichthyic life of the earlier Old Red Sandstone period, must have been comparatively inconspicuous from any sub-aerial point of view elevated but a few hundred feet over the sea-level. Even the few islets of the latter ages of the period, with their ferns, lepidodendra, and coniferous trees, forming, as they did, an exceptional feature in these ages of vast oceans, and of organisms all but exclusively marine, may have well been excluded from a representative diorama that exhibited optically the grand characteristics of the time. Further, it seems equally probable that the introduction of organized existence on our planet was preceded by a change in the atmospheric conditions which had obtained during the previous period, in which the earth had been a desert and empty void. We know that just before the close of the Silurian ages terrestrial plants had appeared, and that before the close of the Old Red Sandstone ages, air-breathing animals had been produced; and infer that the atmosphere in which both could have existed must have been considerably different from that which lay dark and heavy over the bare hot rocks, and tenantless, steam-emitting seas, of the previous time. Under a gray opaque sky, in which neither sun nor moon appear, we are not unfrequently presented with a varied drapery of clouds,—a drapery varied in form, though not in colour; bank often seems piled over bank, shaded beneath and lighter above; or the whole breaks into dappled cloudlets, which bear—to borrow from the poetic description of Bloomfield—the "beauteous semblance of a flock at rest." And if such aerial draperies appeared in this early period, with the clear space between them and the earth which we so often see in gray, sunless days, the optical aspect must have been widely different from that of the previous time, in which a dense vaporous fog lay heavy upon rock and sea, and extended from the earth's surface to the upper heights of the atmosphere.

The third day's vision seems to be more purely geological in its character than either of the previous two. Extensive tracts of dry land appear, and there springs up over them, at the Divine command, a rank vegetation. And we know that what seems to be the corresponding Carboniferous period, unlike any of the preceding ones, was remarkable for its great tracts of terrestrial surface, and for its extraordinary flora. For the first time, dry land, and organized bodies at once bulky enough, and exhibited in a medium clear enough, to render them conspicuous objects in a distant prospect, appear in the Mosaic drama; and we still find at once evidence of the existence of extensive though apparently very flat lands, and the remains of a wonderfully gigantic and abundant vegetation, in what appear to be the rocks of this period. The vision of the fourth day, like that of the second, pertained not to the earth, but to the *heavens;* the sun, moon, and stars become visible, and form the sole subjects of the prophetic description.

And just as during the second period the earth would in all probability have failed to furnish any feature of mark enough to divert a human eye placed on a commanding station from the conspicuous *atmospheric* phenomena of the time, so it seems equally probable that during this fourth period it would have failed to furnish any feature of mark enough to divert a human eye from the still more conspicuous *celestial* phenomena of the time. As has been already incidentally remarked, the Permian and Triassic periods were "epochs"—to employ the language of the late Professor Edward Forbes—"of great poverty of production of generic types." On the other hand, the appearance for the first time of sun, moon, and stars, must have formed a scene well suited to divert the attention of the seer from every other. Nor (as has been somewhat rashly argued by Dr Kitto and several others) does it seem irrational to hold that three very extended *periods* should have elapsed ere the sidereal heavens became visible on earth. Addison's popular illustration, drawn from one of the calculations of Newton, made in an age when comets were believed to be solid bodies, rendered the reading public familiar, considerably more than a century ago, with the vast time which large bodies greatly heated would take in cooling. "According to Sir Isaac Newton's calculation," said the exquisitely classical essayist, "the comet that made its appearance in 1680 imbibed so much heat by its approaches to the sun, that it would have been two thousand times hotter than red hot iron had it been a globe of that metal; and that, supposing it as big as the earth, and at the same distance from the sun, it would be fifty thousand years in cooling before it recovered its natural temper." Such was an estimate of the philosopher, that excited no little wonder in the days of our great grandfathers, for the vast time which it demanded; and, now that the data on which such a calculation ought to be founded are better known than in the age of Newton, yet more time would be required still. It is now ascertained, from the circumstance that no dew is deposited in our summer evenings save under a clear sky, that even a thin covering of cloud,—serving as a robe to keep the earth warm,—prevents the surface heat of the planet from radiating into the spaces beyond. And such a cloud, thick and continuous, as must have wrapped round the earth as with a mantle during the earlier geologic periods, must have served to retard for many ages the radiation, and consequently the reduction, of that internal heat of which it was itself a consequence. Further, the rocks and soils that form the surface of our globe would be much more indifferent conductors of heat than the iron superficies of Newton's ball, and would serve yet more to lengthen out the cooling process. Nor would a planet covered over for ages with a thick screen of vapour be a novelty even yet in the universe. It is doubtful whether astronomers have ever yet looked on the face of Mercury: it is at least very generally held that hitherto only his clouds have been seen. Even Jupiter, though it is thought his mountains have been occasionally detected raising their peaks through openings in his cloudy atmosphere, is known chiefly by the dark shifting bands that, fleaking his surface in the line of his trade-winds, belong not to his body, but to his thick dark covering. It is questionable whether a human eye on the surface of Mercury would ever behold the sun, notwithstanding his near proximity; nor would he be often visible, if at all, from the surface of Jupiter. Nor, yet further, would a warm steaming atmosphere muffled in clouds have been unfavourable to a rank, flowerless vegetation like that of the Coal Measures. There are moist, mild, cloudy days of spring and early summer that rejoice the heart of the farmer, for he knows how conducive they are to the young growth on his fields. The Coal-Measure climate would have consisted of an unbroken series of these, with mayhap a little more of cloud and moisture, and a great deal more of heat. The earth would have been a vast greenhouse covered with smoked glass; and a vigorous though mayhap loosely-knit and faintly-coloured vegetation would have luxuriated under its shade.

The fifth and sixth days,—that of winged fowl and great sea-monsters, and that of cattle and beasts of the earth,—I must regard as adequately represented by those Secondary ages, Oolitic and Cretaceous, during which birds were introduced, and reptiles received their greatest development, and those Tertiary ages during which the gigantic mammals possessed the earth and occupied the largest space in creation. To the close of this latter period,—the evening of the sixth day,—man belongs,—at once the last created of terrestrial creatures, and infinitely beyond comparison the most elevated in the scale; and with man's appearance on the scene the days of creation end, and the Divine Sabbath begins,—that Sabbath of rest from creative labour of which the proper work is the moral development and elevation of the species, and which will terminate only with the full completion of that sublime task on the full accomplishment of which God's eternal purposes and the tendencies of man's progressive nature seem alike directed. Now, I am greatly mistaken if we have not in the six geologic periods all the elements, without misplacement or exaggeration, of the Mosaic drama of creation.

I have referred in my brief survey to extended periods. It is probable, however, that the prophetic vision of creation, if such was its character, consisted of only single representative scenes, embracing each but a point of time; it was, let us suppose, a diorama, over whose shifting pictures the curtain rose and fell six times in succession,—once during the Azoic period, once during the earlier or middle Palæozoic period, once during the Carboniferous period, once during the Permian or Triassic period, once during the Oolitic or Cretaceous period, and finally, once during the Tertiary period. Dr Kurtz holds, taking the Sabbath into the series, that the division into *seven* scenes or stages may have been regulated with reference to the importance and sacredness of the mythic number seven,—the symbol of completeness or perfection; but the suggestion will perhaps not now carry much weight among the theologians of Britain, whatever it might have done two centuries ago. It is true, that creation *might* have been exhibited, not by seven, but by seven hundred, or even by seven thousand scenes; and that the accomplished man of science, skilled in every branch of physics, might have found something distinct in them all. But not the less do the seven, or rather the six, exhibited scenes appear to be not symbolic or mystical, at least not exclusively symbolic or mystical, but truly representative of successive periods, strongly distinctive in their character, and capable, with the three geologic days as given points in the problem, of being treated geologically. Another of the questions raised, both by the German Doctor and the writer in our own country, must be recognised as eminently suggestive. "We treat the history of creation," says Dr Kurtz, "with its six days' work, as a connected series of so many prophetic visions. The appearance and evanishing of each such vision seem to the seer as a morning and an evening, apparently because these were presented to him as an increase and decrease of light, like morning and evening twilight." And we find the Scottish writer taking essentially the same view. "Each day contains," he says, "the description of what he [Moses] beheld in a single vision, and when it faded it was twilight. There is nothing forced in supposing that, after the vision had for a time illumined the fancy of the seer, it was withdrawn from his eyes, in the same way that the landscape becomes dim on the approach of evening. . . . From this point of view, a 'day' can only mean the period during which the divinely-enlightened fancy of the seer was active. When all continued bright and manifest before his entranced but still conscious soul, it was 'day,' or 'light.' When the dimness of departing enlightenment fell upon the scene, it was the evening twilight." The *days*, then, are removed, we find, by the holders of this view, altogether from the province of chronology to the province of prophetic vision; they are represented simply as parts of the exhibited scenery, or rather as forming the measures of the apparent time during which the scenery *was* exhibited. We must also hold, however, that in the character of symbolic days they were as truly representative of the lapse of foregone periods of creation as the scenery itself was representative of the creative work accomplished in these periods. For if the apparent days occurred in only the vision, and were not symbolic of foregone periods, they could not have been transferred with any logical propriety from the vision itself to that which the vision represented, as we find done in what our Shorter Catechism terms "the reason annexed to the Fourth Commandment."[2] The days must have been prophetic days, introduced, indeed, into the panorama of creation as mayhap mere openings and droppings of the curtain, but not the less symbolic of that series of successive periods, each characterized by its own productions and events, in which creation itself was comprised. Nothing more probable, however, than that even Moses himself may have been unacquainted with the *extent* of the periods represented in the vision; nay, he may have been equally unconscious of the actual extent of the seeming days by which they were symbolized. "Visions without dark speeches,"—visions, not of symbolic apparitions, but of actual existences and events, past or present,—may, nay must, have differed from what may be termed the dark hieroglyphic visions; but we find in all visions an element of mere representative value introduced when they deal with time, and that they occur as if wholly outside its pale. These creation "days" seem, in relation to what they typify, to have been, if I may so express myself, the mere *modules* of a graduated scale.

Such a description of the creative vision of Moses as the one given by Milton of that vision of the future which he represents as conjured up before Adam by the archangel, would be a task rather for the scientific poet than for the mere practical geologist or sober theologian. Let us suppose that it took place far from man, in an untrodden recess of the Midian desert, ere yet the vision of the burning bush had been vouchsafed; and that, as in the vision of St John in Patmos, voices were mingled with scenes, and the ear as certainly addressed as the eye. A "great darkness" first falls upon the prophet, like that which in an earlier age fell upon Abraham, but without the "horror;" and, as the Divine Spirit moves on the face of the wildly-troubled waters, as a visible aurora enveloped by the pitchy cloud, the great doctrine is orally enunciated, that "in the beginning God created the heavens and the earth." Unreckoned ages, condensed in the vision into a few brief moments, pass away; the creative voice is again heard, "Let there be light,"and straightway a gray diffused light springs up in the east, and, casting its sickly gleam over a cloud-limited expanse of steaming vaporous sea, journeys through the heavens towards the west. One heavy, sunless day is made the representative of myriads; the faint light waxes fainter,—it sinks beneath the dim undefined horizon; the first scene of the drama closes upon the seer; and he sits awhile on his hill-top in darkness, solitary but not sad, in what seems to be a calm and starless night.

The light again brightens,—it is day; and over an expanse of ocean without visible bound the horizon has become wider and sharper of outline than before. There is life in that great sea,—invertebrate, mayhap also ichthyic life; but, from the comparative distance of the point of view occupied by the prophet, only the slow roll of its waves can be discerned, as they rise and fall in long undulations before a gentle gale; and what most strongly impresses the eye is the change which has taken place in the atmospheric scenery. That lower stratum of the heavens occupied in the previous vision by seething steam, or gray, smoke-like fog, is clear and transparent; and only in an upper region, where the previously invisible vapour of the tepid sea has thickened in the cold, do the clouds appear. But there, in the higher strata of the atmosphere, they lie, thick and manifold,—an upper sea of great waves, separated from those beneath by the transparent firmament, and, like them too, impelled in rolling masses by the wind. A mighty advance has taken place in creation; but its most conspicuous optical sign is the existence of a transparent atmosphere,—of a firmament stretched out over the earth, that separates the waters above from the waters below. But darkness descends for the third time upon the seer, for the evening and the morning have completed the second day.

Yet again the light rises under a canopy of cloud; but the scene has changed, and there is no longer an unbroken expanse of sea. The white surf breaks, at the distant horizon, on an insulated reef, formed mayhap by the Silurian or Old Red coral zoophytes ages before, during the bygone yesterday; and beats in long lines of foam, nearer at hand, against a low, winding shore, the seaward barrier of a widely-spread country. For at the Divine command the land has arisen from the deep,—not inconspicuously and in scattered islets, as at an earlier time, but in extensive though flat and marshy continents, little raised over the sea-level; and a yet further fiat has covered them with the great carboniferous flora. The scene is one of mighty forests of cone-bearing trees,—of palms, and tree-ferns, and gigantic club-mosses, on the opener slopes, and of great reeds clustering by the sides of quiet lakes and dark rolling rivers. There is deep gloom in the recesses of the thicker woods, and low thick mists creep along the dank marsh or sluggish stream.

But there is a general lightening of the sky over-head: as the day declines, a redder flush than had hitherto lighted up the prospect falls athwart fern-covered bank and long withdrawing glade. And while the fourth evening has fallen on the prophet, he becomes sensible, as it wears on, and the fourth dawn approaches, that yet another change has taken place. The Creator has spoken, and the stars look out from openings of deep unclouded blue; and as day rises, and the planet of morning pales in the east, the broken cloudlets are transmuted from bronze into gold, and anon the gold becomes fire, and at length the glorious sun arises out of the sea, and enters on his course rejoicing. It is a brilliant day; the waves, of a deeper and softer blue than before, dance and sparkle in the light; the earth, with little else to attract the gaze, has assumed a garb of brighter green; and as the sun declines amid even richer glories than those which had encircled his rising, the moon appears full-orbed in the east,—to the human eye the second great luminary of the heavens,—and climbs slowly to the zenith as night advances, shedding its mild radiance on land and sea.

Again the day breaks; the prospect consists, as before, of land and ocean. There are great pine woods, reed-covered swamps, wide plains, winding rivers, and broad lakes; and a bright sun shines over all. But the landscape derives its interest and novelty from a feature unmarked before. Gigantic birds stalk along the sands, or wade far into the water in quest of their ichthyic food; while birds of lesser size float upon the lakes, or scream discordant in hovering flocks, thick as insects in the calm of a summer evening, over the narrower seas, or brighten with the sunlit gleam of their wings the thick woods. And ocean has its monsters: great "*tanninim*" tempest the deep, as they heave their huge bulk over the surface, to inhale the life-sustaining air; and out of their nostrils goeth smoke, as out of a "seething pot or cauldron." Monstrous creatures, armed in massive scales, haunt the rivers, or scour the flat rank meadows; earth, air, and water are charged with animal life; and the sun sets on a busy scene, in which unerring instinct pursues unremittingly its few simple ends,—the support and preservation of the individual, the propagation of the species, and the protection and maintenance of the young.

Again the night descends, for the fifth day has closed; and morning breaks on the sixth and last day of creation. Cattle and beasts of the field graze on the plains; the thick-skinned rhinoceros wallows in the marshes; the squat hippopotamus rustles among the reeds, or plunges sullenly into the river; great herds of elephants seek their food amid the young herbage of the woods; while animals of fiercer nature,—the lion, the leopard, and the bear,—harbour in deep caves till the evening, or lie in wait for their prey amid tangled thickets, or beneath some broken bank. At length, as the day wanes and the shadows lengthen, man, the responsible lord of creation, formed in God's own image, is introduced upon the scene, and the work of creation ceases for ever upon the earth. The night falls once more upon the prospect, and there dawns yet another morrow,—the morrow of God's rest,—that Divine Sabbath in which there is no more creative labour, and which, "blessed and sanctified" beyond all the days that had gone before, has as its special object the moral elevation and final redemption of man. And over *it* no evening is represented in the record as falling, for its special work is not yet complete. Such seems to have been the sublime panorama of creation exhibited in vision of old to

> "The shepherd who first taught the chosen seed,
> In the beginning how the heavens and earth
> Rose out of chaos;"

and, rightly understood, I know not a single scientific truth that militates against even the minutest or least prominent of its details.

1. Such is also the view taken by the author of a recently published work, "The Genesis of the Earth and of Man." "Christian philosophers have been compelled to acknowledge," says this writer, "that the Mosaic account of creation is only reconcileable with demonstrated facts, by its being regarded as a record of *appearances;* and if so, to vindicate the truth

of God, we must consider it, so far as the *acts* are concerned, as the relation of a revelation to the *sight,* which was sufficient for all its purposes, rather than as one in words; though the words are perfectly true as describing the revelation itself, and the revelation is equally true as showing man the principal phenomena which he would have seen had it been possible for him to be a witness of the events. Farther, if we view the narrative as the description of a series of visions, while we find it to be perfectly reconcileable with the statement in other parts of Scripture that in six days the Lord made heaven and earth, we remove, with other difficulties, the only strong objection to the opinion of those who regard the 'six days' as periods of undefinable duration, and who may even believe that we are now in the 'seventh day,'—the day of rest or of cessation from the work of creation. Certainly, 'the day of God,' and 'the day of the Lord,' and the 'thousand two hundred and threescore days,' of the Revelation of St John, and the 'seventy weeks' in the Prophecy of Daniel, are not to be understood in their primary and natural senses," &c. &c.

2. "For in six days the Lord made heaven and earth, the sea, and all that in them is, and rested the seventh day: wherefore the Lord blessed the Sabbath day, and hallowed it." (Ex. xx.11)

LECTURE FIFTH.

GEOLOGY IN ITS BEARINGS ON THE TWO THEOLOGIES.

PART I.

THE science of the geologist seems destined to exert a marked influence on that of the natural theologian. For not only does it greatly add to the materials on which the natural theologian founds his deductions, by adding to the organisms, plant and animal, of the present creation the extinct organisms of the creations of the past, with all their extraordinary display of adaptation and design; but it affords him, besides, materials peculiar to itself, in the history which it furnishes both of the appearance of these organisms in time, and of the wonderful order in which they were chronologically arranged. Not only—to borrow from Paley's illustration—does it enable him to argue on the old grounds, from the contrivance exhibited in the *watch* found on the moor, that the watch could not have lain upon the moor for ever; but it establishes further, on different and more direct evidence, that there was a time when absolutely the watch was not there; nay, further, so to speak, that there was a previous time in which no watches existed at all, but only water-clocks; yet further, that there was a time in which there were not even water-clocks, but only sun-dials; and further, an earlier time still in which sun-dials were not, nor any measurers of time of any kind. And this is distinct ground from that urged by Paley. For, besides holding that each of these contrivances must have had in turn an originator or contriver, it adds historic fact to philosophic inference. Geology takes up the master volume of the greatest of the natural theologians, and, after scanning its many apt instances of palpable design, drawn from the mechanism of existing plants and animals, authoritatively decides that not one of these plants or animals had begun to be in the times of the Chalk; nay, that they all date their origin from a period posterior to that of the Eocene.

And the fact is, of course, corroborative of the inference. "That well constructed edifice," says the natural theologian, "cannot be a mere *lusus naturæ*, or chance combination of stones and wood; it must have been erected by a builder." "Yes," remarks the geologist, "it was erected some time during the last nine years. I passed the way ten years ago, and saw only a blank space where it now stands." Nor does the established fact of an absolute beginning of organic being seem more pregnant with important consequences to the science of the natural theologian than the fact of the peculiar order in which they begin to be.

The importance of the now demonstrated fact, that all the living organisms which exist on earth had a beginning, and that a time was when they were not, will be best appreciated by those who know how much, and, it must be added, how unsuccessfully, writers on the evidences have laboured to convict of an absurdity, on this special head, the atheistic assertors of an infinite series of beings. Even Robert Hall (in his famous Sermon on Modern Infidelity) could but play, when he attempted grappling with the subject, upon the words *time* and *eternity*, and strangely argue, that as each member of an infinite series must have begun in *time*, while the succession itself was *eternal*, it was palpably absurd to ask us to believe in a *succession* of beings that was thus infinitely earlier than any of the beings themselves which composed the succession. And Bentley, more perversely ingenious still, could assert, that as each of the individuals in an infinite series must have consisted of many parts,—that as each man in such a series, for instance, must have had ten fingers and ten toes,—it was palpably absurd to ask us to believe in an infinity which thus comprised many infinities,—ten infinities of fingers, for example, and ten infinities of toes. The infidels had the better in this part of the argument. It was surely easy enough to show against the great preacher, on the one hand, that *time* in such a question is but a mere word that means simply a certain limited or definite period which had a beginning, whereas eternity means an unlimited and undefinable period which had no beginning;—that his seeming argument was no argument, but merely a sort of verbal play on this difference of signification in the words;—further, that man could conceive of an infinite series, whether extended in infinite space, or subsisting in infinite time, just as well as he could conceive of any other infinity, and in the same way;—and that the only mode of disproving the possibility of such a series would be to show, what of course cannot be shown, that in conceiving of it in the progressive mode in which, according to Locke, man can alone conceive of the infinite or the eternal, there would be a point reached at which it would be impossible for him to go on adding millions on millions to the previous sum. The symbolic *"ad infinitum"* could be made as adequately representative in the case of an infinite series of men or animals in unlimited time, as of an infinite series of feet or inches in unlimited space, or of an infinite series of hours or minutes in the past eternity. And as for Bentley, on the other hand, he ought surely to have known that all infinities are not equal, seeing that Newton had expressly told him so in the second of his four famous letters; but that, on the contrary, one infinity may be not only ten times greater than another infinity, but even infinitely greater than another infinity; and that so the conception of an infinity of men possessed of ten infinities of fingers and toes is in no respect an absurdity. Of the three infinities possible in space, the second is infinitely greater than the first, and the third infinitely greater than the second. A line infinitely produced is capable of being divided into—*i.e.* consists of—an infinity of given parts; a plane infinitely extended is capable of being divided into an infinity of infinitely divisible lines; and a cube,—*i.e.* a solid, infinitely expanded—is capable of being divided into an infinity of infinitely divisible planes. In fine, metaphysic theology furnishes no argument against the infinite series of the atheist. But geology does. Every plant and animal that now lives upon earth began to be during the great Tertiary period, and had no place among the plants and animals of the great Secondary division. We can trace several of our existing quadrupeds, such as the badger, the hare, the fox, the red deer, and the wild cat, up till the earlier times of the Pleistocene; and not a few of our existing shells, such as the great pecten, the edible oyster, the whelk, and the Pelican's-foot shell, up till the greatly earlier times of the Coraline Crag. But at certain definite lines in the deposits of the past, representative of certain points in the course of time, the existing mammals and molluscs cease to appear, and we find their places occupied by other mammals and molluscs. Even such of our British shells as seem to have enjoyed as species the longest term of life cannot be traced beyond the times of the Pliocene deposits. We detect their remains in a perfect state of keeping in almost every shell-bearing bed, till we reach the Red and Coraline Crags, where we find them for the last time; and, on passing into older and deeper lying beds, we see their places taken by other shells, of species altogether distinct. The very common shell *Purpura lapillus*, for instance, is found in our raised beaches, in our Clyde-beds, in our boulder-clays and mammaliferous crags, and, finally, in the Red Crag, beyond which it fails to appear. And such also is the history of the common edible mussel and common periwinkle; whereas the common edible cockle, and common edible pecten (*P. opercularis*) occur not only in all these successive beds, but in the Coral Crag also. They are older by a whole deposit than their present contemporaries the mussel and periwinkle; and these, in turn, seem of older standing than shells such as *Murex erinaceus*, that has not been traced beyond the times of the mammaliferous crag, or than shells such as *Scrobicularia piperata*, that has not been detected in more ancient deposits than raised sea-beaches of the later periods, and the elevated bottoms of old estuaries and lagoons. We thus know, that in certain periods, nearer or more remote, all our existing molluscs *began* to exist, and that they had no existence during the previous periods; which were, however, richer in animals of the same great molluscan group than the present time. Our British group of recent marine shells falls somewhat short of *four* hundred species;[1] whereas the group characteristic of the older Miocene deposits, largely developed in those districts of France which border on the Bay of Biscay, and more sparingly in the south of England, near Yarmouth, comprises more than *six* hundred species. Nearly an equal number of still older shells have been detected in a single deposit of the Paris basin,—the *Calcaire grossier*; and a good many more in a more ancient formation still, the London Clay. On entering the Chalk, we find a yet older group of shells, wholly unlike any of the preceding ones; and in the Oolite and Lias yet other and different groupes. And thus group preceded group throughout all the Tertiary, Secondary, and Palæozoic periods; some of them remarkable for the number of species which they contained, others for the profuse abundance of their individual specimens, until, deep in the rocks at the base of the Silurian system, we detect what seems to be the primordial group, beneath which only a single animal organism is known to occur,—the *Oldhamia antiqua*,—a plant-like zoophyte, akin apparently to some of our recent sertulariæ. (See fig. 5.) Each of the extinct groupes had, we find, a beginning and an end;—there is not in the wide domain of physical science a more certain fact: and every species of the group which now exists had, like all their predecessors on the scene, their beginning also. The "infinite series" of the atheists of former times can have no place in modern science: all organic existences, recent or extinct, vegetable or animal, have had their beginning;—there was a time when they were not. The geologist can indicate that time, if not by years, at least by periods, and show what its relations were to the periods that went before and that came after; and as it is equally a recognised truth on both sides of the controversy, that as something now exists, something must have existed for ever, and as it must now be not less surely recognised, that that something was not the race of man, nor yet any other of the many races of man's predecessors or contemporaries, the question, What then was that something? comes with a point and directness which it did not possess at any former time. By what, or through whom, did these races of nicely organized plants and animals begin to be? Hitherto at least there has been but one reply to the question originated on the sceptical side. All these races, it is said, have been *developed*, in the long course of ages, into what they now are, as the young animal is developed in the womb, or the young plant is developed from the seed. Topsy, in the novel, "'spected that she was not made, but growed;" and the only class of opponents which the geological theist finds in the field which his science has laid open to the world is a class that hold by the philosophy of Topsy.

Let me briefly remark regarding this development hypothesis, with which I have elsewhere dealt at considerable length, that while the facts of the geologist are demonstrably such, *i.e.* truths capable of proof, the hypothesis is a mere dream, unsupported by a shadow of evidence. A man of a lively imagination could no doubt originate many such dreams; nay, we know that in the dark ages dreams of the kind were actually originated. The *Anser Bernicla*, or barnacle goose, a common winter visitant of our coasts, was once believed to be developed out of decaying wood long submerged in sea-water; and one of our commonest cirripedes or barnacles, *Lepas anatifera*, still bears, in its specific name of the goose-producing *lepas*, evidence that it was the creature specially recognised by our ancestors as the half-developed goose. As if in memory of this old development-legend, the bird still bears the name of the barnacle, and the barnacle of the bird; and we know further, that very intelligent men for their age, such as Gerardes the herbalist (1597), and Hector Boece the historian (1524), both examined these shells, and, knowing but little of comparative anatomy, were satisfied that the animal within was the partially developed embryo of a fowl. Such was one of the fables gravely credited as a piece of natural history in Britain about three centuries ago, and such was the kind of evidence by which it was supported. And we know that the followers of Epicurus received from their master, without apparent suspicion, fables still more extravagant, and that wanted even such a shadow of proof to support them as satisfied the herbalist and the historian. The Epicureans at least professed to believe that the earth, after spontaneously producing herbs and trees, began to produce in great numbers mushroom-like bodies, that, when they came to maturity, burst open, giving egress each to a young animal, which proved the founder of a race; and that thus, in succession, all the members of the animal kingdom were ushered into existence. But whether the dream be that of the Epicureans of classic times, or that of the naturalists of the middle ages, or that of the Lamarckians of our own days, it is equally a dream, and can have no place assigned to it among either the solid facts or the sober deductions of science. Nay, the dream of the Lamarckians labours under a special disadvantage, from which the dreams of the others are free. If some modern Boece or Epicurus were to assert that at certain definite periods, removed from fifteen to fifty thousand years from the present time, all our existing animals were developed from decaying wood, or from a wonderful kind of mushrooms that the earth produced only once every ten thousand years, the assertion, if incapable of proof, would be at least equally incapable of being *dis*-proven. But when the Lamarckian affirms that all our recent species of plants and animals were developed out of previously existing plants and animals of species entirely different, he affirms what, if true, *would* be capable of proof; and so, if it cannot be proven, it is only because it is not true. The trilobites have been extinct ever since the times of the Mountain Limestone; and yet, by series of specimens, the individual development of certain species of this family, almost from the extrusion of the animal from the egg until the attainment of its full size, has been satisfactorily shown. By specimen after specimen has every stage of growth and every degree of development been exemplified; and the Palæontologist has come as thoroughly to know the creatures, in consequence, under their various changes from youth to age, as if they had been his contemporaries, and had grown up under his eye. And had our existing species, vegetable and animal, been derived from other species of the earlier periods, it would have been equally possible to demonstrate, by a series of specimens, *their* relationship. Let us again instance the British shells. Losing certain species in each of the older and yet older deposits at which we successively arrive, we at length reach the Red and Coraline Crags, where we find, mingled with the familiar forms, a large per centage of forms now extinct; then going on to the shells of the Lower Miocene, more than six hundred species appear, almost all of which are strange to us; and then, passing to the Eocene shells of the *Calcaire grossier*, we find ourselves among well nigh as large a group of yet other and older strangers, not one of which we are able to identify with any shell now living in the British area. There would be thus no lack of materials for forming such a genealogy of the British shells, had they been gradually developed out of the extinct species, as that which M. Barrande has formed of the trilobites. But no such genealogy can be formed. We cannot link on a single recent shell to a single extinct one. *Up* to a certain point we find the recent shells exhibiting all their present specific peculiarities, and beyond that point they cease to appear. *Down* to a certain point the extinct shells also exhibit all *their* specific peculiarities, and then they disappear for ever. There are no intermediate species,—no connecting links,—no such connected series of specimens to be found as enables us to trace a trilobite through all its metamorphoses from youth to age. All geologic history is full of the beginnings and the ends of species,—of their first and their last days; but it exhibits no genealogies of development. The Lamarckian sets himself to grapple, in his dream, with the history of all creation: we awaken him, and ask him to grapple, instead, with the history of but a few individual species,—with that of the mussel or the whelk, the clam or the oyster; and we find from his helpless ignorance and incapacity what a mere pretender he is.

But while no hypothesis of development can neutralize or explain away the great geologic fact, that every true species had a beginning independently, apparently, of every preceding species, there was demonstrably a general progress, in the course of creation, from lower to higher forms, which seems scarce less fraught with important consequences to the natural theologian than this fact of *beginning* itself. For while the one fact effectually disposes of the "infinite series" of the atheist, the other fact disposes scarce less effectually of those reasonings on the sceptical side which, framed on the assumption that creation is a "singular effect,"—an effect without duplicate,—have been employed in urging, that from that one effect only can we know aught regarding the producing Cause. Knowing of the Cause from but the effect, and having experience of but one effect, we cannot rationally hold, it has been argued, that the producing Cause could have originated effects of a higher or more perfect kind. The creation which it produced we know; but, having no other measure of its power, we cannot regard it, it has been contended, as equal to the production of a better or nobler creation, or of course hold that it *could* originate such a state of things as that perfect future state

which faith delights to contemplate. It has been well said of the
author of this ingenious argument,—by far the most sagacious of
the sceptics,—that if we admit his premises we shall find it difficult
indeed to set aside his conclusions. And how, in this case, does
geology deal with his premises? By opening to us the history of the
remote past of our planet, and introducing us, through the present,
to former creations, it breaks down that *singularity* of effect on
which he built, and for one creation gives us many. It gives us
exactly that which, as he truly argued, his contemporaries had
not,—an *experience* in creations. And let us mark how, applied to
each of these in succession, his argument would tell.

There was a time when life, animal or vegetable, did not exist
on our planet, and when all creation, from its centre to its
circumference, was but a creation of dead matter. What, in that
early age, would have been the effect of the argument of Hume?
Simply this,—that though the producing Cause of all that
appeared was competent to the formation of gases and earths,
metals and minerals, it would be unphilosophic to deem Him
adequate to the origination of a single plant or animal, even to that
of a spore or of a monad. Ages pass by, and the Palæozoic creation
is ushered in, with its tall araucarians and pines, its highly
organized fishes, and its reptiles of comparatively low standing.
And how now, and with what effect, does the argument apply? It
is now rendered evident, that in the earlier creation the producing
Cause had exerted but a portion of His power, and that He could
have done greatly more than He actually did, seeing that we now
find Him adequate to the origination of vitality and organization
in its two great kingdoms, plant and animal. But, still confining
ourselves with cautious scepticism within the limits of our
argument, we continue to hold that, as fishes of a high and reptiles
of a low order, with trees of the cone-bearing family, are the most
perfect specimens of their respective classes which the producing
Cause has originated, it would be rash to hold, in the absence of
proof, that He *could* originate aught higher or more perfect. And
now, as yet other ages pass away, the creation of the great
Secondary division takes the place of that of the vanished
Palæozoic; and we find in its few dicotyledonous plants, in its

reptiles of highest standing, in its great birds, and in its some two
or three humble marsupial mammals, that in the previous, as in
the earlier creation, the producing Cause had been, if I may so
express myself, working greatly under His strength, and that in
this third creation we have a still higher display of His potency.
With some misgivings, however, we again apply our argument.
And now yet another creation,—that of the Tertiary period, with
its noble forests of dicotyledonous trees and its sagacious and
gigantic mammals,—rises upon the scene; and as our experience in
creations has now become very considerable, and as we have seen
each in succession higher than that which preceded it, we find that,
notwithstanding our assumed scepticism, we had, compelled by
one of the most deeply-seated instincts of our nature, been secretly
anticipating the advance which the new state of things actually
realizes. But applying the argument once more, we at least assume
to hold, that as the sagacious elephant is the highest example of
animal life yet produced by the originating Cause, it would be
unphilosophic to deem Him capable of producing a higher
example. And, while we are thus reasoning, man appears upon
creation,—a creature immeasurably superior to all the others, and
whose very nature it is to make use of his experience of the past for
his guidance in the future. And if that only be solid experience or
just reasoning which enables us truly to anticipate the events
which are to come, and so to make provision for them; and if that
experience be not solid, and that reasoning not just, which would
serve but to darken our discernment, and prevent us from
correctly predicating the cast and complexion of coming events,
what ought to be our decision regarding an argument which, had it
been employed in each of the vanished creations of the past, would
have had but the effect of arresting all just anticipation regarding
the immediately succeeding creation, and which, thus reversing
the main end and object of philosophy, would render the
philosopher who clung to it less sagacious in divining the future
than even the ordinary man? But, in truth, the existing premises,
wholly altered by geologic science, are no longer those of Hume.
The footprint on the sand—to refer to his happy illustration—does
not now stand alone. Instead of one, we see many footprints, each

in turn in advance of the print behind it, and on a higher level; and, founding at once on an acquaintance with the past, extended throughout all the periods of the geologist, and on that instinct of our nature whose peculiar function it is to anticipate at least one creation more, we must regard the expectation of "new heavens and a new earth, wherein dwelleth righteousness," as not unphilosophic, but as, on the contrary, altogether rational and according to experience.

Such is the bearing of geological science on two of the most important questions that have yet been raised in the field of natural theology. Nor does it bear much less directly on a controversy to which, during the earlier half of the last century, there was no little importance attached in Britain, and which engaged on its opposite sides some of the finest and most vigorous intellects of the age and country.

The school of infidelity represented by Bolingbroke, and, in at least his earlier writings, by Soame Jenyns, and which, in a modified form, attained to much popularity through Pope's famous "Essay," assigned to man a comparatively inconsiderable space in the system of the universe. It regarded him as but a single link in a chain of mutual dependency,—a chain which would be no longer an entire, but a broken one, were he to be struck out of it, but as thus more important from his position than from his nature or his powers. You will remember that one of the sections of Pope's first epistle to his "good St John" is avowedly devoted to show what he terms the "absurdity of man's supposing himself the final cause of the creation;" and though this great master of condensed meaning and brilliant point is now less read than he was in the days of our grandfathers, you will all remember the elegant stanzas in which he states the usual claims of the species only to ridicule them. It is human pride personified that he represents as exclaiming,—

> "For me kind Nature wakes her genial power,
> Suckles each herb, and spreads out every flower;
> Annual for me the grape, the rose, renew
> The juice nectarious and the balmy dew.

"For me the mine a thousand treasures brings;
For me health gushes from a thousand springs;
Seas roll to waft me, suns to light me rise;
My footstool earth, my canopy the skies."

You will further remember how the poet, after thus reducing the claims and lowering the position of the species, set himself to show that man, viewed in relation to the place which he occupies, ought not to be regarded as an imperfect being. Man is, he said, as perfect as he ought to be. And, such being the case, the Author of all, looking, it would seem, very little after him, has just left him to take care of himself. A cold, unfeeling abstraction, like the gods of the old Epicurean, the Great First Cause of this school is a being

"Who sees with equal eye, as God of all,
A hero perish or a sparrow fall;
Atoms or systems into ruin hurl'd,
And now a bubble burst, and now a world."

Such, assuredly, was not that God of the New Testament whom the Saviour of mankind revealed to his disciples as caring for all his creatures of the dust, but as caring most for the highest of all. "Are not two sparrows," he said, "sold for a farthing? and one of them shall not fall to the ground without your Father. Fear ye not therefore; ye are of more value than many sparrows."

It was the error of this ingenious but very unsolid school, that it regarded the mere *order* of the universe as itself an end or final cause. It reasoned respecting creation as if it would be true philosophy to account for the origin and existence of some great city, such as the city of Washington in the United States, built, as we know, for purely political purposes, by showing that,—as it was remarkable for its order, for the rectilinear directness of its streets, and the rectangularity of its squares,—it must have been erected simply to be a perfect embodiment of regularity; and to urge further that, save in their character as component parts of a perfect whole, the House of Representatives and the mansion of the President were of no more intrinsic importance, or no more decidedly the *end* of the whole, than any low tavern or out-house in the lesser streets or lanes. The destruction of either the out-house or the House of Representatives would equally form a void in the general plan of the city, regarded as an admirably arranged whole. And it was thus with the grand scheme of creation; for,

> "From nature's chain whatever link we strike,
> Tenth or tenth thousand, breaks the chain alike."

Nor is it in other than due keeping with such a view of creation that its great Author should be represented as a cold abstraction, without love or regard, and equally indifferent to the man and the sparrow, to the atom and the planet. Order has respect to but the *relations* of things or of beings,—not to the things or beings themselves; order is the *figure* which, as mere etched points or strokes, they compose,—the legend which, as signs or characters, they form; and who cares anything for the component strokes or dots irrespective of the print, or for the component letters or words apart from the writing? The "equal eye," in such a scheme, would of necessity be an indifferent one. Against this strange doctrine, though in some measure countenanced by the glosses of Warburton in his defence of Pope, the theologians protested,—none of them, however, more vigorously than Johnson, in his famous critique on the "Free Inquiry" of Soame Jenyns. Nor is it uninteresting to mark with what a purely instinctive feeling of the right some of the better poets, whose "lyre," according to Cowper, was their "heart," protested against it too. Poor Goldsmith, when sitting a homeless vagabond on the slopes of the Alps, could exclaim, in a greatly truer tone than that of his polished predecessor,—

> "Creation's heir, the world, the world is mine!"

And in Cowper himself we find all Goldsmith's intense feeling of appropriation, that "calls the delightful scenery all its own," associated

"With worthy thoughts of that unvaried love
That planned, and built, and still upholds, a world
So clothed with beauty, for rebellious man."

Strange to say, however, it is to the higher exponents of natural science, and in especial to the geologists, that it has been left to deal most directly with the sophistries of Bolingbroke and Pope.

Oken, a man quite as far wrong in some points as either the poet or his master, was the first to remark, and this in the oracular, enigmatical style peculiar to the German, that "man is the sum total of all the animals." Gifted, as all allow, with a peculiarly nice eye for detecting those analogies which unite the animal world into a harmonious whole, he remarked, that in one existence or being all these analogies converge. Even the humbler students of the heavens have learned to find for themselves the star of the pole, by following the direction indicated by what are termed the two pointer stars in the Great Bear. And to the eye of Oken all the groupes of the animal kingdom formed a sphere of constellations, each of which has its pointer stars, if I may so speak, turned towards man. Man occupies, as it were, the central point in the great circle of being; so that those lines which pass singly through each of the inferior animals stationed at its circumference, meet in him; and thus, as the focus in which the scattered rays unite, he imparts by his presence a unity and completeness to creation which it would not possess were he away. You will be startled, however, by the language in which the German embodies his view; though it may be not uninstructive to refer to it in evidence of the fact that a man may be *intellectually* on the very verge of truth, and yet for every moral purpose infinitely removed from it. "Man," he says, "is God manifest in the flesh." And yet it may be admitted that there is a certain loose sense in which man *is* "God manifest in the flesh." As may be afterwards shown, he is God's *image* manifested in the flesh; and an image or likeness *is* a manifestation or making evident of that which it represents, whether it be an image or likeness of body or of mind.

Not less extraordinary, but greatly more sound in their application, are the views of Professor Owen,—supreme in his own special walk as a comparative anatomist. We find him recognising man as exemplifying in his structure the perfection of that type in which, from the earliest ages, nature had been working with reference to some future development, and as *therefore* a fore-ordained existence. "The recognition of an ideal exemplar for the vertebrated animals proves," he says, "that the knowledge of such a being as man must have existed before man appeared. For the Divine mind that planned the archetype also foreknew all its modifications. The archetypal idea was manifested in the flesh, under divers modifications, upon this planet, long prior to the existence of those animal species that actually exemplify it." So far Owen. And not less wonderful is the conclusion at which Agassiz has arrived, after a survey of the geologic existences more extended and minute, in at least the ichthyic department, than that of any other man. "It is evident," we find him saying, in the conclusion of his recent work, "The Principles of Zoology," "that there is a manifest progress in the succession of beings on the surface of the earth. This progress consists in an increasing similarity to the living fauna, and among the vertebrates, especially in their increasing resemblance to man. But this connection is not the consequence of a direct lineage between the faunas of different ages. There is nothing like parental descent connecting them. The fishes of the Palæozoic age are in no respect the ancestors of the reptiles of the Secondary age, nor does man descend from the mammals which preceded him in the Tertiary age. The link by which they are connected is of a higher and immaterial nature; and their connection is to be sought in the view of the Creator himself, whose aim in forming the earth, in allowing it to undergo the successive changes which geology has pointed out, and in creating successively all the different types of animals which have passed away, *was to introduce man upon the surface of our globe*. MAN IS THE END TOWARDS WHICH ALL THE ANIMAL CREATION HAS TENDED FROM THE FIRST APPEARANCE OF THE FIRST PALÆOZOIC FISHES." These, surely, are extraordinary deductions. "In thy book," says the Psalmist, "all my members were written, which in continuance were fashioned when as yet there was none of them." And here is natural science, by the voice of two of its most distinguished professors, saying exactly the same thing.

Of the earliest known vertebrates,—the placoidal fishes of the Upper Silurian rocks,—we possess only fragments, which, however, sufficiently indicate, from their resemblance to the corresponding parts of an existing shark,—the cestracion,—that they belonged to fishes furnished with the two pairs of fins now so generally recognised as the homologues of the fore and hinder limbs in quadrupeds. With the second earliest vertebrates,—the ganoids of the Old Red Sandstone,—we are more directly acquainted, and know that they exhibited the true typical form,—a vertebral column terminating in a brain-protecting skull; and that, in at least the acanth, celacanth, and dipterian families, they had the limb-like fins. In the upper parts of the system the earliest reptiles leave the first known traces of the typical foot, with its five digits. Higher still in one of the deposits of the Trias we are startled by what seems to be the impression of a human hand of an uncouth massive shape, but with the thumb apparently set in opposition, as in man, to the other fingers; we next trace the type upwards among the wonderfully developed reptiles of the Secondary periods; then among the mammals of the Tertiary ages, higher and yet higher forms appear; the mute prophecies of the coming being become with each approach clearer, fuller, more expressive, and at length receive their fulfilment in the advent of man. A double meaning attaches to the term type; and hence some ambiguity in the writings which have appeared on this curious subject. Type means a prophecy embodied in symbol; it means also what Sir Joshua Reynolds well terms "one of the general forms of nature,"—a pattern form, from which all others in the same class or family, however numerous, are recognised as mere exceptions and aberrations. But in the geologic series both meanings converge and become one. The form or number typical as the *general* form or number is found typical also, as a *prophecy*, of the form or number that came at length to be exemplified in the deputed lord of creation. Let us in our examples take typical numbers, as more easily illustrated without diagrams than typical forms.

There are vertebrate animals of the second age of ichthyic existence, that, like the *Pterichthys* and *Coccosteus*, were furnished with but two limbs. The mu--nid-- of recent times have no more; at least one of their number, the mur--na proper, wants limbs altogether; so also do the lampreys. The snakes are equally limbless, save that the boas and pythons possess the rudiments of a single pair; and such also is the condition, among the amphibia, of all the known species of C--cilia. And yet, notwithstanding these exceptional cases, the true typical number of limbs, as shown by a preponderating majority of the vertebrates of all ages of the world, is four. And this typical number is the human number. There is as certainly a typical number of digits too, as of the limbs which bear them. The exceptions are many. All the species of the horse genus possess but a single digit; the cattle family possess but two digits, the rhinoceros three digits, the hippopotamus four digits; many animals, such as the dog and cat, have but four digits on one pair of limbs and five on the other; whereas in some of the fishes the number of digits is singularly great,—from ten to twenty in most species, and in the rays from eighty to a hundred. And yet, as shown in the rocks, in which, however, the aberrations appear early, the true typical number is five on both the fore and hinder limbs. And such is the number in man. There is also, in at least the mammalia, a typical number of vertebr-- in the neck. The three-toed sloth has nine cervical vertebr--; the manati only six; but seven is the typical number. And seven is the human number also. Man, in short, is pre-eminently what a theologian would term the antetypical existence,—the being in whom the types meet and are fulfilled. And not only do typical forms and numbers of the exemplified character meet in man, but there are not a few parts of his framework which in the inferior animals exist as but mere symbols, of as little importance as dugs in the male animal, though they acquire significancy and use in him. Such, for instance, are the many-jointed but moveless and unnecessary bones of which the stiff inflexible *fin* of the dugong and the fore paw of the mole consist, and which exist in his arm as essential portions, none of which could be wanted, of an exquisitely flexible instrument. In other cases, the old types are exemplified serially in the growth and development of certain portions of his frame. Such is specially the case with that all-important portion of it, the organ of thought and feeling. The human brain is built up by a wonderful process, during which it assumes in succession the form of the brain of a fish, of a reptile, of a bird, of a mammiferous quadruped; and, finally, it takes upon it its unique character as a human brain. Hence the remark of Oken, that "man is the sum total of all the animals;" hence, too, a, recognition of type in the *history* of the successive vertebral periods of the geologist, symbolical of the history of every individual man. It is not difficult to conceive how, on a subject of such complexity, especially if approached in an irreverent spirit, grave mistakes and misconceptions should take place. Virgil knew just enough of Hebrew prophecy to misapply, in his *Pollio*, to his great patron Octavius, those ancient predictions which foretold that in that age the Messiah was to appear. And I am inclined to hold, that in the more ingenious speculations of the Lamarckians we have just a similar misapplication of what, emboldened by the views of Owen and Agassiz, I shall venture to term the *Geologic Prophecies*.

The term is new, but the idea which it embodies, though it at first existed rather as a nice poetic instinct than as a scientifically based thought, is at least as old as the times of Herder and Coleridge. In a passage quoted from the former writer by Dr M'Cosh, in his very masterly work on typical forms, I find the profound German remarking of the strange resemblances which pervade all nature, and impart a general unity to its forms, that it would seem "as if on all our earth the form-abounding mother had proposed to herself but one type,—one proto-plasma,—according to which, and for which, she formed them all. Know, then," he continues, "what this form is. It is the identical one which man also wears." And the remark of Coleridge, in his "Aids to Reflection," is still more definite. "Let us carry us back in spirit," he says, "to the mysterious week, the teeming work-days of the Creator (*as they rose in* VISION *before the eye of the inspired historian*), of the operations of the heavens and of the earth in the day that the Lord God made the earth and the heavens. And who that watched their ways with an understanding heart could, as the vision evolved still advanced towards him, contemplate the filial and loyal bee, the home-building, wedded, and divorceless swallow, and, above all, the manifoldly intelligent ant tribes, with their commonwealths and confederacies, their warriors and miners, the husband-folk that fold in their tiny flocks on the honey-leaf, and the virgin sister with the holy instincts of maternal love detached and in selfless purity, and not say in himself, Behold the shadow of approaching humanity, the sun rising from behind in the kindling morn of creation!" There is fancy here; but it is that sagacious fancy, vouchsafed to only the true poet, which has so often proved the pioneer of scientific discovery, and which is in reality more sober and truthful, in the midst of its apparent extravagance, than the gravest cogitations of ordinary men. It is surely no incredible thing, that He who, in the dispensations of the human period, spake by type and symbol, and who, when He walked the earth in the flesh, taught in parable and allegory, should have also spoken in the geologic ages by prophetic figures embodied in the form and structure of animals. Nay, what the poet imagined, though in a somewhat extreme form, the philosophers seem to be on the very eve of confirming. The foreknown "archetypal idea" of Owen,—"the immaterial link of connection" of all the past with all the present, which Agassiz resolves into the fore-ordained design of the Creator,—will be yet found, I cannot doubt, to translate themselves into one great general truth, namely, that the Palæozoic, Secondary, and Tertiary dispensations of creation were charged, like the patriarchal and Mosaic dispensations of grace, with the "shadows of better things to come." The advent of man simply as such was the great event prefigured during the old geologic ages. The advent of that Divine Man "who hath abolished death, and brought life and immortality to light," was the great event prefigured during the historic ages. It is these two grand events, equally portions of one sublime scheme, originated when God took counsel with himself in the depths of eternity, that bind together past, present, and future,—the geologic with the Patriarchal, the Mosaic, and the Christian ages, and all together with that new heavens and new earth, the last of many creations, in which there shall be "no more death nor curse, but the throne of God and the Lamb shall be in it, and his servants shall serve him."

"There is absurdity," said Pope, "in man's conceiting himself the final cause of creation." Unless, however, man had the entire scheme of creation before him, with the farther partially known scheme of which but a part constitutes the grand theme of revelation, how could he pronounce on the absurdity? The knowledge of the geologist ascends no higher than man. He sees all nature in the pre-Adamic past, pointing with prophetic finger towards him; and on even the argument of Hume,—just and solid within its proper limits,—he refuses to acquiesce in the unfounded inference of Pope. In order to prove the absurdity of "man's conceiting himself the final cause of creation," proof of an ulterior cause,—of a higher end and aim,—must be adduced; and of aught higher than man, the geologist as such, knows nothing. The long vista opened up by his science closes with the deputed lord of creation,—with man as he at present exists; and when, casting himself full upon revelation, the veil is drawn aside, and an infinitely grander vista stretches out before him into the future, he sees man—no longer, however, the natural, but the Divine man—occupying what is at once its terminal point and its highest apex. Such are some of the bearings of geologic science on the science of natural theology. Geology has disposed effectually and for ever of the oft-urged assumption of an infinite series; it deals as no other science could have dealt with the assertion of the sceptic, that creation is a "singular effect;" it casts a flood of unexpected light on the somewhat obsolete plausibilities of Bolingbroke and Jenyns, that exhibits their utterly unsolid character; yet further, it exhibits in a new aspect the argument founded on design, and invests the place and standing of man in *creation* with a peculiar significancy and importance, from its relation to the future. But on this latter part of my subject—necessarily of considerable extent and multiplicity, and connected rather with revealed than with natural religion—I must not now expatiate. I shall, however, attempt laying before you on some future evening, a few thoughts on this portion of the general question, which you may at least find suggestive of others, and which, if they fail to elicit new truths,

may have the effect of opening up upon an old truth or two a few
fresh avenues through which to survey them. The character of
man as a fellow-worker with his Creator in the material province
has still to be considered in the light of geology. Man was the first,
and is still the only creature of whom we know anything, who has
set himself to carry on and improve the work of the world's
original framer,—who is a planter of woods, a tiller of fields, and a
keeper of gardens,—and who carries on his work of mechanical
contrivance on obviously the same principles as those on which the
Divine designer wrought of old, and on which He works still. It
may not be wholly unprofitable to acquaint ourselves, through
evidence furnished by the rocks, with the remarkable fact, that the
Creator imparted to man the Divine image before He united to
man's the Divine nature.

1. Forbes and Hanley enumerate one hundred and sixty bivalves, and
two hundred and thirty-two univalves, in all three hundred and ninety-
two species, as the only known shell-bearing molluscs of the existing
British seas.

LECTURE SIXTH.

GEOLOGY IN ITS BEARINGS ON THE TWO THEOLOGIES.

PART II.

Up till the introduction of man upon our planet, the humbler creatures, his predecessors, formed but mere figures in its various landscapes, and failed to alter or affect by their works the face of nature. They were conspicuous, not from what they *did*, but from what they *were*. At a very early period reefs of coral, the work of minute zoophytes, whitened the shallows of the ocean, or encircled with pale, ever-broadening frames, solitary islands green with the shrubs and trees of extinct floras; but, though products of the animal world, they were not built up under the direction of even an instinctive intelligence, but were as entirely the results of a *vegetative* process of mere growth as the forests or reed-brakes of the old Carboniferous savannahs. At a later time an ant-hill might be here and there descried, rearing its squat brown pyramid amid the recesses of some Oolitic forest; or, in a period still more recent, the dam of the gigantic beaver might be seen extending its minute eye-like circlet of blue amid the windings of some bosky ravine of the Pliocene age; or existing as a little mound-skirted pond, with the rude half-submerged *cottage* of the creature, its architect, rising beside it, on some rivulet of the Pleistocene. But how inconsiderable such works, compared with the wide extent of prospect in which they were included! How entirely inconspicuous rather, save when placed in the immediate foreground of the pictures into whose composition they entered! Not until the introduction of man upon earth do we find a creature whose works sensibly affect and modify the aspects of nature. But when man appears, how mighty the change which he effects! Immediately on his creation he takes under his care the vegetable productions of use and show: it becomes his business to keep and dress a garden. He next becomes a tiller of fields, then a planter of vineyards: here he cuts down great forests; there he rears extensive woods. He makes himself places of habitation; and busy cities spring up as the trophies of his diligence and skill. His labours, as they grow upon the waste, affect the appearance of vast continents; until at length, from many a hill-top and tall spire, scarce a rood of ground can be seen on which he has not built, or sown, or planted, or around which he has not erected his walls or reared his hedges. Man, in this great department of industry, is what none of his predecessors upon the earth ever were,—"a fellow-worker" with the Creator. He is a mighty *improver* of creation. We recognise that as improvement which adapts nature more thoroughly to man's own necessities and wants, and renders it more pleasing both to his sense of the æsthetic and to his more material senses also. He adds to the beauty of the flowers which he takes under his charge,—to the delicacy and fertility of the fruits; the seed of the wild grasses become corn beneath his care; the green herbs grow great of root or bulb, or bulky and succulent of top and leaf; the wild produce of nature *sports* under his hand; the rose and lily broaden their disks and multiply their petals; the harsh green crab swells out into a delicious golden-rhinded apple, streaked with crimson; the productions of his kitchen-garden, strangely metamorphosed to serve the uses of his table, bear forms unknown to nature; an occult law of change and development inherent to these organisms meet in him with the developing instinct and ability, and they are re-generated under his surveillance. Nor is his influence over many of the animals less marked. The habits which he imparts to the parents become *nature*, in his behalf, in their offspring. The dog acquires, under his tutelage, the virtues of fidelity to a master and affection to a friend. The ox and horse learn to assist him in the labours of the fields. The udders of the cow and goat distend beneath his care far beyond the size necessary in the wild state, and supply him with rich milk, and the other various products of the dairy. The fleece of the sheep becomes finer of texture and longer of fibre in his pens and folds; and even the indocile silk-worm spins, in his sheltered conservatories, and among the mulberry trees which he has planted, a larger, and brighter, and more glistening cocoon. Man is the great creature-worker of the world,—its one created being, that, taking up the work of the adorable Creator, carries it on to higher results and nobler developments, and finds a field for his persevering ingenuity and skill in every province in which his Maker had expatiated before him. He is evidently—to adopt and modify the remark of Oken—God's image "manifest in the flesh."

Surveyed from the special point of view furnished by this peculiar nature of man, unique in creation, all the past of our planet divides into two periods;—the period, inclusive of every age known to the geologist, during which only the Creator wrought; and the period during which man has wrought, and to which all human history belongs. In such a view we are presented with two sets of works,—those of the Creator-worker, and those of the creature-worker; and the vast fund of materials on which the natural theologian frames his arguments demonstrative of design or contrivance, assumes a new significancy and interest when employed as evidence that there exists a certain correspondence of nature and intellect between the two workers, human and Divine. The ability of accomplishing the same ends by the same means,—in other words, of thinking and acting in the same practical tract,—indicates a similarity, if not identity, of intellectual nature. In the Chinese centre of civilization, for instance, printing, gunpowder, the mariner's compass, with the various chemical and mechanical arts of elegant life, were originated without concert with the European centre of civilization, simply because in China, as in Europe, the same human faculties, prompted by the same tastes and necessities, had expatiated in the same tracts of invention, and had, as a consequence, educed the same results. I was much struck, when spending half an hour in a museum illustrative of the arts in China, by the identity of these with our own, especially in the purely mechanical departments; and again, when similarly employed in that apartment devoted, in the British Museum, to the domestic utensils of the ancient Egyptians. The identity of the more common contrivances which I witnessed, with familiar contrivances in our own country, I regarded as altogether as conclusive of an identity of mind in the individuals who had originated them, as if I had actually seen human creatures at work on them all. One class of productions showed me that the potter's wheel and the turning-lathe had been known and employed as certainly in China and ancient Egypt as in Britain. Another, that their weaving processes must have been nearly the same. The Chinese know, for instance, as well as ourselves, that patterns can be delicately brought out,—as in the damasks,—without the assistance of colour, simply by exposing silken or flaxen fibre at different angles to the light; and they have fallen, as their work shows, on the right methods of producing it. And the Egyptians anticipated us in even our most homely household contrivances. They even fermented their bread and trussed their fowls after the same fashion; and thus gave evidence, in these familiar matters, that they thought and contrived "after the manner of men." Now, in acquainting myself with the organisms of the geologic periods, I have been similarly but more deeply impressed by what I must be permitted to term the *human* cast and character of the contrivances which they exemplified. Not only could I understand the principles on which they were constructed, but further, not a few of them had, I found, been actually introduced into works of human invention ages ere they were discovered in the rock. What the great Creator-worker had originated in the Palæozoic and Secondary periods, had been in after times originated by the little creature-worker, wholly unaware that his contrivance had been anticipated, and was but a repetition of a previously executed design. In the later geologic ages the organization of the various extinct animals so nearly resembled that of the animals which still live, that we may regard it as not inadequately represented by the illustrations of Paley. A few such exceptional contrivances appear among the mammals of the Tertiary as that formed by the huge pick-axe-like tusks of the Dinotherium, or a few such extraordinary modifications of the ordinary mammalian framework as that exhibited in the enormously massive pelvic arches and hinder limbs of the Mylodon and Megatherium. But not until we pass into the deposits of the Secondary period, and get among its cephalopoda, do we find a mechanism altogether unlike any with which we are acquainted among living organisms. As admirably shown by Buckland, the partitions which separate into chambers all the whorls of the ammonite except the outermost one, were exquisitely adapted to strengthen, by the tortuous windings of their outer edges, a shell which had to combine great lightness with great powers of resistance. Itself a continuous arch throughout, it was supported by a series of continuous arches inside, somewhat resembling in form the groined ribs of a Gothic roof, but which, unlike the ponderous stone-work of the mediæval architects, were as light as they were strong. And to this combination of arches there was added, in the ribs and grooves of the shell, yet another element of strength,—that which has of late been introduced into iron roofs, which, by means of their corrugations,—ribs and grooves like those of the ammonite,—are made to span over wide spaces, without the support of beams or rafters. Still more recently, the same principle has been introduced into metallic boats, which, when corrugated, like the old ammonites, are found to be sufficiently strong to resist almost any degree of pressure without the wonted addition of an interior framework. Similar evidences of design appear in the other extinct molluscs peculiar to these geologic ages, such as the hamite and turrilite. The belemnite seems to have united the principle of the float to that of the sinker, as we see both united in some of our

Fig. 94.

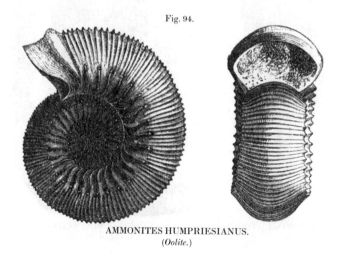

AMMONITES HUMPRIESIANUS.
(*Oolite.*)

modern life-boats, which are steadied on their keels by the one
principle, and preserved from foundering by the other; or as we
find them united by the boy in his mimic smack, which he hollows
out and decks, in order to render it sufficiently light, while at the
same time he furnishes it with a keel of lead, in order to render it
sufficiently steady. The old articulata abound in marks of
ingenious mechanical contrivance. The trilobites were covered
over back and head with the most exquisitely constructed plate
armour; but as their abdomens seem to have been soft and
defenceless, they had the ability of coiling themselves round on the
approach of danger, plate moving on plate with the nicest
adjustment, till the rim of the armed tail rested on that of the
armed head, and the creature presented the appearance of a ball
defended at every point. In some genera, as in Calymene, the tail
consisted of jointed segments till its termination; in others, as in

Fig. 95.

Fig. 96.

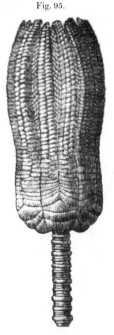

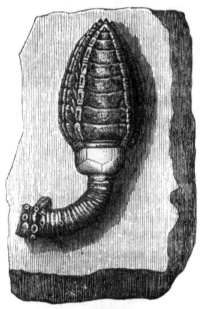

ENCRINITES MONILIFORMIS.
(*Trias.*)

CUPRESSOCRINUS CRASSUS.
(*Old Red Sandstone.*)

Illænus, there was a great caudal shield, that in size and form corresponded to the shield which covered the head; the segments of Calymene, from the flexibility of their joints, fitted close to the cerebral rim; while the same effect was produced in the inflexible shields, caudal and cephalic, of Illænus, by their exact correspondence, and the flexibility of the connecting rings, which enabled them to fit together like two equal-sized cymbals brought into contact at every point by the hand. Nor were the ancient crinoids less remarkable for the amount of nice contrivance which their structures exhibited, than the ancient molluscs or crustaceans. In their calyx-like bodies, consisting always of many parts, we find the principle of the arch introduced in almost every possible form and modification, and the utmost flexibility secured to their stony arms by the amazing number of the pieces of which they were composed, and the nice disposition of the joints. In the Pentacrinites of the Secondary period (see fig. 97.), an immense spread of arms, about a thousand in number, and composed of about a hundred thousand separate pieces, had all the flexibility, though formed of solid lime, of a *drift* of nets, and yet were so nicely jointed, tooth fitting into tooth in all their numerous parts, and the whole so bound together by ligament, that, with all the flexibility, they had also all the toughness and tenacity, of pieces of thread net-work. Human ingenuity, with the same purposes to effect, *i.e.* the sweeping of shoals of swimming animals into a central receptacle, would probably construct a somewhat similar machine; but it would take half a lifetime to execute one equally elaborate.

In carefully examining, for purposes of restoration, some of the earliest ganoidal fishes, I was not a little impressed by the peculiar mechanical contrivances exhibited in their largely developed dermal skeletons. In some cases these contrivances were sufficiently simple, resembling those which we find exemplified in the humbler trades, originated in comparatively unenlightened ages; and yet their simplicity had but the effect of rendering the peculiarly *human* cast of the mind exhibited in their production all the more obvious. The bony scales which covered fishes such as the Osteolepis and Diplopterus of the Old Red Sandstone, or the

Fig. 97.*

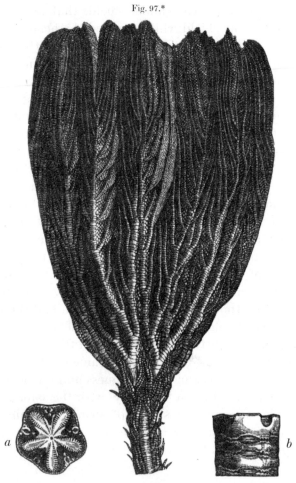

PENTACRINUS FASCICULOSUS.
(*Lias.*)

* *a* Articulating Surface of joint. *b* Fragment of column, exhibiting
laterally the tooth-like processes, so fitted into each other as to admit of
flexure without risk of dislocation. The uppermost joint shows two lateral
cavities for the articulation of auxiliary arms.

Megalichthys of the Coal Measures, were of considerable mass and
thickness. They could not, compatibly with much nicety of finish,
be laid over each other, like the thin horny scales of the salmon or

herring; and so we find them curiously fitted together, not like
slates on a modern roof, but like hewn stones on an ancient one.
There ran on the upper surface of each, along the anterior side and

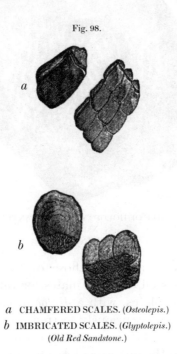

Fig. 98.

a   CHAMFERED SCALES. (*Osteolepis.*)
b   IMBRICATED SCALES. (*Glyptolepis.*)
(*Old Red Sandstone.*)

higher end, a groove of a depth equal to half the thickness of the
scale; and along the posterior side and lower end, on the under
surface, a sort of bevelled chamfer, which, fitting into the grooves
of the scales immediately behind and beneath it, brought their
surfaces to the same line, and rendered the shining coverings of
these strongly armed ganoids as smooth and even as those of the
most delicately coated fishes of the present day. In the scales of the
Celacanth family the arrangement was different. Though
exceedingly massive in some of the genera, they were imbricated,
like those of the Pangolins; and were chiefly remarkable for the
combination of contrivances which they exhibited for securing the
greatest possible amount of strength from the least possible
amount of thickness. The scales of *Holoptychius giganteus* may be

Fig. 99.

SCALE OF HOLOPTYCHIUS GIGANTEUS.
(~Nat. Size.)
(*Old Red Sandstone.*)

selected as representative of those of the family to which it belonged. It consisted of three plates, or rather, like the human skull, of two solid plates, with a *diploe* or spongy layer between. The outer surface was curiously fretted into alternate ridges and furrows; and hence the name of the genus,—*wrinkled scale*; and these imparted to the exterior plate on which they occurred, and which was formed of solid bone, the strength which results from a corrugated or fluted surface. Cromwell, in commissioning a friend to send him a helmet, shrewdly stipulated that it should be a "fluted pot;" and we find that the Holoptychius had got the principle of the fluted pot exemplified in the outer plate of each of its scales, untold ages before. The spongy middle plate must, like the diploe of the skull, have served to deaden the vibrations of a blow dealt from the outside. It was a stratum of sand-bags piled up in the middle of a plank rampart. The innermost table was formed, like the outer, of solid bone, but had a different arrangement. It was properly not one, but several tables, in each of which the osseous fibres, spread out in the general plane of the scale, lay at a diverse angle from those of the table immediately in contact with

Fig. 100.

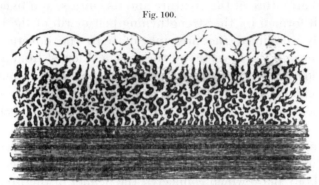

SECTION OF SCALE OF HOLOPTYCHIUS.
(Mag. ~Eight diameters.)

it. The principle was evidently that of the double-woven cloth, or cloth of two incorporated layers, such as *moleskin*, in which, from the arrangement of the threads, what a draper would term the *tear* of the one layer or fold lies at a different angle in the general fabric from that of the other. We are thus presented, in a single fossil scale little more than the eighth part of an inch in thickness, with three distinct strengthening principles,—the principle of Cromwell's "fluted pot,"—the principle of a rampart lined with plank, and filled with sandbags in the centre,—and the principle of the double-woven fabrics of the "moleskin" manufacturer.[1] The contrivances exemplified in the cuirass of the Pterichthys were scarce less remarkable. It was formed of bony plates, strongly arched above, but comparatively flat beneath; and along both its interior and posterior rims a sudden thickening of the plates formed a massive band, which served to strengthen the entire structure, as transverse ribs of stone are found strengthening Gothic vaults of the Norman age. The scale-covered tail of the creature issued from within the posterior rim, which formed around it a complete though irregular ring, arched above and depressed beneath; whereas the anterior rim, to which the head was attached, was incomplete when separated from it. It was, in its detached state, an arch wanting the keystone. A keystone, however, projected outwards from the occipital plate of the head; and, as it had to form at once the bond of connection between the cerebral armature of the creature and its cuirass, and to complete the arch formed by the strengthening belt or rib of the latter, it curiously combined the principle of both the dovetail of the carpenter and the keystone of the mason. Viewed from above, it was a dovetail, forming a strong attachment of the head to the body; viewed in the transverse section, it was an efficient keystone, that gave solidity and strength to the arched belt or rib. Both keystone and dovetail are comparatively simple contrivances; but I know not that they have been united in the same piece, save in the very ancient instance furnished by the strong bony plate which connected the helmet of the Pterichthys with its cuirass.

A brief anecdote, yet further illustrative of the frame-work of this ancient ganoid, may throw some additional light on what I have ventured to term the *human* cast of the contrivances exhibited in the organisms of the old geologic ages. After carefully examining many specimens, I published a restoration of both the upper and under side of Pterichthys fully fifteen years ago. The greatest of living ichthyologists, however, misled by a series of specimens much less complete than mine, differed from me in my conclusions; and what I had represented as the creature's under or abdominal side, he represented as its upper or dorsal side; while its actual upper side he regarded as belonging to another, though closely allied, genus. I had no opportunity, as he resided on the Continent at the time, of submitting to him the specimens on which I had founded; though, at once certain of his thorough candour and love of truth, and of the solidity of my data, I felt confident that, in order to alter his decision, it was but necessary that I should submit to him my evidence. Meanwhile, however, the case was regarded as settled against me; and I found at least one popular and very ingenious writer on geology, after referring to my description of the Pterichthys, going on to say that, though graphic, it was not correct, and that he himself could describe it at least more truthfully, if not more vividly, than I had done. And then there followed a description identical with that by which mine had been supplanted. Five years had passed, when one day our greatest British authority on fossil fishes, Sir Philip Egerton, was struck, when passing an hour among the ichthyic organisms of his princely collection, by the appearance presented by a central plate in the cuirass of the Pterichthys. It is of a lozenge form; and, occupying exactly such a place in the nether armature of the creature as that occupied by the lozenge-shaped spot on the ace of diamonds, it comes in contact with four other plates that lie around it, and represent, so to speak, the white portions of the card. And Sir Philip now found, that instead of lying over, it lay under, the four contiguous plates: they overlapped it, instead of being overlapped by it. This, he at once said, on ascertaining the fact, cannot be the *upper* side of the Pterichthys. A plate so arranged would have formed no proper protection to the exposed dorsal surface of the creature's body, as a slight blow would have at once sent it in upon the interior framework; but a proper enough one to the under side of a heavy swimmer, that, like the flat fishes, kept close to the bottom;—a character which, as shown by the massive bulk of its body, and its small spread of fin, must have belonged to the Pterichthys. Sir Philip followed up his observations on the central plate by a minute examination of the other parts of the creature's armature; and the survey terminated in a recognition of the earlier restoration,—set aside so long before,—as virtually the true one;—a recognition in which Agassiz, when made acquainted with the nature of the evidence, at once acquiesced. Now, here was there a question which had been raised regarding the true mechanism of one of the oldest ganoidal fishes, and settled erroneously on wrong data, again opened up, to be settled anew on one of the most obvious mechanical principles exemplified in the simple art of the slater or tiler. The argument of Sir Philip amounted simply to this:—If the accepted restoration be a true one, then the Creator of the Pterichthys must have committed a mistake in mechanics which an ordinary slater would have avoided; but as the Creator commits no such blunders, the mistake probably occurs in but the restoration. I may mention, that the dorsal surface of this ancient fish had also its central plate,—a lozenge truncated at its two longer ends; and that, moulded to meet the necessities of its position, it was not flat, like the under one, but strongly arched; and that on four of its six sides it overrode by a squamose suture the lower plates with which it came in contact.

These are but humble illustrations of the designing principle, as exhibited of old; and yet they impress none the less strongly on that account. Among the many contrivances of the Chinese Museum, to which I have already referred, none seemed more to excite the curiosity of visitors than a set of tall-backed, elaborately-carved chairs, exceedingly like those which were used in our own country two centuries ago, and which Cowper so exquisitely describes. For thousands of miles in the wide tract that spreads out between European Christendom and the great wall, the inhabitants squat upon mats or carpets, or loll on divans; and the contrivance of the chair is unknown: it re-appears in China, however, and re-appears, not as a mere seat or stool, but as, in every bar and limb, the identical chair of Europe arrested a century or two back in its development. And every corresponding tenon and mortise exhibited by the Chinese and European examples of this simple piece of furniture served more forcibly to show an identity of character in the minds which had originated them in countries so far apart, than the more elaborate contrivances which, though illustrative of the same principles of invention, were less easily understood. It is so with the more simple and familiar instances of adaptation furnished by the works of the Creator. We infer from them, more directly than from the complex mechanisms, that He who wrought of old after the manner of a man must have in his intellectual character, if I may so express myself, certain man-like qualities and traits. In all those works on Natural Theology that treat, like the work of Paley, on the argument of design, the assumption of a certain unity of the intellectual nature of the Creator and creature is made, tacitly at least, the basis of all the reasonings; and it is in the cases in which the design is most simple that the argument is most generally understood. It is in the lower *skirts* of the Divine nature that we most readily trace the resemblance to the nature of man,—an effect, mayhap, of the narrow reach of our faculties in their present infantile state.

But the resemblance is not restricted to the constructive

department. Both in the Chinese collection and among the Egyptian antiquities exhibited in the British Museum, I found colour as certainly as mechanical contrivance. And the colour furnished not only a practical example from both the early and the remote peoples of the same sort of chemical science as exists at the present time among ourselves in our dye works and pigment manufactories, but it also showed a certain identity with our own of their sense of beauty. The Chinese satins are gorgeous with green, blue, yellow, scarlet, crimson, and purple, and have fringes heavy with thread of gold. Gilding is as common among this distant people as among ourselves, and at once shows a familiarity with the art of the gold-beater, and a sensibility to the beauty of a golden surface; and in the painted ornaments I detected the rich tints of vermilion and crimson lake, with the mineral blues, yellows, and greens. In the Egyptian department, though the blanching influences of three thousand years had dimmed the tints and tarnished the metals, I found evidence of the same regard to hue and lustre as exists still in China and among ourselves: all that now pleases the eye in London and Pekin had pleased it in Thebes during the times of the earlier Pharaohs. And just as we infer from the mechanical contrivances of the Creative Worker that He possesses a certain identity of mind in the *constructive* department with his creature-workers, and this upon the principle on which we infer an identity of mind between the creature-workers of China, ancient Egypt, and our own country, seeing that their works are identical, must we not also infer, on the same principle, that He possesses in the *æsthetic* department a certain identity with them also. True, this region of the beautiful, ever surrounded by an atmosphere of obscure, ill-settled metaphysics, is greatly less clear than that mechanical province of whose various machines, whether of Divine or human contrivance, it can be at least affirmed that machines they *are*, and that they effect their purposes by contrivances of the same or of resembling kinds. And yet the appearance in nature, age after age, of the same forms and colours of beauty which man, in gratifying his taste for the lovely in shape and hue, is ever reproducing for himself, does seem to justify our inference of an identity of mind in this province also.

The colours of the old geologic organisms, like those of the
paintings of ancient Egypt, are greatly faded. A few, however, of
the Secondary, and even Palæozoic shells, still retain the rich
prismatic hues of the original nacre. Many of the Tertiary division
still bear the distinctive painted spots. Some of the later fossil
fishes, when first laid open in the rock, exhibit the pearly gleam
that must of old have lighted up the green depths of the water as
they darted through. Not a few of the fossil corals preserve enough
of their former colour to impart much delicacy of tint to the
marbles in which they occur. But it is chiefly in form, not in shade
or hue, that we find in the organisms of the geologic ages examples
of that beauty in which man delights, and which he is ever
reproducing for himself. There is scarce an architectural ornament
of the Gothic or Grecian styles which may not be found existing as
fossils in the rocks. The Ulodendron was sculptured into gracefully
arranged rows of pointed and closely imbricated leaves, similar to
those into which the Roman architects fretted the torus of the
Corinthian order. The Sigillaria were fluted columns ornately

Fig. 101.

SIGILLARIA GRŒSERI.
(*Coal Measures.*)

carved in the line of the channelled flutes; the Lepidodendra bore, according to their species, sculptured scales, or lozenges, or egg-like hollows, set in a sort of frame, and relieved into knobs and furrows; all of them furnishing examples of a delicate diaper-work, like that so admired in our more ornate Gothic buildings, such as

Fig. 102.

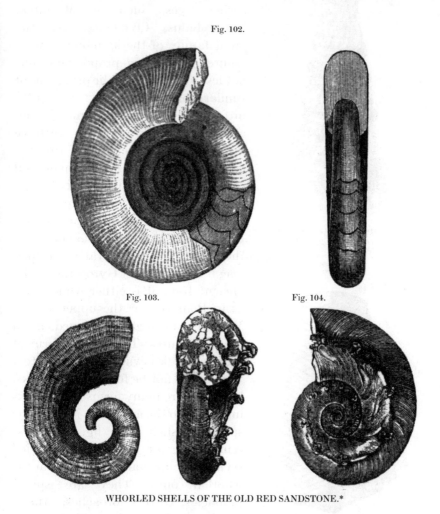

Fig. 103.   Fig. 104.

WHORLED SHELLS OF THE OLD RED SANDSTONE.*

* Fig. 102, Clymenia Sedgwicki; fig. 103, Gyroceras Eifelensis; fig. 104, Cirrus Goldfussii

Fig. 105.

MURCHISONIA BIGRANULOSA.
(*Old Red Sandstone.*)

Fig. 106.

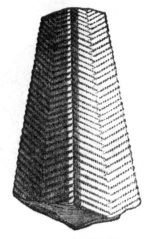

CONULARIA ORNATA.
(*Old Red Sandstone.*)

Westminster Abbey or Canterbury and Chichester Cathedrals, only greatly more exquisite in their design and finish. The scroll shells, a very numerous section of the class in the earlier ages, such as Maclurea, Euomphalus, Clymenia, and the great family of the ammonites, were volutes of varying proportions, but not less graceful than the ornament of similar proportions so frequently introduced into Greek and Roman architecture, and of which we have such prominent examples in the capitals of the Ionic, Corinthian, and composite orders. In what is known as the modern Ionic the spiral of the volute is not all on one plane; it is a Euomphalus: in the central volutes of the Corinthian the spiral is an open one; it is a Lituite or Gyroceras: in the ancient Ionic it is either wholly flat, as in Planorbis or the upper side of Maclurea, or slightly relieved, as in the ammonites. There is no form of the volute known to the architect which may not be found in the rocks, but there are many forms in the rocks unknown to the architect. Nor are the spire-like shells (see fig. 105.) less remarkable for the rich and varied style of their ornamentation than the whorled ones. They are spires, pinnacles, turrets, broaches; ornate, in some instances, beyond the reach of the architect, and illustrative, in almost all, of his happiest forms and proportions. We detect among the fossils the germs of numerous designs developed in almost every department of art; but merely to enumerate them would require a volume. One form of the old classic lamp was that of the nautilus; another, that of *Gryphœa incurva*; the zig-zag mouldings of the Norman Gothic may be found in the carinated oysters of the Greensand; the more delicate frettings of similar form which roughened the pillars of a somewhat later age occur on Conularia and the dorsal spines of Gyracanthus. The old corals, too, abound in ornamental patterns, which man, unaware of their existence at the time, devised long after for himself. In an article on calico printing, which forms part of a recent history of Lancashire, there are a few of the patterns introduced, backed by the recommendation that they were the most successful ever tried. Of one of these, known as "Lane's Net," there sold a greater number of pieces than of any other pattern

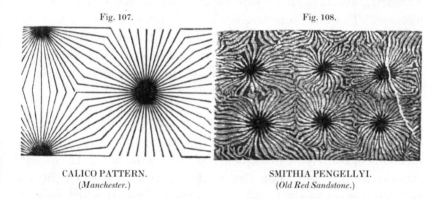

Fig. 107.   Fig. 108.

CALICO PATTERN.   SMITHIA PENGELLYI.
(*Manchester.*)   (*Old Red Sandstone.*)

ever brought into the market. It led to many imitations; and one of the most popular of these answers line for line, save that it is more stiff and rectilinear, to the pattern in a recently-discovered Old Red Sandstone coral, the *Smithia Pengellyi*. The beautifully-arranged lines which so smit the dames of England, that each had to provide herself with a gown of the fabric which they adorned, had been stamped amid the rocks *eons* of ages before. And it must not be forgotten, that all these forms and shades of beauty which once filled all nature, but of which only a few fragments, or a few faded tints, survive, were created, not to gratify man's love of the æsthetic, seeing that man had no existence until long after they had disappeared, but in meet harmony with the tastes and faculties of the Divine Worker, who had in his wisdom produced them all.

You will, I trust, bear with me should I seek, in depths where the light shed by science becomes obscure, to guide my steps by light derived from another and wholly different source. In an assembly such as that which I have now the honour of addressing, there must be many shades of religious opinion. I shall, however, assail no man's faith, but simply lay before you a few deductions which, founded on my own, have supplied me with what I deem a consistent theory of the curious class of phenomena with which this evening we have been mainly dealing. First, then, I must hold that we receive the true explanation of the *man*-like character of the Creator's workings ere man was, in the remarkable text in which we are told that "God made man in his own image and likeness." There is no restriction here to moral quality: the moral image man had, and in large measure lost; but the intellectual image he still retains. As a geometrician, as an arithmetician, as a chemist, as an astronomer,—in short, in all the departments of what are known as the strict sciences,—man differs from his Maker, not in kind, but in degree,—not as matter differs from mind, or darkness from light, but simply as a mere portion of space or time differs from *all* space or *all* time. I have already referred to mechanical contrivances as identically the same in the Divine and human productions; nor can I doubt that, not only in the pervading sense of the beautiful in form and colour which it is our privilege as men in some degree to experience and possess, but also in that perception of harmony which constitutes the *musical* sense, and in that poetic feeling of which Scripture furnishes us with at once the earliest and the highest examples, and which we may term the *poetic* sense, we bear the stamp and impress of the Divine image. Now, if this be so, we must look upon the schemes of Creation, Revelation, and Providence, not as schemes of mere adaptation to man's nature, but as schemes also specially adapted to the nature of God as the pattern and original nature. Further, it speaks, I must hold, of the harmony and unity of one sublime scheme, that, after long ages of immaturity,—after the dynasties of the fish, the reptile, and the mammal should in succession have terminated,—man should have at length come upon the scene in the image of God; and that, at a still later period, God himself should have come upon the scene in the form of man; and that thus all God's workings in creation should be indissolubly linked to God himself, not by any such mere likeness or image of the Divinity as that which the first Adam bore, but by Divinity itself in the Second Adam; so that on the rainbow-encircled apex of the pyramid of created being the Son of God and the Son of Man should sit enthroned for ever in one adorable person. That man should have been made in the image of God seems to have been a meet preparation for God's after assumption of the form of man. It was perhaps thus secured that *stock* and *graft*, if I may venture on such a metaphor, should have the necessary affinity, and be capable of being united in a single person. The false gods of the Egyptians assumed, it was fabled, the forms of brutes: it was the human form and nature that was assumed by the true God;—so far as we know, the only form and nature that could have brought Him into direct union with at once the matter and mind of the universe which he had created and made,—with "true body and reasonable soul." Yet further, I learn by inevitable inference from one of the more distinctive articles of my creed, that as certainly as the dynasty of the fish was predetermined in the scheme of Providence to be succeeded by the higher dynasty of the reptile, and that of the reptile by the still higher dynasty of the mammal, so it was equally predetermined that the dynasty of responsible, fallible man should be succeeded by the dynasty of glorified, immortal man; and that, in consequence, the present mixed state of things is not a mere result, as some theologians believe, of a certain human act which was perpetrated about six thousand years ago, but was, virtually at least, the effect of a God-determined decree, old as eternity,—a decree in which that act was written as a portion of the general programme. In looking abroad on that great history of life of which the latter portions are recorded in the pages of revelation, and the earlier in the rocks, I feel my grasp of a doctrine first taught me by our Calvinistic

Catechism at my mother's knee, tightening instead of relaxing. "The decrees of God are his eternal purposes," I was told, "according to the counsel of his will, whereby for his own glory He hath fore-ordained whatsoever comes to pass."And what I was told early I still believe. The programme of Creation and Providence, in all its successive periods, is of God, not of man. With the arrangements of the old geologic periods it is obvious man could have had nothing to do: the primæval ages of wondrous plants and monster animals ran their course without counsel taken of him; and in reading their record in the bowels of the earth, and in learning from their strange characters that such ages there were, and what they produced, we are the better enabled to appreciate the impressive directness of the sublime message to Job, when the "Lord answered him out of the whirlwind, and said, Where wast thou when I laid the foundations of the earth? Declare if thou hast understanding." And I can as little regard the present scene of things as an ultimate consequence of what man had willed or wrought, as even any of the pre-Adamic ages. It is simply one scene in a fore-ordained series,—a scene intermediate in place between the age of the irresponsible mammal and of glorified man; and to provide for the upward passage to the ultimate state, we know that, in reference to the purposes of the Eternal, He through whom the work of restoration has been effected was in reality what He is designated in the remarkable text, "The Lamb slain from the *foundations* of the world." First in the course of things, man in the image of God, and next, in meet sequence, God in the form of man, have been equally from all eternity pre-determined actors in the same great scheme.

I approach a profound and terrible mystery. We can see how in the pre-Adamic ages higher should have succeeded lower dynasties. To be low was not to be immoral; to be low was not to be guilt-stained and miserable. The sea anemone on its half-tide rock, and the fern on its mossy hill-side, are low in their respective kingdoms; but they are, notwithstanding, worthy, in their quiet, unobtrusive beauty, of the God who formed them. It is only when the human period begins that we are startled and perplexed by the problem of a lowness not innocent,—an inferiority tantamount to moral deformity. In the period of responsibility, to be low means to be evil; and how, we ask, could a lowness and inferiority resolvable into moral evil have had any place in the decrees of that Judge who ever does what is right, and in whom moral evil can have no place? The subject is one which it seems not given to man thoroughly to comprehend. Permit me, however, to remark in reply, that in a sense so plain, so obvious, so unequivocally true, that it would lead an intelligent jury, impannelled in the case, conscientiously to convict, and a wise judge righteously to condemn, all that is evil in the present state of things man may as certainly have wrought out for himself, as the criminals whom we see sentenced at every justiciary court work out for themselves the course of punishment to which they are justly subjected.

It has been well said of the Author of all by the poet, that, "binding nature fast in fate," He "left free the human will." And it is this freedom or independency of will operating on an intellect moulded after the image and likeness of the Divinity that has rendered men capable of being what the Scriptures so emphatically term "fellow-workers with God." In a humble and restricted sense, as I have already remarked,—humble and restricted, but in that restricted sense obviously true,—the surface of the earth far and wide testifies to this fact of fellowship in working. The deputed lord of creation, availing himself of God's natural laws, does what no mere animal of the old geologic ages ever did, or ever could have done,—he adorns and beautifies the earth, and adds tenfold to its original fertility and productiveness. In this special sense, then, he is a fellow-worker with Him who, according to the Psalmist, "causeth the grass to grow for the cattle, and herb for the service of man, and wine that maketh glad the heart of man, and oil that maketh his face to shine, and bread which strengtheneth man's heart." But it is in a greatly higher sense, and in reference to God's moral laws, that he is fitted to be his fellow-worker in the Scriptural sense. And his proper employment in this department is the elevation and development, moral and intellectual, of himself and his fellow-men, both in adaptation to the demands of the present time, and in preparation for a future state.

All experience, however, serves to show that in this paramount department man greatly fails; nay, that he is infinitely less true to his proper end and destiny than the beasts that perish to their several instincts. And yet it may be remarked, that such of the lower animals as are guided by pure instinct are greatly more infallible within their proper spheres than the higher, half-reasoning animals. The mathematical bee never constructs a false angle; the sagacious dog is not unfrequently *out* in his calculations. The higher the animal in the scale, the greater its liability to error. But it is not the less true, that no fish, no reptile, no mammal, of the geologic or the recent ages, ever so failed in working out the purposes it was created to serve, as man has failed in working out *his*; further, in no creature save in man does there exist that war of the mind between appetite and duty of which the Apostle so consciously complained. And we must seek an explanation of these twin facts in that original freedom of the will which, while it rendered man capable of being *of choice* God's fellow-worker, also conferred on him an ability of choosing *not* to work with God. And his choice of not working with Him, or of working against Him, being once freely made, we may see how, from man's very constitution and nature, as an intelligence united to matter that increases his kind from generation to generation in virtue of the original law, the ability of again working with God might be for ever destroyed. And thus man's general condition as a lapsed creature may be as unequivocally a consequence of man's own act, as the condition of individuals born free, but doomed to slavery in punishment of their offences, is a consequence of *their* own acts. A brief survey of the many-coloured and variously-placed human family, as at present distributed on the earth, may enable us in some degree to conceive of a matter which, involving, as it does, that master problem of moral science, the origin of evil, seems, as I have said, not to be given to man fully to comprehend.

"The different races of mankind," says Humboldt, employing, let me remark, the language of the distinguished German naturalist Müller, to give expression to the view which he himself adopts,—"the different races of mankind are not different species of a genus, but forms of one sole species." "The human species," says Cuvier, "appears to be single." "When we compare," says Pritchard, "all the facts and observations which have been heretofore fully established as to the specific instincts and separate psychical endowments of all the distinct tribes of sentient beings in the universe, we are entitled to draw confidently the conclusion, that all human races are of one species and one family." "God hath made of one blood," said the Apostle Paul, in addressing himself to the *elite* of Athens, "all nations, for to dwell on the face of all the earth." Such, on this special head, is the testimony of Revelation, and such the conclusion of our highest scientific authorities. The question has, indeed, been raised in these latter times, whether each species of animals may not have been originally created, not by single pairs or in single centres, but by several pairs and in several centres, and, of course, the human species among the rest? And the *query*,—for in reality it amounts to nothing more,—has been favourably entertained on the other side of the Atlantic, where there are uneasy consciences, that would find comfort in the belief that Zambo the blackamoor, who was lynched for getting tired of slavery and hard blows, was an animal in no way akin to his master. And on purely scientific grounds it is of course difficult to prove a negative in the case, just as it would be difficult to prove a negative were the question to be, whether the planet Venus was not composed of quartz-rock, or the planet Mars of Old Red Sandstone. But the portion of the problem really solvable by science,—the identity of the human race under all its conditions, and in all its varieties,—science *has* solved. It has determined that all the various tribes of man are but forms of a single species. And in the definition of species,—waiving the American *doubt* until it shall at least become something more,—I am content to follow the higher authorities. "We unite," says M. de Candolle, "under the designation of a *species*, all those individuals that mutually bear to each other so close a resemblance as to allow of our supposing that they may have proceeded originally from a single being or a single pair." "A *species*," says Buffon, "is a constant succession of individuals similar to and capable of reproducing each other." "A *species*," says Cuvier, "is a succession of individuals which reproduces and perpetuates itself."

Now, all history and all tradition, so far as they throw light on
the question at all, agree in showing that the centre in which the
human species originated must have been somewhere in the
temperate regions of the east, not far distant from the Caucasian
group of mountains. All the old seats of civilization,—that of
Nineveh, Babylon, Palestine, Egypt, and Greece,—are spread out
around this centre. And it is certainly a circumstance worthy of
notice, and surely not without bearing on the *physical* condition of
primæval humanity, that in this centre we find a variety of the
species which naturalists of the highest standing regard as
fundamentally typical of the highest races of the globe. "The
natives of the Caucasus," says Cuvier, "are even now considered as
the handsomest on earth." And wherever man has, if I may so
speak, *fallen* least,—wherever he has retained, at least
intellectually, the Divine image,—this Caucasian type of feature
and figure, with, of course, certain national modifications, he also
retains. It was developed in a remarkable degree among the old
Greeks, as may be seen from the busts of some of their handsomer
men; and still more remarkably in their *beau ideal* of beauty, as
exemplified in the statues of their gods. We see it also, though
dashed with a shade of severity, in the strong forms and stern
features of monarchs that reigned of old in Nineveh and Babylon,
as brought to light in their impressive effigies by the excavations of
Rawlinson and Layard. And further, though somewhat modified
by the African dash, we detect it in the colossal statues of Egypt.
Nor, as shown by Egyptian paintings still fresh in colour and
outline, was it less traceable in the ancient Jewish countenance
and figure. It is still palpable, too, amid all the minor peculiarities
of national physiognomy, in the various peoples of Europe. We
may see it in our own country, though, as Sir Walter Scott truly
tells us,—

> "The rugged form may mark the mountain band,
> And harsher features and a mien more grave."

It walks, however, the boards of our Parliament House here in a
very respectable type of Caucasian man; and all agree that

nowhere else in modern Europe is it to be found more true to its original contour than among the high-bred aristocracy of England, especially among the female members of the class. Looking, then, at the entire evidence,—at the admitted fact that the Circassians of the present day are an eminently handsome people,—that the old Greeks, Ninevites, Egyptians, Jews, Romans, and with these all the modern nations of Europe, are but the varieties of the central race that have retained in greatest perfection the original traits,—I do not see how we are to avoid the conclusion that this Caucasian type was the type of Adamic man. Adam, the father of mankind, was no squalid savage of doubtful humanity, but a noble specimen of man; and Eve a soft Circassian beauty, but exquisitely lovely beyond the lot of fallen humanity.

> "The loveliest pair
> That ever yet in love's embraces met:
> Adam, the goodliest man of men since born
> His sons; the fairest of her daughters Eve."

I know not whether I should add what follows. It has been said that Luke, the "beloved physician," was also a painter. It has been said that that traditionary, time-honoured form, which we at once recognise in the pictures of the old masters as that of the Saviour of mankind, He in reality bore when He walked this earth in the flesh. I know not what degree of probability attaches to the belief. I know not whether the traditionary form be in reality the true one. This, however, I know, that *if* such was the form which the adorable Redeemer assumed when he took to himself a real body and a reasonable soul, the second Adam, like the first, exemplified, when upon earth, the perfect type of Caucasian man.

Let me next remark, that the further we remove from the original centre of the race, the more degraded and sunk do we find the several varieties of humanity. We must set wholly aside, in our survey, the disturbing element of modern emigration. Caucasian man has been pressing outwards. In the backwoods of America, in Southern Africa, in Australia, and in the Polynesian islands, the old Adamic type has been asserting its superiority, and annihilating before it the degraded races. But taking into account merely the aboriginal varieties, it seems to be a general rule, that the farther we remove in any direction from the Adamic centre, the more animalized and sunk do we find the various tribes or races. Contrary to the conceptions of the assertors of the development hypothesis, we ascertain, as we proceed outwards, that the course is not one of progression from the low to the high, but of descent from the high to the low. Passing northwards, we meet, where the lichen-covered land projects into the frozen ocean, with the diminutive Laps, squat, ungraceful, with their flat features surmounted by pyramidal skulls of small capacity, and, as a race, unfitted for the arts either of peace or war. We meet also with the timid Namollas, with noses so flat as to be scarce visible in the women and children of the race; and with the swarthy Kamtschatkans, with their broad faces, protuberant bellies, and thin, ill-formed legs. Passing southwards, we come to the negro tribes, with their sooty skins, broad noses, thick lips, projecting jaw-bones, and partially webbed fingers. And then we find ourselves among the squalid Hottentots, repulsively ugly, and begrimmed with filth; or the still more miserable Bushmen. Passing eastwards, after taking leave of the Persian and Indian branches of the Caucasian race, we meet with the squat Mongolian, with his high cheek-bones set on a broad face, and his compressed, unintellectual, pig-like eyes; or encounter, in the Indian Archipelago or the Australian interior, the pitiably low Alforian races, with their narrow retreating foreheads, slim, feeble limbs, and baboon-like faces. Or, finally, passing westwards, we find the large-jawed, copper-coloured Indians of the New World, vigorous in some of the northern tribes as animals, though feeble as men, but gradually sinking in southern America, as among the wild Caribs or spotted Araucans; till at the extremity of the continent we find, naked and shivering among their snows, the hideous, small-eyed, small-limbed, flat-headed Fuegians, perhaps the most wretched of human creatures. And all these varieties of the species, in which we find humanity "fallen," according to the poet, "into disgrace," are varieties that have lapsed from the original Caucasian type. They are all the descendants of man as God created him; but they do not exemplify man as God created him. They do not represent, save in hideous caricature, the glorious creature moulded of old by the hand of the Divine Worker. They are fallen,—degraded; many of them, as races, hopelessly lost. For all experience serves to show, that when a tribe of men falls beneath a certain level, it cannot come into competition with civilized man, pressing outwards from his old centres to possess the earth, without becoming extinct before him. Sunk beneath a certain level, as in the forests of America, in Van Dieman's Land, in New South Wales, and among the Bushmen of the Cape, the experience of more than a hundred years demonstrates that its destiny is extinction,—not restoration. Individuals may be recovered by the labours of some zealous missionary; but it is the fate of the race, after a few generations, to disappear. It has fallen too hopelessly low to be restored. There remain curious traces in the New World of these perished tribes. The Bible, translated into an old Indian language, from which the devoted David Brainerd taught so successfully a nation of Red Men, still exists; but it speaks in a dead tongue, which no one can now understand; for the nation to whom he preached has become extinct. And Humboldt tells us, in referring to a perished tribe of South America, that there lived in 1806, when he visited their country, an old parrot in Maypures, which could not be understood, because, as the natives informed him, it spoke the language of the Atures. Tribes of the aborigines of Australia have wholly disappeared during the present generation; and I remember seeing it stated in a newspaper paragraph, which appeared a few years ago, that the last male survivor of the natives of Tasmania was at that time in the latter stages of consumption.

But if man, in at least the more degraded varieties of the race, be so palpably *not* what the Creator originally made him, by whom, then, was he made the poor lost creature which in these races we find him to be? He was made what he is, I reply, by man himself; and this, in many instances, by a process which we may see every day taking place among ourselves in individuals and families, though, happily, not in races. Man's nature, again,—to employ the condensed statement of the poet,—has been bound fast in fate, but his will has been left free. He is free either to resign himself to the indolence and self-indulgence so natural to the species; or, "spurning delights, to live laborious days;"—free either to sink into ignorant sloth, dependent uselessness, and self-induced imbecility, bodily and mental, or to assert by honest labour a noble independence,—to seek after knowledge as for hidden treasures, and, in the search, to sharpen his faculties and invigorate his mind. And while we see around us some men addressing themselves with stout brave hearts to what Carlyle terms, with homely vigour, their "heavy job of work," and, by denying themselves many an insidious indulgence, doing it effectually and well, and rearing up well-taught families in usefulness and comfort to be the stay of the future, we see other men yielding to the ignoble solicitations of appetite or of indolence, and becoming worse than useless themselves, and the parents of ignorant, immoral, and worse than useless families. The wandering vagrants of Great Britain at the present time have been estimated at from fifteen to twenty thousand souls; the hereditary paupers of England,—a vastly more numerous class,—have become, in a considerable degree, a sept distinct from the general community; and in all our large towns there are certain per centages of the population,—unhappily ever-increasing per centages,—that, darkened in mind and embruted in sentiment, are widely recognised as emphatically the dangerous classes of the community. And let us remember, that we are witnessing in these instances no new thing in the history of the species: every period since that of the vagabond Cain has had its waifs and stragglers, who fell behind in the general march. In circumstances such as obtained in the earlier ages of the human family, all the existing nomades and paupers of our country would have passed into distinct races of men. For in the course of a few generations their forms and complexions would begin to tell of the self-induced degradation that had taken place in their minds; and in a few ages more they would have become permanent varieties of the species. There are cases in which not more than from two to three centuries have been found sufficient thoroughly to alter the original physiognomy of a race. "On the plantation of Ulster in 1611, and afterwards, on the success of the

British against the rebels in 1641 and 1689," says a shrewd writer of the present day, himself an Irishman, "great multitudes of the native Irish were driven from Armagh and the south of Down, into the mountainous tract extending from the Barony of Fleurs eastward to the sea; on the other side of the kingdom the same race were exposed to the worst effects of hunger and ignorance, the two great brutalizers of the human race. The descendants of these exiles are now distinguished physically by great degradation. They are remarkable for open projecting mouths, with prominent teeth and exposed gums; and their advancing cheek-bones and depressed noses bear barbarism on their very front. In Sligo and northern Mayo the consequences of the two centuries of degradation and hardship exhibit themselves in the whole physical condition of the people, affecting not only the features, but the frame. Five feet two inches on an average,—pot-bellied, bow-legged, abortively featured, their clothing a wisp of rags,—these spectres of a people that were once well-grown, able-bodied, and comely, stalk abroad into the daylight of civilization, the annual apparition of Irish ugliness and Irish want."

Such is man as man himself has made him,—not man as he came from the hand of the Creator. In many instances the degradation has been voluntary; in others it has been forced upon families and races by the iron hand of oppression; in almost all,—whether self-chosen by the parents or imposed upon them,—the children and the children's children have, as a matter of inevitable necessity, been born to it. For, whatever we may think of the scriptural doctrine on this special head, it is a fact broad and palpable in the economy of nature, that parents *do* occupy a federal position, and that the lapsed progenitors, when cut off from civilization and all external interference of a missionary character, become the founders of a lapsed race. The iniquities of the parents are visited upon the children. And in all such instances it is *man* left to the freedom of his own will that is the deteriorator of man. The doctrine of the Fall, in its purely theologic aspect, is a doctrine which must be apprehended by faith; but it is at least something to find that the analogies of science, instead of running counter to it, run in exactly the same line. It is one of the inevitable consequences of that nature of man which the Creator "bound fast in fate," while he left free his will, that the free will of the parent should become the destiny of the child.

But the subject is one in which we can see our way as but "through a glass darkly." Nay, it is possible that the master-problem which it involves no created intelligence can thoroughly unlock. It has been well said, that the "poet's heart" is informed by a "terrible sagacity;" and I am at times disposed to regard Milton's conception of the perplexity of the fallen spirits, when reasoning on "fixed fate, free-will, foreknowledge absolute," and finding "no end in wandering mazes lost," much rather as a sober truth caught from the invisible world, than as merely an ingenious fancy. The late Robert Montgomery has rather unhappily chosen Satan as one of the themes of his muse; and in his long poem, designated in its second title "Intellect without God," he has set that personage a-reasoning in a style which, I fear, more completely demonstrates the absence of God than the presence of intellect. It has, however, sometimes occurred to me, that a poet of the larger calibre, who to the divine faculty and vision added such a knowledge of geologic science as that which Virgil possessed of the natural history of his time, or as that which Milton possessed of the general learning of *his*, might find, in a somewhat similar subject, the materials of a poem which "posterity would not willingly let die." There is one of the satirists justly severe on a class of critics

> "Who, drily plain, without invention's aid,
> Write dull receipts how poems may be made."

But at some risk of rendering myself obnoxious to his censure, I shall attempt indicating at least the general scope and character of what the schoolmen might term a *possible* poem; which, if vivified by the genius of some of the higher masters of the lyre, broad of faculty, and at once great poets and great men, might prove one precious boon more to the world, suited, conformably to the special demands of these latter times, to

"assert Eternal Providence,
And justify the ways of God to man."

There has been war among the intelligences of God's spiritual creation. Lucifer, son of the morning, has fallen like fire from heaven; and our present earth, existing as a half-extinguished hell, has received him and his angels. Dead matter exists, and in the unembodied spirits vitality exists; but not yet in all the universe of God has the vitality been united to the matter: animal life, to even the profound apprehension of the fallen angel, is an inconceivable idea. Meanwhile, as the scarce reckoned centuries roll by, vacantly and dull, like the cheerless days and nights over the head of some unhappy captive, the miserable prisoners of our planet become aware that there is a slow change taking place in the condition of their prison-house. Where a low, dark archipelago of islands raise their flat backs over the thermal waters, the heat glows less intensely than of old; the red fire bursts forth less frequently; the dread earthquake shakes more rarely; save in a few centres of intenser action, the great deep no longer boils like a pot; and, though the heavens are still shut out by a gray ceiling of thick vapour, through which sun or moon never yet appeared, a less gloomy twilight struggles at noonday through the enveloping cloud, and falls more cheerfully than heretofore upon land and sea. At length there comes a morning in which great ocean and the scattered islands declare that God the Creator had descended to visit the earth. The hitherto verdureless land bears the green flush of vegetation; and there are creeping things among the trees. Nor is the till now unexampled mystery of animal life absent from the sounds and bays. It is the highest intelligences that manifest the deepest interest in the works of the All-Wise. Nor can we doubt that on that morning of creative miracle in which matter and vitality were first united in the bonds of a strange wedlock, the comprehensive intellect of the great fallen spirit—profound and active beyond the lot of humanity—would have found ample employment in attempting to fathom the vast mystery, and in vainly asking what these strange things might mean.

With how much of wonder, as scene succeeded scene, and creation followed creation,—as life sprang out of death, and death out of life,—must not that acute Intelligence have watched the course of the Divine Worker,—scornful of spirit and full of enmity, and yet aware, in the inner depths of his intellect, that what he dared insultingly to depreciate, he yet failed, in its ultimate end and purpose, adequately to comprehend! Standing in the presence of unsolved mystery, under the chill and withering shadow of that secret of the Lord which was not with him, how thoroughly must he not have seen, and with what bitter malignity felt, that the grasp of the Almighty was still upon him, and that in the ever-varying problem of creation, which, with all his powers, he failed to unlock, and which, as age succeeded age, remained an unsolved problem still, the Divine Master against whom he had rebelled, but from whose presence it was in vain to flee, emphatically spake to him, as in an after age to the patriarch Job, and, with the quiet dignity of the Infinite, challenged him either to do or to know! "Shall he that contendeth with the Almighty instruct Him? He that reproveth God, let him answer. Knowest thou the ordinances of Heaven? or canst thou set the dominion thereof in the earth?" With what wild thoughts must that restless and unhappy spirit have wandered amid the tangled mazes of the old carboniferous forests! With what bitter mockeries must he have watched the fierce wars which raged in their sluggish waters, among ravenous creatures horrid with trenchant teeth, barbed sting, and sharp spine, and enveloped in glittering armour of plate and scale! And how, as generation after generation passed away, and ever and anon the ocean rolled where the land had been, or the land rose to possess the ancient seats of the ocean,—how, when looking back upon myriads of ages, and when calling up in memory what once had been, the features of earth seemed scarce more fixed to his view than the features of the sky in a day of dappled breeze-borne clouds,—how must he have felt, as he became conscious that the earth was fast ripening, and that, as its foundations became stable on the abyss, it was made by the Creator a home of higher and yet higher forms of existence,—how must he have felt, if, like some old augur looking into the inner mysteries of animal life, with their strange prophecies, the truth had at length burst upon him, that reasoning, accountable man was fast coming to the birth,—man, the moral agent,—man, the ultimate work and end of creation,—man, a creature in whom, as in the inferior animals, vitality was to be united to matter, but in whom also, as in no inferior animal, responsibility was to be united to vitality! How must expectancy have quickened,—how must solicitude have grown,—when, after the dynasty of the fish had been succeeded by the dynasty of the reptile, and that of the reptile by the dynasty of the sagacious mammal, a time had at length arrived when the earth had become fixed and stable, and the proud waves of ocean had been stayed,—when, after species and genera in both kingdoms had been increased tenfold beyond the precedent of any former age, the Creative Hand seemed to pause in its working, and the finished creation to demand its lord! Even at this late period, how strange may not the doubts and uncertainties have been that remained to darken the mind of the lost spirit! It was according to his experience,—stretched backwards to the first beginnings of organic vitality, and co-extensive, at a still earlier period, with God's spiritual universe,—that all *animals* should die,—that all *moral agents* should live. How, in this new creation,—this prodigy of creation, who was to unite what never before had been united,—the nature of the animals that *die* with the standing and responsibility of the moral agents that *live*,—how, in this partaker of the double nature, was the discrepancy to be reconciled? How, in this matter, were the opposite claims of life and death to be adjusted, or the absolute *immortality*, which cannot admit of degrees, to be made to meet with and shade into the *mortality* which, let us extend the term of previous vitality as we may, must for ever involve the antagonistic idea of final annihilation and the ceasing to be?

At length creation receives its deputed monarch. For, moulded by God's own finger, and in God's own likeness, man enters upon the scene, an exquisite creature, rich in native faculty, pregnant with the yet undeveloped seeds of all wisdom and knowledge, tender of heart and pure of spirit, formed to hold high communion with his Creator, and to breathe abroad his soul in

sympathy over all that the Creator had made. And yet, left to the
freedom of his own will, there is a weakness in the flesh that
betrays his earthly lineage. It is into the dust of the ground that
the living soul has been breathed. The son of the soil, who, like the
inferior animals, his subjects, sleeps and wakes, and can feel thirst
and hunger, and the weariness of toil, and the sweets of rest, and
who comes under the general law, "increase and multiply,"
promulgated of old to them, stands less firmly than the immaterial
spirits stood of old; and yet even they rebelled against Heaven,
and fell. There awakes a grim hope in the sullen lord of the first
revolt. Ages beyond tale or reckoning has this temple of creation
been in building. Long have its mute prophecies in fishes and in
creeping things, in bird and in beast, told of coming man, its final
object and end. And now there needeth but one blow, and the
whole edifice is destroyed, God's purposes marred and frustrated,
and this new favourite of earth dashed back to the dust out of
which he was created, and brought, like the old extinct races,
under the eternal law of death. Armed with the experience in evil
of unsummed ages, the Tempter plies his work; nor is it to low or
ignoble appetites that he appeals. It is to the newly-formed
creature's thirst for knowledge; it is to his love stronger than
death. The wiles of the Old Serpent prevail; man falls prostrate
before him; creation trembles; and then from amid the trees of the
garden comes the voice of God. And lo! in an enigma mysterious
and dark a new dispensation of prophecy begins. Victims bleed;
altars smoke; the tabernacle arises amid the white tents of the
desert; the temple ascends all glorious on the heights of Mount
Zion; prophet after prophet declares his message. At length, in the
fulness of time, the Messiah comes; and, in satisfying the law, and
in fulfilling all righteousness, and in bringing life and immortality
to light, abundantly shows forth that the terminal destiny of all
creation had been of old fore-ordained, ere the foundations of the
world, to possess for its eternal lord and monarch, not primæval
man, created in the image of God, but God, made manifest in the
flesh, in the form of primæval man. But how breaks on the baffled
Tempter the sublime revelation? Wearily did he toil,—darkly did
he devise, and take, in his great misery, deep counsel against the

Almighty; and yet all the while, while striving and resisting as an enemy, has he been wielded as a tool; when, glaring aloof in his proud rebellion, the grasp of the Omnipotent has been upon him, and the Eternal Purposes have encompassed him, and he has been working out, all unwittingly, the fore-ordained decree. "For our God maketh the wrath of the wicked to praise Him, and the remainder thereof doth He restrain."

But enough, for the present, of the poems that might be. Permit me, however, to add, in the words of one of the most suggestive, and certainly not least powerful, of English thinkers, that "a fall of some sort or other,—the creation, as it were, of the non-absolute,—is the fundamental postulate of the moral history of man. Without this hypothesis," he adds, "man is unintelligible,—with it every phenomenon is explicable. The mystery itself is too profound for human insight." Such, in this matter, was the ultimate judgment of a man who in youth had entertained very opposite views,—the poet Coleridge.

It has been said that the inferences of the geologist militate against those of the theologian. Nay, not those of our higher geologists and higher theologians,—not what our Murchisons and Sedgwicks infer in the one field, with what our Chalmerses and Isaac Taylors infer in the other. Between the Word and the Works of God there can be no actual discrepancies; and the seeming ones are discernible only by the men who see worst.

> "Mote-like they flicker in unsteady eyes,
> And weakest his who best descries."

The geologist, as certainly as the theologian, has a province exclusively his own; and were the theologian ever to remember that the Scriptures could not possibly have been given to us as revelations of scientific truth, seeing that a single scientific truth they never yet revealed, and the geologist that it must be in vain to seek in science those truths which lead to salvation, seeing that in science these truths were never yet found, there would be little danger even of difference among them, and none of collision. Nay, there is, I doubt not, a time coming in which the Butlers and

Chalmerses of the future will be content to recognise the geologic field as that of their richest and most pregnant analogies. It is with the history of the pre-Adamic ages that geology sets itself to deal; and by carefully conning the ancient characters graven in the rocks, and by deciphering the strange inscriptions which they compose, it greatly extends the record of God's doings upon the earth. And what more natural to expect, or rational to hold, than that the Unchangeable One should have wrought in all time after one general type and pattern, or than that we may seek, in the hope of finding, meet correspondences and striking analogies between his revealed workings during the human period, and his previous workings of old during the geologic periods,—correspondences and analogies suited to establish the identity of the worker, and, of course, from that identity to demonstrate the authenticity of the revelation? Permit me to bring out, in conclusion, what I have often thought on this subject, but have not been able so tersely to express, in a brief quotation from one of the most instructive works of the present age, the "Method of the Divine Government," by the Rev. Dr M'Cosh:—"Science has a foundation," says this solid thinker and accomplished writer, "and so has religion. Let them unite their foundations, and the basis will be broader, and they will be two compartments of one great fabric reared to the glory of God. Let the one be the outer and the other the inner court. In the one let all look, and admire, and adore; and in the other let those who have faith kneel, and pray, and praise. Let the one be the sanctuary where human learning may present its richest incense as an offering to God, and the other, the holiest of all, separated from it by a veil now rent in twain, and in which, on a blood-sprinkled mercy-seat, we pour out the love of a reconciled heart, and hear the oracles of the living God."

1. Perhaps one strengthening principle more might be enumerated as occurring in this curious piece of mechanism. In the layers of the nether plate, the fibres, instead of being laid in parallel lines, like the threads in the moleskin of my illustration, seem to be felted together,—an arrangement which must have added considerably to their coherency and powers of resistance.

LECTURE SEVENTH.

THE NOACHIAN DELUGE.

PART I.

THERE are events so striking in themselves or from their accompaniments, that they powerfully impress the memories of children but little removed from infancy, and are retained by them in a sort of troubled recollection ever after, however extended their term of life. Samuel Johnson was only two and a half years old when, in accordance with the belief of the time, he was touched by Queen Anne for the "Evil;" but more than seventy years after, he could call up in memory a dream-like recollection of the lady dressed in a black hood, and glittering with diamonds, into whose awful presence he had been ushered on that occasion, and who had done for the cure of his complaint all that legitimate royalty could do. And an ancient lady of the north country, who had been carried, when a child, in her nurse's arms, to witness the last witch execution that took place in Scotland, could distinctly tell, after the lapse of nearly a century, that the fire was surrounded by an awe-struck crowd, and that the smoke of the burning, when blown about her by a cross breeze, had a foul and suffocating odour. In this respect the memory of infant tribes and nations seems to resemble that of individuals. There are characters and events which impress it so strongly, that they seem never to be forgotten, but live as traditions, sometimes mayhap very vague, and much modified by the inventions of an after time, but which, in floating downwards to late ages, always bear about them a certain strong impress of their pristine reality. They are shadows that have become ill-defined from the vast distance of the objects that cast them,—like the shadows of great birds flung, in a summer's day, from the blue depths of the sky to the landscape far below,—but whose very presence, however diffused they may have become, testifies to the existence of the remote realities from which they are thrown, and without which they could have had no being at all. The old mythologies are filled with shadowy traditions of this kind,—shadows of the world's "gray fathers,"—which, like those shadows seen reflected on clouds by travellers who ascend lofty mountains, are exaggerated into the most gigantic proportions, and bear radiant glories around their heads.

There is, however, one special tradition which seems to be more deeply impressed and more widely spread than any of the others. The destruction of well nigh the whole human race, in an early age of the world's history, by a great deluge, appears to have so impressed the minds of the few survivors, and seems to have been handed down to their children, in consequence, with such terror-struck impressiveness, that their remote descendants of the present day have not even yet forgotten it. It appears in almost every mythology, and lives in the most distant countries, and among the most barbarous tribes. It was the laudable ambition of Humboldt,—first entertained at a very early period of life,—to penetrate into distant regions, unknown to the natives of Europe at the time, that he might acquaint himself, in fields of research altogether fresh and new, with men and with nature in their most primitive conditions. In carrying out his design, he journeyed far into the woody wilderness that surrounds the Orinoco, and found himself among tribes of wild Indians whose very names were unknown to the civilized world. And yet among even these forgotten races of the human family he found the tradition of the deluge still fresh and distinct; not confined to single tribes, but general among the scattered nations of that great region, and intertwined with curious additions, suggestive of the inventions of classic mythology in the Old World. "The belief in a great deluge," we find him saying, "is not confined to one nation singly,—the Tamanacs: it makes part of a system of historical tradition, of which we find scattered notions among the Maypures of the great cataracts; among the Indians of the Rio Erevato, which runs into the Caura; and among almost all the tribes of the Upper Orinoco. When the Tamanacs are asked how the human race survived this great deluge,—'the *age of water*' of the Mexicans,—they say, a man and woman saved themselves on a high mountain called Tamanacu, situated on the banks of the Asiveru, and, *casting behind them over their heads* the fruits of the mauritia palm-tree, they saw the seeds contained in these fruits produce men and women, who re-peopled the earth. "Thus," adds the philosophic traveller, "we find in all simplicity, among nations now in a savage state, a tradition which the Greeks embellished with all the charms of imagination." The resemblance is certainly very striking. "Quit the temple," said the Oracle to Deucalion and Pyrrha, when they had consulted it, after the great deluge, regarding the mode in which the earth was to be re-peopled,—"veil your heads, unloose your girdles, and throw behind your backs the bones of your grandmother." Rightly interpreting what seemed darkest and most obscure in the reply, they took "stones of the earth," and, casting them behind them, the stones flung by Deucalion became men, and those by Pyrrha became women, and thus the disfurnished world was peopled anew. The navigator always regards himself as sure of his position when he has *two* landmarks to determine it by, or when in the open ocean he can ascertain, not only his latitude, but his longitude also. And this curious American tradition seems to have its two such marks,—its two bisecting lines of determination,—to identify it with the classic tradition of the Old World that refers evidently to the same great event.

There are other portions of America in which the tradition of the Flood is still more distinct than among the forests of the Orinoco. It is related by Herrera, one of the Spanish historians of America, that even the most barbarous of the Brazilians had some knowledge of a general deluge; that in Peru the ancient Indians reported, that many years before there were any Incas, all the people were drowned by a great flood, save six persons, the progenitors of the existing races, who were saved on a float; that among the Mechoachans it was believed that a single family was preserved, during the outburst of the waters, in an ark with a sufficient number of animals to replenish the new world; and, more curious still, that it used to be told by the original inhabitants of Cuba, that "an old man, knowing the deluge was to come, built a great ship, and went into it with his family and abundance of animals; and that, wearying during the continuance of the flood, he sent out a crow, which at first did not return, staying to feed on the dead bodies, but afterwards returned bearing with it a green branch." The resemblance borne by this last tradition to the Mosaic narrative is so close as to awaken a doubt whether it may not have been but a mere recollection of the teaching of some early missionary. Nor can its genuineness now be tested, seeing that the race which cherished it has been long since extinct. It may be stated, however, that a similar suspicion crossed the mind of Humboldt when he was engaged in collecting the traditions of the Indians of the Orinoco; but that on further reflection and inquiry he dismissed the doubt as groundless. He even set himself to examine whether the district was not a fossiliferous one, and whether beds of sea-shells, or deposits charged with the petrified remains of corals or of fishes, might not have originated among the aborigines some mere myth of a great inundation sufficient to account for the appearances in the rocks. But he found that the region was mainly a primary one, in which he could detect only a single patch of sedimentary rock, existing as an unfossiliferous sandstone. And so, though little prejudiced in favour of the Mosaic record, he could not avoid arriving at the conclusion, simply in his character as a philosophic inquirer, who had no other object than to attain to the real and the true, that the legend of the wild Maypures and Tamanacs regarding a great destructive deluge was simply one of the many forms of that oldest of traditions which appears to be well-nigh co-extensive with the human family, and which, in all its varied editions, seems to point at one and the same signal event. Very varied some of these editions are. The inhabitants of Tahiti tell, for instance, that the Supreme God, a long time ago, being angry, dragged the earth through the sea, but that by a happy accident *their* island broke off and was preserved; the Indians of Terra Firma believe, that when the great deluge took place, one man, with his wife and children, escaped in a canoe; and the Indians of the North American lakes hold, that the father of all their tribes being warned in a dream that a flood was coming, built a raft, on which he preserved his family, and pairs of all the animals, and which drifted about for many months, until at length a new earth was made for their reception by the "Mighty Man above."

In that widely-extended portion of the Old World over which Christianity has spread in its three great types,—Greek, Romish, and Protestant,—and in the scarce less extended portion occupied by the followers of Mohammed, the Scriptural account of the deluge, or the imperfect reflection of it borrowed by the Koran, has, of course, supplanted the old traditions. But outside these regions we find the traditions existing still. One of the sacred books of the Parsees (representatives of the ancient Persians) records, that "the world having been corrupted by Ahriman the Evil One, it was thought necessary to bring over it a universal flood of waters, that all impurity might be washed away. Accordingly the rain came down in drops as large as the head of a bull, until the earth was wholly covered with water, and all the creatures of the Evil One perished. And then the flood gradually subsided, and first the mountains, and next the plains, appeared once more." In the Scandinavian Edda, between whose wild fables and those of the sacred books of the Parsees there has been a resemblance traced by accomplished antiquaries such as Mallet, the tradition of the deluge takes a singularly monstrous form. On the death of the great giant Ymir, whose flesh and bones form the rocks and soils of the earth, and who was slain by the early gods, his blood, which now constitutes the ocean, rushed so copiously out of his wounds, that all the old race of the lesser giants, his offspring, were drowned in the flood which it occasioned, save one; and he, by escaping on board his bark with his wife, outlived the deluge. The tradition here is evidently allegorized, but it is by no means lost in the allegory.

Sir William Jones, perhaps the most learned and accomplished man of his age (such at least was the estimate of Johnson), and the first who fairly opened up the great storehouse of eastern antiquities, describes the tradition of the Deluge as prevalent also in the vast Chinese empire, with its three hundred millions of people. He states that it was there believed that, just ere the appearance of Fohi in the mountains, a mighty flood, which first "flowed abundantly, and then subsided, covered for a time the whole earth, and separated the higher from the lower age of mankind." The Hindu tradition, as related by Sir William, though disfigured by strange additions, is still more explicit. An evil demon having purloined the sacred books from Brahma, the whole race of men became corrupt except the seven Rishis, and in especial the holy Satyavrata, the prince of a maritime region, who, when one day bathing in a river, was visited by the God Vishnu in the shape of a fish, and thus addressed by him:—"In seven days all creatures who have offended me shall be destroyed by a deluge; but thou shalt be secured in a capacious vessel, miraculously formed. Take, therefore, all kinds of medicinal herbs and esculent grain for food, and, together with the seven holy men, your respective wives, and pairs of all animals, enter the ark without fear: then shalt thou know God face to face, and all thy questions shall be answered." The god then disappeared; and after seven days, during which Satyavrata had conformed in all respects to the instructions given him, the ocean began to overflow the coasts, and the earth to be flooded by constant rains, when a large vessel was seen coming floating shorewards on the rising waters; into which the Prince and the seven virtuous Rishis entered, with their wives, all laden with plants and grain, and accompanied by the animals. During the deluge Vishnu preserved the ark by again taking the form of a fish, and tying it fast to himself; and when the waters had subsided, he communicated the contents of the sacred books to the holy Satyavrata, after first slaying the demon who had stolen them. It is added, however, that the good man having, on one occasion long after, by "the act of destiny," drunk mead, he became senseless, and lay asleep naked, and that Charma, one of three sons who had been born to him, finding him in that sad state, called on his two brothers to witness the shame of their father, and said to them, "What has now befallen? In what state is this our sire?" But by the two brothers,—more dutiful than Charma,—he was hidden with clothes, and recalled to his senses; and, having recovered his intellect, and perfectly knowing what had passed, he cursed Charma, saying, "Thou shalt be a servant of servants." It would be difficult certainly to produce a more curious legend, or one more strikingly illustrative of the mixture of truth and fable which must ever be looked for in that tradition which some are content to accept even in religion as a trustworthy guide. In ever varying tradition, as in those difficult problems in physical science which have to be wrought out from a multitude of differing observations, it is, if I may so express myself, the mean result of the whole that must be accepted as approximately the true one. And the mean result of those dim and distorted recollections of the various tribes of men which refer to the Flood is a result which bears simply to this effect,—that in some early age of the world a great deluge took place, in which well nigh the whole human family was destroyed.

The ancient traditions which have come down to us embalmed in classic literature form but a small portion of what seems once to have existed in the wide region now overspread by Christianity and Mohammedanism. A second deluge, more fatal to at least the productions of the human mind than the first had been, overspread the earth during what are known as the Middle Ages; and so signal was the wreck which it occasioned, that of seven heathen writers[1] whose testimony regarding the Flood Josephus cites as corroborative of his own, not one has descended in his writings to these later times. We learn, however, from the Jewish historian, that one of their number, Berosus, was a Chaldean; that two of the others, Hieronymus and Manetho, were Egyptians; and that a third, Nicolaus, whose history he quotes, was a citizen of Damascus. "There is," said this latter writer, in his perished history, "a great mountain in Armenia, over Minyas, called Baris, upon which it is reported that many who fled at the time of the Deluge were saved; and that one who was carried in an ark came on shore on the top of it; and that the remains of the timber were a great while preserved. This might be the man," added this forgotten writer, "about whom Moses, the legislator of the Jews, wrote." The works of the Chaldean, Berosus, have long since been lost, all save a few extracts preserved by the patristic writers. One of these, however, which embodies the Chaldean tradition of the Flood, is very remarkable. Like the Scandinavian legend, it represents the antediluvians as giants, all of whom, save one, became exceedingly impious and depraved. "But there was one among the giants," says Berosus, "that reverenced the gods, and was more wise and prudent than all the rest. His name was Noa, he dwelt in Syria, with his three sons, Sem, Japet, Chem, and their wives, the great Tidea, Pandora, Noela, and Noegla. This man, fearing the destruction which, he foresaw from the stars, would come to pass, began, in the seventy-eighth year before the inundation, to build a ship, covered like an ark. Seventy-eight years from the time he began to build this ship, the ocean of a sudden broke out, and all the inland seas and the rivers and fountains bursting from beneath (attended by the most violent rains from heaven for many days), overflowed all the mountains; so that the whole human race was buried in the waters, except Noa and his family, who were saved by means of the ship, which, being lifted up by the waters, rested at last upon the top of the Gendyae or Mountain, on which, it is reported, there now remaineth some part, and that men take away the bitumen from it, and make use of it by way of charm or expiation, to avoid evil." A more general Assyrian tradition, somewhat different in its details, also survives.[2] The god Chronus, it was said, appeared in a vision to Xisuthrus, the tenth king of Babylon; and, warning him that on a certain day there would be a great flood upon the earth, by which mankind would be destroyed, he enjoined him to build a vessel, and to bring into it his friends and relatives, with everything necessary to sustain life, and all the various animals, birds, and quadrupeds. In obedience to the command, the king built a vessel about three quarters of a mile in length and half a mile in breadth, which he loaded with stores and the different kinds of animals; and into which, on the day of the flood, he himself entered, accompanied by his wife and children, and all his friends. The flood broke out. After, however, accomplishing its work of destruction, it abated; and the king sent out birds from the vessel, which, at first finding no food or place of rest, returned to him; but which, when, after the lapse of some days, he sent them forth again, came back to him with their feet tinged with mud. On a third trial they returned no more; upon which, judging that the surface of the earth was laid dry, he made an opening in the vessel, and, looking forth, found it stranded on a mountain of the land of Armenia.

There seems to exist no such definite outline of the Egyptian tradition referred to by Josephus as that preserved of the Chaldean one. Plato, in his "Timæus" makes the Egyptian priest whom he introduces as discoursing with Solon, to attribute that clear recollection of a remote antiquity which survived in Egypt, to its comparative freedom from those great floods which had at various times desolated Greece, and destroyed the memory of remote events by the destruction of the people and their records; and Bacon had evidently this passage in view when he poetically remarked, in his magnificent essay on the "Vicissitude of Things," that "the great winding-sheets that bury all things in oblivion are two,—deluges and earthquakes; from which two destructions it is to be noted," he adds, "that the remnant of people that happen to be preserved are commonly ignorant and mountainous people, that can give no account of the time past." Even in Egypt, however, the recollection of the Deluge seems to have survived, though it lay entangled amid what seem to be symbolized memories of unusual floodings of the river Nile. "The Noah of Egypt," says Professor Hitchcock, in his singularly ingenious essay (Historical and Geological Deluges Compared), "appears to have been Osiris. Typhon, a personification of the ocean, enticed him into an ark, which being closed, he was forced to sea; and it is a curious fact, that he embarked on the seventeenth day of the month Athyr,—the very day, most probably, when Noah entered the ark." The classical tradition of Greece, as if the events whence it took its rise had been viewed through a multiplying-glass, appears to have been increased from one to many. Plutarch enumerates no fewer than five great floods; and Plato makes his Egyptian priest describe the Greek deluges as oft-repeated and numerous. There was the flood of Deucalion, the flood of Ogyges, and several other floods; and no little time and learning have been wasted in attempting to fix their several periods. But, lying far within the mythologic ages,—the last of them to which any determining circumstances are attached, in the days of that Prometheus who stole fire from heaven, and was chained by Jupiter to Mount Caucasus,—it appears greatly more probable that the traditions respecting them should be the mere repeated and re-repeated echoes of one signal event, than that many wide-spread and destructive floods should have taken place in the obscure, fabulous ages of Grecian story, while not one such flood has happened during its two thousand five hundred years of authentic history. Nor is it difficult to conceive how such repetitions of the original tradition *should* have taken place. The traditions of the same event preserved by tribes living in even the same tract of country come in course of time considerably to differ from each other in their adjuncts and circumstances; those, for instance, of the various tribes of the Orinoco do so; and should these tribes come to be fused ultimately into one nation, nothing seems more probable than that their varying editions, instead of being also fused together, should remain distinct, as the recollection of separate and independent catastrophes. And thus the several deluges of Grecian mythology may in reality testify, not to the occurrence of several floods, but to the existence merely of several independent tribes, among whom the one great tradition has been so altered and modified ere they came to possess a common literature, that when at length they became skilful enough to place it on record, it appeared to them not as one, but as many. The admirable reflection of Humboldt suggested by the South American traditions seems, incidentally at least, to bear out this view. "Those ancient traditions of the human race," he says, "which we find dispersed over the whole surface of the globe, like the relics of a vast shipwreck, are highly interesting in the philosophical study of our own species. How many different tongues belonging to branches that appear totally distinct transmit to us the same facts! The traditions concerning races that have been destroyed, and the renewal of nature, scarcely vary in reality, though every nation gives them a local colouring. In the great continents, as in the smallest islands of the Pacific Ocean, it is always on the loftiest and nearest mountain that the remains of the human race have been saved; and this event appears the more recent in proportion as the nations are uncultivated, and as the knowledge they have of their own existence has no very remote date." And it seems at least not improbable, that the several traditions of apparently special deluges,—deluges each with its own set of circumstances, and from which the progenitors of one nation were saved on a hill-top, those of another on a raft, and those of yet another in an ark or canoe, and which in one instance destroyed only giants, and had in another the loss which they occasioned repaired by date-stones, and in yet another by stones of the earth,—should come to be regarded among a people composed of various tribes, and but little accustomed to sift the evidence on which they founded, rather as all diverse narratives of diverse events, than as in reality but varied accounts of one and the same tremendous catastrophe.

Taking it for granted, then, that the several Greek traditions refer to but one great event, let us accept that which records what is known as the flood of Deucalion, as more adequately representative of the general type of its class, especially in the edition given by Lucian (in his work "De Dea Syria"), than any of the others. "The present world," says this writer, "is peopled from the sons of Deucalion. In respect to the former brood, they were men of violence, and lawless in their dealings; they regarded not oaths, nor observed the rites of hospitality, nor showed mercy to those who sued for it. On this account they were doomed to destruction; and for this purpose there was a mighty eruption of water from the earth, attended with heavy showers from above, so that the rivers swelled and the sea overflowed, till the whole earth was covered with a flood, and all flesh drowned. Deucalion alone was preserved, to people the world. This mercy was shown him on account of his justice and piety. His preservation was effected in this manner: he put all his family, both his sons and their wives, into a vast ark which he had provided, and he then went into it himself. At the same time, animals of every species,—boars, horses, lions, serpents,—whatever lived upon the face of the earth,—followed him by pairs; all which he received into the ark, and experienced no evil from them." Such is the tradition of Deucalion, as preserved by Lucian. It is added by his contemporary Plutarch, that "Deucalion, as his voyage was drawing to a close, sent out a dove, which coming in a short time back to him, indicated that the waters still covered the earth; but which on a second occasion failed to return; or, as some say, returned to him with mud-stained feet, and thus intimated the abatement of the flood." It cannot, I think, be rationally doubted that we have in this ancient legend one other tradition of the Noachian Deluge. Even as related by Ovid, with all the licence of the poet, we find in it the great leading traits that indicate its parentage. I quote from the vigorous translation of Dryden.

> "Impetuous rain descends;
> Nor from his patrimonial heaven alone
> Is Jove content to pour his vengeance down;
> But from his brother of the seas he craves
> To help him with auxiliary waves.
> Then with his mace the monarch struck the ground;
> With inward trembling earth received the wound,
> And rising streams a ready passage found.
> Now seas and earth were in confusion lost,—
> A world of waters, and without a coast.
> A mountain of tremendous height there stands
> Betwixt the Athenian and Bœotian lands:
> Parnassus is its name, whose forky rise
> Mounts through the clouds, and mates the lofty skies.
> High on the summit of this dubious cliff
> Deucalion, wafting, moor'd his little skiff:
> He, with his wife, were only left behind
> Of perished man; they two were human kind:
> The most upright of mortal men was he,—
> The most serene and holy woman she."

Such are some of the traditions of that great catastrophe which overtook the human family in its infancy, and made so deep an impression on the memories of the few awe-struck survivors, that the race never forgot it. Ere the dispersal of the family it would have of course existed as but one unique recollection,—a single reflection on the face of an unbroken mirror. But the mirror has since been shattered into a thousand pieces; and we now find the object, originally but one, pictured in each broken fragment, with various degrees of distinctness, according to the various degrees of injury received by the reflecting medium. *Picture*, too, scarce less certainly than language spoken and written, testifies to the wide extent of the tradition. Its symbols are found stamped on coins of old classical Greece; they have been traced amid the ancient hieroglyphics of Egypt, recognised in the sculptured caves of Hindustan, and detected even in the far west, among the picture-writings of Mexico. The several glyphic representatives of the tradition bear, like its various written or oral editions, a considerable resemblance to each other. Even in the rude paintings of the old Mexican, the same leading idea may be traced as in the classic sculpture of the Greek. On what is known to antiquaries as the Apamæan medal, struck during the reign of Philip the elder, we find the familiar name of *Noe* inscribed on a floating chest or ark, within which a man and woman are seen seated, and to which a bird on the wing is represented as bearing a branch.[3] And in an ancient Mexican painting, figured by Humboldt, "the man and

Fig. 109.   Fig. 110.

APAMÆAN MEDAL.   OLD MEXICAN PICTURE.
                                          (*Humboldt.*)

woman who survived the age of water" are shown similarly
inclosed in a leaf-tufted box, or hollow trunk of a tree; while a
gigantic female,—Matalcueje, the goddess of water,—is seen
pouring down her floods around them and upon an overwhelmed
human figure, representative apparently of the victims of the
catastrophe. All is classical in the forms of the one representation,
and uncouth in those of the other. They bear the same sort of
artistic relation to each other that the rude Tamanac tradition
bears, in a *literary* point of view, to the well-constructed story and
elegant verse of Ovid; but they are charged apparently with the
same meaning, and shadow forth the same event.

The tradition of the Flood may, I repeat, be properly regarded
as universal; seeing there is scarce any considerable race of man
among which, in some of its many forms, it is not to be found.
Now, it has been argued by some of the older theologians, with a
not very cogent logic, that the universality of the tradition
establishes the universality of the Flood,—that where the
tradition *is to be found*, the Flood *must have been*;—an argument
which would have force if it could also be shown that each tribe
had had its own Noah, saved by ark, raft, or canoe, or on some tall
mountain summit, in the region in which his descendants
continued to reside; but of no force whatever if the Noah of the
race was but one, and if the scene of his danger and deliverance
was restricted, as of necessity it must have been in that case, to a
single locality. Further, if, as we believe, there was but one
Noah,—if, according to the Scriptural account, condensed into a
single sentence by the Apostle, only "eight souls" were saved in the
great catastrophe of the race,—there could have existed no human
testimony to determine whether the exterminating deluge that
occasioned their destruction was a universal deluge, or merely a
partial one. It could not be known by men shut up in an ark, nor
even though from a mast-top they could have swept the horizon
with a telescope, whether the waters that spread out on every side
of them, covering the old familiar mountains, and occupying the
entire range of their vision, extended all around the globe, or found
their limits some eight or ten hundred miles away. The point is one

respecting which, as certainly as respecting the creation of the world itself, or of the world's inhabitants, there could have existed no human *witness-bearing*: contemporary man, left to the unassisted evidence of his senses, *must* of necessity have been ignorant of the extent of the Deluge. True, what man could never have known of himself, God could have told him, and in many cases *has* told him; but then God's revelations have in most instances been made to effect exclusively moral purposes; and we know that those who have perilously held that along with the moral facts definite physical facts, geographic, geologic, or astronomical, had also been imparted, have almost invariably found themselves involved in monstrous error. And in this matter of the Flood, though it be a fact of great moral significancy that God in an early period of the human history destroyed the whole race for their wickedness,—all save one just man and his family,—it is not in the least a matter of moral significancy whether or no the deluge by which the judgment was effected covered not only the parts of the earth occupied by man at the time, but extended also to Terra del Fuego, Tahiti, and the Falkland Islands. In fine, though the question whether the Noachian Deluge was universal, or merely partial, is an interesting question in physics, it is in no higher degree a moral one than those questions which relate to the right figure or age of the earth, or to the true motions of the heavenly bodies. And it will be found that the only passages in Scripture which refer to this strictly physical subject, instead of determining the geographic extent of the Flood, serve only to raise a question regarding their own extent of meaning.

It is known to all students of the sacred writings, that there is a numerous class of passages in both the Old and New Testaments in which, by a sort of metonymy common in the East, a considerable part is spoken of as the whole, though in reality often greatly less than a moiety of the whole. Of this class are the passages in which it is said, that on the day of Pentecost there were Jews assembled at Jerusalem "*out of every nation under heaven;*" "that the gospel was preached to *every creature under heaven;*" that the Queen of Sheba came to hear the wisdom of Solomon from the *"uttermost parts of the earth;"* that God put the dread and fear of the children of Israel upon the nations that were *"under the whole heavens;"* and that *"all countries* came into Egypt to Joseph to buy corn." And of course the universally admitted existence of such a class of passages, in which words are *not* to be accepted in their rigidly literal meanings, but with certain great modifications, renders the task of determining and distinguishing such passages from others in which the meaning is definite and strict, not only legitimate, but also laudable; and justifies us in inquiring whether those passages descriptive of the Flood or its effects, in which it is said that the "waters prevailed exceedingly on the earth," so that *"all* the high hills that were under *the whole heavens* were covered," or that *"all* flesh died that moved upon the earth," belong to their number or no. There are some instances in which the Scriptures themselves reveal the character and limit the meaning of the metonymic passages. They do so with respect to the passage already quoted regarding the stranger Jews assembled in Jerusalem at the Pentecostal feast,—"out of every nation under heaven." For further on we read that these Jews had come from but the various countries extending around Judea, as far as Italy on the one hand, and the Persian Gulf on the other;—an area large, indeed, but scarce equal to a one fiftieth part of the earth's surface. But there is no such explanation given to limit or restrict most of the other passages; the modifying element must be sought for outside the sacred volume,—in ancient history or ancient geography. The reader must, for instance, acquaint himself with the progress of discovery in early ages, or the boundaries of the Roman Empire under the first Cæsars, ere he can form a probable conjecture regarding the extent of that "all the earth" which sought the presence of Solomon, or a correct estimate respecting the limits of that "all the world" which Cæsar Augustus could have taxed. And to this last class, which fail to explain themselves, the passages respecting the Flood evidently belong. Like the passages cited, and, with these, almost all the texts of Scripture in which questions of physical science are involved, the limiting, modifying,

explaining facts and circumstances must be sought for in that
outside region of secular research, historic and scientific, from
which of late years so much valuable biblical illustration has been
derived, and with which it is so imperatively the duty of the
Church to keep up an acquaintance at least as close and intimate
as that maintained with it by her gainsayers and assailants.

That the Noachian Deluge might have been but partial, not
universal, was held, let me here remark, by distinguished
theologians in our own country, at least as early as the seventeenth
century. It was held, for instance, by the learned biblical
commentator old Matthew Poole, whom we find saying, in his
Synopsis on Genesis, that "it is not to be supposed that the entire
globe of the earth was covered with water;" for "where," he adds,
"was the need of overwhelming those regions in which there were
no human beings?" It was held also by that distinguished
Protestant churchman of the reign of Charles II., Bishop
Stillingfleet, whom Principal Cunningham of Edinburgh well
describes, in his elaborate edition of the Bishop's work, "The
Doctrines and Practices of the Church of Rome," as a divine of
"great talents and prodigious learning." "I cannot see," says the
Bishop, in his "Origines Sacra," "any urgent necessity from the
Scriptures to assert that the Flood did spread over all the surface
of the earth. That all mankind, those in the ark excepted, were
destroyed by it, is most certain, according to the Scriptures. The
Flood was universal as to mankind; but from thence follows no
necessity at all of asserting the universality of it as to the globe of
the earth, unless it be sufficiently proved that the whole earth was
peopled before the Flood, which I despair of ever seeing proved."
It was not, however, until the comparatively recent times in which
the belief entertained by Poole and Stillingfleet was adopted and
enforced by writers such as Dr Pye Smith, and Professor
Hitchcock of the United States, that there was any show of
argument displayed against the theory of a partial deluge which
would now be deemed worthy of consideration. And these modern
objections may be found ingeniously arrayed by the late Dr John
Kitto, in his "Daily Bible Illustrations," published only six years

ago (in 1850), and by the learned Dr William Hamilton of Mobile, in his "Friend of Moses," published in 1852. Both these writers, however, virtually agree with their opponents in holding that the strict meaning of the terms employed by Moses in describing the Deluge is to be determined on considerations apart from the mere philological ones. After marshalling his objections to the theory of a local flood, Dr Kitto goes on to say, "We yield our judgment to what appears to us the *force of these arguments* as to the *meaning* of Scripture;" and we find Dr Hamilton prefacing his objections as follows:—"Were the mere universality of some of the terms employed in the Mosaic narrative the *sole* ground of objection to the hypothesis of a *local* inundation only in the days of Noah, that hypothesis might perhaps be deemed admissible. But there are," he adds, "other and more serious difficulties attending it." Let us, then, briefly examine these supposed difficulties and objections; and as they have been better and more amply stated by Dr Kitto than by any other writer with whom I am acquainted,—for Dr Hamilton takes up rather the arguments in favour of a universal, than the objections against a merely partial flood,—let us take them as they occur in his writings, especially in the excellent work now before me,—his "Daily Bible Illustrations." It will scarce be suspected that such an accomplished writer, who did so much for Biblical illustration, and whose admirable Pictorial Bible formed, with but four works more, what Chalmers used to term with peculiar emphasis his "Biblical Library,"[4] would do injustice to any cause, or any line of argument which he adopted, if it was in reality a good and sound one.

It may be well, however, not to test too rigidly the value of the remark,—meant to be at least of the nature of argument,—when we find him saying that "a plain man sitting down to read the Scripture account of the Deluge would have no doubt of its universality." Perhaps not. But it is at least equally certain, that plain men who set themselves to deduce from Scripture the figure of the planet we inhabit had as little doubt, until corrected by the geographer, that the earth was a great plane—not a sphere; that plain men who set themselves to acquire from Scripture some notion of the planetary motions had no doubt, in the same way, until corrected by the astronomer, that it was the earth that rested, and the sun that moved round it; and that plain men who have sought to determine from Scripture the age of the earth have had no doubt, until corrected by the geologist, that it was at most not much more than six thousand years old. In fine, when plain men, who, according to Cowper, "know, and know no more, their Bible true," have in perhaps every instance learned from it what it was in reality intended to teach,—the way of salvation,—it seems scarce less certain, that in every instance in which they have sought to deduce from it what it was *not* intended to teach,—the truths of physical science,—they have fallen into extravagant error. And as any question which, bearing, not on the punitory extent and ethical consequences of the Flood, but merely on its geographic limits and natural effects, is not a moral, but a purely physical question, it would be but a fair presumption, founded on the almost invariable experience of ages, that the deductions from Scripture of the "plain men" regarding it would be, not true, but false deductions. Of apparently not more real weight and importance is the Doctor's further remark, that there seems, after all, to be a marked difference between the terms in which the universality of the Deluge is spoken of, and the terms employed in those admittedly metonymic passages in which the whole is substituted for a part. "What limitation," he asks, "can we assign to such a phrase as this:—'all the high hills that were UNDER THE WHOLE HEAVENS were covered?' If here the phrase had been, 'upon the face of the whole earth,' we should have been told that 'the whole earth' had sometimes the meaning of 'the whole land;' but, as if designedly to obviate such a limitation of meaning, we have here the largest phrase of universality which the language of man affords,—'under the whole heavens!'" So far Dr Kitto. But his argument seems to be not more valuable in this case than in the other. It was upon the nations that were "UNDER THE WHOLE HEAVENS" that Deity represented himself as putting the fear and dread of the children of Israel; but he would be certainly a very "plain man" who would infer from the universality of a passage so evidently metonymic, that that fear extended to the people of Japan on the one hand, or to the Red Indians of the Rocky Mountains on the other. The phrase *"under the whole heavens"* seems to be but co-extensive in meaning with the phrase "upon the face of the whole earth." The "whole earth" is evidently tantamount to the whole terrestrial floor,—the "whole heavens," to the whole celestial roof that arches over it; and on what principle the whole terrestrial floor is to be deemed less extensive than the floor under the whole celestial roof, really does not appear. Farther, nothing can be more certain than that both the phrases contrasted by Dr Kitto are equally employed in the metonymic form.

When, however, the Doctor passes to argument based upon natural science, we find what he adduces worthy of our attention, were it but for the inquiries which it suggests. "If the deluge were but local," we find him saying, "what was the need of taking *birds* into the ark; and among them birds so widely diffused as the raven and the dove? A deluge which could overspread the region which these birds inhabit could hardly have been less than universal. If the deluge were local, and all the birds of these kinds in that district perished,—though we should think they might have fled to the uninundated regions,—it would have been useless to encumber the ark with them, seeing that the birds of the same species which survived in the lands not overflowed would speedily replenish the inundated tract as soon as the waters subsided." It will be found that the reasoning here is mainly based upon an error in natural science, into which even naturalists of the last century, such as Buffon, not unfrequently fell, and which was almost universal among the earlier voyagers and travellers,—the error of confounding as identical the merely allied birds and beasts of distant countries, and of thus assigning to *species* wide areas in creation which in reality they do not occupy. The grouse, for instance, is a widely-spread genus, or rather *family*; for it consists of more genera than one. It is so extensively present over the northern hemisphere, that Siberia, Norway, Iceland, and North America, have all their grouse,—the latter continent, indeed, from five to eight different kinds; and yet so restricted are some of the

species of which they consist, that, were the British islands to be
submerged, one of the best known of the family,—the red grouse,
or moorfowl (*Lagopus Scoticus*),—would disappear from creation.
This bird, which, rated at its money-value, is one of the most
important in Europe,—for the barren moors which it frequents in
the Highlands of Scotland alone are let every season almost
entirely for its sake for hundreds of thousands of pounds,—is
exclusively a British bird; and, unless by miracle a new migratory
instinct were given to it, a complete submersion of the British
islands would secure its destruction. If the submergence amounted
to but a few hundred miles in lateral extent, the moorfowl would to
a certainty not seek the distant uninundated land. Nor is it at all
to be inferred, that in a merely local but wide-spread deluge, birds
occupying a more extensive area than that overspread by the
Flood would, according to Dr Kitto, "speedily replenish the
inundated tract as soon as the waters had subsided." The
statement must have been hazarded in ignorance of the peculiar
habits of many of the non-migratory birds. Up till about the
middle of the last century, the capercailzie, or great cock of the
woods, was a native of Scotland. It was exterminated, however,
about the time of the last Rebellion, or not long after: the last
specimen seen among the pine forests of Strathspey was killed, it is
said, in the year 1745: the last specimen seen among the woods of
Strathglass survived till the year 1760. Pennant relates that he saw
in 1769 a specimen, probably a stuffed one, that had been killed
shortly before in the neighbourhood of Inverness. But from at
least that time the species disappeared from the British islands;
and, though it continued to exist in Norway, did not "replenish the
tracts from which it had been extirpated." The late Marquis of
Breadalbane was at no small cost and trouble in re-introducing the
species, and to some extent he succeeded; but the capercailzie is, I
understand, still restricted to the Breadalbane woods. I have seen
the golden eagle annihilated as a species in more than one district
of the north of Scotland; nor, though it still exists in other parts of
the kingdom, and is comparatively common among the mountains
of Norway, have I known it in any instance to spread anew over

the tracts from which it had been extirpated. So much for the general reasonings of Dr Kitto. Further, we find him stating, that a deluge which could overspread the region inhabited by birds so widely diffused as the raven and the dove, could hardly have been less than universal. The Doctor, however, ought to have known that the *dove* is a *family*, not a *species*. All the American species of doves, for example, differ from the six European species, three of which are to be found in Scotland. Of even the American passenger pigeons (*Ectopistes migratoria*), which occur in such numbers in their native country as actually to eclipse, during their migratory flights, the light of day, only a single straggler,—the one whose chance visit has been recorded by Dr Fleming,—seems to have been ever seen in Britain. And the East has also its own peculiar species, unknown to Europe. The golden-green pigeons and the great crowned pigeons of the Indian isles are never seen in northern and western latitudes, save in stuffed specimens in a museum. The Vinago pigeons, with their vividly bright plumes, though they exist in several species, are all restricted to the woods of the torrid zone. Even the collared dove of Africa and the Levant rarely visits, and then only as a straggler, the western and northern parts of Europe. The bluecapped turteline pigeon is restricted, as a species, to the island of Celebes; the blue and green turteline pigeon is a native of New Guinea; the Cape turtle occurs in but the southern parts of Africa; the Nicobar ground pigeon in but the Indian Archipelago; the magnificent fruit pigeon in the eastern parts of Australia; and the crowned goura pigeon, the giant of its family, in the Molucca Islands. No single species of dove seems to be so widely spread but that it might be exterminated in a merely partial deluge; and of course conjecture may in vain weary itself in striving to determine what that particular species was which Noah sent forth as a messenger from the ark, or in inquiring what was the extent of the area which it occupied? The common raven is more widely spread than any single species of pigeon. Even the raven, however, seems restricted to the northern hemisphere. India and Southern Africa have both their ravens; but the species differ from each other, and from the widely-spread northern one. It is a question whether even the pied raven of the Faroe Isles be not a distinct bird from the black raven of our own country: if not an independent species, it is at least a very remarkable variety. Further, when extirpated in a district, it is found that, as in the case of the capercailzie and the golden eagle, the neighbouring regions in which the raven continues to exist fail for ages to furnish a fresh supply. There are counties in England in which the raven is now never seen; and I am acquainted with a district in the north of Scotland from which, when a pair that were known to breed for more than a century in a tall cliff were destroyed by the fowler, the species disappeared.[5] Such, when examined, are the arguments drawn by Dr Kitto from natural science; nor is he in any degree happier when he resorts to arguments more restrictedly physical. "If," we find him saying, "the waters of the Deluge rose fifteen cubits above all the mountains of the countries which the raven and the dove inhabit, *the level must have been high enough to give universality to the Deluge.*" The only point here not already dealt with,—for I have just shown that certain species of the dove and the raven might have of necessity been inmates of the ark, though the Flood had been only a partial one,—is that which refers to the submergence of the hills over at least an extensive tract, and to the inference, evident in the passage, that if lofty mountains were covered in one portion of the globe, mountains of similar altitude must have been equally covered in every other portion of it.

The inference here seems to be founded on a common but altogether mistaken view of some of the grandest operations of nature with which modern science has brought us acquainted. It has been well remarked, that when two opposing explanations of extraordinary natural phenomena are given,—one of a simple and seemingly common-sense character, the other complex and apparently absurd,—it is almost always safer to adopt the apparently absurd than the seemingly common-sense one. Dr Kitto's "plain man," yielding to the dictates of what he would deem common sense,—which, of course, in questions of natural science is tantamount to common nonsense,—would be sure to go wrong. And we find the remark not inaptly illustrated by the now well-established fact, that while the medium level of the ocean is one of the most fixed lines in nature, the level of the great continents, with their table-lands and mountains, is an ever-fluctuating line. It may seem strange that land should be less stable than water. We see the tide rising and falling twice every twenty-four hours, and the rock ever remaining in its place;—we speak of the fixed earth and the unstable sea. And yet, while we have no evidence whatever that the sea-level has changed during at least the ages of the Tertiary formations, and absolutely know that it could not have varied more than a few yards, or at most a few fathoms, we have direct evidence that during that time great mountain chains, many thousand feet in height, such as the Alps, have arisen from the bottom of the ocean, and that great continents have sunk beneath it and disappeared. The larger part of northern Europe and America have been covered by the sea since our present group of shells began to exist; and it seems not improbable that the lower portion of the valley of the Jordan was depressed to its present low level of thirteen hundred feet beneath the Mediterranean since the times of the Deluge. On several parts of the coasts of Britain and Ireland the voyager can look down through the clear sea, in depths to which the tide never falls, on the remains of submerged forests; and it is a demonstrable fact, that even during the present age there are certain extensive tracts of land which have sunk beneath the sea-level, while certain other extensive tracts have been elevated over it. In 1819, a wide expanse of country in the delta of the Indus, containing fully two thousand square miles of flat meadow, was converted by a sudden depression of the land, accompanied by an earthquake, into an inland sea; and the tower of a small fort, which occupied nearly the middle of the sunken area, and on which many of the inhabitants of a neighbouring village succeeded in saving themselves, may still be seen raising its shattered head over the surface,—the only object visible in a waste of waters of which the eye fails to determine the extent. About three years after this event, a tract of country, interposed between the foot of the Andes and the Pacific,

more than equal in area to all Great Britain, was elevated from two
to seven feet over its former level, and rocks laid bare in the sea,
which the pilots and fishermen of the coast had never before seen.
On the Indian coast the sea *seemed* to be rising at nearly the same
time when it *appeared* to be falling on the American one; and on
the latter such was the actual impression entertained by the
people. It is stated by Sir Charles Lyell, in his "Elements," that he
was informed by Mr Cruickshanks, an English botanist who
resided in Chili at the time, "that it was the general belief of the
fishermen and inhabitants, *not* that the land had risen, but that
the ocean had permanently retreated." But if it had retreated from
the Chilian shore, how could it have risen on the Indian one? In
like manner the sea appears to be receding from the north-eastern
shores of Sweden at the rate of nearly four vertical feet in the
century; while it seems to be advancing on the western coasts of
Greenland at apparently a rate more considerable, though there
the ratio of its rise has not been marked with equal care. It seems
to be rising on even the Swedish province of Scania; while all the
time, however, the actual motion,—upwards in one region,
downwards in another,—is in the solid earth,—not in the unstable
water, which merely serves as a sort of hydrostatic *level*, to indicate
this fact of subsidence or elevation in the land. And of course all
the reasoning, founded on mere appearances, that would reverse
the process by assigning permanency to the level of the land, and
fluctuation to that of the sea, would lead to inevitable error.

Let us, for the illustration's sake, suppose that the British
islands had been the scene of the Deluge; and that it had been
occasioned by a gradual depression in the earth's surface of about
fifteen hundred miles in length, a thousand miles in breadth, five
thousand feet in depth in its centre, and which gradually trended
all around towards the sides. Such a depression would form a
scarce appreciable inequality on the surface of even a three-feet
globe; in a twelve-inch globe it might be represented by the
abrasion of a small patch of the varnish; nor would it have in
nature one sixth the depth, or one sixteenth the area, of the bed of
the Atlantic Ocean. Let us suppose further, that it had been

produced by an equable sinking of the surface, prolonged for forty days at the rate of one hundred and twenty-five feet per day,—a motion not equal to that of the minute-hand of a clock whose dial-plate measures two feet in diameter. Further, let us suppose that a thoroughly intelligent man,—let us say Dr Kitto himself,—secure from all personal danger in an ark perched on some such commanding eminence as Arthur's Seat, had been a witness of the catastrophe; and that, instead of having merely to reason respecting it, after the lapse of more than four thousand years, he had been enabled to bear testimony regarding it from the evidence of his senses. In the first place, let me remark that the sinking or downward motion of the earth's crust would be altogether inappreciable by sense; in the next, that the depression, even when it had reached its acme, would in no sensible degree affect the contour of surrounding objects. Even at the end of the forty days, when the five thousand feet of depression had been reached, the gradient of declination across the sunken area would not exceed *ten* feet per mile, and across the larger diameter would amount to but *six feet eight inches* per mile. Of course, at the end of the twentieth day the gradients would be represented by but one-half these sums, and would be altogether inappreciable in the landscape; the hills would seem quite as high as before, and the valleys not more profound. The only sensible sign felt or visible of what was taking place would be simply a persistent rising of the sea at somewhat less than twice its rate of flow during stream tides. Ocean, as if forgetful of its ancient bounds, would continue to encroach upon the land. On the second day the greater part of what is now the site of Edinburgh would be covered; on the seventh day the tide would have reached the vessel perched on the top of the hill now known as Arthur's Seat; on the sixteenth day the highest peak of the Pentlands would have disappeared; and in nine days more, the distant summit of Ben Lomond. From the roof of the slowly drifting ark nothing would then have appeared save a shoreless ocean. But it would have taken yet other eleven days ere the proud crest of Ben Nevis, the highest land in the British islands, would have been submerged; and the eve of the fortieth day would have seen it covered by little more than five hundred feet of water. An actual witness, in such circumstances, however intelligent, could have but testified to the persistent rise of the sea, accompanied mayhap by rain and tempest; he could but tell how that for many days together it had been flood without ebb, as if the fountains of the great deep had been broken up; and that at length he was encompassed by what seemed a shoreless ocean. But he would certainly depart perilously from his position as a witness-bearer were he to argue that when his ark had begun to float on a hill eight hundred feet in height, all hills upon the surface of the globe of a corresponding altitude must have been also covered; or that, from what was in reality but a local depression, a universal deluge might be legitimately inferred. His error would be of the same nature (though of course immensely greater) as that of the native of Chili who held, that because the ocean had retreated from the coasts of his own country, it had of necessity also retreated from the delta of the Indus; or as that of the inhabitant of Cutch, who held, that as the sea had risen high over his native districts, it had also of necessity overflowed the coasts of Chili and Aracan.

Dr Kitto brings forward but one other objection to a Flood only partial, and that the one virtually disposed of by Bishop Stillingfleet in the terminal half of a short sentence. The Bishop "despaired," as he well might, "of ever seeing it proved that the whole earth had been peopled before the Deluge." "It has been much urged of late," says Dr Kitto, "that the Deluge was not universal, but was confined to a particular region, which man inhabited. It may be freely admitted that, seeing the object of the Flood was to drown mankind, there was no need that it should extend beyond the region of man's habitation. But this theory necessarily assigns to the world before the Flood a lower population, and a more limited extension of it, than we are prepared to concede." He then goes on to argue that, as the species increased very rapidly immediately after the Deluge, it must have increased in a ratio at least equally rapid before that catastrophe took place. But how gratuitous the assumption! It would be quite as safe to infer, that as the human race multiplied greatly in Ireland during the first half of the present century, it must have also multiplied greatly in Italy, a much finer country, during the first half of the fifth century, or in the wealthier portions of Kurdistan during the first half of the thirteenth. Ere applying, however, the Irish ratio of increase to either the Italy of thirteen hundred years ago, or to the Kurdistan of five hundred years ago, it would surely be necessary to take into account the important fact, that these were the ages of Zingis Khan and of Attila; of Zingis Khan, who, on possessing himself of the three capitals of the one country, coolly butchered four millions three hundred and forty-seven thousand persons, their inhabitants; and of that Attila, "the scourge of God," who used to say, more especially in reference to the other country, that "wherever his horse-hoofs had once trod, the grass never afterwards grew," and before whose ravages the human race seemed melting away. The terms in which the great wickedness of the antediluvians is described indicate a period of violence and outrage;—the age which preceded the Flood was an age of "giants" and of "mighty men," and of "men of renown,"—forgotten Attilas, Alarics, and Zingis Khans, may-hap,—"giants of mighty bone and bold emprize," who became famous for their "infinite manslaughter," and the thousands whom they destroyed. Such is decidedly the view which the brief Scriptural description suggested to the poets; and certainly, when a question comes to be one of guesswork, no other class of persons guess half so sagaciously as they. It has not unfrequently occurred to me,—and in a question of this kind one suggestion may be quite as admissible as another,—that the Deluge may have been more a visitation of mercy to the race than of judgment. Even in our own times, as happened in New Zealand during the present century, and in Tahiti about the close of the last, tribes restricted to one tract of country, when seized by the madness of conquest, have narrowly escaped extermination. We know that in some instances better have been destroyed by worse races,—that the more refined have at times yielded to the more barbarous,—yielded so entirely, that all that survived of vast populations and a comparatively high civilization have been broken temples and great burial mounds locked up in the solitudes of deep forests; and further, that whole peoples, exhausted by their vices, have sunk into such a state of depression and decline, that, unable any longer to supply the inevitable waste of nature, they have dropt into extinction. And such may have been the condition of the human race during that period of portentous evil and violence which preceded the Deluge. We know that the good came at length to be restricted to a single family; and even the evil, instead of being numbered, as now, by hundreds of millions, may have been comprised in a few thousands, or at most a few hundred thousands, that were becoming fewer every year, from the indulgence of fierce and evil passions, in a time of outrage and violence. The Creator of the race may have dealt with it on this occasion of judgment, as a florist does with some decaying plant, which he cuts down to the ground in order to secure a fresh shoot from the root. At all events, the *proof* of an antediluvian population at once enormously great and very largely spread must rest with those who hold, with Dr Kitto, that its numbers and extent were such as to militate against the probability of a deluge merely partial; and any such proof we may, with the good old Bishop of Worcester, well "despair of ever seeing" produced. Even admitting, however, for the argument's sake, that the inhabitants of the Old World may have been as numerous as those of China are now,—a number estimated by the recent authorities at more than three hundred and fifty millions,—and the admission is certainly greatly larger than there is argument enough on the other side to extort,—a comparatively partial deluge would have been sufficient to secure their destruction. In short, it may be fairly concluded, that if there be a show of reason against the theory of a flood merely local, it has not yet been exhibited. Even Dr Kitto, with all his ingenuity and learning, has failed to array against it arguments of any real weight or cogency; and in my next address I may be perhaps able to show you that the objections which, on the other hand, bear against the antagonist hypothesis, are at once solid and numerous. I may be mistaken in my estimate; but for some years past I have regarded them as altogether insurmountable.

1. Berosus, Hieronymus, Mnaseas, Nicolaus, Manetho, Mochus and Hestæus.

2. See Cory's "Ancient Fragments."

3. As was common in Bible illustrations published in our own country a century and a half ago, the old Greek artist has introduced into his medal two points of time. Two of the figures represent *Noe* and his wife quitting the ark; while the other two exhibit them as seated within it. An English print of the death of Abel, now before me, which dates a little after the times of the Revolution, shows, on the same principle, the two brothers, represented by four figures,—two of these quietly offering up their respective sacrifices in the background, and the other two grappling in deadly warfare in front.

4. "In preparing the 'Horæ Biblicæ Quotidianæ,' he [Dr Chalmers] had beside him, for use and reference, the Concordance, the Pictorial Bible, Poole's Synopsis, Henry's Commentary, and Robertson's Researches in Palestine. These constituted what he called his Biblical Library. 'There,' said he to a friend, pointing, as he spoke, to the above-named volumes as they lay together on his library table, with a volume of the 'Quotidianæ,' in which he had just been writing, lying open beside them,—'these are the books I use: all that is Biblical is there.'"—*Dr Hanna's Preface to "Daily Scripture Readings"*.

5. The raven is said to live for more than a hundred years. I am, however, not prepared to say that it was the same pair of birds that used year after year to build on the same rock shelf among the precipices of Navity, from the times of my great grandfather's boyhood to those of my own.

LECTURE EIGHTH.

THE NOACHIAN DELUGE.

PART II.

A century has not yet gone by since all the organic remains on which the science of Palæontology is now founded were regarded as the wrecks of a universal deluge, and held good in evidence that the waters had prevailed in every known country, and risen over the highest hills. Intelligent observers were not wanting at even an earlier time who maintained that a temporary flood could not have occasioned phenomena so extraordinary. Such was the view taken by several Italian naturalists of the seventeenth century, and in Britain by the distinguished mathematician Hooke, the contemporary, and in some matters rival, of Newton. But the conclusions of these observers, now so generally adopted, were regarded both in Popish and Protestant countries as but little friendly to Revelation; and so strong was the opposite opinion, and so generally were petrifactions regarded as so many proofs of a universal deluge, that Voltaire felt himself constrained, first in his Dissertation drawn up for the Academy at Bologna, and next in his article on shells in the Philosophical Dictionary, to take up the question as charged with one of the evidences of that Revelation which it was the great design of his life to subvert. And with an unfairness too characteristic of his sparkling but unsolid writings, we find him arguing, that all fossil-shells were either those of fresh-water lakes and rivers evaporated during dry seasons, or of land-snails developed in unusual abundance during wet ones; or that they were shells which had been dropped from the hats of pilgrims on their way from the Holy Land to their homes; or that they were shells that had gone astray from cabinets and museums; or, finally, that they were not shells at all, but mere shell-like forms, produced by some occult process of nature in the bowels of the earth. In fine, in order to destroy the credibility of the Noachian Deluge, the brilliant Frenchman exhausted every expedient in his attempts to neutralise that Palæontologic evidence on which geologists now found some of their most legitimate conclusions. But he only succeeded, instead, in producing compositions of which every sentence contains either an absurdity or an untruth, and in raising a re-action against the special school of infidelity which he had founded, that at length bore it down. He wrote in the middle of the Paris basin, with its multitude of fossil-shells and bones; and, when penning his article for the Encyclopædia, he had, he tells us, a boxful of the shell-charged soil of the Faluns of Touraine actually before him; but the Deluge had to be put down, whatever the nature or bearing of the facts; and so he could find in either no evidence of a time when the sea had covered the land. He found instead, only "some mussels, because there were ponds in the neighbourhood." As for "the spiral petrifactions termed *cornu ammonis*," of which the Jurassic Alps are full, they were not nautili, he said; they could be nothing else than reptiles; seeing that reptiles take almost always the form of a spiral when not in motion; and it was surely more likely, that when petrified they should still retain the spiral disposition, than that "the Indian Ocean should have long ago overflowed the mountains of Europe." Were there not, however, real shells of the Syrian type in France and Italy? Perhaps so. But ought "we not to recollect," he asked, "the numberless bands of pilgrims who carried their money to the Holy Land, and brought back shells? or was it preferable to think that the sea of Joppa and Sidon had covered Burgundy and Milanais?" As for the seeming shells of the less superficial deposits, "are we sure," he inquired, "that the soil of the earth cannot produce fossils?" Agate in some specimens contains its apparent sprigs of moss, which, we know, never existed as the vegetable they resemble; and why should not the earth have, in like manner, produced its apparent shells? Or are not many of these shells mere lake or river petrifactions?—one never sees among them "true marine substances"!! "If there *were* any, why have we never seen bones of sea-dogs, sharks, and whales?"!!! And thus he ran on, in the belief apparently that he had to deal with but an ignorant priesthood, too little acquainted with the facts to make out a case against him in behalf of the Mosaic narrative, and whom at least, should argument fail him, he could vanquish with a joke.

There was, however, a young German, who had not at the time quite made up his mind either for the French school or against it, who was no uninterested reader of Voltaire's disquisitions on fossil-shells. And this young man was destined to be in the coming age what the Frenchman had been in the closing one,—the leading mind of Europe. He, too, had been looking at fossils; and having no case to make out either for or against Moses, or any one else, he had received in a fair and candid spirit the evidence with which they were charged. And the gross dishonesty of Voltaire in the matter formed so decided a turning point with him, that from that time forward he employed his great influence in bearing down the French school of infidelity, as a school detestably false and hollow;—a warning, surely, to all, whether they stand up for Revelation or against it, of the danger of being, like the witty Frenchman, "wicked overmuch." "To us youths," says Goethe, in his Autobiography, "with our German love of truth and nature, the factious dishonesty of Voltaire, and the perversion of so many worthy subjects, became more and more annoying, and we daily strengthened ourselves in our aversion from him. He could never have done with degrading religion and the sacred books for the sake of injuring priestcraft, as he called it; and had thus produced in me many an unpleasing sensation. But when I now learned, that to weaken the tradition of a Deluge, he had denied all petrified shells, and only admitted them as *lusus naturæ*, he entirely lost my confidence; for my own eyes had on the Baschberg plainly enough shown me that I stood on the bottom of an old dried-up sea, among the *exuviæ* of its ancient inhabitants. These mountains had certainly been once covered with waves,—whether before or during the Deluge did not concern me: it was enough that the valley of the Rhine had been a monstrous lake,—a bay extending beyond the reach of eyesight: out of this I was *not* to be talked. I thought much more of advancing in the

knowledge of lands and mountains, let what would be the result."
I know not in the whole history of opinion a more instructive
passage than this. Little could Voltaire have known what he was in
reality doing, or how egregiously he was overreaching himself,
when, in labouring to bear down the evidence borne by fossils to
the ancient upheavals and cataclysms, he suffered himself to make
use of assertions and arguments so palpably unfair. And those who
employ, in their zeal against the geologists, what is still
exceedingly common,—the Voltairean style of argument,
—especially if they employ it in what they deem the behalf of
religion, might do well to inquire whether they are not in some
little danger of producing the Voltairean result.

No man acquainted with the general outlines of Palæontology,
or the true succession of the sedimentary formations, has been able
to believe, during the last half century, that any proof of a general
deluge can be derived from the *older* geologic systems,—Palæozoic,
Secondary, or Tertiary. It has been held, however, by
accomplished geologists, within even the last thirty years, that
such proof might be successfully sought for in what are known as
the superficial deposits. Such was the belief of Cuvier,—a man
who, even in geologic science, which was certainly not his peculiar
province, exerted a mighty influence over the thinking of other
men. "I agree with MM.Deluc and Dolomieu in thinking," we find
him saying, in his widely-famed "Theory of the Earth," "that if
anything in geology be established, it is, that the surface of our
globe has undergone a great and sudden revolution, the date of
which cannot be referred to a much earlier period than five or six
thousand years ago." But from the same celebrated work we learn
that Cuvier held that this sudden catastrophe,—occasioned, as he
supposed, by an elevation of the sea-bottom and a submergence of
the previously existing land,—had *not* been universal; seeing he
could entertain the belief that the three great races of the human
family,—Ethiopian, Mongolian, and Caucasian,—had all escaped
from it in several directions. In referring to the marked
peculiarities of the Mongolian race, so very distinct from the
Caucasian, he merely intimates, that he was "tempted to believe

their ancestors and ours had escaped the great catastrophe on different sides;" but in dwelling on the still more marked peculiarities of the negroes, we find him explicitly stating, that "all their characters clearly show that they had escaped from the overwhelming deluge at another point than the Caucasian and Altaic races; from which they had perhaps been separated," he adds, "for a long time previous to the occurrence of that event." For a season, geologists of high standing in our own country, such as Buckland and Conybeare, followed Cuvier so far as to hold, that the superficial deposits bore evidence everywhere to a great cataclysm, the last of the geologic catastrophes; and which might be identified, they believed, with the Noachian Deluge. Against this view one of the most distinguished of Scottish naturalists, Dr John Fleming, raised a vigorous protest as early as the year 1826, and conclusively showed that no temporary flood could have produced the existing appearances. And so thoroughly were his facts and reasonings confirmed by subsequent discovery, that the geologists of name who had acquiesced, wholly or in part, in the Cuvierian view, read in succession their recantations: Dr Buckland in especial, who had written most largely on the subject, and committed himself most thoroughly, did so a very few years after: nor does the hypothesis of Cuvier appear to have been since adopted by any writer of scientific reputation. Instead, therefore, of contending with arguments or inferences which there are now no parties in the field to maintain, I shall briefly refer to a few of the leading characteristics of those superficial deposits on which the abandoned conclusions were originally based, and show, in the passing, that they are not such as a temporary deluge could have produced.

The superficial deposits include what is known as the mammaliferous crag, the drift, the boulder and brick clays, the stratified sands and gravels, the travelled rocks, the ösars, and moraines of the *higher* latitudes. For it is a fact very significant in its bearings on the diluvial controversy, that it is in the higher latitudes in both hemispheres that these peculiar deposits are chiefly to be found. They have been traced in Patagonia in the one hemisphere, from the southern limits of the country to the forty-first degree of south latitude; and in Europe in the other, to the fortieth; and in America to even the thirty-eighth degree of north latitude. But in the great belt, nearly eighty degrees in breadth, which, encircling the globe from east to west, includes with the torrid the warmer portions of the temperate zones, they have scarce any existence at all, or exist at least in different forms and exceedingly reduced proportions. The superficial deposits, in their most characteristic conditions, are deposits of the colder portions of the globe, and in many parts indicate that there prevailed during their formation a much severer climate than now obtains in the regions in which they occur. The shells which they contain in Britain, for instance, though almost all of existing species, are many of them such as are not now to be found in the British seas, but in seas about ten degrees farther to the north; and there is evidence that the line of perpetual snow must have descended at the time to a lower level than that attained by our second-class hills, and that almost every Highland valley had its glacier. They represent, too, vast periods of time;—earlier periods, during which the land gradually sank, till only its higher eminences were uncovered, and great floats of icebergs went careering over its submerged plains and lower hills; and later periods, during which the land as gradually arose, after apparently many pauses and oscillations, until at length, when it had reached a level scarce eighty feet higher than that which it at present maintains, the climate softened, and the glaciers which had formed in the later times among its hills ultimately disappeared. Beds of sea-shells of the boreal type, that belong to those ice ages, may be still found occupying the places in which they had lived and died, many miles inland, and hundreds of feet over the sea-level. Boring shells, such as the pholodadidæ, may be detected far out of sight of the ocean, still occupying the cells which they had scooped out for themselves in hard limestone or yielding shale; and serpula and nuliporate encrustations may be seen still adhering to rocks raised to giddy elevations over the sea. The group of mammals, however, which lived during this period, and to whose abundant tusks and skeletons one of its older deposits (the mammaliferous crag) owes its name, was marked by so peculiar a character, that evidence of a universal deluge has been often sought for in their remains. The group,—that which immediately preceded the animals of our own times, and included not a few of the indigenous species which still inhabit our country,—was chiefly remarkable for containing many genera, all of whose existing species are exotic. It had its great elephant, its two species of rhinoceros, its hippopotamus, its hyæna, its tiger, and its monkey; and much ingenious calculation has been employed by writers such as Granville Penn, in attempting to show how these remains might have been transported from the intertropical regions during the Flood, not only to Britain, but even to the northern wastes of Siberia,—a voyage of from four to five thousand miles. There are instances on record in which the bodies of the drowned have been drifted from ninety to a hundred and fifty miles from the spot where they had been first submerged; but they have always been found, in these cases, in a condition of sad mutilation and decay; whereas the carcase of the ancient elephant which was discovered, a little ere the commencement of the present century, locked up in ice in Siberia, three thousand six hundred miles from where elephants now live, was in such a state of excellent keeping, that the bears and dogs fed upon its flesh. It seems a significant circumstance, too, that the remains of these fossil elephants, tigers, and hyænas, should be associated in even our own country with those of well-known northern species,—with the remains of the rein-deer, of the red-deer, of the Lithuanian auroch, of the European beaver, of the European wolf, of the wild cat, the fox, and the otter. Writers, however, such as Mr Penn got over both difficulties. He showed, for instance, how a ship had once run across the Atlantic under bare poles, during an almost continued hurricane, at the rate of two hundred and eighty-eight miles in the twenty-four hours,—nearly the rate at which the great American steamers cross the same ocean now; and why, he asked, might not the carcases of elephants have drifted northwards at an equal rate on the tides of the Deluge? And as for the mixed character of the group with which these remains are found associated, *that* was exactly what Mr Penn would have expected in the circumstances. It was the result of a tumultuary flood, which had brought together in our northern region the floating carcases of the animals of all climates, to sink in unwonted companionship, when putrefaction had done its work, into the same deposits. He had, however, unluckily overlooked the fact, that comparative anatomy is in reality a science; and further, that it is a science of which men such as Cuvier and Owen know a great deal more than the men who never studied it, however respectable. It is the recorded decision of these great anatomists,—a decision which has been many times tested and confirmed,—that the northern species of elephant, rhinoceros, tiger, and hyæna, were entirely different from the intertropical species; that they differed from them very considerably more than the ass differs from the horse, or the dog from the wolf; and that, while there is a preponderating amount of evidence to show that they were natives of the countries in which their remains are now found, there is not a shadow of evidence to show that they had ever lived, or *could* have lived, in an intertropical country. Of the northern elephant, it is positively known from the Siberian specimen, that it was covered, like many other subarctic animals, with long hair, and a thick crisp undergrowth of wool, about three inches in length,—certainly not an intertropical provision; and so entirely different was it in form from either of the existing species, African or Indian, that a child could be taught in a single lesson to distinguish it by the tusks alone. In fine, the assumption that challenges the remains of the old Pleistocene carnivora and pachydermata as those of intertropical species brought northwards by a universal deluge, is about as well based and sound as if it challenged the bones of foxes occasionally found in our woods for the remains of dogs of Aleppo or Askalon brought into Britain by the Crusaders, or as if it pronounced a dead ass to be one of the cavalry horses of the fatal charge of Balaklava, transported to England from the Crimea as a relic of the fight. The hypothesis confounds as a species the Rosinante of Quixote with the Dapple of Sancho Panza, and frames its argument on the mistake.

That this extinct group of animals inhabited for ages the countries in which their remains are now embedded, is rendered evident by their great numbers in some localities, and from their occurrence in various states of preservation, and in beds of various ages. The five hundred mammoths whose tusks and grinders were dragged up in thirteen years by the oyster dredgers of the Norfolk coast from a tract of submerged drift, could not all have been contemporary in a small corner of England, but must have represented several generations. And of course the two thousand grinders brought up from the exposed surface of the drift must have borne but a small proportion to the thousands still dispersed throughout the entire depth of the deposit. Any argument, however, founded on the mere numbers of these elephantine tusks and grinders, and which evaded the important question of species, might be eluded, however unfairly, by the assertors of a universal deluge. Floods certainly do at times accumulate, in great heaps, bodies of the same specific gravity; and why might not a universal flood have accumulated on this special tract of drift, the carcases of many elephants? But it will be found greatly more difficult to elude the ingenious argument on the general question of Professor Owen. Next, perhaps, to the extinct elephant, one of the most numerous animals of this ancient group was the great Irish elk, *Megaceros Hibernicus*, a creature that, measured to the top of its enormous antlers, stood ten feet four inches in height, and exceeded in bulk and size the largest horses. Like all other species of the deer family, the creature annually shed and renewed its horns; "and a male deer may be reckoned," says Professor Owen, "to have left about eight pairs of antlers, besides its bones, to testify its former existence upon the earth. But as the female has usually no antlers, our expectations might be limited to the discovery of four times as many pairs of antlers as skeletons in superficial deposits of the countries in which such deer have lived and died. The actual proportion of the fossil antlers of the great extinct species of British Pliocene deer (which antlers are proved by the form of their base to have been shed by the living animals)

Fig. 111.

MEGACEROS HIBERNICUS.
(*Irish Elk.*)

to the fossil bones of the same species, is somewhat greater than in the above calculation. Although, therefore, it may be contended that the swollen carcase of a drowned exotic deer might be borne along a diluvial wave to a considerable distance, and its bones ultimately deposited far from its native soil, *it is not credible that all the solid shed antlers of such species of deer could be carried by the same cause to the same distance*; or that any of them could be rolled for a short distance, with other heavy debris of a mighty torrent, without fracture and signs of friction. But the shed antlers of the large extinct species of deer found in this island and in Ireland have commonly their parts or branches entire as when they fell;

and the fractured specimens are generally found in caves, and *show marks of the teeth of the ossivorous hyænas* by which they had been gnawed; thus at the same time revealing the mode in which they were introduced into those caves, and *proving the contemporaneous existence in this island of both kinds of mammalia.*"

But the contents of the bone caves, consisting in large part of the extinct mammals, ought of themselves to be decisive in this question. As the opening of the Kirkdale cavern is only about four feet each way, a diluvial wave, charged with the wreck of the lower latitudes, could scarce have washed into such an orifice any considerable number of the intertropical animals. And yet there has been found in this cave,—with the teeth of a very young mammoth, of a very great tiger, of a tiger-like animal whose genus is extinct, of a rhinoceros, and of a hippopotamus,—the fragmentary remains of from two to three hundred hyænas. Further, even supposing, what is impossible, that a diluvial wave had swept them all from the tropics into the four-feet hole, on what principle is it to be explained that the bones thus washed into the cave should be all gnawed bones, even those of the hyænas themselves, whereas the bones of the same creatures found in the mammaliferous deposits of the country bear no marks of teeth? Mr Granville Penn, however, gets over the difficulty of the cave, which is hollowed, I may mention, in a limestone of the Oolitic series, inclosing the ammonite and belemnite, by asserting that its mammaliferous contents may be *somewhat older than itself!* The limestone existed, he holds, as but a mere unformed pulp at the time the intertropical animals came floating northwards: they sank into it; the gases evolved during putrefaction blew up the plastic lime above them into a great oblong bubble, somewhat as a glass-blower blows up a bottle; and hence the Kirkdale cavern, with its gnawed bones and its amazing number of teeth. And certainly a *geologic* argument of this ingenious character has one signal advantage,—it is in no danger whatever of being answered by the geologists. Mr Penn, in a second edition of his work, expressed some surprise that an Edinburgh Reviewer should have merely stated his *argument* without replying to it!!

But I need not dwell on the arguments for a universal deluge which have been derived from the superficial deposits. They all belong to an immature age of geologic science, and are of no value whatever. Let us pass rather to the consideration of the facts and arguments which militate against the universality of the catastrophe.

The form and dimensions of Noah's ark are definitely given in the sacred record. It seems to have been a great oblong box, somewhat like a wooden granary, three storeys high, and furnished with a roof apparently of the ordinary angular shape, but with a somewhat broader ridge than common; and it measured three hundred cubits in length, fifty cubits in breadth, and thirty cubits in height. A good deal of controversy has, however, arisen regarding the cubit employed; some holding, with Sir Walter Raleigh, and most of the older theologians, such as Shuckford and Hales, that the Noachian cubit was what is known as the common or natural cubit, "containing," says Sir Walter, "one foot and a half, or a length equal to that of the human fore-arm measured from the sharp of the elbow to the point of the middle finger;" others contending that it was the palm-cubit, "which taketh," adds my authority, "one handful more than the common;" yet others, the royal or Persian cubit of twenty-one inches; and so on; for there are, it seems, five several kinds of cubit to choose from, all differing each from the others. The controversy is one in which there is exceeding little footing for any party. I am inclined, however, to adopt, with Raleigh and Hales, the *natural* cubit, for the following reason. The given dimensions of the ark form the oldest example of measurement of which we have any record; and all, or almost all, the older and simpler standards of measure bear reference to portions of the human frame. There is the span, the palm, the hand-breadth, the thumb-breadth (or inch), the hair-breadth, and the *foot*. The simple fisherman on our coasts still measures off his fathoms by stretching out both his arms to the full; the village sempstress still tells off her cloth-breadths by finger-lengths and *nails*; the untaught tiller of the soil still estimates the area of his little field by *pacing* along its sides. Man's

first and most obvious expedient, when he sets himself to measure,
is to employ his own person as his standard; and the first or
common cubit was a measure of this natural description equal in
length to the extended fore-arm and hand. All the other cubits
were artificial compounds of after introduction; and so, in the
absence of direct evidence on the point, I accept the most natural
and oldest cubit as in all probability the one employed in the oldest
recorded piece of cubit measurement. And the ark, if measured by
the common or natural cubit, must have been a vessel four
hundred and fifty feet in length, seventy-five feet in breadth, and
forty-five feet in height. Dr Kitto, however, though we find him
remarking that in computations of Scripture measures the cubit
may be regarded as half a yard (Sir Walter's estimate), adopts, in
his own computation of the size of the ark, without assigning any
reason why, the palm-cubit, or cubit of twenty-one inches and
nearly nine lines (21.888 inches); and, waiving all controversy on
the question, let us, for the argument's sake, admit the larger
measure. Let us,—however much inclined to hold with Raleigh,
Shuckford, and Hales,—agree with Dr Kitto that the ark was five
hundred and forty-seven feet in length, by ninety-one feet in
breadth. Such dimensions, multiplied by three, the number of
storeys in the vessel, would give an area equal to about one
seventh that of the great Crystal Palace of 1851. Or, to take a more
definite illustration from the same vast building, the area of the
three floors of the ark, taken together, would fall short, by about
twenty-eight thousand square feet, of that of the northern gallery
of the Palace, which measured one thousand eight hundred and
forty-eight feet in length, by ninety-six feet in breadth. And thus,
yielding to our opponents their own large measurements, let us
now see whether the non-universality of the Deluge cannot be
fairly predicated from the dimensions of the ark.

I may first remark, however, that measures so definite as those
given by Moses (definite, of course, if we waive the doubt regarding
the cubit employed) were effectual in setting the arithmeticians to
work in all ages of the Church, in order to determine whether all
the animals in the world, by sevens and by pairs, with food

sufficient to serve them for a twelvemonth, could have been
accommodated in the given space. It was a sort of stock problem,
that required, it was thought, no very high attainments to solve.
Eighty years have not yet passed since kind old Samuel Johnson,
in writing to little Miss Thrale a nice little letter, recommending
her to be a good girl, and to mind her arithmetic, advised her to try
the ark problem. "If you can borrow 'Wilkins' Real Character,'"
we find him saying to the young lady, "a folio which perhaps the
booksellers can let you have, you will have a very curious
calculation, *which you are qualified to consider*, to show that Noah's
ark was capable of holding all the known animals of the world,
with provision for all the time in which the earth was under
water." Unluckily, however, though the dimensions of the ark
were known, the animals of the world were not; and so the
question, in at least one of its terms, had to be very frequently re-
stated. Let us take it as we find it presented (drawn, however, from
a much older source), in Sir Walter Raleigh's magnificent "History
of the World." "If in a ship of such greatness," says this
distinguished man, "we seek room for eighty-nine distinct species
of beasts, or, lest any should be omitted, for a hundred several
kinds, we shall easily find place both for them and for the birds,
which in bigness are no way answerable to them, and for meat to
sustain them all. For there are three sorts of beasts whose bodies
are of a quantity well known; the beef, the sheep, and the wolf; to
which the rest may be reduced by saying, according to Aristotle,
that one elephant is equal to four beeves, one lion to two wolves,
and so of the rest. Of beasts, some feed on vegetables, others on
flesh. There are one-and-thirty kinds of the greater sort feeding on
vegetables, of which number only three are clean according to the
law of Moses, whereof seven of a kind entered into the ark, namely,
three couples for breed, and one odd one for sacrifice; the other
eight-and-twenty kinds were taken by two of each kind; so that in
all there were in the ark one-and-twenty great beasts clean, and
six-and-fifty unclean; estimable for largeness as ninety-one beeves;
yet, for a supplement (lest, perhaps, any species be omitted), let
them be valued as an hundred and twenty beeves. Of the lesser

sort feeding on vegetables were in the ark six-and-twenty kinds, estimable, with good allowance for supply, as fourscore sheep. Of those which devour flesh were two-and-thirty kinds, answerable to three score and four wolves. All these two hundred and eighty beasts might be kept in one storey or room of the ark, in their several cabins; their meat in a second; the birds and their provision in a third, with space to spare for Noah and his family, and all their necessaries." Such was the calculation of the great voyager Raleigh,—a man who had a more practical acquaintance with *stowage* than perhaps any of the other writers who have speculated on the capabilities of the ark; and his estimate seems sober and judicious. It will be seen, however, that from the vast increase in our knowledge of the mammals which has taken place since the age in which the "History of the World" was written, the calculation which embraced all the eighty-nine known animals of that time would embrace those of but a single centre of creation now; and that the estimate of Sir Walter tells, in consequence, on the side, not of a universal, but of a partial deluge.

As man extended his acquaintance with the mammals, he found their number greatly increasing on his hands. Buffon, like Raleigh, though a professed naturalist, and a writer of admirable genius, had no very distinct notions of species. He was inclined to question whether even the ass might not be merely a degraded horse; and confounded many of the mammals of the New World with their representative cogeners in the Old. And yet, in summing up his history of the mammaliferous division, he could state, that though it included descriptions of "a hundred and thirty-four different species of creatures that suckled their young, many of which had not been observed or described before," it was necessarily incomplete, as there were still others to add to the list, for whose history there existed no materials. At the same time he remarked, however, that the "number of quadruped animals whose existence is certain and well established does not amount to more than two hundred on the surface of the known world." Yet here was the extreme estimate made by Raleigh, with what he deemed large allowance for the unknown animals, fairly doubled;

and under the hands of more discriminating naturalists, and in the inevitable course of discovery, the number has so enormously increased, that the "eighty-nine distinct species" known to the great voyager have been represented during the last thirty years by the one thousand mammals of Swainson's estimate, the one thousand one hundred and forty-nine mammals of Charles Bonaparte's estimate, the one thousand two hundred and thirty mammals of Winding's estimate, and the one thousand five hundred mammals of Oken's estimate. In the first edition of the admirable "Physical Atlas" of Johnston (published in 1848) there are one thousand six hundred and twenty-six different species of mammals enumerated; and in the second edition (published in 1856), one thousand six hundred and fifty-eight species. And to this very extraordinary advance on the eighty-nine mammals of Raleigh and the two hundred mammals of Buffon we must add the six thousand two hundred and sixty-six birds of Lesson, and the six hundred and fifty-seven reptiles of Charles Bonaparte; or at least,—subtracting the sea-snakes, and perhaps the turtles, as fitted to live outside the ark,—his six hundred and *forty-two* reptiles.[1]

Such is the number of the known vertebrates, exclusive of the fishes, with which in this question we have now to deal. Still, however, there are a few lingering theologians, some of them very intelligent men, who continue to regard the ark as quite big enough for them all. Dr Hamilton of Mobile, for instance, after fairly stating Swainson's estimate, namely, one thousand mammalia, six thousand birds, and one thousand five hundred reptiles and amphibiæ, goes on to say, that "it must not be forgotten, that of all these, the vastly greater proportion are small; and that numbers of them could be placed together in the same compartment of the ark." This, however, permit me to say with all respect, is not meeting the real difficulty. No doubt many of the birds are small,—many of the reptiles are small,—many even of the mammals are small,—many small animals were known in the days of Raleigh, and a much greater number of small animals are known now; but the question proper to the case seems to be, What

proportions do both the large and the small animals now known
bear to the large and small animals known in the days of Raleigh
or Buffon; and how much additional accommodation-room would
they require during their supposed voyage of a twelvemonth?
There are two different ways in which the list of the known
animals has been increased, especially of the known mammals.
They have been increased in a certain appreciable proportion by
discovery; and as discovery has been made chiefly in islands,—for
the great continents had been previously known,—and as the
mammals of islands, as has been well remarked by Cuvier, are
usually small, of this appreciable proportion the bulk is
comparatively not great. The great kangaroo (*Macropus
giganteus*), though the inhabitant of an island which ranks among
the continents, would not much exceed in bulk, tried by Raleigh's
quaint scale of measurement, a sheep and a half, or at most two
sheep; and yet I know not that discovery in the islands has added a
larger animal to the previously known ones than the great
kangaroo. Mr Waterhouse, when he published, in 1841, his
"History of the Marsupialia," reckoned up one hundred and five
distinct species of pouched animals; and eighteen species
more,—in all one hundred and twenty-three,—have been since
added to the order. With the exception of an opossum or two, all
these marsupiata may be regarded as discoveries made since the
time of Buffon; most of them, as I have said, are small. And such,
generally, has been the nature of the revelations made during the
last seventy years by positive *discovery*. It is not, however, by
discovery, but by scientific scrutiny into the true nature and
distinctions of species, that the recent enormous increase in the
number of the known mammals has mainly taken place. And in
these cases it will generally be found that the new species, which
had been previously confounded with some old ones, so nearly
resembles the latter in bulk as well as aspect, as to justify in some
degree the mistake. Let us take two of the greatest animals as
examples,—the elephant and the rhinoceros. Buffon confounded
the African with the Asiatic elephant. We now know that they
represent two well-marked species, *Elephas Africanus* and *Elephas*

Indicus; and that an ark which contained the ancestors of all the existing animals would require to have its *two* pair of elephants, not the one pair only which would have been deemed sufficient eighty years ago. Again, with respect to the rhinoceros, Buffon was acquainted with the single-horned animal, and had *heard* of the animal with two horns; and so, though by no means certain that the "*variety* was constant," he yet held that "two distinct species might possibly be established." But we now know that there are six species of rhinoceros (seven, according to the "Physical Atlas"),—*Rh. Indicus, Rh. Javanus, Rh. Sumatrensis, Rh. Africanus, Rh. simus,* and *Rh. ketloa*; and that, instead of *possibly* four, at least twelve, or more probably fourteen, animals of the genus would require, on the hypothesis of a universal deluge, to have been accommodated in the ark. Buffon even held that the bison of America might be identical with not simply the auroch of Europe, which it closely resembles, but with even the European ox, which it does *not* resemble. But it is now known, that while the European aurochs are provided by nature with but fourteen pairs of ribs, the American bison is furnished with fifteen. Of each of the ruminants that divide the hoof there were *seven* introduced into the ark; and it may be well to mark how, even during the last few years, our acquaintance with this order of animals has been growing, and how greatly the known species, in their relation to human knowledge, have in consequence increased. In 1848 (in the first edition of the "Physical Atlas") Mr Waterhouse estimated the oxen at thirteen species; in 1856 (in the second edition) he estimates them at twenty. In 1848 he estimated the sheep at twenty-one species; in 1856 he estimates them at twenty-seven. In 1848 he estimated the goats at fourteen species; in 1856 he estimates them at twenty. In 1848 he estimated the deer at thirty-eight species; in 1856 he estimates them at fifty-one. In short, if, excluding the lamas and the musks as doubtfully *clean*, tried by the Mosaic test, we but add to the sheep, goats, deer, and cattle, the forty-eight species of unequivocally *clean* antelopes, and multiply the whole by seven, we shall have as the result a sum total of one thousand one hundred and sixty-two individuals,—a number more than four times greater than that for which Raleigh made provision in the ark, and considerably more than twice greater than that provided for by the students of Buffon. Such is the nature and amount of the increase which has taken place during the last half-century in the mammaliferous fauna. In so great a majority of cases has it increased its *bulk* in the ratio in which it has increased its numbers, that if one ark was not deemed more than sufficient to accommodate the animal world known to the French naturalist of eighty years ago, it would require at least from five to six arks to accommodate the animal world known in the present day.

Even in the days of Buffon, however, and at a still earlier period, the ark, regarded as a natural means of preservation from death by *drowning*, was usually coupled, in the case of at least the carnivorous animals, with certain miraculous provisions against death by *starving*. It seems to have been generally taken for granted, that the flesh-eating animals, when introduced to the shelter of the ark, entirely changed the nature indicated by their form of teeth, the character of their stomachs, and the shortness of their bowels, and fed, for the time they remained in it, exclusively on vegetable substances, which, in ordinary circumstances, their lacteals could not have converted into chyle. Certain figurative expressions in Scripture taken literally, which refer to a class of wild animals whose real destiny is rather, it would seem, to be extirpated than to be changed, coupled with the belief, now no longer tenable, that there was a time, ere man had sinned, when there was no death among the inferior creatures, and of course no eaters of flesh, rendered the belief easy of reception; but it involved a miracle nowhere recorded; and the burden of the proof that such a miracle actually took place in the circumstances lies of necessity on the assertors of a universal deluge. Further, of even the creatures that live on vegetables, many are restricted in their food to single plants, which are themselves restricted to limited localities and remote regions of the globe. Dr Hamilton has not referred, in his list of animals, to the insects,—a class which, though they were estimated in 1842 to consist of no fewer than five hundred and fifty thousand species, might yet be accommodated in a comparatively limited space. But how extraordinary an amount of miracle would it not require to bring them all together into any one centre, or to preserve them there! Many of them, like the myriapoda and the thysanura, have no wings, and but feeble locomotive powers; many of them, such as the ephemera and the male ants, live after they have got their wings only a few hours, or at most a few days; and there are myriads of them that can live upon but single plants that grow in very limited botanic centres. Even supposing them all brought into the ark by miracle as eggs, what multitudes of them would not, without the exertion of further miracle, require to be sent back to their proper habitats as wingless grubs, or as insects restricted by nature to a few days of life! Or, supposing the eggs all left in their several localities to lie under water for a twelvemonth amid mud and debris,—though certain of the hardier kinds might survive such treatment, by miracle alone could the preponderating majority of the class be preserved. And be it remembered, that the expedient of having recourse to supposititious miracle in order to get over a difficulty insurmountable on every natural principle, is not of the nature of argument, but simply an evidence of the want of it. Argument is at an end when supposititious miracle is introduced.

But the very inadequate size of the ark, though a conclusive proof that all, or nearly all, the progenitors of our existing animals could not have harboured within it from any general cataclysm, does not furnish a stronger argument against the possibility of any such assemblage, than the peculiar manner in which we now find these animals distributed over the earth's surface. Linnæus held, early in the last century, that all creatures which now inhabit the globe had proceeded originally from some such common centre as the ark might have furnished; but no zoologist acquainted with the distribution of species can acquiesce in any such conclusion now. We now know that every great continent has its own peculiar fauna; that the original centres of distribution must have been, not one, but many; further, that the areas or circles around these centres must have been occupied by their pristine animals in ages long anterior to that of the Noachian Deluge; nay, that in even the latter geologic ages they were preceded in them by animals of the same general type. There are fourteen such areas or provinces enumerated by the later naturalists. It may be well, however, instead of running any risk of losing ourselves amid the less nicely defined provinces of the Old World, to draw our illustrations from two and a half provinces of later discovery, whose limits have been rigidly fixed by nature. "The great continents," says Cuvier, "contain species peculiar to each; insomuch that whenever large countries of this description have been discovered, which their situation had kept isolated from the rest of the world, the class of quadrupeds which they contained has been found extremely different from any that had existed elsewhere. Thus, when the Spaniards first penetrated into South America, they did not find a single species of quadruped the same as any of Europe, Asia, or Africa. The puma, the jaguar, the tapir, the cabiai, the lama, the vicuna, the sloths, the armadilloes, the opossums, and the whole tribe of sapajous, were to them entirely new animals, of which they had no idea. Similar circumstances have occurred in our own time, when the coasts of New Holland and the adjacent islands were first explored. The various species of kangaroo, phascolomys, dasyurus, and perameles, the flying phalangers, the ornithorynchi, and echidnæ, have astonished naturalists by the strangeness of their conformations, which presented proportions contrary to all former rules, and were incapable of being arranged under any of the systems then in use." New Zealand, though singularly devoid of indigenous mammals and reptiles,—for the only native mammal seems to be a peculiar species of rat, and the only native reptile a small, harmless lizard,—has a scarce less remarkable fauna than either of these great continents. It consists almost exclusively of birds, some of them so ill provided with wings, that, like the *wika* of the natives, they can only run along the ground. And it is a most significant fact, that both in the two great continents and the New Zealand islands there existed, in the later geologic ages, extinct faunas that bore the peculiar generic characters by which their recent ones are still distinguished. The sloths and armadilloes of

Fig. 112.

MYLODON ROBUSTUS.

Fig. 113.

GLYTODON CLAVIPES.

South America had their gigantic predecessors in the enormous megatherium and mylodon, and the strongly armed glyptodon; the kangaroos and wombats of Australia had their extinct predecessors in a kangaroo nearly twice the size of the largest living species, and in so huge a wombat, that its bones have been mistaken for those of the hippopotamus; and the ornithic inhabitants of New Zealand had their predecessors in monstrous birds, such as the dinornis, the aptornis, and the palapteryx,—wingless creatures like the ostrich, that stood from six to twelve feet in height. In these several regions two *generations* of species of the genera peculiar to them have existed,—the recent generation, by whose descendants they are still inhabited, and the extinct gigantic generation, whose remains we find locked up in their soils and caves. But how are such facts reconcileable with the hypothesis of a universal deluge?

The Deluge was an event of the existing creation. Had it been universal, it would either have broken up all the diverse centres, and substituted one great general centre instead,—that in which the ark rested; or else, at an enormous expense of miracle, all the animals preserved by *natural* means by Noah would have had to be returned by *supernatural* means to the regions whence by means *equally supernatural* they had been brought. The sloths and armadilloes,—little fitted by nature for long journeys,—would have required to be ferried across the Atlantic to the regions in which the remains of the megatherium and glyptodon lie entombed; the kangaroo and wombat, to the insulated continent that contains the bones of the extinct macropus and phascolomys; and the New Zealand birds, including its heavy flying quails and its wingless wood-hen, to those remote islands of the Pacific in which the skeletons of *Palapteryx ingens* and *Dinornus giganteus* lie entombed. Nor will it avail aught to urge, with certain assertors of a universal deluge, that during the cataclysm, sea and land changed their places, and that what is now land had formed the bottom of the antediluvian ocean, and, *vice versa*, what is now sea had been the land on which the first human inhabitants of the earth increased and multiplied. No geologist who knows how very various the ages of the several table-lands and mountain-chains in reality are could acquiesce in such an hypothesis; our own Scottish shores,—if to the term of the existing we add that of the ancient coast-line,—must have formed the limits of the land from a time vastly more remote than the age of the Deluge. But even supposing, for the argument's sake, the hypothesis recognised as admissible, what, in the circumstances of the case, would be gained by the admission? A continuous tract of land would have stretched,—when all the oceans were continents and all the continents oceans,—between the South American and the Asiatic coasts. And it is just possible that, during the hundred and twenty years in which the ark was in building, a pair of sloths might have crept by inches across this continuous tract, from where the skeletons of the great megatheria are buried, to where the great vessel stood. But after the flood had subsided, and the change in sea and land had taken place, there would remain for them no longer a roadway; and so, though their journey outwards might, in all save the impulse which led to it, have been altogether a natural one, their voyage homewards could not be other than miraculous. Nor would the exertion of miracle have had to be restricted to the transport of the *remoter* travellers. How, we may well ask, had the Flood been universal, could even such islands as Great Britain and Ireland have ever been replenished with many of their original inhabitants? Even supposing it possible that animals such as the red deer and the native ox *might* have swam across the Straits of Dover or the Irish Channel, to graze anew over deposits in which the bones and horns of their remote ancestors had been entombed long ages before, the feat would have been surely far beyond the power of such feeble natives of the soil as the mole, the hedge-hog, the shrew, the dormouse, and the field-vole.

Dr Pye Smith, in dealing with this subject, has emphatically said, that "all land animals having their geographical regions, to which their constitutional natures are congenial,—many of them being unable to live in any other situation,—we cannot represent to ourselves the idea of their being brought into one small spot from the polar regions, the torrid zone, and all the other climates of Asia, Africa, Europe, and America, Australia, and the thousands of islands,—their preservation and provision, and the final disposal of them,—without bringing up the idea of miracles more stupendous than any that are recorded in Scripture. The great decisive miracle of Christianity," he adds,—"the resurrection of the Lord Jesus,—sinks down before it." And let us remember that the preservation and re-distribution of the land-animals would demand but a portion of the amount of miracle absolutely necessary for the preservation, in the circumstances, of the entire fauna of the globe. The freshwater fishes, molluscs, crustacea, and zoophytes, could be kept alive in a universal deluge only by miraculous means. It has been urged that, though the living individuals were to perish, their spawn might be preserved by natural means. It must be remembered, however, that even of some fishes whose proper habitat is the sea, such as the salmon, it is essential for the maintenance of the species that the spawn should be deposited in fresh water, nay, in running fresh water; for in still water, however pure, the eggs in a few weeks addle and die. The eggs of the common trout also require to be deposited in running fresh water; while other fresh-water fishes, such as the tench and carp, are reared most successfully in still reedy ponds. The fresh-water fishes spawn, too, at very different seasons, and the young remain for very different periods in the egg. The perch and grayling spawn in the end of April or the beginning of May; the tench and roach about the middle of June; the common trout and powan in October and November. And while some fishes, such as the salmon, remain from ninety to a hundred days in the egg, others, such as the trout, are extruded in five weeks. Without special miracle the spawn of all the fresh-water fishes could not be in existence *as such* at one and the same time; without special miracle it could not maintain its vitality in a universal deluge; and without special miracle, even did it maintain its vitality, it could not remain in the egg-state throughout an entire twelvemonth, but would be developed into fishes of the several species to which it belonged at very different periods. Farther, in a universal deluge, without special miracle vast numbers of even the salt-water animals could not fail to be extirpated; in particular, almost all the molluscs of the littoral and laminarian zones. Nor would the vegetable kingdom fare greatly better than the animal one. Of the one hundred thousand species of known plants, few indeed would survive submersion for a twelvemonth; nor would the seeds of most of the others fare better than the plants themselves. There are certain hardy seeds that in favourable circumstances maintain their vitality for ages; and there are others, strongly encased in water-tight shells or skins, that have floated across oceans to germinate in distant islands; but such, as every florist knows, is not the general character of seeds; and not until after many unsuccessful attempts, and many expedients had been resorted to, have the more delicate kinds been brought uninjured, even on shipboard, from distant countries to our own. It is not too much to hold that, without special miracle, at least three-fourths of the terrestrial vegetation of the globe would have perished in a universal deluge that covered over the dry land for a year. Assuredly the various vegetable centres or regions,—estimated by Schouw at twenty-five,—bear witness to no such catastrophe. Still distinct and unbroken, as of old, either no effacing flood has passed over them, or they were shielded from its effects at an expense of miracle many times more considerable than that at which the Jews were brought out of Egypt and preserved amid the nations, or Christianity itself was ultimately established.[2]

There is, however, a class of learned and thoroughly respectable theologians who seem disposed to accept rather of any amount of unrecorded miracle, than to admit of a merely partial deluge, co-extensive with but the human family. "Were the difficulty attending this subject tenfold greater, and seemingly beyond all satisfactory explanation," says Dr William Hamilton, "if I yet find it recorded in the Book of Revelation, that in the Deluge *'every living thing in which is the breath of life perished, and Noah only remained alive, and they which were with him in the ark,'* I could still believe it implicitly, satisfied that the difficulty of explanation springs solely from the imperfection of human knowledge, and not from any limitation in the power or the wisdom of God, nor yet from any lack of trustworthiness in the document given us in a revelation from God,—a document given to men by the hands of Moses, the learned, accomplished, and eminently devout Jewish legislator." Here again, however, Dr Hamilton seems to have mistaken the question actually at issue. The true question is, not whether or no Moses is to be believed in the matter, but whether or no we in reality understand Moses. The question is, whether we are to regard the passages in which he describes the Flood as universal, as belonging to the very numerous metonymic texts of Scripture in which a part—sometimes a not very large part—is described as the whole, or to regard them as strictly and severely literal. Or, in other words, whether we are, with learned and solid divines of the olden time, such as Poole and Stillingfleet, and with many ingenious and accomplished divines of the passing age, such as the late Dr Pye Smith and the Rev. Professor Hitchcock, to regard these passages as merely metonymic; or, with Drs Hamilton and Kitto, to regard them as strictly literal, and to call up in support of the literal reading an amount of supposititious miracle, compared with which all the recorded miracles of the Old and New Testaments sink into insignificance. The controversy does not lie between Moses and the naturalists, but between the *readings* of theologians such as Matthew Poole and Stillingfleet on the one hand, and the *readings* of theologians such as Drs Hamilton and Kitto on the other. And finding all natural science arrayed against the conclusions of the one class, and in favour of those of the other, and believing further, that there has been always such a marked economy shown in the exercise of miraculous powers, that there has never been more of miracle employed in any one of the dispensations than was needed,[3] I must hold that the theologians who believe that the Deluge was but coextensive with the moral purpose which it served are more in the right, and may be more safely followed, than the theologians who hold that it extended greatly farther than was necessary. It is not with Moses or the truth of revelation that our controversy lies, but with the opponents of Stillingfleet and of Poole.

To only one of the other arguments employed in this controversy need I at all refer. The cones of volcanic craters are formed of loose incoherent scoriæ and ashes; and, when exposed, as in the case of submarine volcanoes, such as Graham's Island and the islands of Nyoe and Sabrina, to the denuding force of waves and currents, they have in a few weeks, or at most a few months, been washed completely away. And yet in various parts of the world, such as Auvergne in central France, and along the flanks of Ætna, there are cones of long extinct or long slumbering volcanoes, which, though of at least triple the antiquity of the Noachian Deluge, and though composed of the ordinary incoherent materials, exhibit no marks of denudation. According to the calculations of Sir Charles Lyell, no devastating flood could have passed over the forest zone of Ætna, during the last twelve thousand years,—for such is the antiquity which he assigns to its older lateral cones, that retain in integrity their original shape; and the volcanic cones of Auvergne, which inclose in their ashes the remains of extinct animals, and present an outline as perfect as those of Ætna, are deemed older still. Graham Island arose out of the sea early in July 1831; in the beginning of the following August it had attained to a circumference of three miles, and to a height of two hundred feet; and yet in less than three months from that time the waves had washed its immense mass down to the sea-level; and in a few weeks more it existed but as a dangerous shoal. And such inevitably would have been the fate of the equally incoherent cone-like craters of Ætna and Auvergne during the seven and a half months that intervened between the breaking up of the fountains of the great deep and the re-appearance of the mountain-tops, had they been included within the area of the Deluge. It is estimated that even the newer Auvergne lavas are as old as the times of the Miocene. It is at least a demonstrable fact, that the slow action of streams had hollowed them in several places into deep chasms nearly two thousand years ago; for the remains of Roman works of about that age survive, to show that they had then, as now, to be spanned over by bridges, and that baths had been erected in their denuded recesses; and yet the craters out of which these lavas had flowed retain well nigh all their original sharpness of outline. No wave ever dashed against their symmetrically sloping sides. Now, I have in no instance seen the argument derivable from this class of facts fairly met. The supposed mistake of the Canonico Recupero, or rather of Brydone, who argued that the "lowest of a series of seven distinct lavas of Ætna, most of them covered by thick intervening beds of rich earth, must have been fourteen thousand years old," has been often referred to in the controversy. Brydone or the Canon mistook, it has been said, beds of brown ashes, each of which might have been deposited during a single shower, for beds of rich earth, each of which would have taken centuries to form. The oldest of the series of lava-beds, therefore, instead of being fourteen thousand, might be scarce fourteen hundred years old. And if Brydone or the Canon were thus mistaken in their calculations, why may not the modern geologists be also mistaken in theirs? Now, altogether waiving the question as to whether the ingenious traveller of eighty-six years ago was or was not mistaken in his estimate,—for to those acquainted with geologic fact in general, or more particularly with the elaborate descriptions of Ætna given during the last thirty years by Elie de Beaumont, Hoffmann, and Sir Charles Lyell, the facts of Brydone, in their bearing on either the age of the earth or the age of the mountain, can well be spared,—waiving, I say, the question whether the traveller was in reality in mistake, I must be permitted to remark, that the concurrent testimony of geologists cannot in fairness be placed on the same level as the testimony of a man who, though accomplished and intelligent, was not only no geologist, but who observed and described ere geology had any existence as a science. Further, I must be allowed to add, that geology *is* now a science; and that individuals unacquainted with it in its character as such place themselves in positions greatly more perilous than they seem to think, when they enter on the field of argument with men who for many years have made it a subject of special study. It is not by "bidding down" the age of the extinct or quiescent volcanoes by a species of blind haggling, or by presuming mistake in the calculations regarding them simply because mistakes are possible and have sometimes been made, that that portion of the cumulative evidence against a universal deluge which they furnish is to be neutralized or set aside. The argument on the general question *is* a cumulative one; and while many of its component portions are of themselves so conclusive, that only supposititious miracle, and not presentable argument, can be arrayed against them, its aggregate force seems wholly irresistible. In passing, however, from the facts and reasonings that bear against the hypothesis of a universal deluge, to indicate in a few sentences both the possible mode in which a merely partial flood might have taken place, and the probable extent of area which it covered, I shall have to remove from very strong to comparatively weak ground,—from what can be maintained as argument, to what can at best be but offered as conjecture.

There is a remarkable portion of the globe, chiefly in the Asiatic continent, though it extends into Europe, and which is nearly equal to all Europe in area, whose rivers (some of them, such as the Volga, the Oural, the Sihon, the Kour, and the Amoo, of great size) do not fall into the ocean, or into any of the many seas which communicate with it. They are, on the contrary, all *turned inwards*, if I may so express myself; losing themselves, in the eastern parts of the tract, in the lakes of a rainless district, in which they supply but the waste of evaporation, and falling, in the western parts, into seas such as the Caspian and the Aral. In this region there are extensive districts still under the level of the ocean. The shore-line of the Caspian, for instance, is rather more than eighty-three feet beneath that of the Black Sea; and some of the great flat steppes which spread out around it, such as what is known as the Steppe of Astracan, have a mean level of about thirty feet beneath that of the Baltic. Were there a trench-like strip of country that communicated between the Caspian and the Gulf of Finland to be depressed beneath the level of the latter sea, it would *so open up the fountains of the great deep* as to lay under water an extensive and populous region, containing the cities of Astracan and Astrabad, and many other towns and villages. Nor is it unworthy of remark, surely, that one of the depressed steppes of this peculiar region is known as the "Low Steppe of the Caucasus," and forms no inconsiderable portion of the great recognised centre of the human family. The Mount Ararat on which, according to many of our commentators, the ark rested, rises immediately on the western edge of this great hollow; the Mount Ararat selected as the scene of that event by Sir Walter Raleigh, certainly not without some show of reason, lies far within it. Vast plains, white with salt, and charged with sea-shells, show that the Caspian Sea was at no distant period greatly more extensive than it is now. In an outer region, which includes the vast desert of Khiva, shells also abound; but they seem to belong, as a group, rather to some of the later Tertiary eras than to the recent period. It is quite possible, however, that,—as on parts of the western shores of our own country, where recent marine deposits lie over marine deposits of the Pleistocene age, while a terrestrial deposit, representative of an intervening paroxysm of upheaval, lies between,—it is possible, I say, that in this great depressed area, the region covered of old by a Tertiary sea, which we know united the Sea of Aral with the Caspian, and rolled over many a wide steppe and vast plain, may have been again covered for a brief period (after ages of upheaval) by the breaking in of the great deep during that season of judgment when, with the exception of one family, the whole human race was destroyed. It seems confirmatory of this view, that during even the historic period, at least one of the neighbouring inland seas, though it belongs to a different system from that of the Caspian and the Aral, covered a vastly greater area than it does now,—a consequence, apparently, of a more considerable depression in the Caucasian region than at present exists. Herodotus, as quoted by Cuvier in his "Theory of the Earth," represents the Sea of Azoff as equal in extent to the Euxine.

With the known facts, then, regarding this depressed Asiatic region before us, let us see whether we cannot originate a theory of the Deluge free from at least the palpable monstrosities of the older ones. Let us suppose that the human family, still amounting to several millions, though greatly reduced by exterminating wars and exhausting vices, were congregated in that tract of country which, extending eastwards from the modern Ararat to far beyond the Sea of Aral, includes the original Caucasian centre of the race: let us suppose that, the hour of judgment having at length arrived, the land began gradually to sink, as the tract in the run of Cutch sank in the year 1819, or as the tract in the southern part of North America known as the "sunk country," sank in the year 1821: farther, let us suppose that the depression took place slowly and equably for forty days together, at the rate of about four hundred feet per day,—a rate not twice greater than that at which the tide rises in the Straits of Magellan, and which would have rendered itself apparent as but a persistent inward flowing of the sea: let us yet farther suppose, that from mayhap some volcanic outburst coincident with the depression, and an effect of the same deep-seated cause, the atmosphere was so affected, that heavy drenching rains continued to descend during the whole time, and that, though they could contribute but little to the actual volume of the flood,—at most only some five or six inches per day,—they at least *seemed* to constitute one of its main causes, and added greatly to its terrors, by swelling the rivers, and rushing downwards in torrents from the hills. The depression, which, by extending to the Euxine Sea and the Persian Gulf on the one hand, and to the Gulf of Finland on the other, would open up by three separate channels the fountains of the great deep, and which included, let us suppose, an area of about two thousand miles each way, would, at the end of the fortieth day, be sunk in its centre to the depth of sixteen thousand feet,—a depth sufficiently profound to bury the loftiest mountains of the district; and yet, having a gradient of declination of but sixteen feet per mile, the contour of its hills and plains would remain apparently what they had been before,—the doomed inhabitants would see but the water rising along the mountain sides, and one refuge after another swept away, till the last witness of the scene would have perished, and the last hill-top would have disappeared. And when, after a hundred and fifty days had come and gone, the depressed hollow would have begun slowly to rise,—and when, after the fifth month had passed, the ark would have grounded on the summit of Mount Ararat,—all that could have been seen from the upper window of the vessel would be simply a boundless sea, roughened by tides, now flowing outwards, with a reversed course, towards the distant ocean, by the three great outlets which, during the period of depression, had given access to the waters. Noah would of course see that "the fountains of the deep were stopped," and "the waters returning from off the earth continually;" but whether the Deluge had been partial or universal, he could neither see nor know. His prospect in either case would have been equally that described by the poet Bowles:—

> "The mighty ark
> Rests upon Ararat; but nought around
> Its inmates can behold, save o'er the expanse
> Of boundless waters the sun's orient orb
> Stretching the hull's long shadow, or the moon
> In silence through the silver-curtained clouds
> Sailing, as she herself were lost, and left
> In hollow loneliness."

Let me farther remark, that in one important sense a partial flood, such as the one of which I have conceived as adequate to the destruction, in an early age, of the whole human family, could scarce be regarded as miraculous. Several of our first geologists hold, that some of the formidable cataclysms of the remote past may have been occasioned by the sudden upheaval of vast continents, which, by displacing great bodies of water, and rolling them outwards in the character of enormous waves, inundated wide regions elevated hundreds of feet over the sea-level, and strewed them over with the rock-boulders, clays, gravels, and organic debris of deep sea-bottoms. And these cataclysms they regard as perfectly natural, though of course very unusual, events. Nor would the gradual depression of a continent, or, as in the supposed case, of a portion of a continent, be in any degree less natural than the sudden upheaval of a continent. It would, on the contrary, be much more according to experience. Nay, were such a depression and elevation of the great Asiatic basin to take place during the coming twelvemonth as that of which I have conceived as the probable cause of the Deluge, though the geologists would have to describe it as beyond comparison the most remarkable oscillation of level which had taken place within the historic period, they would certainly regard it as no more miraculous than the great earthquake of Lisbon, or than that exhibition of the volcanic forces which elevated the mountain of Jorullo in a single night sixteen hundred feet over the plain. And why have recourse, in speculating on the real event of four thousand years ago, to supposititious miracle, if an event of apparently the same kind would not be regarded as miraculous now? May we not in this matter take our stand beside the poet, who, when recognising a Providence in the great Calabrian earthquake, and in the overwhelming wave by which it was accompanied, pertinently inquired of the sceptics,

> "Has not God
> Still wrought by means since first he made the world?
> *And did He not of old employ his means*
> *To drown it?* What is His creation less
> Than a capacious reservoir of means,
> Formed for His use, and ready at His will?"

The revelation to Noah, which warned him of a coming Flood, and taught him how to prepare for it, was evidently miraculous: the Flood itself may have been purely providential. But on this part of the subject I need not dwell. I have accomplished my purpose if I have shown, as was attempted of old by divines such as Stillingfleet and Poole, that there "seems to be no reason why the Deluge should be extended beyond the occasion of it, which was the corruption of man," but, on the contrary, much reason against it; and that, on the other hand, a Flood restricted and partial, and yet sufficient to destroy the race in an early age, while still congregating in their original centre, cannot be regarded as by any means an incredible event. The incredibility lies in the mere human glosses and misinterpretations in which its history has been enveloped. Divested of these, and viewed in its connection with those wonderful traditions which still float all over the world regarding it, it forms, not one of the stumbling-blocks, but one of the evidences, of our faith; and renders the exercise a not unprofitable one, when, according to the poet,

> "Back through the dusk
> Of ages Contemplation turns her view,
> To mark, as from its infancy, the world
> Peopled again from that mysterious shrine
> That rested on the top of Ararat."

1. The following estimate of the air-breathing vertebrates (that of the "Physical Atlas," second edition, 1856) may be regarded as the latest. It will be seen that it does not include the cetacea or the seals:—

	SPECIES.		
Quadrumana	170		
Marsupialia	123		
Edentata	28		
Pachydermata	39		
Terrestrial Carnivora	514		
Rodentia	604		
Ruminantia	180		
	---	1658	
Birds		6266	
Reptiles	657		
Turtles 8			
Sea-Snakes 7	15		
	---	672	

Great as is this number of animals, compared with those known a century ago, there are indications that the list is to be increased rather than diminished. Even by the latest European authorities the reindeer is represented as consisting of but a single species, common to the subarctic regions of both the Old and New Worlds; whereas in the "Canadian Naturalist" for 1856 I find it stated, on what seems to be competent authority, that America has its two species of reindeer, and that they both differ from the European species.

2. If I do not introduce here the argument founded on the great age of certain gigantic trees, such as the Baobab of intertropical Africa, or the Taxodium of South America, it is not because I have any reason to challenge the estimates of Adanson or Candolle. The one tree may have lived its five thousand, the other its six thousand, years; but as the grounds have been disputed on which the calculations respecting their vast age have been founded, and as they cannot be re-examined anew by the reader, I wholly omit the evidence in the general question which they have been supposed to furnish.

3. The following excellent remarks on the economy of miracle, by Chalmers, bear very directly on this subject:– "It is remarkable that God is sparing of miracles, and seems to prefer the ordinary processes of

nature, if equally effectual for the accomplishment of his purposes. He might have saved Noah and his family by miracles; but He is not prodigal of these, and so He appointed that an ark should be made to bear up the living cargo which was to be kept alive on the surface of the waters; and not only so, but He respects the laws of the animal physiology, as He did those of hydrostatics, in that He put them by pairs into the ark, male and female, to secure their transmission to after ages, and food was stored up to sustain them during their long confinement. In short, He dispenses with miracles when these are not requisite for the fulfilment of his ends; and He never dispenses with the ordinary means when these are fitted, and at the same time sufficient, for the occasion."—*Daily Scripture Readings*, vol. i. p. 10.

LECTURE NINTH.

THE DISCOVERABLE AND THE REVEALED.

IT seems natural, nay inevitable, that false revelations, which have descended from remote, unscientific ages, should be committed to a false science. Natural phenomena, when of an extraordinary character, powerfully impress the untutored human mind. In operating, through the curiosity or the fears of men, upon that instinct of humanity—never wholly inactive in even the rudest state—which cannot witness any remarkable effect without seeking to connect it with its producing cause, they excite into activity in the search the imaginative faculty,—always of earlier development than the judgment in both peoples and individuals, and which never fails, when so employed, to conduct to delusions and extravagances. And this state of mind gives birth simultaneously to both false religion and false science. Great tempests, inundations, eclipses, earthquakes, thunder and lightning, famine and pestilence, the births of monsters, or the rare visitation of strange fishes or wild animals, come all to be included in the mythologic domain. Even the untutored Indian "sees God in clouds, and hears him in the wind." And when an order of priesthood springs up, a portion of the leisure of the class is usually employed in speculating on these phenomena; and to their speculations they give the form of direct revelation. Thus almost all the false religions of the old world—not grafted, like Mohammedanism, on the true one—have their pretended revelations regarding the form, structure, and origin of the earth, the mechanism of the heavens, the electric and meteoric phenomena, and even the arrangement of oceans and continents on the surface of our planet.

The old extinct forms of heathenism,—Etrurian, Egyptian, Phœnician, and Babylonian,—had all their cosmogonies.[1] In the wild mythology of ancient Scandinavia, of which we find such distinct traces in the languages and superstitions of northern

Europe, and which even in our own country continues to give the names of its uncouth deities to the days of our week, there is a strange genesis of not only the heavens and earth, but of the gods also. It has, besides, its scheme of the universe in its great mundane tree of three vast roots,—celestial, terrestrial, and infernal,—which supports the land, the sea, the sky, and all things. The leading religions of the East which still survive, such as Buddhism, Brahminism, and Parseeism, have all their astronomy, geography, meteorology, and geology, existing as component parts of their several systems. Nor have there been wanting ingenious men who, though little tolerant of the various attempts made to reconcile the Mosaic account of creation with the discoveries of modern science, have looked with a favourable eye on the wild science of the false religions, and professed to detect in it at least striking analogies with the deductions of both the geologist and the astronomer. When the sceptical wits of the last century wished to produce, by way of foil, a morality vastly superior, as they said, to that of Christianity, they had recourse to the Brahmins and the Chinese. And though we hear less of the ethics of these peoples since we have come to know them better, we are still occasionally reminded of the superiority of their science. Hinduism has been regarded as furnishing examples of the geologic doctrine of a succession of creations extended over immensely protracted geologic periods; and Buddhism represented as charged with both the geologic doctrine and the perhaps less certain astronomic deduction of a plurality of worlds. And before entering on our general argument, it may be well to show by specimen what mere chance hits these are, and how enormous the amount of the nonsense and absurdity really is in which they are set.

When Brahma, wearied with the work of producing and maintaining the universe, goes to sleep, say the Hindus,—an occurrence which happens at the end of every four millions of years,—a deluge of water rises high above the sun and moon, and the worlds and their inhabitants are destroyed. When he awakes, however, he immediately sets himself to produce anew; and another universe springs up, consisting, like the former one, of ten worlds placed over each other, like the storeys of a tall building, and replenished with plants and animals. Of these our own world is the eighth in number, reckoning from the ground-floor upwards: there are seven worlds worse than itself beneath it, and two better ones above; with a few worlds more higher up still, to which the destroying flood does not reach, save once or twice in an eternity or so; and which, in consequence, have not to be re-created each time with the others. The special forms which the upper and nether worlds exhibit do not seem to be very well known; but that which man inhabits is "flat, like the flower of the water-lily, in which the petals project beyond each other;" and it has in all, including sea and land, a diameter of several hundred thousand *millions* of miles. It has its many great oceans,—one of these (unfortunately the only one in contact with man's place of habitation) of salt water, one of sugar-cane juice, one of spirituous liquor, one of clarified butter, and one of sour curds. It has, besides, its very great ocean of sweet water. And around all, forming a sort of gigantic hoop or ring, there extends a continent of pure gold. Of all the luminaries that rise over this huge world, the sun is the nearest: the distance of the moon is twice as great; the lesser fixed stars occur immediately beyond; then Mercury, then Venus, then Mars, then Jupiter, then Saturn; and finally, the great bear and the polar star. And such is that cosmogony and astronomy of the Brahmins to which their religion, in its character as a revelation, stands committed, and in which a very lenient criticism has found the geologic revolutions. Let me draw my next illustration from Buddhism, the most ancient and most widely-spread religion of the east; for, though partially overlaid in the great Indian peninsula by the more modern monstrosities of Brahminism, it extends in one direction from 'the Persian Gulf to Formosa and Japan, and in the other from the wastes of Siberia to the Gulf of Siam. Scarce any of the other forms of heathenism darken so large a portion of the map as Buddhism,—a superstition which is estimated to include within its pale nearly one-third of the whole human species.

It has been held, I need scarce say, by most astronomers since the times of Newton, that the universe consists of innumerable systems of worlds, furnished each with its own sun; and held by

most geologists during the last fifty years, that the past duration of
our earth was divided into periods of vast extent, each of which
had a creation of its own. And certainly in Buddhism we find both
these ideas,—the idea of the existence of separate systems, each
with its own sun; and the idea of successive periods, each with its
own creation. We ascertain on examination, however, that in the
superstition they are not scientific ideas at all, but mere chance
guesses, set, like those of Brahminism, in a farago of wild and
monstrous fable. Each of the many systems of which the universe
is composed consists, say the Buddhists, of three worlds of a
circular form, joined together at the edges, so that there intervenes
between them an angular interspace, which constitutes their
common hell; and to each of these systems there is a sun and moon
apportioned, that take their daily journeys over them, returning
at night through a void space underneath. And each of the bygone
successive creations was a creation originated, it is added, out of
chaos, through the stored-up merits of the Buddhas, and the
effects of a life-invigorating rain, and which sank into chaos again
when the old stock of merit, accumulated in the previous period,
was exhausted. The creatures of each period, too, whether brute or
human, were animated by but the souls of former creatures
embodied anew. In the centre of each of the three worlds of which
a system or *sackwala* consists, there is a vast mountain, more than
forty thousand miles in height, surrounded by a circular sea, which
is in turn surrounded by a ring of land and rock. Another circular
sea lies outside the ring, and a second solid ring outside the sea;
and thus rings of land and water alternate from the centre to the
circumference. According to the geography of the Buddhas, a
model of our own earth would exactly resemble that old-fashioned
ornament,—a work of the turning-lathe,—which some of my
auditors must have seen roughening the upper board of the ornate
parlour bellows of the last century, and which consisted of a large
central knob, surrounded by alternate circular rings and furrows.
And as in the old-fashioned bellows each ring flattened, and each
furrow became shallower, in proportion as it was removed from the
centre, so in the Buddhist earth, the seas, from being many
thousand miles deep in the inner rings, shallow so greatly, that in

the outer rings their depth is only an inch; while the continents, from being forty thousand miles high, sink into mere plains, almost on the level of the surrounding ocean. Such is the geography to which this religion pledges itself. Its astronomy, on the other hand, is not quite so bad as that to which Father Cullen has affixed his imprimatur, seeing that, though it gives the same sort of diurnal journey to the sun, it confers upon it a diameter, not of only six feet, but of four hundred miles. Nor is its geology a great deal worse than that of many Christians. It makes the earth consist, reckoning from its foundations upwards, of a layer of wind, a layer of water, a layer of a substance resembling honey, a layer of rock, and a layer of soil. Such is a small portion of the natural science of Buddhism: the minute details of its monstrous cosmogony, with its descriptions of fabulous oceans, inhabited by fishes thousands of miles in length, and of wonderful forests abounding in trees four hundred miles high, and haunted by singing lions that leap two miles at a bound, occupy many chapters of the sacred volumes. Every form of faith has its heretics; and there are, it would seem, heretics among even the Buddhists, who, instead of adopting the nonsense of the priests in this physical department, originate a nonsense equally gross of their own. The error of concluding that the worlds of the universe are finite in number, say the sacred books, is the heresy *antawada*; the error of concluding that the world itself is infinite is the heresy *anantawada;* the error of concluding that the world is finite vertically but infinite horizontally is the heresy *anantanantawada*; and the error of concluding the world to be neither finite nor infinite is the heresy *nawantanantawada*. A name equally formidable would be, of course, found for the students of modern astronomy and the other kindred sciences, among the professed believers in Buddh, did not these contrive to get over the difficulty by observing, "that certain things, as stated in the *Sastras*, must have been so formerly; but great changes have taken place in these in latter times; and for astronomical purposes astronomical rules must be followed."

Believers in Buddhism may be still found by tens of millions on the shores of the Yellow Sea. Let me select my third specimen of a universe-fashioning mythology from a faith, long since extinct, that had its seat on the opposite side of the Old World, along the coasts of the Northern Atlantic. The old Teutonic religion professed to reveal, like that of Buddh and of Brahma, *how* the heavens and earth were formed, and of *what*.

Ymir, the great frost-giant, a being mysteriously engendered out of frozen vapour, was slain by the god Odin and his brothers; and, dragging his body into the middle of the universe, they employed the materials of which it was composed in forming the earth. Of his blood they made the vast ocean, and all the lakes and rivers; of his flesh they constructed the land, placing it in the midst of the waters; of his bones they built up the mountains; his teeth and jaws they broke up into the stones and pebbles of the earth and shore; of his great skull they fashioned the vault of the heavens; and, tossing his brains into the air, they became the clouds. Earth, sea, and sky, however, thus made, were supported by the great ash-tree Yggdrasill, which, with its roots anchored deep in the primordial abyss, rose up through the vast central mountains of the world, and, stretching forth its branches to the farthest heaven, bore the stars as its fruit. Encircling the whole earth like a ring, lay the huge snake Midgard,—always hidden in the sea, save when half drawn forth on one occasion by the god Thor; outside the snake a broader ring of ice-mountains swept round both land and ocean, and formed the outer frame of the world,—for there lay only blank space beyond; and over all, the sun and moon performed their journeys, chased through the sky by ravenous wolves, that ever sought to devour them. Such was the wild dream of our Scandinavian ancestors,—a dream, however, that occupied as prominent a place in their Edda as any of their other religious beliefs, and which, with the first dawn of science, would not only have fallen itself, but would have also dragged down the others along with it.

Now this physical department has ever proved the vulnerable portion of false religions,—the portion which, if I may use the metaphor, their originators could not dip in the infernal river. The ability of drawing the line, in the early and ignorant ages of the world, between what man can of himself discover and what he cannot, is an ability which man cannot possibly possess. The ancient Chaldeans, who first watched the motions of the planets, could not possibly have foreseen, that while on the one hand men would be one day able of themselves to measure and weigh these bodies, and to determine their distances from the earth and from each other, men might never be able of themselves to demonstrate the fact of their authorship, or to discover the true character of their Author. Nay, if they could have at all thought on the subject, the latter would have seemed to them by much the simpler discovery of the two. To know at such a time what was in reality discoverable and what was not, would be to know by anticipation what is not yet known,—the limits of all human knowledge. It would be to trace a line nonexistent at the period, and untraceable, in the nature of things, until the history of the human race shall be completed. It was held by even the sagacious Socrates, that men cannot arrive at any certainty in questions respecting the form or motion of the earth, or the mechanism of the heavens; and so he set himself to elucidate what he deemed much simpler matters,—to prove, for instance, as we find in the Phedon, that human souls existed ere they came to inhabit their mortal bodies, and retained faint recollections of great misfortunes that had overtaken them ere their embodiment as men, and of sufferings to which they had been subjected in a primevous state. And lacking this ability of distinguishing between the naturally discoverable and what cannot be naturally discovered, the originators of the old mythogic beliefs obtruded into provinces in which ultimately the lawless nature of the obtrusion could not fail to be detected; and thus, by making their false science a portion of their false religion, they created what was afterwards to prove its weakest and most vulnerable part. We absolutely know that the course at present pursued by enlightened Christian missionaries in India is to bring scientific truth into direct antagonism with the monstrously false science of the pretended revelations of Parseeism, Brahminism, and Buddhism; and that by this means the general falsity of these systems has been so plainly shown, that it has become a matter of doubt whether a single educated native of any considerable ability in reality believes in them. They seem to have lost their hold of all the minds capable of appreciating the weight and force of scientific evidence.

Let us farther remark, that since it seems inevitable that pretended revelations of ancient date should pledge themselves to a false science, the presumption must be strong that an ancient revelation of great multiplicity of detail, which has *not* so pledged itself, is not a false, but a true revelation. Nay, if we find in it the line drawn between what man can know of himself and what he cannot know, and determine that this line was traced in a remote and primitive age, we have positive evidence in the circumstance, good so far as it extends, of its Divine origin. Now, it will be ultimately found that this line was drawn with exquisite precision in the Hebrew Scriptures,—not merely the most ancient works that profess to be revelations, but absolutely the most ancient of all writings. Unfortunately, however, what God seems to have done for His Revelation, influential theologians of both the Romish and orthodox Churches have laboured hard to undo; and, from their mistaking, in not a few remarkable passages, the scope and object of the vouchsafed message, they have at various times striven to pledge it to a science as false as even that of Buddhist, Teuton, or Hindu. And so, not only has the argument been weakened and obscured which might be founded on the rectitude of the line drawn of old between what ought and what ought not to be the subject of revelation, but even a positive argument has been furnished to the infidel,—ever ready to identify the glosses of the theologian with the enunciations of Revelation itself,—similar to that which the Christian missionary directs against the false religions of India. It may be well briefly to inquire how this unlucky mistake has originated.

It is of first importance often to the navigator that he should have a good chronometer, seeing that his ability of determining his exact position on wide seas, and, in consequence, of determining also the exact place and bearing of the rocks and reefs which he must avoid, and of the lands and harbours on which he must direct his course, must very much depend on the rectitude of his instrument. But it may be of very little importance to him to know how chronometers are made. And so a friend may reveal to him where the best chronometers are to be purchased, with the name of the maker, without at the same time revealing to him the principle on which they are constructed. Let us suppose, however, that from some peculiarity in the mode of the revelation, the navigator has come to believe that it includes both items,—an enunciation regarding the place where and the maker from whom the best chronometers are to be had, and a farther enunciation regarding the true mechanism of chronometers. Let us suppose farther, that while the good faith and intelligence of his friend are unquestionable, the supposed revelation regarding the construction of chronometers, which he thinks he owes to him, is altogether erroneous and absurd. The chronometer mainly differs from the ordinary watch in being formed of a mixture of metals, which preserve so nice a chemical balance, that those changes of temperature which quicken or retard the movements of common timepieces fail to affect it. Now, let us suppose that the friend and adviser of the sailor had said to him,—using a common metonymy,—there are no chronometers anywhere constructed that so *completely neutralize the temperature* as the ones I recommend to you; and that the sailor had at once leaped to the conclusion, that the remark was authority enough for holding that it is the principle of chronometers, not to be composed of such counteractive combinations of metals as that the expansion of one shall be checked by the contraction of another, but to keep up an equal temperature within through a heat-engendering quality in the amalgamated metals. Such a mistake might be readily enough originated in this way; and yet it would be a very serious mistake indeed; seeing that it would substitute an active for a passive principle,—a principle of equalizing the temperature by acting upon it, for a principle of inert impassibility to the temperature. And of course not only would the sailor himself be in error in taking such a view, but he might seriously compromise the intelligence or integrity of his friend in the judgment of all who held, on his testimony, that it was with his friend, and not from his own misconception of his friend's meaning, that the view had originated. And how, let us ask, ere dismissing our lengthened illustration, is an error such as the supposed one here to be tested, and its erroneousness exposed? There can be but one reply to such a query. It might be wholly in vain to fall back upon the *ipsissima verba* of the revelation made by the sailor's friend. Though in reality but an enunciation regarding the *authorship* of certain chronometers, it might possibly enough appear, from its metonymic character, to be also a revelation regarding the *construction* of chronometers. The sailor's error respecting the construction of chronometers is to be tested and exposed, not by any references to what his friend had said, but by the art of the chronometer-maker. The demonstrable principles of the art, as practised by the makers of chronometers, must be the test of all supposed *revelations* regarding the principles and mechanism of chronometer-making.

Now, it will be found that those mistakes of the theologians to which I refer have been exactly similar to that of the navigator in the supposed case, and that they are mistakes which must be corrected on exactly the same principle. The departments in which the mistakes have been made have, as in the false religions, been

Fig. 114

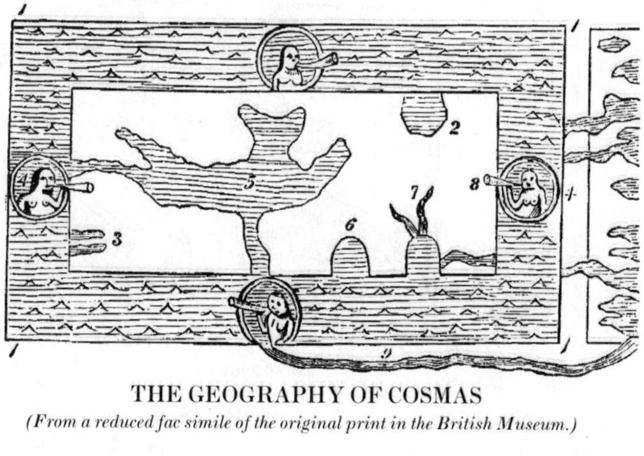

THE GEOGRAPHY OF COSMAS
(From a reduced fac simile of the original print in the British Museum.)

* 1. The great surrounding oceans.
  2. Caspian Sea.
  3. River Phison.
4-4. Points of the Compass.
  5. Mediterranean Sea.
  6. Red Sea.
7-8. Persian Gulf, with the rivers
     Tigris and Euphrates.
  9. River Gihon.

chiefly three,—the geographic, astronomic, and geologic provinces. The geographic errors are of comparatively ancient date. They belong mainly to the later patristic and earlier middle ages, when the monk Cosmas, as the geographer of the Church, represented the earth as a parallelogrammical plain, twice longer than it was broad, deeply indented by the inland seas,—the Mediterranean, the Caspian, the Red Sea, and the Persian Gulf,—and encompassed by a rectangular trench occupied by the oceans. Some of my audience will, however, remember, that of the council of clergymen which met in Salamanca in 1486 to examine and test the views of Christopher Columbus, a considerable portion held it to be grossly heterodox to believe that by sailing westwards the eastern parts of the world could be reached. No one could entertain such a view without also believing that there were antipodes, and that the world was round, not flat,—errors denounced by not only great theologians of the golden age of ecclesiastical learning, such as Lactantius and St Augustine, but

Fig. 115.

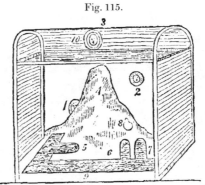

THE HEAVENS AND THE EARTH OF COSMAS
(Sectional View)

* 1. The sun occident.
  2. The sun orient.
  3. The heavens.
  4. Great mountain behind which the sun is hidden when it is night.
  5. The Mediterranean Sea.
  6. Red Sea.
  7. Persian Gulf.
  8. Garden of Eden.
  9. Great surrounding ocean.
  10. The Creator looking down upon his work, and seeing that all was good.

also directly opposed, it was said, to the very letter of Scripture. "They observed," says Washington Irvine, in his "Life of Columbus," "that in the Psalms the heavens are said to be extended like a hide,—that is, according to commentators, the curtain or covering of a tent, which among the ancient pastoral nations was formed of the hides of animals; and that St Paul, in his Epistle to the Hebrews, compares the heavens to a tabernacle or tent extended over the earth, which they thence inferred must be flat." In the sectional view of Cosmas the heavens are represented as a semi-circular vault or tent raised on perpendicular walls; a vast mountain beyond the "Great Sea," lofty as the innermost continent of the Buddhist cosmogony, rises immediately under it; when the sun passed behind this mountain it was night, and when it emerged from it, it was day. And certainly under the crystal box of the monk it would be in vain to attempt, by passing westwards, to arrive at the far east. The cosmogony of Cosmas was also that of the doctors of Salamanca; and the views of Columbus were denounced as heterodox because they failed to conform to it. Such was one of the earlier mistakes of the theologians. When merely told regarding the authorship of the chronometer, they held that they had been told also respecting the mechanism of the chronometer. Attaching literal meanings to what we now recognise as merely poetic or oratorical figures, they believed that not only was it revealed to them that God had created the heavens and earth, but also that He had created the earth in the form of an extended plain, and placed a semi-globular heavens over it, just as one places a semi-globular case of glass over a piece of flower-plot or a miniature thicket of fern. And how, I ask, was this error ultimately corrected? Simply by that science of the geographer which demonstrates that the earth is not flat, but spherical, and that the heavens have not edges, like a skin-tent or glass-case, to come anywhere in contact with it, but consist mainly of a diffused atmosphere, with illimitable space beyond.

The second great error to which the theologians would fain have pledged the truth of Scripture was an error in the astronomical province. I need scarce refer to the often-adduced case of Galileo. The doctrine which the philosopher had to "abjure, curse, and detest," and which he was never again to teach, "because erroneous, heretical, and contrary to Scripture," was the doctrine of the earth's motion and the sun's stability. But to the part taken by our Protestant divines in the same controversy,—men still regarded as authorities in their own proper walk,—I must be allowed to refer, as less known, though not less instructive, than that enacted by the Romish Church in the case of Galileo. "This, we affirm, *i.e.* that the earth rests, and the sun moves daily around it," said Voetius, a great Dutch divine of the middle of the seventeenth century, "with all divines, natural philosophers, Jews and Mohammedans, Greeks and Latins, excepting one or two of the ancients, and the modern followers of Copernicus." And we detect Heideggeri, a Swiss theologian, who flourished about half an age later, giving expression, a few years ere the commencement of the last century, to a similar view, as the one taken by himself and many others, and as a view "from which," he states, "our pious reverence for the Scriptures, the word of truth, will not allow us to depart." A still more remarkable instance occurs in Turrettine, whom we find in one of his writings arguing in the strictly logical form, "in opposition to certain philosophers," and in behalf of the old Ptolemaic doctrine that the sun moves in the heavens and revolves round the earth, while the earth itself remains at rest in the midst. "*First,*" he remarks, "the sun is said in Scripture to move in the heavens, and to rise and set. 'The sun is as a bridegroom coming out of his chamber, and rejoiceth as a strong man to run a race.' 'The sun knoweth his going down.' 'The sun also ariseth, and, the sun goeth down.' *Secondly,* The sun by a miracle stood still in the time of Joshua; and by a miracle it went back in the time of Hezekiah. *Thirdly,* The earth is said to be fixed immoveably. 'The earth is also established that it cannot be moved.' 'Thou hast established the earth, and it abideth.' 'They continue this day according to their ordinance.' *Fourthly,* Neither could birds, which often fly off through an hour's circuit, be able to return to their nests. *Fifthly,* Whatever flies or is suspended in the air ought (by this theory) to move from west to east; but this is proved not to be true, from birds, arrows shot forth, atoms made manifest in the sun, and down floating in the atmosphere." The theologian, after thus laying down the law, sets himself to meet objections. If it be urged that the Scriptures in natural things speak according to the common opinion, Turrettine answers, "*First,* The Spirit of God best understands natural things. *Secondly,* that in giving instruction in religion, He meant these things should be used, not abused. *Thirdly,* That He is not the author of any error. *Fourthly,* Neither is He to be corrected on the pretence of our blind reason." If it be farther urged, that birds, the air, and all things, are moved with the earth, he answers, "*First,* That this is a mere fiction, since air is a fluid body; and *secondly,* if so, by what force would birds be able to go from east to west?"

Now this I must regard as a passage as instructive as it is extraordinary. Turrettine was one of the most accomplished theologians of his age; nor is that age by any means a remote one. Tycho Brahe, Kepler, and Galileo, had all finished their labours long ere he published this passage; nay, at the time when his work issued from the Amsterdam press (1695), Isaac Newton had attained his fifty-third year; and fully ten years previous, Professor David Gregory, nephew of the inventor of the Gregorian telescope, had begun to teach, from his chair in the University of Edinburgh, the doctrine of gravitation and the true mechanism of the heavens, as unfolded in the Newtonian philosophy. The learned theologian, had he applied himself to astronomical science, could have found at the time very enlightened teachers; but falling into exactly the mistake of the sailor of my illustration, or into that which, two centuries before, the doctors of Salamanca had fallen, he set himself, instead, to contend with the astronomers, and, to the extent of his influence, laboured to pledge revelation to an astronomy as false as that of the Buddhist, Hindu, or old Teuton. His mistake, I repeat, was exactly that of the sailor. Though in the Scriptures only the fact of the *authorship* of the great chronometer set in the heavens "to be a sign for seasons, and for days and years," is revealed, he regarded himself as also informed respecting the principles on which the chronometer was constructed, or at least respecting the true nature of its movements; and several very important deductions may, I think, be drawn from the carefully constructed passage in which he so unwittingly records his error, and the grounds of it. In the first place, we may safely hold that the texts of Scripture quoted by so able a theologian are those which have most the appearance of being revelations to men respecting the motions of the heavenly bodies. We may conclusively infer, that if *they* do not reveal the character of those motions, then nowhere in Scripture is their character revealed. In the second place, it is obvious that the cited texts do *not* reveal the nature of the motions. It would be as rational to hold that our best almanacs reveal the Ptolemaic astronomy. In the scientific portion of our almanacs there occur many phrases which are perfectly well understood, and indicate very definitely what the writer really intends to express by them, that yet, taken literally, are not scientifically true. The words "Sun rises," and "Sun sets," and "Moon rises," and "Moon sets," occur in every page; there are two pages—those devoted to the months of March and September—in which the phrase occurs, "Sun crosses the equinoctial line;" and further, in the other pages, such phrases as "Sun enters Aries," "Sun enters Taurus," "Sun enters Gemini," &c. &c. are not unfrequent. The phrase "New moon" is also of common occurrence. And these phrases, interpreted after the manner of Turrettine, and according to their strict grammatical meaning, would of course imply that the sun has a motion round our planet,—that the moon moves round it every twenty-four hours,—and that the earth is provided every month with a new satellite. And yet we know that none of these ideas are in the mind of the writer who, in compiling the almanac, employs the phrases. He employs them to indicate, not the nature of the heavenly motions, but the exact time when, from the several motions of the earth, the sun and moon are brought into certain apparent positions with respect to either the earth itself or to the celestial signs; or to indicate the time at which the moon completes its monthly revolution, and presents a wholly darkened disk to the earth. The commentator skilful enough to pledge the almanac, in virtue of the literal meaning of the specified phrases, to the old Ptolemaic hypothesis, would pledge it to a false science, which its author never held. And such, evidently, has been the part enacted by Turrettine and the elder theologians. The Scriptural phrases are in no degree more express respecting the motion of the sun and the other heavenly bodies than those of the almanac, which, we know, do not refer to motion at all, but to time. Nor are we less justified in holding that the cited Scriptures do not refer to *motion*, but to *authorship*. In the third place, however, it is not by any mere reconsideration of the adduced passages that the error, once made, is to be corrected. In a purely astronomic question the appeal lies, not to Scripture, but to astronomic science. And in the fourth place, the reasonings of Turrettine, when, quitting his own proper walk, he discourses, not as a theologian, but as a natural philosopher, are such as to read a lesson not wholly unneeded in the present day. They show how in a department in which it demanded the united life-long labours of a Kepler, Galileo, and Newton to elicit the truth, the hasty guesses of a great theologian, rashly ventured in a polemic spirit, gave form and body to but ludicrous error. It is not after a fashion so impetuous and headlong that the elaborately-wrought key must be plied which unlocks the profound mysteries of nature. But of this more anon.

Let me remark in the passing, that while Turrettine, one of the greatest of theologians, failed, as we have seen, to find in Scripture the fact of astronomic *construction,* La Place, one of the greatest of the astronomers, failed in a manner equally signal to find in his science the fact of astronomic *authorship.* The profound Frenchman (whom Sir David Brewster well characterizes as "the philosopher to whom posterity will probably assign the place next to Newton") by demonstrating that certain irregularities in the motion of the heavenly bodies, which had been supposed to indicate a future termination to the whole, were but mere oscillations, subject to periodic correction, and indicative of no such termination in consequence, demonstrated also that, from all that appears, the present astronomical movements might go on for ever. And as he could find in the solar system no indications of an end, so was he unable, he said, to find in it any trace of a beginning. He failed in discovering in all astronomy the fact of authorship, just as Turrettine had failed in finding in all Scripture the fact of astronomic construction. And here lies, I am inclined to think, the true line between revelation and science,—a line drawn of old with a God-derived precision, which can be rightly appreciated neither by mere theologians like Turrettine, nor by mere men of science like La Place, but which is notwithstanding fraught with an evidence direct in its bearing on the truth of Scripture. That great fact, moral in its influence, of the authorship of the heavens and earth, which the science of La Place failed of itself to discover, and which was equally unknown to the ancient philosophers, God has revealed. It is "through faith we understand that the worlds were formed by the word of God, so that things which are seen were not made of things which do appear." And, on the other hand, the great truths, physical in their bearing, to the discovery of which science is fully competent, God did not reveal, but left them to be developed piecemeal by the unassisted human faculties. And that ability of nicely drawing the line between the two classes of truths in a very remote age of the world, which we find manifested in the oldest of the Scriptural books, I must regard as an ability which could have been derived only through inspiration, and from God alone.

Let us, however, pursue our argument. Questions of geography, such as those entertained by the theologians of Salamanca, must be tested, we conclude, not by a revelation never intended by its Divine Author to teach geography, but by the findings of geographic science. Questions in astronomy, such as those which Turrettine and the opponents of Galileo entertained, must be tried, we hold, not by a revelation never intended to teach astronomy, but by the findings of astronomic science. But how deal, I next ask, with the theologian who holds that geologic fact has been revealed to him? Geology is as thoroughly a physical science as either geography or astronomy. Its facts are equally capable of being educed and established by the unassisted human intellect. It seems quite as unlikely that it should have been made a special subject of revelation, in its character as a science, as either of these sciences, or that the line so nicely maintained with respect to *them* should have been transgressed with regard to *it*. In short, in order satisfactorily to answer our query, it seems but necessary satisfactorily to answer another, namely, What, in this special department, are truth and fact scientifically ascertained?

There are, however, certain texts that appear to have a more direct bearing on the successive periods of the geologist than any of those that were once held to refer to the form of the earth, or to the nature of the heavenly bodies, are now believed to have on geography or astronomy. No one now holds that there is a geography revealed in Scripture, or regards the cavils of the Salamanca doctors as other than mere aberrations of the human mind. Nor, save mayhap in the darker corners of the Greek and Romish Churches, are there men in the present day who hold that there is a revealed astronomy. The texts so confidently quoted by Turrettine, such as "The sun also ariseth and the sun goeth down," are regarded in every Protestant Church as simply tantamount, in their bearing on the question at issue, to the "Sun rises" and "Sun sets" of the almanac. But while the Scriptures do not reveal the form of the earth or the motions of the planets, they do reveal the fact that the miracle of creation was effected, not by a single act, but in several successive acts. And it is with the organisms produced by successive acts of creation, and the formations deposited during the periods in which these acts took place, that the geologist is called on by his science to deal. And hence, while there are now no attempts made to reconcile geographic or astronomic fact with the Scripture passages which refer, in the language of the time, to the glory of the heavens or the stability of the earth, just because it is held that there is really nothing geographic or astronomic in the passages to conflict with the geographic or astronomic facts, we still seek to reconcile the facts of geologic science with what is termed the Mosaic geology. We inquire whether, in its leading features, the Mosaic does not correspond with the geologic record; and whether the *days* of the retrospective prophecy of creation are to be regarded as co-extensive with the vast periods of the geologist, or as merely representative portions of them, or as literal days of twenty-four hours each? But though we thus seek to harmonize the two records, we continue to regard their grounds and objects as entirely different. The object of geology is simply the elucidation of the history of the earth, and of the story of its various creations;

and its grounds are, like those of astronomy or geography, or of any other physical science, facts and inferences scientifically determined or deduced; while, on the other hand, the grounds of the Mosaic record are those on which the other Scriptures rest, and which have been so well laid down in what we may term the higher literature of the "Evidences;" while at least some of its objects,—for who shall declare them all?—seem to be, first, to establish the all-important fact of the Divine authorship of the universe, and to show that all its various forces are not self-existent, but owe their origin to a Great First Cause; next, to exhibit the progressive character of God's workings,—a character which equally applies to his works of creation and providence; and, in the third place, to furnish a basis and precedent in the Divine example for that institution of the Sabbath which bears not only a prophetic reference to the great dynasty to come,—last of all the dynasties, and of which re-created men are to be the happy subjects, and the Divine Man the adorable Monarch,—but which has also been specially established in order that right preparation may be made for the terminal state which it symbolizes and foreshadows. Here, as certainly as in the other physical sciences, the line has been drawn with perfect precision between what man could and what he could not have known of himself. What he could have known, and in part already knows, is geologic science; what in all probability he never could have known is the fact of the Divine authorship of the universe, and the true nature of the institution of the Sabbath, as a time of preparation for the final state, and as alike representative of God's workings in the past, and of his eternally predetermined scheme for the future. "Is it not certain," Socrates is represented as inquiring, in "the first Alcibiades" of his gay and confident pupil, "that you know nothing but what has been told you by others, or what you have found out for yourself?" There is at once exquisite simplicity and great terseness in this natural division of the only modes in which men can acquire knowledge; and we find it wonderfully exemplified in all Revelation. Scripture draws practically a broad line between the two modes; and while it tells man all that is necessary to his wants and welfare as a religious creature, it does not communicate to him a single scientific fact which he is competent to find out for himself.

About an age previous to the times of Turrettine, the danger of "corrupting philosophy through an intermixed divinity" was admirably shown by Bacon in his "Novum Organum;" and the line indicated was exactly what we now find was laid down of old with such precision in Scripture. "To deify error and to adore vain things," said the great philosopher, "may be well accounted the plague of the understanding. Some modern men, guilty of much levity, have so indulged this vanity, that they have essayed to find natural philosophy in the first chapter of Genesis, the Book of Job, and other places of holy writ, seeking the living among the dead. Now this vanity is so much the more to be checked and restrained, because, by unadvised mixture of divine and human things, not only a phantastical philosophy is produced, but also an heretical religion. Therefore it is safe to give unto Faith, with a sober mind, the things that are Faith's." The passage, partially quoted, has been not unfrequently misapplied, as if it bore, not against theologians such as Turrettine and the Franciscans, but against theologians such as Chalmers, Dr Bird Sumner, and Dr Pye Smith,—not against the men who derive a false science from Scripture, into which God never introduced natural science of any kind, but against the men who, having sought and acquired their science where it is alone to be found, have striven to bring Scripture, in the misinterpreted passages, into harmony with its findings. Taken, however, as a whole, its true meaning is obvious. It is the men who have "essayed to find natural philosophy" positively revealed in Genesis and the other sacred books,—not the men who have merely shown that there is nothing in Scripture which conflicts with the natural philosophy legitimately found elsewhere,—that are obnoxious to the censure conveyed in the remark. It is they only, and not the others, that are *"phantastical"* in their philosophy and *"heretical"* in their religion. I say heretical in their religion. The Ptolemaic doctrine which ascribed to the earth a central place in the universe was only scientifically false, whereas the same doctrine in Turrettine and the Franciscans, from the circumstance that they pledged the Scripture to its falsity, and professed to derive it direct from revelation, was not only scientifically false, but a heresy to boot. And, in like manner, it is the class who term themselves the "Mosaic geologists,"—men such as the Granville Penns, Moses Stewarts, Eleazar Lords, Dean Cockburns, and Peter Macfarlanes,—who essay to "find natural philosophy in the first chapter of Genesis," and that too a demonstrably false natural philosophy, who are obnoxious to the Baconian censure now. No true geologist ever professes to deduce his geology from Scripture. It is from the earth's crust, with its numerous systems, always invariable in their order, and its successive groupes of fossil remains, always (in accordance with their place and age) of a certain determinable character,—not in a revelation never intended by its Divine Author to teach any natural science as such,—that he derives the materials with which he builds. Had there been no Divine Revelation, geology would be as certainly what it now is as either geography or astronomy. That it comes in the present time more in contact with revealed truth than either of these sciences, is, as I have shown, merely a consequence of the fact that there is a history given in the opening passages of Scripture, for far other than geological purposes, of the authorship of the heavens and earth, and of the successive stages of creation; and further, from the circumstance that, from various motives, men are ever and anon inquiring how the geologic agrees with the Scriptural record. It may be well here to remind the anti-geologists, in connection with this part of my subject, of what at the utmost they may hope to accomplish. Judging from all I have yet seen of their writings, they seem to be as certainly impressed by the belief that they are settling textually the geologic question of the world's antiquity, as the doctors of Salamanca held that they were settling textually the question of the world's form; or Turrettine and the Franciscans, that they were settling textually the question of the world's motion, or rather want of motion. But the mistake is quite as gross in their case as in that of Turrettine and the doctors. Geology rests on a broad, ever-extending basis of evidence, wholly independent of the revelation on which they profess, very unintelligently, in all the instances I have yet known, to found their objections. What they need at most promise themselves is, to defeat those attempts to reconcile the two records which are made by geologists who respect and believe the Scripture testimony,—not a very laudable feat, even could it be accomplished, and certainly worthy of being made rather a subject of condolence than of congratulation. And though, of course, men should pursue the truth simply for its own sake, and independently either of the consequences which it may be found to involve, or of the company with which it may bring them acquainted, the anti-geologists might be worse employed than in scanning the character and aims of the associates with whom they virtually league themselves when they declare war against the Christian geologist.

There are three different parties in the field, either directly opposed, or at least little friendly, to the men who honestly attempt reconciling the Mosaic with the geologic record. First, there are the anti-geologists,—men who hold that geological questions are to be settled now as the Franciscans contemporary with Galileo held that astronomical questions were to be settled in the seventeenth century, or as the doctors of Salamanca contemporary with Columbus held that geographic questions were to be settled in the fifteenth. And *they* believe that geology, as interpreted by the geologists, is entirely false, because, as they think, irreconcileable with Scripture; further, that our planet had no existence some seven or eight thousand years ago,—that the apparent antiquity of the various sedimentary systems and organic groupes of the earth's crust is wholly illusive,—and that the very oldest of them cannot be more than a few days older than the human period. In fine, just as it was held two centuries ago by Turrettine and the Franciscans, that the Bible as interpreted by *them* was the only legitimate authority in astronomic questions, so this class now hold that the Bible as interpreted by *them* is the only legitimate authority in geologic questions; and further, that the Bible being, as they contend, wholly opposed to the deductions of the geologist, these deductions must of necessity be erroneous.

Next, there is a class, more largely represented in society than in literature, who, looking at the general bearings of the question, the character and standing of the geologists, and the sublime nature of their discoveries, believe that geology ranks as certainly among the sciences as astronomy itself; but who, little in earnest in their religion, are quite ready enough, when they find theologians asserting the irreconcileability of the geologic doctrines with those of Scripture, to believe them; nay, not only so, but to repeat the assertion. It is not fashionable in the present age openly to avow infidelity, save mayhap in some modified rationalistic or pantheistic form; but in no age did the thing itself exist more extensively; and the number of individuals is very great who, while they profess an outward respect for Revelation, have no serious quarrel with the class who, in their blind zeal in its behalf, are in reality undermining its foundations. Nor are there avowed infidels awanting who also make common cause with the party so far as to assert that the results of geologic discovery conflict irreconcileably with the Mosaic account of creation. But there is yet another class, composed of respectable and able men, who, from the natural influence of their acquirements and talents, are perhaps more dangerous allies still, and whom we find represented by writers such as Mr Babbage and the Rev. Baden Powell. It is held by both these accomplished men, that it is in vain to attempt reconciling the Mosaic writings with the geologic discoveries: both are intimately acquainted with the evidence adduced by the geologist, and entertain no doubt whatever regarding what *it* establishes; but though in the main friendly to at least the moral sanctions of the New Testament, both virtually set aside the Mosaic cosmogony; the one (Mr Babbage) on the professed grounds that we really cannot arrive with any certainty at the meaning of that old Hebrew introduction to the Scriptures in which the genesis of things is described; and the other (Mr Powell) on the assumption that that introduction is but a mere picturesque myth or parable, as little scientifically true as the parables of our Saviour or of Nathan the seer are historically so. Now, I cannot think that the anti-geologists are quite in the place in which they either ought or intend to be when engaged virtually in making common cause with either of these latter classes.[2]

Be this as it may, however, it may be not uninstructive, and perhaps not wholly unamusing, to examine what the claims really are of some of our later anti-geologists to be recognised as the legitimate and qualified censors of geologic fact or inference. It will be seen, that in the passage which I have quoted from Turrettine, the theologian, in three of his five divisions, restricts himself to the theologic province, and that when in his own proper sphere even his errors are respectable; but that in the two concluding divisions he passes into the province of the natural philosopher, and that there his respectability ceases for the time, and he becomes eminently ridiculous. The anti-geologists,—men of considerably smaller calibre than the massive Dutch divine of the seventeenth century,—also enter into a field not their own. Passing from the theologic province, they obtrude into that of the geologist, and settle against him, apparently after a few minutes' consideration, or as mere special pleaders, questions on which he has been concentrating the patient study and directing the laborious explorations of years. And an exhibition by specimen of the nonsense to which they have in this way committed themselves in their haste may not be wholly uninstructive. But I must defer the display till another evening. I shall do them no injustice; but I trust it will be forgiven me should I exhibit as they have exhibited themselves, a class of writers to whose assaults I have submitted for the last fourteen years without provocation and without reply.

1. For a brief but masterly view of these ancient cosmogonies, see the Rev. D. Macdonald's "Creation and the Fall" Edinburgh: Constable & Co.

2. The very different terms which Mr Powell employs in characterizing the anti-geologists, from those which he makes use of in denouncing the men honestly bent on reconciling the enunciations of revelation with the findings of geologic science,—a class which included in the past, divines

such as Chalmers, Buckland, and Pye Smith, and comprises divines such as Hitchcock and the Archbishop of Canterbury now,—is worthy of being noted. In two sermons, "Christianity without Judaism," written by this clergyman of the Church of England, to show that all days of the week are alike, and the Christian Sabbath a mere blunder, I find the following passage:—"Some divines have consistently rejected all geology and all science as profane and carnal; and some even, when pretending to call themselves men of science, have stooped to the miserable policy of tampering with the truth, investing the real facts in false disguises, to cringe to the prejudices of the many, and to pervert science into a seeming accordance with popular prepossessions." I cannot believe that this will be regarded as justifiable language: it seems scarce worthy of a man of science; and will, I fear, only be accepted as good in evidence that the *odium theologicum* is not restricted to what is termed the orthodox side of the Church.

LECTURE TENTH.

THE GEOLOGY OF THE ANTI-GEOLOGISTS.

It has been well remarked, that that writer would be equally in danger of error who would assign very abstruse motives for the conduct of great bodies of men, or very obvious causes for the great phenomena of nature. The motives of the masses,—on a level always with the average comprehension,—are never abstruse; the causes of the phenomena, on the other hand, are never obvious. And when these last are hastily sought after, not from any devotion to scientific truth, or any genuine love of it, but for some purpose of controversy, we may receive it as a sure and certain fact that they will not be found. Some mere plausibility will be produced instead, bearing on its front an obviousness favourable mayhap to its reception for the time by the vulgar, but in reality fatal to its claims in the estimate of all deep thinkers; while truth will meanwhile lie concealed far below, in the bottom of her well, until patiently solicited forth by some previously unthought of process, in the character of some wholly unanticipated result. Such, in the history of science, has been the course and character of error on the one hand, and of actual discovery on the other: the error has been always comparatively obvious,—the discovery unexpected and abstruse. And as men descend in the scale of accomplishment or intellect, a nearer and yet nearer approximation takes place between their conceptions of the causes of the occult processes of nature, and the common and obvious motives which influence large masses of their fellows; until at length the sublime contrivances of the universe sink, in their interpretation of them, into the clumsy expedients of a bungling mechanism.

Tested by their reading of the phenomena on this principle, we find curious gradations between the higher and the humbler orders of minds. The vortices of Descartes, for instance, involve but a simple idea, that might have been struck out by almost any

individual of a tolerably lively fancy, who had walked by the side
of a winding river, and seen sticks and straws revolving in its
eddies. But no fancy, however active, or no reach of mere common
sense, however respectable, could have originated, or conducted to
a successful conclusion, that profound contemplation into which
Newton fell in the garden at Woolsthorpe, when he saw the
loosened apple drop from the tree, and succeeded in demonstrating
that the planets are retained in their orbits by the same law which
impels a falling pebble towards the ground. So little obvious,
indeed, was the Newtonian scheme, that most of the contemporary
generation of philosophers,—some of them, such as Fontenelle and
his brother academicians of France, men of no mean
standing,—died rejecting it. And the objections of Turrettine to
the motion of the earth on its axis are, we find, still more obvious
than even the idea of the vortices. It does at first seem natural
enough to suppose, that if the earth's surface be speeding
eastwards at the rate of several hundred miles in the hour (a
thousand miles at the equator), the birds which flutter over it
should be somewhat in danger of being left behind; and that atoms
and down-flakes floating in the atmosphere in a time of calm,
instead of appearing, as they often do, either in a state of rest, or
moving with equal freedom in every direction, ought to be seen
hurrying westwards, as if puffed by the breath of a tornado. Such
an objection must for a time have appeared as just as it seems
obvious, especially in one's study on a Saturday night, with much
of one's lecture still to write, and the Sabbath too near to permit of
verification or experiment. Fontenelle, however, though he could
not get over the difficulty of conceiving how the same gravitation
which made a stone fall also kept the moon in its place, fairly
surmounted that which puzzled Turrettine; and in his "Plurality
of Worlds,"—a publication of the same age as the "Compendium
Theologiæ,"—he makes his Marchioness surmount it too. "But I
have a difficulty to solve," he represents the lady as saying, "and
you must be serious. As the earth moves, the air changes every
moment; so we breathe the air of another country. 'Not at all,'
replied I; 'for the air which encompasses the earth follows with us,
and turns with us. Have you not seen the labours of the silkworm?

The shell or cocoon which it weaves around itself with so much art is of a down very loose and soft; and so the earth, which is solid, is covered, from the surface twenty leagues upwards, with a kind of down, which is the air, and, like the shell of the silkworm, turns along with it.'" Even Turrettine, however, was as far in advance of some of our contemners of science in the present day, as Fontenelle was in advance of Turrettine, or Newton in advance of Fontenelle. The old theologian could scarce have held, with a living ecclesiastic of the Romish Church in Ireland, Father Cullen, that the sun is *possibly* only a fathom in diameter; or have asserted with a most Protestant lecturer who addressed an audience in Edinburgh little more than three years ago, that, though God created all the wild animals, it was the devil who made the flesh-eaters among them fierce and carnivorous; and, of course, shortened their bowels, lengthened their teeth, and stuck formidable claws into the points of their digits.[1] Further, the error of Turrettine was but that of his age, whereas our modern decriers of scientific fact and inference are always men greatly in the rear of theirs, and as far inferior to the ancient assertors of the same errors as the few untutored peasants and fishermen of our own time, located in remote parts of the country, who still retain the old faith in witchcraft, are inferior to the great lawyers, poets, and divines,—the Fairfaxes, Henry Mores, Judge Haleses, and Sir George Mackenzies,—who in the seventeenth century entertained a similar belief. And so it may seem somewhat idle work to take any pains in "scattering" such a "rear of darkness thin" as this forlorn phalanx composes. "Let them alone," said a lunatic in the lucid fit, to a soldier who had told him, when asked why he carried a sword, that it was to kill his enemies,—"let them alone, and they will all die of themselves." But though very inconsiderable, there is a comparatively large proportion of the class perilously posted, on both sides of the Atlantic, in what used to be termed of old in Scotland "the chair of verity;" and there they sometimes succeed in doing harm, all unwittingly, not to the science which they oppose, but to the religion which they profess to defend. I was not a little struck lately by finding in a religious periodical of the United States, a worthy Episcopalian clergyman bitterly complaining, that whenever his sense of duty led him to denounce from his pulpit the gross infidelity of modern geology, he could see an unbelieving grin rising on the faces of not a few of his congregation. Alas! who can doubt that such ecclesiastics as this good clergyman must virtually be powerful preachers on the sceptical side, to all among their people who, with intelligence enough to appreciate the geologic evidence, are still unsettled in their minds respecting that of the Christian faith. And so on this consideration alone it may be found not uninstructive to devote the address of the present evening to an exposure of the errors and nonsense of our modern anti-geologists,—the true successors and representatives, in the passing age, of the Franciscan and Salamanca doctors of the fifteenth and seventeenth centuries.

Let me first remark, that no one need expect to be original simply by being absurd. There is a cycle in nonsense, as certainly as in opinion of a more solid kind, which ever and anon brings back the delusions and errors of an earlier time: the follies of the present day are transcripts, unwittingly produced, and with of course a few variations, of follies which existed centuries ago; and it seems to be on this principle,—a consequence, mayhap, of the limited range of the human mind, not only in its elucidations of truth, but also in its forms of error,—that scarce an explanation of geologic phenomena has been given by the anti-geologists of our own times, that was not anticipated by writers of the sixteenth and seventeenth centuries. It was held, for instance,—in opposition to the great painter, Leonardo da Vinci, who flourished early in the sixteenth century, and was one of the first who, after the revival of learning, asserted the true character of organic remains,—that fossils were formed in the rocks through the planetary influences, or a certain plastic force in nature, and had never entered into the composition of living creatures or plants. And this view obtained very generally till about the middle of the seventeenth century, when, save for a brief space long after, in the times of Voltaire, it ceased to be regarded as any longer tenable. Curiously enough, however, it was virtually reproduced by one of the extant anti-geologists,—a clergyman of the English Church,—only three years ago, in a publication written, he says, to counteract "the immense mischief occasioned by the infidel works of geologists, *especially among the lower classes,*" and which he has termed "a brief and complete refutation" of their "anti-scriptural theory."[2] "Fossils," says this courageous writer, "were not necessarily animated structures:" some of them were in all probability "formed of stone from the very first;" others, of inanimate flesh and bone. "The mammoth found under the ice in arctic regions had not necessarily been a living creature: it was created under the ice, and then preserved in that peculiar form of preservation, instead of being transmuted into stone, like the rest of its class." Such was the state of keeping of this famous mammoth when discovered a little ere the beginning of the present century, that, as I had occasion formerly to remark, dogs and bears fed upon its flesh; and its bones, and part of its skin, covered with long red hair, are now in the Museum of Petersburg. But there is no evidence whatever, according to this writer, that it had ever been a living creature: it was simply a created carcase. All organisms are, he holds, models or archetypes, fashioned during the first day in the depths of chaos, to typify or foreshadow the living plants and animals that were to be called into existence a few days later. "What," he asks, "do the cocoa-nuts, melons, and gourds, which have been found in the strata, show, but that the vegetable had its perfect archetype in chaos as well as the animal?" Nay, further, the geologist has but got into the apartment in which the original architect stored up his plans and models,—many of them, however, rejected ones. For "though every animal is formed after his archetype," we find him saying, "the converse is not true, that every chaotic structure is represented by its living *fac-simile.*" But they typify, if not living organisms, much more important things,—"they represent," says our writer, "the land of the shadow of death;" and the strata containing them, which geologists have opened, are symbolical of the "gates of death." "The state of preservation in which most fossils are, instead of having mouldered away, foreshadows immortality. The gradation, too, from the organisms whose types are *said to be* lost or destroyed, and confused in innumerable heaps, up to the perfect and complete specimen, is no fanciful representation of the resurrection; while the isolated bones and parts of skeletons which, though found far apart, as they were created, have been fitted together by the skill of the accomplished anatomist, give assurance of the fact that our scattered dust—our *membra disjecta*—shall come together at the sound of the last trump." And this is "geology on Scripture principles," soberly expounded by a man who respects facts, while he gives no place to fancy.

The "English clergyman" then goes on to show in his pamphlet, that the Coal Measures furnish no evidence of the earth's antiquity. They were formed, he says, by the finger of the Creator, "immediately and at once. A carboniferous tree of gigantic size has been discovered," he adds, "in the interior of the earth, of such a shape as entirely to prove the absurdity of a theory [that of the earth's antiquity] which has not a single valid argument to support it. It is described as having its trunk rising from the earth perpendicularly ten feet, and then bending over and extending horizontally sixty feet. Now, what living tree thus lopsided could support such a weight in such a direction? It seems to have been *created on purpose to silence the* HORRID BLASPHEMIES *of geologists*; for it proves to a demonstration, that the upper, nether, and surrounding matter came into existence with it at the same instant; for how else could it have been preserved in such a position?" The triumph secured by the carboniferous tree, however,—though it does not seem wholly impossible that a tree might in any age of the world have been broken over some ten feet from its root, and bent in a horizontal position,—seems in some danger of being neutralized, as we read on, by the circumstance that geologists find not unfrequently, among their fossils, the dung of the carnivorous vertebrates, charged in many instances with the teeth, bones, and scales of the creatures on which they had preyed, and strongly impressed, in at least the coprolites of the larger Palæozoic ganoids, and of the enaliosaurs of the Secondary period, by the screw-like markings of a spiral intestine, similar in form to that now exemplified by the sharks and rays. And in maintaining his hypothesis that most fossils are mere archetypes—mere plans or models—of existences to be, the archetypal dung proves rather a stumbling-block, and the English clergyman waxes exceedingly wroth against the geologists. "We cannot," he says, "believe in such things as coprolites. They are only a curious form of matter commanded by Him who has made the flower to assume all shapes as well as all hues. He who would not allow so much as a tool to be lifted up on the stones that composed his altar, would certainly not allow the *work* of animals to compose his creation, much less, then, their dung. The geological assertion that the Creator of this world formed it in some parts of coprolites savours very much of Satan or Beelzebub, the god of dung. Geologists could scarcely have made a more unfortunate self-refuting assertion than this." I question, however, whether the clergyman does well to be angry with the geologists here. That fossils are mere models and archetypes, is *his* hypothesis, not theirs; and so it is he himself who is answerable, not they, for what he deems the impiety of the archetypal dung. His next statement is of a kind suited somewhat to astonish the practical geologist. *"It is the constant language of the geologists,"* he says, in giving the result of their discoveries, *"that no young have been found!!!* while the larger fossils have been detected isolated, or in the company of others, all differing in kind." "Archetypal resemblances of ova have been found, and such things as *moths*; but these are distinct and perfect in their kind. The occurrence of the young, which are imperfect, is a fact which has not been, and never can be, established; *therefore it can never be proved that this world has had a longer existence than six thousand years."* It is "the constant language of geologists" that "no young have been found" in the fossil state. Amazing assertion! "Therefore it never can be proved that this world has had a longer existence than six thousand years." Astonishing inference! There is not a tyro in geology who ever looked over a set of fossils, or ever spent an hour in exploring a fossiliferous deposit, who does not know that the remains of organisms in every stage of growth may be found lying side by side in the same bed,—that almost every museum contains its series of molluscs, crustaceans, fishes, and corals, formed to illustrate species in their various stages of growth,—that, in especial, among the ammonites of the Secondary ages, and the trilobites of the Palæozoic ones, these series have been made with great care, in order to prevent the erroneous multiplication of species,—and that, in short, every richly fossiliferous stratum in the earth's crust repeats the lesson so often deduced from our churchyards, where graves of all sizes, from that of the infant of a day to that of the aged adult, may be found lying side by side. What the English clergyman represents as "the constant language of geologists," is a language which *no* geologist ever yet used, or ever will. And his inference is in every way worthy of his premises. The flourish with which he concludes his pamphlet would be infinitely amusing had his language been just a little less solemn. "The writer of the above remarks has felt it his duty," we find him saying, "to publish them, not only to refute the arguments of the vain and puffed-up geologist, who fancies himself wiser than God, but also to prevent, by God's blessing, the evils that must ensue from tampering with the sacred text. And now, what has Satan to say? Why, THE TABLES ARE TURNED. Let men beware. Why did not the British Association, at their twenty-third meeting, in September 1853, acknowledge their error as a body, in applauding so loudly the assertion of one of their geological members at a previous meeting, that this earth existed ages before man? They may now have the satisfaction of thinking that, in spite of themselves, those impious plaudits have been turned by the wrath of God into hisses." Strange as the fact may seem, this passage was written, not in grave joke, but in serious earnest.

The belief that fossil remains had never entered into the composition of living organisms, but had been formed in the rocks just as we find them, gradually gave place, during the seventeenth century, to the belief that they were the debris of the Noachian Deluge, and evidences, as they occurred in almost every known country, and were found on the top of lofty hills, of at once its universality and the height to which its waters had prevailed. And this hypothesis, like the others, has been reproduced by some of the anti-geologists of the present day. The known fact,—a result of modern science,—that the several formations (always invariable in their order of succession) have their groupes of organisms peculiar to themselves, has, however, interposed a difficulty from which the earlier cosmogonists were exempt. It has become necessary to show that the Noachian cataclysm was strangely selective, in burying in the beds which it is held by the class to have formed, now one group of plants and animals, now quite another group, and anon yet another and different group still; and all this many times repeated with such nice care and discrimination, that not a single organism of the lower beds is to be detected in the middle ones, nor yet a single organism of either the middle or lower in the beds that lie above. Even this task, however, just a little lightened by here and there a suppression of the facts, has been attempted by the redoubtable Dean of York.[3] Fire and water were, he conceives, equally agents in the great catastrophe that destroyed the old world,—a circumstance which, if true, would have furnished with an admirable apology the class of persons who, according to the wit, would have cried out "Fire, fire," at the Deluge. The Dean conceives that at the commencement of the Flood, when torrents of rain were falling upon the land, numerous submarine volcanoes began to disgorge their molten contents into the sea, destroying the fish, and all other marine productions, by the intensity of the heat, and at the same time locking them up in strata formed of the erupted matter. This process took place ere the land-floods, laden with the spoils of island and continent, and the accompanying mud and sand, could arrive at the remoter depths; which, however, they ultimately reached, and formed a second formation, overlying the first. There were thus two formations originated,—a marine formation below, and a terrestrial or fresh-water formation above; but as these two deposits could not be made to include all the geological phenomena with which even the Dean was acquainted, he had nicely to parcel out the work of his volcanoes on the one hand, and that of his land-floods on the other, into separate fits or paroxysms, each of which served to entomb a distinct class of creatures, and originate a definite set of rocks. Thus, the first work of his volcanoes was to form the Transition series of strata. As a commencement of the whole, the internal fire blew up from the bed of the ocean, in tremendous explosions, vast quantities of pulverized rock mixed with clay, which, slowly subsiding, and covering up, as it sank, shells, stone-lilies, and trilobites, formed the Silurian rocks. A second explosion brought up the vents of the volcanoes to the level of the ocean; and while the Old Red Sandstone, thus produced, and charged with fish killed by the heat, was settling on their flanks, they themselves, as if seized by black vomit, began to disgorge in vast quantities, coal in the liquid state. Very opportunely, just ere it cooled, enormous quantities of vegetables, washed out to sea by the extraordinary land-floods, were precipitated immediately over it; and, sticking in its viscid surface, or sinking into its substance through cracks formed in it during the cooling, they became attached to it in such considerable masses, as to lead long after to the very mistaken notion that coal itself was of vegetable origin. Then there ensued another deposit of red sand, with salt boiled into it; and then a deposition of lime and clay. The land-floods still continuing, the great Sauroid reptiles which had haunted the rivers and lower plains began to yield to their force, and their carcases, floating out to sea, sank amid the slowly subsiding lime and clay, now known as the Lias. The volcanoes too were still very active; and the lighter shells, ammonites, and the like, which had been previously bobbing up and down on the boiling surface, now sank by myriads; for the viscid argillaceous mud thrown up by the fiery ebullitions from beneath stuck fast to them, and dragged them down. Then came the formation of the Oolite, rolled into little egg-like pellets by the waves; and last of all, the Green-sand and Chalk; after which the waters ran off, and sank into the deep hollow which now forms the bed of the ocean, but which previous to the cataclysm had been the place of the land. The Dean, as he went on, fell into some little confusion regarding the true place of some of his animals, such as the Megatherium, which arrived in his arrangement a little too soon. He spoke, too—if a newspaper report is to be credited—of a heavy creature soon overtaken and drowned by the rising waters, which he termed the *pterogactylus*, and which does not seem to have turned up, either in the body or out of it, since it was lost on that memorable occasion. Nor did he make any provision in his arrangement for the formation of the various Tertiary deposits. But then all these are slight matters, that could be very easily woven into his hypothesis. As the flood rose along the hill-sides, first such of the weightier animals would perish as could not readily climb steep acclivities; and then the oxen, the horses, the deer, and the goats, with the lighter carnivora, who, as they would die last,—some of them not until the final disappearance of the hill-tops,—would of course be entombed in the upper deposits. Such is the hypothesis of the Dean of York,—a hypothesis of which it may be justly affirmed, that it is well nigh as ingenious as the circumstances of the case permit, and against which little else can be urged than that it must seem rather cumbrous and fanciful to the class who do not know geology, and, on the whole, somewhat inadequate to the class who do.

The Flood, however, is not left to do the whole geologic work, by even such of the anti-geologists as assign to it the largest share. A great unrecorded convulsion which accompanied the Fall is held by some of their number to have greatly assisted, by laying down the older formations of the fossiliferous rocks; and very much is said to have been done during the extended antediluvian period that succeeded it. One of perhaps the most amusing though least known of the writers that take this special view is a Scotchman, resident in a secluded provincial town, who for the last twelve or fifteen years has been printing ingenious little books against the infidel geologists, and getting letters of similar character inserted in such of our country newspapers as are ambitious of rendering their science equal to their literature. And from the great trouble which he has taken with the writings of the individual who now addresses you, he seems to regard them as peculiarly unsolid and dangerous. According to this profound cosmogonist, the world before the Fall was rather more than twice its present size, and very artificially constructed.[4] It was a hollow ball, supported inside by a frame-work of metal wrought into hexagonal reticulations, somewhat like the frame-work of the great iron bridge over the river Wear at Sunderland; and which had an open space in its centre, occupied by a vast tubular furnace lying direct south and north, which threw out huge volumes of flame towards the poles. Over the reticulated frame-work there rose a great thick *firmament* of metal, which formed the inner shell of the globe; over the metal there lay a considerably thicker shell of granite; and over the granite, a thinner shell of a substance not specified, perhaps not known, but which, from its being completely water-tight, served the purpose of the layer of asphalt or *terra cotta* which the architect spreads over his flat roofs, or on the tops of his sloping terraces, afterwards to be covered with soil and laid out into gardens. Such, it seems, was that portion of the framework of our great globe which corresponded to the hollow lath and plaster frame-work of the little globes used in schools; while its uppermost layer,—correspondent with the slips of the map which the geographer pastes on the model and then varnishes,—was formed of earth and water, economically laid out into "most useful and tasteful configurations,"—the earth into pretty little rising grounds and valleys, and the water into seas and lakes of no great extent, but which formed, from their very handsome combinations, "a terraqueous surface all over PERFECTLY PARADISAICAL." Over this exquisitely neat earth there lay an enveloping atmosphere, greatly thinner and less dense than the air at present is, and incapable, in consequence, of being agitated by storms; while directly over the northern and southern extremities of the world the polar auroras, now so fitful and broken, extended in a permanent arch, and gave light, during the long dark winters, to the regions lying below. And as warmth was as necessary to the paradisaical perfection of these districts as light, they received the necessary heat from the great double-acting furnace in the interior, which, belching out flames at both ends, acted powerfully against the polar portions of the metallic crust or shell, and thus maintained the necessary glow in the absence of the sun, on the principle on which a frying-pan or Scotch *girdle* is heated when placed by the cook-maid over the fire. And such, according to this excellent world-fashioner and very zealous man, was the construction of that unblighted and unbroken earth which was of old pronounced to be "very good." The Fall, however, produced a most remarkable and singularly disastrous change. The earth was somehow partially crushed and broken, contemporaneously with the event,—like a strong fishing-basket when it accidentally falls from a coach-top under the wheel; and, from a most interesting coloured copperplate that illustrates one of the author's treatises (for he draws as well as he writes), the exact damage which it received can be minutely estimated. The interior network was compressed into all sorts of irregular polygons; the iron firmament was broken into great fragments,—some of which may be seen in the print hanging down into the hollow interior, like patches of broken plaster dangling from a ceiling, suspended by the hairs originally employed to give the necessary tenacity to the lime. The great granitic shell was also broken, but broken so nicely on the principle of the arch, that the pieces remained in nearly their original places. Finally, vast rents are seen to occur in the cement and soil of the outer crust; and those great rents, which must have formed enormous gulfs and deep interminable ravines, were destined, it would seem, to perform a most important part in the future geology of the globe. Forming impassable lines of demarcation between the several portions into which they broke up the earth's surface, they imprisoned the recently-created animals in separate groupes, kept as completely from mixing together as the fallow-deer of one loftily-walled park are kept from mixing with the white oxen of another loftily-walled park, or as the kangaroos or duck-billed quadrupeds of Australia are kept by the surrounding ocean from mixing with the tigers of Sumatra or the tortoises of Madagascar. I employ the writer's own happy illustration:—"In some places these fragments" of the earth's crust "would be piled more or less above each other, and in others quite detached and isolated, like fragments of ice on the bank of a river after a thaw." They would of course be on very different levels, each having, as I have said, a distinct group of animals of its own; and when, after the lapse of nearly two thousand years, the great catastrophe of the Flood came on, it would necessarily find, as it rose along the levels, and submerged platform after platform in succession, a different and yet different set of creatures to kill. To borrow from the description of this ingenious cosmogonist, "those on the lower fragments would be first engulphed, and their races completely extinguished from off the surface, and deposited in the earth; then those on higher and higher upwards, till the whole became submerged. And we have only to suppose that man, with the present survivors, were those that occupied one of the higher table-lands when the Flood commenced (and of course in that case

Noah could collect into the ark only out of those of his own country); then the result would be, that man and his present contemporaries would be among the last overwhelmed. This will sufficiently account for the fact of his and their remains not being found deep in the earth." .... "The two most interesting geological facts therefore, namely, that distinct organisms are to be found in distinct formations respectively; and secondly, *that no remains of man, and few or none of the other races at present surviving, are to be found in any but comparatively recent formations,*—these two grand facts of geology, we say, instead of pointing back to vast cycles of ages before the creation, seem to point merely to the peculiar physical circumstances of the fallen planet in the interval between those two eventful stages in its history, the Fall and Flood, and the natural consequences of these circumstances in causing distinct divisions, and some of these of different elevations, among the organic living creatures, during the interval." One other circumstance completes this really original and beautiful hypothesis. The cosmogonist holds that the Flood,—no mere tranquil rising of the waters, as some suppose,—was accompanied by terrible convulsions, which reduced to utter ruin the already shattered earth. The granitic dome fell inwards upon the central furnace; and the fires, bursting outwards under the enormous pressure, found vent at the surface, and made the volcanoes. And this collapsed and diminished world, scarce half the bulk of the old one,—with no heating furnace under its polar regions, nor aught save the merest tatters of an aurora flitting occasionally over them,—greatly too dense in itself, and surrounded by a greatly too dense atmosphere,—with its huge mountains, vast oceans, wide steppes, and arid deserts, with its snows, its frosts, its drenching rains, its horrible tempests, its terrible thunder-storms, and devastating earthquakes,—all alike frightful defects, not in the original plan,—is not only, unlike the primæval world, not very good, or, unlike the antediluvian world, tolerably good, but not good at all. "On taking a bird's-eye view of the geographical and hydrographical features or superficies of the globe," says this bold writer, "any unprejudiced person must at once admit, that in either of these departments there is scarce a trace of that beautiful,

tasteful, and economical design which we have a right to expect
from the admitted qualities of the great Author, and his avowed
object in the structure and report of it when newly finished." It is
added, however, that "its *present object*, as the *Siberia*—the penal
settlement—of expatriated rebels, it is in its *present state* well
calculated to fulfil."

It may be worth mentioning, that the writer who sets himself
after a fashion so peculiar to assert and justify the ways of
Providence against the geologists resides in one of the loveliest
districts in Scotland,—a district, however, shaggy with rock, and
overshadowed by great mountains, and occasionally visited by
earthquake tremors, and both snow and thunder-storms, and so,
with all its wild beauty to other eyes, merely, I must suppose, one
of the rougher districts of the penal Siberia in his. He is, indeed,
particularly severe upon mountains; though not, as he tells us,
wholly devoid of a lurking prejudice in their favour. But what
weak prejudice might palliate or plead for, his better judgement
condemns. "See," says this judicious writer, "vast districts of the
globe disfigured by tremendous masses of rugged and almost
barren mountains. . . What! cry some, would you bury as
deformities the lofty peak and rugged mountain-brow, nature's
palaces,—generally the grandest and most sublime objects in
natural scenery! We cordially assure the reader we are by no
means prejudiced against these grand objects; *for if prejudice we
have on the subject, it is rather on the other side.* It is therefore the
force of evidence alone makes us,—reluctantly we admit,—give up
these to rank among the derangements and deformities of nature.

She, according to her usual *taste* and *economy*, would never be
at the *expense* of rearing, and that upon ground *that might have been
otherwise much better occupied*, such unwieldy, useless masses of
matter, merely for the sake of gratifying the taste for grandeur and
sublimity in a few of her sons, nor, indeed, for any other use we
ever heard ascribed to them. . . According to *our* test, a rich and
gently undulatory surface, intersected with rivulets and sheets of
water, in the places taken up by these elevations, would be far
better, as combining in the highest degree the *utile cum dulce.*"[5] To
such of my audience as are familiar with Dr Thomas Burnet's

"Sacred Theory of the Earth" (1684), that revolution in the cycle of hypothesis to which I have referred, and through which the visionaries of the later ages return to the dreams which had occupied the visionaries of an earlier time, must be sufficiently apparent in this passage. For not only does Burnet speak after the same manner of hills and mountains, but also of an idle, ill-founded prejudice entertained in their favour. We find him thus summing up a general survey of the mountains of the globe:—"Look upon these great ranges: in what confusion do they lie! They have neither form, nor beauty, nor shape, nor order, no more than the clouds in the air. Then, how barren, how desolate, how naked are they! How they stand neglected by nature! Neither the rains can soften them, nor the dews from heaven make them fruitful. I give this short survey of the mountains of the earth *to help remove that prejudice we are apt to have,* or that conceit that the present earth is regularly formed. . . There is nothing in nature," adds this writer, "more shapeless and ill figured than an old rock or a mountain."

I leave it to my audience to determine how far this depreciatory view,—whether regarded as that of Dr Burnet or of the modern anti-geologist,—agrees with the estimate of the higher minds, or whether it manifests the proper respect for the adorable Being who, in his infinite wisdom, made our world what it is. Let me next show that some of even the abler and more respectable anti-geologists exhibit no very profound veneration for the letter of Scripture, when, instead of bearing, as they think, against the deductions of their opponents, they find it directly opposed to fancies of their own. It is held by not a few among them, that at the Deluge the sea and land changed places. When the waters receded, it was found, they allege, that the old land had become ocean, and the old ocean had become land; and as there are certain rivers which are described in Scripture as flowing beside Eden, and which, judging by the names given them, still exist, it has become imperative on the assertors of the hypothesis to show that the rivers which now drain tracts of what they hold was then sea, and that fall into seas which they hold were then land, could not by any possibility have formed the boundaries of the old Adamic garden. Let us mark how Mr Granville Penn,—certainly one of the

most extensively informed of his class,—deals with this difficulty.[6]
There are, he argues, certain great corruptions of Scripture. What
had been at first written as marginal notes by uninspired men, and
were in some cases very erroneous and absurd, came in the course
of transcription to be transferred, wholly by mistake, from the side
of the page into the body of the text; and thus, in at least a few
places, the Scriptures were vitiated, and now declare, instead of
Divine truth, what is neither sense nor fact. And on this very
general, and certainly most perilous ground, he goes on to argue,
unsupported by a single ancient manuscript, and solely on what he
terms internal evidence, that the verses in Genesis which conflict
with his hypothesis must be regarded as mere idle glosses,
ignorantly or surreptitiously introduced into the text by the
ancient copyists. "In the second chapter of Genesis," we find him
saying, "*there appears an internal critical evidence* of an insertion of
the 11th, 12th, 13th, and 14th verses, similar to that of the 4th
verse of the 5th chapter of St John, and constituting, in a similar
manner, a *parenthesis* intersecting the thread of the narrative, and
introduced solely for a similar purpose of illustration. It does not
wear the character of the simple narrative in which it appears, but
of *the surcharge of the gloss or note of a later age, founded upon the
fanciful traditions then prevailing with respect to the situation of the
ancient Paradise.*" This certainly is cutting the knot; and, if erected
into a precedent by the geologist, would no doubt greatly facilitate
the labour of reconciliation. It would, however, be perilous work
for *him*. "A wolf," says Plutarch, "peeping into a hut where a
company of shepherds were assembled, saw them regaling
themselves with a joint of mutton. 'Ye gods!' he exclaimed, 'what
a clamour these men would have raised if they had caught *me* at
such a banquet.'" I need scarcely add, that the hypothesis in
whose behalf Scripture is thus divested of its authority, and
recklessly cast aside, is entirely a worthless one; and that the
various continents of the globe, instead of all dating from one
period little more than four thousand years back, are of very
various ages,—some of them comparatively modern, though
absolutely old in relation to human history; and some of so hoar an
antiquity, that the term since man appeared upon earth might be

employed as a mere unit to measure it by.

It need not surprise us that a writer who takes such strange liberties with a book which he professes to respect, and which he must have had many opportunities of knowing, should take still greater liberties with a science for which he entertains no respect whatever, and of whose first principles he is palpably ignorant. And yet the wild recklessness of some of his explanations of geological phenomena must somewhat astonish all sufficiently acquainted with the science to know that the place and relations of its various formations have been long since determined, and now as certainly form the regulating data of the practical miner, as the places and relations long since determined by the geographer form the regulating data of the practical navigator or engineer. It is as certain, for instance, that the Oolitic system underlies the Green Sand and the Chalk, with all the various formations of the Tertiary division,—Eocene, Miocene, Pliocene, and Pleistocene,—as that York is situated to the south of Edinburgh, or that both those cities lie very considerably to the north of London and Paris. And the anti-geologist who would argue, in the heat of controversy, that the Oolite and the Pleistocene were contemporaneous deposits, would be no more worthy of reply than the anti-geographer who would assert, in order to serve some argumentative purpose, that the North Cape lies in the same latitudinal parallel as South California, or that Terra del Fuego is but a day's sailing from Iceland. And yet such, as I intimated on a former evening, is the line taken up by Mr Granville Penn, in dealing with the difficulties of the Kirkdale Cave, so remarkable for its accumulations of gnawed bones of the Pleistocene ages,—especially for its bones of hyænas, tigers, bears, wolves, rhinoceroses, and elephants. The cave occurs in the moorlands of Yorkshire, in a limestone rock of that Oolitic division to which the Oxford Clay and the Coral Rag belong, and contains corals and shells that had passed into extinction long even ere the Tertiary period began; while in the cave itself, mixed with bones of the extinct mammals of the geologic age in immediate advance of the present one, there have been found the contemporary remains of animals that still live in our fields and woods, such as the hare, the rabbit, the weasel, and the water-rat. And we find Mr Penn assigning both the Oolitic rock, in which the cave is hollowed, and the mammalian remains of the cave itself, equally to the period of the Deluge. The limestone existed at that time, it would seem, as a soft calcareous paste, into which the animal remains, floated northwards from intertropical regions on the waters of the Flood, were precipitated in vast quantities, and sank, and then, fermenting under the putrefactive influences, the gas which they formed blew up the yielding lime and mud around them into a long narrow cave, just as a glass-blower blows up a bottle, or as a little yeast blows up into similar but greatly smaller cavities, a bit of leaven. And the stalactites and stalagmites which encrust the Kirkdale Cave are, Mr Penn holds, simply the last runnings of the lime that exuded after the general mass had begun to set. Certainly any one disposed to take such liberties with the Bible on the one hand, and with geologic science on the other, as those taken in the given instances by this most formidable of the anti-geologists, could have but little difficulty in making either Scripture as geological or geology as Scriptural as he had a mind. His chief danger would be that of making the sounder theologians just a little angry, and of escaping, unless quoted for the joke's sake, the notice of the geologists altogether. In truth, the extreme absurdity of our later anti-geologists in virtually contending, in the controversy, that *their* ignorance of an interesting science, founded on millions of determined facts, ought to be permitted to weigh against the knowledge of the men who have studied it most thoroughly, forms their best defence. It secures them against all save neglect. As, however, some of their number are well-meaning men, who would not be ridiculous if they could help it, and only oppose themselves to the geologists because they deem them mischievous and in error, it may be worth while showing them, by an example or two, the ludicrous nature of the positions which in their honest ignorance they permit themselves to occupy, and the real scope and bearing of the arguments which they unwittingly permit themselves to use. I shall adduce two several instances of reasoning, directed by the anti-geologists *against* their antagonists (as they themselves believed), but which, from their ignorance of the true state of the argument, and of the bearing of the facts with which they dealt, in reality made out for these antagonists as strong a case as they could possibly have made out for themselves. And I am sure that, rather than be found siding with their opponents, the anti-geologists would be content even to acquire a little geology.

I shall select my first instance from the records of the annual controversy which used to rage some ten or fifteen years ago, in sermons, newspapers, and magazines, immediately after every meeting of the British Association. A religious Dublin newspaper,—the "Statesman and Record,"—since extinct, took always an active part in these discussions on the anti-geological side, and boldly affirmed, as in a number now before me, that geology had the devil for its author. A learned correspondent of the paper, who was, however, somewhat more charitable, thought that at least, the *facts* of the science might be exempted from a condemnation so sweeping; nay, that, well interpreted, they might be found decidedly opposed to at least the more mischievous deductions of the geologists; and in illustrating the point, we find him thus arguing, from certain appearances in the valley of the Nile, that the globe which we inhabit cannot possibly be more than six thousand years old.[7] "The valley of the Nile," says this writer, "is known to be covered with a bed of slime which the river has deposited in its periodical inundations, and which rests on a foundation of sand, like that of the adjacent desert. The French savans who accompanied Bonaparte in his Egyptian expedition made several experiments to ascertain the thickness and depth of this superincumbent bed. They dug about two hundred pits, and carefully measured the thickness in the transversal section of the valley, where the deposit had been free from obstacles, and had not been materially increased or lessened by local causes. They found the mean of all these measurements to be six and a half metres, or rather more than twenty feet. M. Gironde endeavoured to determine the quantity of slime deposited in a century; and he found that the elevation of soil in that period was rather less than four inches and a half! Dividing the total thickness of the bed by the centenary elevation, he found the quotient 56.50; whence it followed that the inundations had commenced 5650 years before the year 1800, when the experiments were made,—a number which only differed 159 years from the Mosaic date. The difference is not very important, when it is considered that the most trifling error, whether in the measure of the entire superincumbent bed, or in the valuation of the quantity of slime deposited in a century, affects the final results. Notwithstanding this, the coincidence between the sacred historian and the computations of science is remarkable, and furnishes one proof more of the harmony existing between nature and revelation. An honest experimentalist was constrained to arrive at this conclusion at a period when the infidel school of our continental neighbours was in high feather. I am sorry to add, that the result of his own calculation had not that effect on the philosopher himself, or his freethinking associates, which, for their own sakes, was desirable; but it is no less valuable to us on that account; for we know that an unwilling witness to the truth is worth a score of evidences already prejudiced in its favour."

Now, this is clear, distinct statement; and nothing can be more evident than that the theologian who makes it holds he is reasoning with conclusive effect in behalf of what may be termed the short chronology,—not in its legitimate connection with the recent introduction of the human species, but in its supposed bearing on the age of the earth. And in doing so he commits himself to the apparent positive fact, determined on what may be regarded as geologic data, that the river Nile has been flowing over its bed for about as many years as have elapsed, according to the Hebrew chronology adopted by Usher, since the creation of man, and no more. To the integrity of this inference he pledges himself, as an inference to which the infidel ought to have yielded, as conclusive in its bearing on the question of the earth's age, and as of singular value to the believer who sets himself to deal with the evidences of his faith. Now, without referring to the circumstance that the data on which the French savans under Napoleon founded have since been challenged by geologists, such as Lieutenant Newbold and Sir G. Wilkinson, who have carefully surveyed the rocks and soils of Egypt with the assistance of clearer

light than existed at the commencement of the century, let us, for
the argument's sake, hold the inference to be quite as good as this
theologian regards it. And see, we urge upon him, that you yourself
do not suffer it to drop should you find that it commits you to the
other side of the argument. Be at least as fair and honest as you
say the infidels ought to have been. The six and a half metres of silt
and slime,—representative, let us hold, of from five to six
thousand years,—rest, you say, on "a foundation of sand like that
of the adjacent desert." But have you ascertained on what the
sand rests? I know nothing of that, replies the theologian; I had
not even thought of that. But the geologist has thought of it, we
reply; and has spent much time under the hot sun in ascertaining
the point. For nearly three hundred miles,—from the inner
boundaries of the delta to within a few hours' journey of the
cataracts,—the silt and sand rest on what is known as the
"marine" or nummulitic limestone,—a formation of great extent,
for it runs into the Nubian desert on the one hand, and into the
Libyan desert on the other; and which, though it abounds in the
animalcules of the European chalk, is held to belong, in at least its
upper beds, which are charged with nummulites, to the earlier
Eocene. Over this marine limestone there rests a newer formation,
of later Tertiary age, which contains the casts of sea-shells, and
whole forests of dicotyledonous trees, converted into a flint-like
chert; and over all repose the sands and gravels of the desert.
Underneath the silt of the river, then, and the sand of the desert,
lie these two formations of the Tertiary division. The lower, which
is of great thickness, must have been of slow formation. It is
composed almost exclusively, in many parts, of microscopic
animals, and abounds in others in fossil shells,—nautili, ostreadæ,
turritella, and nummulites, with corals, sponges, the remains of
crustacea, and the teeth of fishes. And between the period of its
deposition and that of the formation which rests upon it the
surface of what is now Egypt must have been elevated over the
surface of the sea, to be covered, in the course of ages, by great
forests, which, ere the land assumed its present form and level,
were submerged by another oscillation of the surface, and petrified
amid beds of a siliceous sand at the bottom of the ocean. Nor is the

underlying marine limestone by any means the oldest of the sedimentary rocks of Egypt. It rests on a sandstone of Permian or Triassic age; the sandstone rests, in turn, on the famous Breccia de Verde of Egypt; and the Breccia on a group of Azoic rocks, gneisses, quartzes, mica schists, and clay slates, that wrap round the granitic nucleus of Syene. The formations of Egypt constitute a well-determined part of that great series of systems which compose the upper portion of the earth's crust: its silt is by far the most inconsiderable of its deposits; and if five thousand six hundred and fifty years were exhausted in laying down layer after layer of the twenty feet which form *its* average thickness, what enormous periods must we not demand in addition for the laying down of the forest formation, of the marine limestone formation, of the New Red Sandstone formation, of the Breccia de Verde formation, and, in short, for the some ten miles of fossiliferous rock of which these deposits form such definite, well-determined portions; besides the time necessary for the production of the enormously developed Azoic rocks which lie under all! The theologian, in this instance, instead of reasoning, as he himself supposed, in behalf of the short chronology, has been making out a very formidable case for the long one; and all that the geologist can have to urge upon him in the circumstances is simply that he should act as he holds the infidel ought to have done, and yield to the force of evidence. I may mention in the passing, that some of the most ancient buildings of Egypt are formed of the Tertiary

Fig. 116.

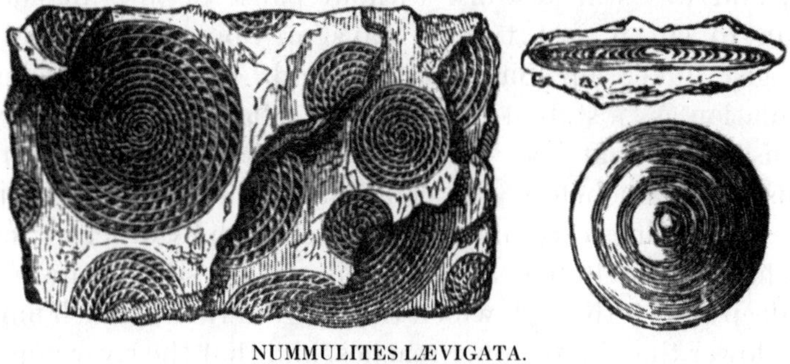

NUMMULITES LÆVIGATA.
(*Pharoah's Beans.*)

marine limestones of the country; the stones of the pyramids are charged with nummulites, known to the Arabs as "Pharaoh's beans;" and these organisms stand out in high relief on the weathered portions of the Great Sphinx. Some of the oldest things in the world in their relation to human history,—erections, many of which had survived the memory of their founders even in the days of Herodotus,—are formed of materials so modern in their relation to the geologic epochs, that they had no existence as rock until after the Palæozoic and Secondary ages had gone by. Not only the Carboniferous sandstone of the High Church and Parliament House of Edinburgh, but even the Oolitic (*i.e.* Portland stone) of Somerset House and St Paul's, are of an antiquity incalculably vast compared with the stone out of which the oldest of the pyramids were fashioned.

The second example which I shall adduce is one with which many of my auditors must be already familiar. The Falls of Niagara are gradually eating their way through an elevated tract of table-land, upwards towards Lake Erie, at the rate of about fifty yards in forty years; and it has been argued by Sir Charles Lyell, that as they are now seven miles distant from Queenston, where the elevation of the plateaux begins, they must have taken about ten thousand years to scoop out their present deep channel through that space.[8] Ten thousand years ago the Falls were, he infers, at Queenston; and the grounds on which he reasons are exactly those on which one would infer that a labourer who had cut a ditch two hundred yards long at the rate of ten yards per day, and was still at work without pause or intermission, had begun to cut it just twenty days previous. A reverend anti-geologist takes up Sir Charles;[9] and, after denouncing the calculation as "a stab at the Christian religion," seeing it involves the assertion that the "Falls were actually at Queenston four thousand years before the creation of the world according to Moses," he brings certain facts, adduced both by other writers and Sir Charles himself, to bear on the calculation, such as the fact that the deep trench through which the Niagara runs is much narrower in its lower than in its upper reaches, and that the river must have performed its work of excavation when the breadth was less, at a greatly quicker rate than now. And thus the work of excavating the trench is brought fairly within the six thousand years. Nor is the principle of the reasoning bad. In our illustration of the ditch excavated by the labourer we of course take it for granted that it is a ditch of the same depth and breadth throughout, and excavated in the same sort of soil; for if greatly narrower and shallower at one place than at another, or dug in a greatly softer mould, the rate of its excavation at different times might be very different indeed, and the general calculation widely erroneous, if based on the ratio of progress when it went on most slowly, taken as an average ratio for the whole. But the anti-geologist provokes only a smile when, in his triumph, he exultingly exclaims, "It is on grounds such as these that the most learned and voluminous among English geologists disputes the Mosaic history of the Creation and Deluge,—a strong proof that even men of argument on other subjects often reason in the most childish and ridiculous manner, and on grounds totally false, when they undertake to deny the truth of the Holy Scriptures." Now, it must be wholly unnecessary to remark here, that it is surely one thing to "undertake to deny the truth of the Holy Scriptures," and quite another and different thing to hold that the Niagara Falls may have been at Queenston ten thousand years ago; or further, that it seems not in the least wise to stake the truth of Revelation on any such issue. Let me request you, however, to observe, that in one important respect this writer resembles the former one. The former, ignorant of the various phenomena exhibited by the great deposits of Egypt, exhausted all his five thousand six hundred years of available time in accounting for the formation of one of the least of them,—the silt of the Nile; and the latter, though he bids down Sir Charles some four thousand four hundred years or so in the one item of scooping out the bed of the St Lawrence, at least expends the remainder of the ten thousand,—his five thousand six hundred years,—in that work of excavation alone, and leaves himself no farther sums to set off against the various geologic processes that may have preceded it.

In this case, as in the other, let us grant, for the argument's sake, all the facts. Let us admit that the trench through which the

St Lawrence now flows has been cut by the river in somewhat less than six thousand years. But through what, let us ask, has it been cut? There can exist no doubt on the subject: it has been cut through an ancient graveyard of the Upper Silurian system, charged with the peculiar fossils characteristic of what are known as the Clinton and Niagara groupes, and common, many of them, to the Upper Silurian of our own country and of the European continent. *Leptæna depressa* and *Pentamerus oblongus*, two of the most frequent shells of the deposit, occur also in equal abundance in the Dudley and Caradoc formations of England; its prevailing encrinite, *Ichthyocrinus lævis*, is scarce distinguishable from an encrinite which I have often picked up in the quarries of the "Wren's Nest" (*Ichthyocrinus pyriformis*); while its prevailing trilobite, *Phacops limulurus*, seems to be but a transatlantic variety of our well-known *Asaphus (Phacops) caudatus*. Farther, the sequence of the various formations both above and below the Niagara group is shown with remarkable distinctness in that part of the world along the shores of the great lakes. They may be traced downward, on the one hand, along the Lower Silurian deposits, to the non-fossiliferous base on which the system rests, and upwards, on the other, through the Old Red Sandstone and the Carboniferous Limestone, to the workable Coal Measures. Both stratigraphically and palæontologically the place in the scale of the Niagara graveyard can be definitely determined; and a superficial deposit on the heights in its immediate neighbourhood shows that the river did not begin its work of excavation among its long extinct shells, trilobites, and corals, until after not only the great Palæozoic, but also the Secondary and Tertiary divisions had been laid down, and the recent period ushered in. The superficial shells of the adjacent heights belong to the Pleistocene age, and show that in even that comparatively modern time the lower lands of Upper Canada were submerged beneath the level of the ocean, and that a series of deep seas, connected by broad sounds, occupied the place of the great lakes. Not until the last upheaval of the land was the river now known as the St Lawrence called into existence, to begin its work of excavation; and ere that event took place, fully ten miles of fossiliferous rock had been deposited on the earth's surface, charged with the remains of many succeeding creations. The deposit through which the St Lawrence is slowly mining its way is older than the river itself by the vast breadth of the four Tertiary periods, by that of all the Secondary ages,—Cretaceous, Oolitic, and Triassic,—by the periods, too, of the Permian system, of the Carboniferous system, of the Old Red system, and of the uppermost beds of the Upper Silurian system. But a simple illustration may better serve to show the true character of the conclusion urged here by the opponent of Sir Charles, than any such line of statement as that which I employ, however clear to the geologist. In the year 1817, Prince's Street, in Edinburgh, was opened up to the Calton Hill, and the Calton burying-ground cut through to the depth of many feet by the roadway. Let us suppose that when the excavation has been carried a hundred yards into the cemetery, a geologist, finding the labourers cutting on the average about a yard per day, simply intimates as his opinion that the labourers have been a hundred days at work. "No," replies a controversialist on the anti-geological side; "for the first fifty yards, so soft was the subsoil, and so shallow the covering of mould, that the labourers must have cut at the rate of *two* yards a-day: it has been merely for the last fifty yards that they have been excavating at the present slow rate: they cannot have been more than seventy-five days at work. I marvel exceedingly at the absurdity of geological reasoners: *palpably the burying-ground of the Calton is only seventy-five days old.*" Now, such, in no exaggerated, but, on the contrary, greatly modified form, is the argument that would limit the age of the earth to the period during which the St Lawrence has been scooping out a channel for itself, from Queenston to Niagara, through an ancient Silurian burying-ground. Both arguments alike confound the age of the ancient burying-grounds with the date of the modern excavations opened up through them; but in order to render the argument of my illustration equally absurd with the other, it would be not only necessary to infer that the Calton cemetery was only seventy-five days old, but also that the rock on which it rested was no older.

But enough of follies such as these! I had marked a good many other passages of similar character in the writings of the recent anti-geologists, and would have little difficulty in filling a volume with such, but it would be a useless, though mayhap curious work, and is much better exhibited by specimen than as a whole. A little folly is amusing; but much of it fatigues. There is a time coming, and now not very distant, when the vagaries of the anti-geologists will be as obsolete as those of the geographers of Salamanca, or as those of the astronomers who upheld the orthodoxy of Ptolemy against Galileo and Newton; and when they will be regarded as a sort of curious fossils, very monstrous and bizarre, and altogether of an extinct type, but which had once not only life, but were formidable. It will then be seen by all what a noble vestibule the old geologic ages form to that human period in which moral responsibility first began upon earth, and a creature destined to immortality anticipated an eternal hereafter. There is always much of the mean and the little in the worlds which man creates for himself, and in the history which he gives them. Of all the abortions of the middle ages which have come down to us, I know not a more miserable one,—at once ludicrous and sad,—than that heavens and earth of Cosmas *Indicopleustes*, the monk, which I illustrated by diagrams in my last lecture (figs. 114, 115.) They are just such heavens and earth as a monk might have made, and made too at a sitting. The heavens, represented as a solid arch raised on tall walls, resemble, as a whole, the arch which figures in the middle of a freemason's apron, or, more homely still, the section of a wine-cellar; while the earth lies beneath as a great plain or floor, with a huge hill in the distance, behind which the sun passes when it is night. And yet this scheme gave law to the world for more than six centuries, and lay like a nightmare on physical discovery, astronomic and geographical. The anti-geologists have been less mischievous, for they live in a more enlightened age; and we already see but the straggling remains of the body, and know that the time cannot be far distant when it will be as completely extinct as any of the old faunas. The great globe, ever revolving on itself, and journeying in space round the sun, in obedience to laws which it immortalized a Newton to discover and demonstrate, is an infinitely more sublime and noble object than the earth of Cosmas the monk, with its conical mountain and its crypt-like firmament;

nor can I doubt that its history throughout the long geologic ages,—its strange story of successive creations, each placed in advance of that which had gone before, and its succeeding organisms, vegetable and animal, ranged according to their appearance in time, on principles which our profounder students of natural science have but of late determined,—will be found in an equal degree more worthy of its Divine Author than that which would huddle the whole into a few literal days, and convert the incalculably ancient universe which we inhabit into a hastily run-up erection of yesterday.

1. The gentleman here referred to lectured no later than October 1853 against the doctrines of the geologists; and modestly chose as the scene of his labours the city of Hutton and Playfair. What he set himself specially to "demonstrate" was, as he said, that the geologic "theories as to antiquity of the earth, successive eras, &c. were not only fallacious and unphilosophical, but rendered nugatory the authority of the Sacred Scriptures." Not only, however, did he exert himself in demolishing the geologists as infidel, but he denounced also as unsound the theology of good old Isaac Watts. The lines taught us in our infancy,—

> "Let dogs delight to bark and bite,
>   For God hath made them so,"—

were, he remarked, decidedly heterodox. They ought to have run instead—

> "Let dogs delight to bark and bite,
>   *Satan* hath made them so." !!!

2. "A Brief and Complete Refutation of the Anti-Scriptural Theory of Geologists." by a Clergyman of the Church of England. London: Wertheim & Macintosh. 1853.

3. Newspaper Report of Meeting of the British Association held at York in September 1844.

4. See "Primary and Present State of the Solar System, particularly of our own planet;" and "Exposure of the Principles of Modern Geology." By P. M'Farlane, Author of the "Primary and Present State of the Solar System." Edinburgh: Thomas Grant.

5. One of the more brilliant writers of the present day,—a native of the picturesque village in which this anti-geologist resides,—describes in a recent work, with the enthusiasm of the poet, the noble mountains which rise around it. I know not, however, whether my admiration of the passage was not in some degree dashed by a few comic notions suggestive of an "imaginary conversation," in the style of Landor, between this popular author and his anti-geologic townsman, on the merits of hills in general, and in especial on the claims of those which encircle Comrie "as the mountains are round about Jerusalem." The two gentlemen would, I suspect, experience considerable difficulty in laying down, in such a discussion, their common principles.

6. "Comparative Estimate of the Mineral and Mosaical Geologies." By Granville Penn, Esq. London, 1825.

7. "Statesman and Record," October 6th 1846.

8. Sir Charles Lyell's statement is by no means so express or definite as it is represented to be in this passage, in which I have taken the evidence of his opponents regarding it. What he really says (see his "Principles," second edition, 1832) is what follows:—"*If* the ratio of recession had never exceeded fifty yards in forty years, it must have required nearly ten thousand years for the excavation of the whole ravine; but no probable conjecture can be offered as to the quantity of time consumed in such an operation, because the retrograde movement may have been much more rapid when the whole current was confined within a space not exceeding a fourth or fifth of that which the Falls now occupy." In the eighth edition of the same work, however, published in 1850, after he had examined the Falls, there occurs the following re-statement of the case:—"After the most careful inquiries I was able to make during my visit to the spot in 1841-42, I came to the conclusion that the average [recession] of one foot a-year would be a much more probable conjecture than that of one and a quarter yards. In that case it would have required *thirty five thousand years* for the retreat of the Falls from the escarpment of Queenston to their present site. It seems by no means improbable that

such a result would be no exaggeration of the truth, although we cannot assume that the retrograde movement has been uniform. At some points it may have receded much faster than at present; but in general its progress was probably slower, because the cataract, when it began to recede, must have been nearly twice its present height."

9. "Scottish Christian Herald," 1838, vol.iii. p.766.

LECTURE ELEVENTH.

ON THE LESS KNOWN FOSSIL FLORAS OF SCOTLAND.*

PART I.

SCOTLAND has its four fossil floras,—its flora of the Old Red Sandstone, its Carboniferous flora, its Oolitic flora, and that flora of apparently Tertiary age of which his Grace the Duke of Argyll found so interesting a fragment overflown by the thick basalt beds and trap tuffs of Mull. Of these, the only one adequately known to the geologist is the gorgeous flora of the Coal Measures,—probably the richest, in at least individual plants, which the world has yet seen. The others are all but wholly unknown; and the Association may be the more disposed to tolerate the comparative meagreness of the few brief remarks which I purpose making on two of their number,—the floras of the Old Red Sandstone and the Oolite,—from the consideration that that meagreness is only too truly representative of the present state of our knowledge regarding them; and that if my descriptions be scanty and inadequate, it is only because the facts are still few. How much of the lost may yet be recovered I know not; but the circumstance that two great floras,—remote predecessors of the existing one,—which once covered with their continuous mantle of green the dry land of what is now Scotland, should be represented by but a few coniferous fossils, a few cycadaceous fronds, a few ferns and

* The substance of this and the following lecture was originally given in a single paper, before the Geological Section of the British Association, held at Glasgow in September 1855. So considerable have been the additions, however, that the one paper has swelled into two lectures. Most of the added matter was at first thrown into the form of notes; but it was found, that from their length and frequency, they would have embarrassed the printer, mayhap the reader also; and so most of the larger ones have been introduced into the text within brackets.

club mosses, must serve to show what mere fragments of the past history of our country we have yet been able to recover from the rocks, and how very much in the work of exploration and discovery still remains for us to do. We stand on the farther edge of the great floras of by-past creations, and have gathered but a few handfuls of faded leaves, a few broken branches, a few decayed cones.

The Silurian deposits of our country have not yet furnished us with any unequivocal traces of a terrestrial vegetation. Professor Nicol of Aberdeen, on subjecting to the microscope the ashes of a Silurian anthracite which occurs in Peeblesshire, detected in it minute tubular fibres, which seem, he says, to indicate a higher class of vegetation than the algæ; but these may have belonged to a marine vegetation notwithstanding. I detected some years ago, in the Trilobite-bearing schists of Girvan, associated with graptolites of the Lower Silurian type, a vegetable organism somewhat resembling the leaf of one of the pond-weeds,—an order of plants, some of whose species, such as Zostera, find their proper habitats in salt water. I have placed beside this

Fig. 117.

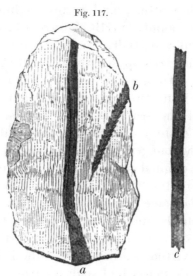

a. SILURIAN ORGANISM.   *b.* GRAPTOLITE.
c. PORTION OF THE LEAF OF ZOSTERA MARINA.

specimen a fragment of the same graptolite-bearing rock, across which I have pasted part of a leaf of *Zostera marina*, the only plant of our Scottish seas which is furnished with true roots, bears real flowers inclosed in herbaceous spathes, and produces a well-formed farinaceous seed. It will be seen, that in the few points of comparison which can be instituted between forms so exceedingly simple, the ancient very closely resembles the recent organism. It is not impossible, therefore, that the Silurian vegetable may have belonged to some tribe of plants allied to Zostera; and if so, we can easily conceive how the Silurian anthracite of our country may be altogether of marine origin, and may yet exhibit in its microscopic tubular fibres vestiges of a vegetation higher than the algæ.

[It were well, in dealing with the very ancient floras, in which equivocal forms occur that might have belonged to either the land or the sea, to keep in view those curious plants of the present time, the habitats of which are decidedly marine, but which are marked by many of the peculiarities of the seed-bearing plants of the land. The superiority of Zostera to the common sea-weeds of our coasts appears to have struck in the north of Scotland eyes very little practised in such matters, and seems to have given rise, in consequence, to a popular myth. *Zostera marina* abounds on a series of sand-banks, partially uncovered by the larger stream tides, which lie directly opposite the town of Cromarty, near the spot pointed out by tradition as the site of an earlier town, which was swept away some two or three hundred years ago by the encroachments of the sea. And these banks, with their thick covering of green Zostera, used to be pointed out by the fishermen of the place, in my younger days, as the *meadows* of the old town, still bearing their original coverings of vegetation,—a vegetation altered no doubt by the "sea change" that had come over it, but still essentially the same, it was said, as that which had smiled around the old burgh, and not at all akin to the brown kelp or tangle that every storm from the boisterous north-east heaps along the shore. It was virtually affirmed that the luxuriant terrestrial grasses of ancient Cromarty had made a virtue of necessity in their altered circumstances; and that, settling down into grasses of the sea, they remained to testify that an ancient Cromarty there had *once been. Zostera marina*, like most plants of the land, ripens its seeds towards the close of autumn; and I have seen a smart night's frost at this season, when coincident with a stream-tide that laid bare the beds, nip its seed-bearing stems by thousands; and have found them strewed along the beach a few days after, with all their grass-like spikes fully developed, and their grain-like seeds charged with a farinaceous substance, which one would scarce expect to find developed in the sea. In the higher reaches of the Cromarty Frith, the Zostera beds, which are of great extent, are much frequented, during the more protracted frosts of a severe winter, by wild geese and swans, that dig up and feed upon the saccharine roots of the plant. The Zostera of the warmer latitudes attain to a larger size than those of our Scottish seas. "A southern species," says Loudon, "*Zostera oceanica*, has leaves a foot long and an inch broad. It is used as a thatch, which is said to last a century; bleaches white with exposure; and furnishes the rush-like material from which the envelops of Italian liquor-flasks are prepared." The simple rectilinear venation of ribbon-like fronds, usually much broken, that occurs in the Lower Old Red Sandstone, has often reminded me of that exhibited by this exotic species of Zostera.]

Associated with the earliest ichthyic remains of the Old Red Sandstone, we find vegetable organisms in such abundance, that they communicate often a fissile character to the stone in which they occur. But, existing as mere carbonaceous markings, their state of keeping is usually so bad, that they tell us little else than that the antiquely-formed fishes of this remote period swam over sea-bottoms darkened by forests of algæ. The prevailing plant was one furnished with a long, smooth stem, which, though it threw off, in the alternate order, numerous branches at least half as stout as itself, preserved its thickness for considerable distances without diminution,—a common fucoidal characteristic. We find its remains mixed in the rock, though sparingly, with those of a rough-edged plant, knobbed somewhat like the thong-like receptacles of *Himanthalia lorea*, which also threw off branches like the other, but diminished more rapidly. A greatly more minute vegetable organism of the same beds, characterized by its bifid partings, which strike off at angles of about sixty, somewhat

Fig. 118.

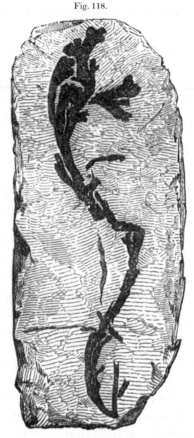

FUCOID.

resembles the small-fronded variety of *Dictyota dichotoma*, save that the slim terminations of the frond are usually bent into little hooks, like the tendrils of the pea just as their points begin to turn. Another rather rare plant of the period, existing as a broad, irregularly-cleft frond, somewhat resembling that of a modern *Cutleria* or *Nitophyllum*, betrays at once, in its outline and general appearance, its marine origin; as does also an equally rare contemporary, which, judging from its appearance, seems to have been a true fucus. It exists in the rock as if simply drawn in Indian ink; for it exhibits no structure, though, as in some of the ferns of

the Coal Measures, what were once the curls of its leaflets continue
to exist as sensible hollows on the surface. It broadens and divides

Fig. 119.

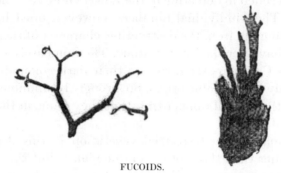

FUCOIDS.

atop into three or four lobes, and these, in turn, broaden and
divide into minor lobes, double or ternate, and usually rounded at
their terminations. In general appearance the plant not a little
resembles those specimens of *Fucus vesiculosus* which we find
existing in a diminutive form, and divested of both the receptacles
and the air-vessels, at the mouth of rivers. Of two other kinds of
plants I have seen only confused masses, in which the individuals
were so crowded together, and withal so fragmentary and broken,
that their separate forms could not be traced. In the one the
general appearance was such as might be produced by compressed
and tangled masses of *Chorda filium*, in which the linear and even
tubular character of the plant could be determined, but not its
continuous, cord-like aspect; in the other, the fragments seemed
well nigh as slim as hairs, and the appearance was such as might be
produced by branches of that common ectocarpus, *E. littoralis,*
which may be seen on our rocky coasts roughening at low water
the stems of laminaria. When highly magnified, a mesial groove
might be detected running along each of the hair-like lines. With
these marine plants we occasionally find large rectilinear stems,
resolved into a true coal, but retaining no organic character by
which to distinguish them. As I have seen some of these more than
three inches in diameter, and, though existing as mere fragments,

several feet in length, they must, if they were also plants of the sea, have exceeded in size our largest laminaria.* And such are the few vegetable organisms, of apparently aquatic origin, which I have hitherto succeeded in detecting in the Lower Old Red Sandstone of Scotland.† Their individual numbers, however, must have been very great, though, from the destructible character of their tissues, their forms have perished in the stone. The immensely developed flagstones of Caithness seem to owe their dark colour to organic matter mainly of vegetable origin. So strongly bituminous, indeed, are some of the beds of dingier tint, that they flame in the fire like slates steeped in oil.

The remains of a terrestrial vegetation in this deposit are greatly scantier than those of its marine plants; but they must be regarded as possessing a peculiar interest, as, with the exception of the spore cases of the Ludlow rocks, the oldest of their class, in at least the British islands, whose true place in the scale can be satisfactorily established. In the flagstones of Orkney there occurs,

* A curious set of these, with specimens of the smooth-stemmed fucoid collected by Mr John Miller of Thurso,—a meritorious labourer in the geologic field,—were exhibited at Glasgow to the Association. The larger stems were thickly traversed in Mr J. Miller's specimens by diagonal lines, which seemed, however, to be merely lines of rhomboidal fracture in the glassy coal into which the plants were converted, and not one of their original characters.

† I must, however, add, that there was found in the neighbourhood of Stromness about fifteen years ago, by Dr John Fleming, a curious nondescript vegetable organism, which, though equivocal in character and appearance, was in all probability a plant of the sea. It consisted of a flattened cylinder, in some of the specimens exceeding a foot in length by an inch in breadth, and traversed on both the upper and under sides by a mesial groove extending to the extremities. It bore no external markings, and the section exhibited but an indistinct fibrous structure, sufficient however, to indicate its vegetable origin. I have not hitherto succeeded in finding for myself specimens of this organism, which has been named provisionally by Dr Fleming *Stroma obscura*; but it seems not improbable that certain supposed fragments of wood, detected by Mr Charles Peach in the Caithness Flagstones, but which do not exhibit the woody structure, may have belonged to it.

Fig. 120.

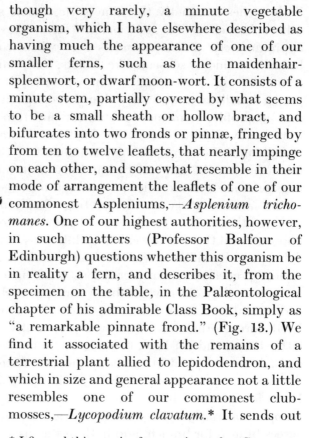

though very rarely, a minute vegetable organism, which I have elsewhere described as having much the appearance of one of our smaller ferns, such as the maidenhair-spleenwort, or dwarf moon-wort. It consists of a minute stem, partially covered by what seems to be a small sheath or hollow bract, and bifurcates into two fronds or pinnæ, fringed by from ten to twelve leaflets, that nearly impinge on each other, and somewhat resemble in their mode of arrangement the leaflets of one of our commonest Aspleniums,—*Asplenium trichomanes.* One of our highest authorities, however, in such matters (Professor Balfour of Edinburgh) questions whether this organism be in reality a fern, and describes it, from the specimen on the table, in the Palæontological chapter of his admirable Class Book, simply as "a remarkable pinnate frond." (Fig. 13.) We find it associated with the remains of a terrestrial plant allied to lepidodendron, and which in size and general appearance not a little resembles one of our commonest club-mosses,—*Lycopodium clavatum.** It sends out

* I figured this species from an imperfect Cro-marty specimen fifteen years ago. (See "Old Red Sandstone," first edition; 1841, Plate VII fig. 4.) Of the greatly better specimens now figured I owe the larger one (fig. 120) to Mrs Mill, Thurso, who detected it in the richly fossiliferous flagstones of the locality in which she resides, and kindly made it over to me; and the specimen of which I have given a magnified representation (fig. 12.), to my friend Mr Robert Dick. I have, besides, seen several specimens of the same organism, in a better or worse state of keeping, in the interesting collection of the Rev. Charles Clouston, Sandwick, near Stromness.

its branches in exactly the same style,—some short and simple, others branched like the parent stem,—in an arrangement approximately alternate; and is everywhere covered, stem and branch, by thickly set scale-like leaflets, that, suddenly narrowing, terminate in exceedingly slim points. It has, however, proportionally a stouter stem than Lycopodium; its leaves, when seen in profile, seem more rectilinear and thin; and none of its branches yet found bear the fructiferous stalk or spike. Its resemblance, however, to this commonest of the Lycopodia,—a plant that may be gathered by handfuls on the moors by which the flagstones are covered,—is close enough to suggest a new reading of the familiar adage on the meeting of extremes. Between the times of this ancient fossil,—one of the oldest of land-plants yet known,—and those of the existing club-moss that now scatters its light spores by millions over the dead and blackened remains of its remote predecessor, many creations must have intervened, and many a prodigy of the vegetable world appeared, especially in the earlier and middle periods,—Sigillaria, Favularia, Knorria, and Ulodendron,—that have had no representatives in the floras of latter times; and yet here, flanking the immense scale at both its ends, do we find plants of so nearly the same form and type, that it demands a careful survey to distinguish their points of difference. Here, for instance, to illustrate the fact, is there a specimen of *Lycopodium clavatum*, from one of these Caithness moors, that agrees branch for branch, and both in the disposition of its scales and in general outline, with the specimen in the stone. What seems to be an early representative of the Calamites occurs in the same beds. Some of the specimens are of large size,—at least from nine inches to a foot in circumference,—and retain their thickness, though existing as fragments several feet in length, with but little diminution throughout. They resembled the interior casts of Calamites in being longitudinally furrowed; but the furrows are flatter, and are themselves minutely striated lengthwise by lines as fine as hairs; and, instead of presenting any appearance of joints, there run diagonally across the stems, interrupted and very irregular lines of knobs. These I find referred to by Dr Joseph Hooker, in describing a set of massive but ill-preserved remains of the same organism detected in South Ness quarry, near Lerwick, by the Hon. Mr Tuffnell, as taking, in two of the specimens, "the appearance of transverse knobs and bars (mayhap spirally arranged) that cross the striæ obliquely. But though the knobs," he adds, "may perhaps indicate a peculiar character of the plants, they have more probably been caused by pressure during silicification." As, however, they also occur in the best preserved fragment of the plant which I have yet seen,—a Thurso specimen which I owe to my friend Mr Dick,—I deem it best to regard them, provisionally at least, as one of the characteristics of the plant. I may mention, that while I disinterred one of my specimens from the Thurso flagstones, where it occurred among remains of Dipterus and Asterolepis, I derived another specimen from the great overlying formation of pale Red Sandstone to which the lofty hills of Hoy and the tall mural precipices of Dunnet Head belong; and that this plant is the only organism which has yet been found in this uppermost member of the Lower Old Red, to at least the north of the Moray Frith. Another apparently terrestrial organism of the lower formation, of, however, rare occurrence, very much resembles a sheathing bract or spathe. It is of considerable size,—from four to six inches in length, by from two to three inches in breadth,—of a broadly elliptical and yet somewhat lanceolate form, deeply but irregularly corrugated, the rugæ exhibiting a tendency to converge towards both its lower and upper terminations, and with, in some instances, what seems to be the fragment of a second spathe springing from its base. Another and much smaller vegetable organism of the same beds presents the form of a spathe-enveloped bud or unblown flower wrapped up in its calyx; but all the specimens which I have yet seen are too obscure to admit of certain determination. I may here mention, that curious markings, which have been regarded as impressions made by vegetables that had themselves disappeared, have been detected during the last twelvemonth in a quarry of the Lower Old Red Sandstone near Huntly, by the Rev. Mr Mackay of Rhynie. They are very curious and very puzzling; but though some of the specimens present the appearance of a continuous midrib, that throws off, with a certain degree of regularity, apparent leaflets, I

am inclined to regard them rather as lying within the province of
the ichnologist than of the fossil botanist. They bear the same sort
of resemblance to a long, thickly-leaved frond, like that of the
"hard fern," that the cast of a many-legged annelid does to a club-
moss; and I was struck, on my first walk along the Portobello
beach, after examining a specimen kindly sent me by Mr Mackay,
to see how nearly the tract of a small shore crab (*Carcinus Mœnas*)
along the wet sand resembled them, in exhibiting what seemed to
be an obscure midrib fringed with leaflets.

But the genuine vegetable organism of the formation,
indicative of the highest rank of any yet found in it, is a true wood
of the cone-bearing order. I laid open the nodule which contains
this specimen, in one of the ichthyolite beds of Cromarty, rather
more than eighteen years ago; but though I described it, in the first
edition of my little work on the Old Red Sandstone, in 1841, as
exhibiting the woody fibre, it was not until 1845 that, with the
assistance of the optical lapidary, I subjected its structure to the
test of the microscope. It turned out, as I had anticipated, to be
the portion of a tree; and on my submitting the prepared specimen
to one of our highest authorities,—the late Mr William Nicol,—he
at once decided that the "reticulated texture of the transverse
section, though somewhat compressed, clearly indicated a
coniferous origin." I may add, that this most ancient of Scottish
lignites presents several peculiarities of structure. Like some of the
Araucarians of the warmer latitudes, it exhibits no lines of yearly
growth; its medullary rays are slender, and comparatively
inconspicuous; and the discs which mottle the sides of its sap-
chambers, when viewed in the longitudinal section, are
exceedingly minute, and are ranged, so far as can be judged in
their imperfect state of keeping, in the alternate order peculiar to
the Araucarians. On what perished land of the early Palæozoic
ages did this venerably antique tree cast root and flourish, when
the extinct genera Pterichthys and Coccosteus were enjoying life
by millions in the surrounding seas, long ere the flora or fauna of
the Coal Measures had begun to be?

I may be here permitted to mention, that in a little volume,
written in reply to a widely known and very ingenious work on the

Development hypothesis, I described and figured this unequivocally genuine lignite, in order to show that a true wood takes its place among the earliest terrestrial plants known to the geologist. I at the same time mentioned,—desirous, of course, that the facts of the question should be fairly stated, whatever their bearing,—that the nodule in which it occurred had been partially washed out of the fish-bed in which I found it, by the action of the surf; and my opponent, fixing on the circumstance, insinuated, in the answer with which he honoured me, that it had *not* belonged to the bed at all, but had been derived from some other formation of later date. He ought, however, to have taken into account my further statement, namely, that the same nodule which enclosed the lignite contained part of another fossil, the well-marked scales of *Diplacanthus striatus*, an ichthyolite restricted, like the Coccosteus (a specimen of which occurred in a neighbouring nodule), to the Lower Old Red Sandstone exclusively. If there be any value whatever in palæontological evidence, this Cromarty lignite must have been deposited in a sea inhabited by the Coccosteus and Diplacanthus. It is demonstrable that, while yet in the recent state, a Diplacanthus lay down and died beside it; and the evidence in the case is unequivocally this, that in the oldest portion of the oldest terrestrial flora yet known, there occurs the fragment of a tree quite as high in the scale as the stately Norfolk Island pine, or the noble cedar of Lebanon.

[I have failed hitherto in finding any remains of terrestrial plant-covered surfaces in the Old Red Sandstone of Scotland, though decided traces of desiccated sub-aerial ones are not rare. Shallows and banks seem to have been numerous during the period of at least the Lower formation. The flagstones of Caithness and Orkney, and the argillaceous fish-beds of Cromarty and Ross, not only abound in the ripple-marked surfaces of a shallow sea, but also in cracked and flawed planes that must have dried and split into polygonal partings in the air and the sun. The appearance of these in the neighbourhood of the town of Thurso, about half a mile to the east of the river, is not a little curious. Bearing throughout the general dingy hue of the flagstones, they yet consist of alternating beds of two distinct characters and qualities.

The one kind, fissile, finely grained, and sharply ripple-marked, seems to have been deposited in shallow water; the other, not fissile, but, if I may so speak, felted together so as to yield with difficulty to the hammer in any direction, and traversed by polygonal partings, filled up usually by the substance of the overlying stratum, appears to have had a different origin. The state of keeping, too, in which the ichthyic remains of these alternating beds occur is always very different. The smaller and more delicately organized fishes are never found entire, save in the fissile, finely-grained beds; in the others we detect only scattered fragments; and even these, unless they belonged to the robust Asterolepis or his cogeners,—which, however, in these beds they usually do,—much broken. The polygonal partings seem to indicate that these toughly-felted beds, whose very style of weathering,—rough, gnarled, fretted into globose protuberances and irregular hollows,—shows that it had not been formed by quiet deposition, must have had their broad backs raised for a time above the surface of the water, to be desiccated in the hot sun. And the fragmentary state of the fossils which they contain seems to point, with the roughnesses of their weathered surfaces, to some peculiarity in their origin. The recollection which they awoke in my mind with each visit I paid them for three years together, may probably indicate what that origin was. I had a relation who died more than a quarter of a century ago, who passed many years in British Guiana, in the colony of Berbice, and whose graphic description of that part of South America made a strong impression upon me when a boy, and still dwells in my memory. He was settled on a cotton plantation near the coast-side; and so exceedingly flat was the surrounding country, that the house in which he dwelt, though nearly two miles distant from the shore, stood little more than five feet above its level. The soil consisted of a dark gray consolidated mud; and in looking seawards from the margin of the land, there was nothing to be seen when the tide fell, save dreary mud-flats whole miles in extent, with the line of blue water beyond stretching along the distant horizon. These mud-flats were much frequented by birds of the wader family, that used to come and fish in the shallow pools for the small fry that had lingered behind when the tide fell; and my cousin, a keen sportsman in his day, has told me that he used to steal upon them in his mud-shoes,—flat boards attached to the soles, like the snow-shoes of the higher latitudes,—and enjoy rare sport in knocking down magnificent game, such as "the roseate spoonbill" and "gorgeous flamingo." There were times, however, when the mud-shoe proved of no avail, and the flat expanse remained impassable for weeks,—

> "A boggy syrtis, neither sea
> Nor good dry land."

The coast,—directly impinged on by the drift current, and beaten by the long roll of waves which had first begun to rise under the impulsions of the trade-winds on the African coast two thousand miles away,—was much exposed to tempests; and after every fresh storm from the east, a huge bank of mud used to come rolling in from the sea, three or four feet abreast, and remain wholly impassable until, during some two or three neap tides, its surface had been exposed to a tropical sun, and partially consolidated by the heat. And then the waste would become passable as before, and the chopped and broken surface, exposed to the ordinary action of the sea, and to gradual depositions during flood, would begin to be smoothed over, and the birds would find themselves no longer safe. Now, I am inclined to think that we have here the conditions necessary to the formation of the Thurso deposits. Let us suppose, near where Thurso now stands, a wide tract of flat mudbanks in a sea so shallow as to be laid dry at ebb for miles together. Let us farther suppose periods of tranquil deposition or re-arrangement, during which one ripple-marked stratum is laid quietly down over another, and the fish, killed by accident, or left stranded by the evaporation of the little pools, are covered up, like the plants in a botanist's drying-book, in a state of complete entireness. Let us yet farther suppose great mud-banks driven by occasional tempests from the deeper water beyond, and so heaped up over these sedimentary beds as to be exposed during even the flood of neap tides to the desiccating influences of the atmosphere and the sun, until the surface has become hard as a sun-burned brick, and has chopped into polygonal partings, with wide rents between. And finally, let us suppose the whole in this state laid under water at the return of stream tides, and exposed to the ordinary sedimentary action. Does it not seem probable that the alternating beds in all their conditions would be given us by such a process? In the stratum represented by the mud-bank, the stone would be of what I have termed a *felted*, not a fissile character; its organic remains would exist in a fragmentary and scattered state,—for, torn up from their places of original deposition, and rolled onwards in the storm-impelled mud, they could not fail to be broken up and dispersed; and farther, they would be in large part those of bulky deep-sea fishes. And lastly, the surface of these beds would be polygonally cracked and flawed, and the wider cracks filled up by the substance of the overlying strata. And these overlying strata, on the other hand,—the result of a period of quiet deposition in shallow water,—would be regularly bedded, and their ichthyic remains, consisting mainly of small littoral fishes, would be preserved in a state of comparative entireness. For, however, such numerous repetitions of alternately *felted* and fissile ripple-marked strata as we find in the neighbourhood of Thurso,—repetitions carried on for hundreds of feet in vertical extent,—we require yet another condition,—that condition of gradual subsidence in the general crust which can alone account for the fact so often pressed upon the geologist in exploring the Coal Measures, that in deposits thousands of feet in thickness, each stratum in succession had been laid down in a shallow sea.]

It is a curious circumstance, that the Old Red flagstones which lie along the southern flanks of the Grampians, and are represented by the gray stone known in commerce as the Arbroath Pavement, have not, so far as is yet known, an organism in common with the Old Red flagstones of the north. I at one time supposed that the rectilinear, smooth-stemmed fucoid already described, occurred in both series, as the gray stones have also their smooth-stemmed, rectilinear, tape-like organism; but the points of resemblance were too few and simple to justify the conclusion that they were identical, and I have since ascertained that they were entirely different plants. The fucoid of the Caithness flagstones threw off, as I have shown, in the alternate order, numerous ribbon-like branches or fronds; whereas the ribbon-like fronds or branches of the Forfarshire plant rose by dozens from a common root, like the fronds of Zostera, and somewhat resembled a scourge of cords fastened to a handle. Contemporary with this organism of the gray flagstone formation, and thickly occupying the planes on which it rests, there occur fragments of twisted stems, some of them from three to four inches in diameter (though represented by but mere films of carbonaceous matter), and irregularly streaked, or rather *wrinkled*, longitudinally, like the bark of some of our forest trees, though on a smaller scale. With these we find in considerable abundance irregularly-shaped patches, also of carbonaceous matter, reticulated into the semblance of polygonal, or, in some instances, egg-shaped meshes, and which remind one of pieces of ill-woven lace. When first laid open, these meshes are filled each with a carbonaceous speck; and, from their supposed resemblance, in the aggregated form, to the eggs of the frog in their albuminous envelop, the quarriers term them "puddock [frog] spawn." The slabs in which they occur, thickly covered over with their vegetable impressions, did certainly remind me, when I first examined them some fifteen years ago, of the bottom of some stagnant ditch beside some decaying hedge, as it appears in middle spring, when paved with fragments of dead branches and withered grass, and mottled with its life-impregnated patches of the gelid substance regarding which a provincial poet tells his readers, in classical Scotch, that

> "Puddock-spue is fu' o' e'en,
> An' every e'e's a pu-head."*

* "Frog-spawn is full of eyes [*i.e.* black eye-like points], and every eye is a tadpole."

Higher authorities than the quarriers,—among the rest, the late Dr Mantell,—have been disposed to regard these polygonal markings as the fossilized spawn of ancient Batrachians; but there now seems to be evidence enough from which to conclude that they are the remains, not of the eggs of an animal, but of the seed of a plant. Such was the view taken many years ago by Dr Fleming,—the original discoverer, let me add, of fossils both in those Upper and Middle Old Red Sandstone deposits that lie in Scotland to the south of the Grampians. "These organisms," we find him saying, in a paper published in "Cheek's Edinburgh Journal" (1831), "occur in the form of circular flat patches, not equalling an inch in diameter, and composed of numerous smaller contiguous pieces. They are not unlike what might be expected to result from a compressed berry, such as the bramble or the rasp. As, however, they are found adjacent to the narrow leaves of gramineous [looking] vegetables, and chiefly in clay slate, originally lacustrine silt, it is probable that they constituted the conglobate panicles of extinct species of the genus Juncus or Sparganium." From specimens subsequently found by Dr Fleming, and on which he has erected his species *Parka decipiens,*

Fig. 121.

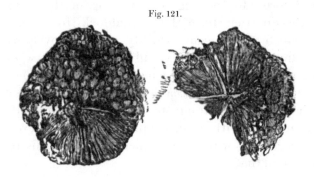

PARKA DECIPIENS.

it seems evident that the nearly circular bodies (which in all the better preserved instances circumscribe the small polygonal ones) were set in receptacles somewhat resembling the receptacle or calyx of the strawberry or rasp. Judging from one of the specimens, this calyx appears to have consisted of five pieces, which united in a central stem, and were traversed by broad irregularly diverging striæ. And the spawn-like patches of Carmylie appear to be simply ill-preserved specimens of this fruit, whatever its true character, in which the minute circular portions, divested of the receptacle and stem, had been thrown into irregular forms by the joint agency of pressure and decay. The great abundance of these organisms,—for so abundant are they, that visitors to the Carmylie quarries find they can carry away with them as many specimens as they please,—may be regarded as of itself indicative of a vegetable origin.* It is not in the least strange, however, that they should have been taken for patches of spawn. The large-grained spawn of fishes, such as the lumpfish, salmon, or sturgeon, might be readily enough mistaken, in even the recent state, for the detached spherical seed-vessels of fruit, such as the bramble-berry, the stone-bramble, or the rasp. "Hang it!" I once heard a countryman exclaim, on helping himself at table to a spoonful of Caviare, which he had mistaken for a sweetmeat, and instantly, according to Milton, "with sputtering noise rejected,"—"Hang it for nasty stuff!—I took it for bramble-berry jam."

Along with these curious remains Dr Fleming found an organism which in form somewhat resembles the spike of one of the grasses, save that the better preserved bracts terminate in fan or kidney-shaped leaflets, with a simple venation radiating from the base. It is probably a fern, more minute in its pinnules than even our smaller specimens of true maiden-hair. Its stipes, however, seems proportionally stouter than that of any of the smaller ferns with which I am acquainted. But the state of keeping of the specimen is not good, nor do I know that another has yet been found. Further, in the same beds Dr Fleming found a curious non-descript vegetable, or rather part of a vegetable, with smooth narrow stems, resembling those of the smooth-stemmed organism of the Caithness flagstones, but unlike it in the circumstance that

---

* Mr Page figures, in his "Advanced Text Book of Geology" (p. 127), a few circular markings from the Forfarshire beds, which he still regards as spawn, probably that of a Crustacean, and which certainly differ greatly in appearance from the markings found enclosed in the apparent spathes.

Fig. 122.

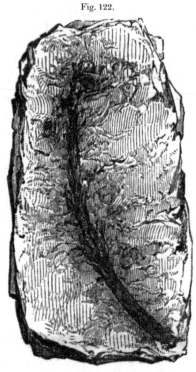

its detached nearly parallel stalks anastomose with each other by means of cross branches, that unite them in the middle, somewhat in the style of the Siamese twins. I have heard the Doctor suggest, but know not whether he has placed the remark on record, that these parallel stems may have been but the internal fibres of some larger plant, whose more succulent portions have disappeared; and certainly, while such instances of anastomosis are rare among the *stems* of plants, they are common enough among their *internal fibres*, as all who have examined the macerated *debris* of a kitchen-garden or a turnip-field must have had occasion to remark. We sometimes, however, find cases of anastomosis among the stems of even the higher plants. I have seen oftener than once, in neglected hawthorn hedges, the branch of one plant entering into the stem of another, and becoming incorporated with its substance; and we are told by Professor Balfour, that this kind of chance adhesion is

Fig. 123.

often seen in the branches of the ivy; and that not unfrequently, by a similar process, the roots of contiguous trees are united. Nor does it seem improbable, that what occasionally takes place among the higher plants of the present time may have been common among some of the comparatively low plants of so ancient a period as that of the Middle Old Red Sandstone. This formation of the gray tilestones has furnished one vegetable organism apparently higher in the scale than those just described, in a well-marked Lepidodendron, which exhibits, like the Araucarian of the Lower Old Red, though less distinctly, the internal structure. It was found about sixteen years ago in a pavement quarry near Clockbriggs,—the last station on the Aberdeen and Forfar Railway as the traveller approaches the town of Forfar from the north. I owe my specimen of this ancient Lepidodendron to Mr William Miller, banker, Dundee, an accomplished geologist, who has taken no little trouble in determining its true history. He has ascertained that it occurred deep in the rock, seventy-one feet from the surface; that the beds which rested over it were composed, in the descending order, first, of a conglomerate thirty feet thick; secondly, of a red rock four feet thick; thirdly, of twenty-eight feet of the soft shaly substance known to the quarriers as caulm; and fourthly, of more than nine feet of gray pavement, immediately under which, in a soft, argillaceous stratum, lay the organism. It was about four feet in length, bulged out at the lower end into a bulb-like protuberance, which may have been, however, merely an accidental result of its state of keeping; and threw off, at an acute angle, two branches about a foot from the top. It was covered with a bark of brittle coal, which is, however, wanting in all the fragments that have been preserved; and was resolved internally into a brown calcareous substance of about the hardness of ordinary marble, and very much resembling that into which the petrifactive agencies have consolidated the fossil trees of Granton and

Craigleith. From the decorticated condition of the surviving fragments, and the imperfect preservation of the interior structure, in all save the central portions of its transverse sections, it yields no specific marks by which to distinguish it; but enough remains in its irregular network of cells, devoid of linear arrangement, and untraversed by medullary rays, to demonstrate its generic standing as a Lepidodendron.

[It has been questioned whether the lower place in the Old Red System should be assigned to the flagstones of Caithness and Ross, with their characteristic Dipterus and Coccosteus beds, or to the gray tilestones of Forfar and Kincardineshires, with their equally characteristic Cephalaspis. The evidence on the point is certainly not so conclusive as I deemed it fifteen years ago, when our highest authority on the subject not only regarded the tilestone of the Silurian regions of England as a member of the Old Red Sandstone (an arrangement which I am still disposed to deem the true one), but also held further, that there had been detected in this formation near Downton Castle, Herefordshire, broken remains of *Dipterus macrolepidotus,* one of the best marked ichthyolites of the flagstones of Caithness and Orkney. A great and unbroken series of fossiliferous rocks, with Dipterus at its base, Cephalaspis in its medial spaces, and Holoptychius at its top, might well be regarded as the analogue of the Old Red of Scotland, with the Caithness flagstones ranged at its bottom, the Cephalaspis beds of Forfarshire placed in its middle, and the Holoptychius beds of Scot-Crag and Clashbinnie on its upper horizon; but since that time the tilestones have been transferred to the Upper Silurian division of rocks, and the evidence furnished by their supposed Dipterus has not been confirmed. And as the Old Red Sandstones of Scotland have no true fossiliferous base, but rest on primary rocks both to the south and north of the Grampians, it may be regarded as in some degree a moot point whether the lowest fossiliferous beds to the north be older or newer than those to the south, or, what is quite possible, of the same age. Provisionally, however, I have arranged my paper on the supposition that the Coccostean formation of the north is the lowest and oldest of the three; and this from the following considerations. In the first place, the Coccosteus and its contemporaries appear in the north at a very short distance above the base of the system. I have disinterred an Osteolepis from a fish-bed near Cromarty only thirty-three feet over the great conglomerate, and only a hundred and twenty-nine feet over the granitic gneiss beneath; whereas the Cephalaspis beds occur high above the primary base of the system in the south,—at some distance over even the thick conglomerate of Stonehaven and Dunnottar; and under this conglomerate, as shown in the section furnished by the valley of the North Esk, there lies a pale red sandstone member of the system, estimated by Colonel Imrie at seven hundred and eighty feet in thickness. The conglomerate itself he estimates at twelve hundred feet. Adopting as correct Colonel Imrie's section, taken along the banks of the North Esk,—and the Colonel was unquestionably a truthful observer,—the Cephalaspis beds of the south lie nearly two thousand (nineteen hundred and eighty) feet above the Azoic slates on which the Old Red Sandstone of Forfarshire rests, whereas the Coccosteus and Osteolepis beds of the north lie only one hundred and twenty-nine feet over the Azoic gneiss on which the Old Red Sandstone of Cromarty rests. There is thus at least *room* in the south for an underlying fossiliferous formation between that of the Cephalaspis and the base of the system, but none in the north beneath that of the Coccosteus and its base. In the north we find the *room* lying above between the Coccostean and Holoptychian formations, and represented by that great unfossiliferous deposit of pale sandstone to which the hills of Hoy and the rocks of Duncansbay Head and of Tarbet Ness belong. Further, in the second place, while the upper or Holoptychian formation is found *directly* overlying that of the Coccosteus in only one locality,—Moray,—we find it directly overlying that of the Cephalaspis in *two* widely-separated localities;—in the vast band of Old Red which runs diagonally across the island from sea to sea, parallel to the Grampian chain; and in the immensely developed Red Sandstones of England and Wales. And it is of course more probable that the two corroborative instances should represent the natural succession of the formations, and the single instance the accidental gap in the scale consequent on the missing formation, than that, *vice versa*, the solitary instance should represent the natural succession, while the two mutually corroborative ones should represent, in localities widely apart, the mere accident of the gap. But, in the third place, I attach more weight to a conclusion founded on the positive character of the groupes of organic remains by which the three great formations of the Old Red System are characterized, than I do to either of these considerations. The organisms of the Cephalaspian deposits differ *generically*, and in their whole aspect, from both those of the Coccostean and Holoptychian formations; whereas the organisms of the Coccostean formations, while they resemble generically and in the group those of the Holoptychian one, mainly differ from them *specifically*. The extreme *generic* difference in the one case argues evidently a great difference in *condition*,—the lesser specific difference in the other, a great difference in point *of time*. The Cephalaspian formation might, as a fresh-water formation, be nearly contemporary with either of the other two, or, as seems more probable, interposed between them; while they themselves, on the other hand, generically similar and decidedly marine in their character, must have been so widely separated in time, that all the species of the lower group became extinct ere those of the upper one had been ushered into being. And such are some of the considerations that still lead me, notwithstanding the failure of previous evidence, to hold, at least provisionally, that our Scottish flagstones to the north of the Grampians occupy a lower horizon than our Scottish tilestones to the south. It must, however, be stated, on the other hand, that the crustaceans of the gray tilestones of Forfar and Kincardine not a little resemble those of the Upper Silurian and red-tilestone beds of England; and that, judging from the ichthyodorulites found in both, their fishes must have been at least generically allied. The crustaceans of the Upper Silurian of Lesmahagow, too, seem certainly much akin to those of the Forfarshire tilestones.]

Above this gray tilestone formation lies the Upper Old Red Sandstone, with its peculiar group of ichthyic organisms, none of which seem specifically identical with those of either the Caithness or the Forfarshire beds. For it is an interesting circumstance, suggestive surely of the vast periods which must have elapsed during its deposition, that the great Old Red System has, as I have just said, its three distinct platforms of organic existence, each wholly different from the others. Generically and in the group, however, the Upper fishes much more closely resemble, I repeat, the fishes of the Lower or Caithness and Cromarty platform, than they do those of the Forfarshire and Kincardine one. The vegetable remains of the Upper formation in Scotland are both rare and ill preserved. I have seen what I deemed fucoidal markings dimly impressed on the planes of some of the strata, not in the carbonaceous form so common in the other two formations, but as mere coloured films of a deeper red than the surrounding matrix. Further, I have detected in the same beds, and existing in the same state, fragments of a striated organism, which may have formed part of either a true calamite, like those of the Coal Measures, or of some such striated but jointless vegetable as that of the Lower Old Red of Thurso and Lerwick.* With these

* Since these sentences were written I have seen a description of both the plants of the Upper Old Red to which they refer, in an 'interesting sketch of the geology of Roxburghshire by the Rev. James Duncan, which forms part of a recent publication devoted to the history and antiquities of the shire. "In the red quarry of Denholm Hill there occurs," says Mr Duncan, " a stratum of soft yellowish sandstone, which contains impressions of an apparent fucoid in considerable quantity. One or several linear stems diverge from a point, and throw off at acute angles, as they grow upwards, branches or leaves very similar to the stem, which are in turn subdivided into others. The width of the stalks is generally about a quarter of an inch, the length often a foot. The colour is brown, blackish-brown, or grayish. The same plant also occurs in the white-stone quarry [an overlying bed] in the form of Carbonaceous impressions. There can be little doubt that it is a fucoid. The general mode of growth greatly resembles that of certain sea-weeds; and in some specimens we have seen the branches dilated a little at the extremities, like those of such of the living fuci as expand in order to afford space for the fructification. It is deserving of remark, that the plant is seldom observed lying horizontally on the rock in a direction parallel to its stratification, but rising up through the layers, so as only to be seen when

markings ferns are occasionally found; and to one of these, fróm
the light which it throws on the true place in the scale of a series of
deposits in a sister country, there attaches no little interest. I owe
my specimen to Mr John Stewart of Edinburgh, who laid it open in
a micaceous red sandstone in the quarry of Prestonhaugh, near
Dunse, where it is associated with some of the better-known
ichthyic organisms of the Upper Old Red Sandstone, such as
Pterichthys major and *Holoptychius Nobilissimus.* Existing as but a
deep red film in the rock, with a tolerably well-defined outline, but
without trace of the characteristic venation on which the fossil
botanist, in dealing with the ferns, founds his generic distinctions,
I could only determine that it was either a Cyclopterus or
Neuropterus. My collection was visited, however, by the late
lamented Edward Forbes, only a few weeks before his death; and

the stone is broken across; as if it had been standing erect or kept
buoyant in water, while the stony matter to which it owes its
preservation was deposited around it." Mr Duncan, after next referring to
the remains of what he deems a land plant, derived from the same
deposit, and which, though sadly mutilated, presents not a little of the
appearance of the naked framework of a frond of Cyclopterus Hibernicus
divested of the leaflets, goes on to describe the apparent calamite of the
formation. "The best preserved vegetable remain yet found in Denholm
Hill quarry," he says, "is the radical portion of what we cannot hesitate
to call a species of calamite. The lower part is regularly and beautifully
rounded, bulging and prominent nearly four inches in diameter. About an
inch from the bottom it contracts somewhat suddenly in two separate
stages, and from the uppermost sends up a stem about an inch in
diameter, and nearly of the same length, where it is broken across. At the
origin of this stem the small longitudinal ridges are distinctly marked;
and the whole outline of the figure, though converted into stone, is as well
defined as it could have been in the living plant." Mr Duncan
accompanies his description with a figure of the organism described,
which, however, rather resembles the bulb of a liliaceous plant than the
root of a calamite, which in all the better preserved specimens contracts,
instead of expanding as it descends. The apparent expansion, however, in
the Old Red specimen may be simply a result of compression in its upper
part; the under part certainly much resembles, in the dome-like
symmetry of its outline, the radical termination of a solitary calamite.

Fig. 124.

CYCLOPTERUS HIBERNICUS.

he at once recognised in my Berwickshire fern, so unequivocally an organism of the Upper Old Red, the *Cyclopterus Hibernicus* of those largely developed beds of yellow sandstone which form so marked a feature in the geology of the south of Ireland, and whose true place, whether as Upper Old Red or Lower Carboniferous, has been the subject of so much controversy. I had been previously introduced by Professor Forbes, in the Museum of Economic Geology in Jermyn Street, London, to an interesting collection of plants from these yellow beds, and had an opportunity afforded me of examining the only ichthyic organism hitherto found associated with them; and was struck, though I could not identify its species, with its peculiarly Old Red aspect; but the evidence of the Cyclopterus is of course more conclusive than that of the fish; and we may, I think, legitimately conclude, that in Ireland, as in our own country, it was a contemporary of the great Pterichthys (*P. major*),—the hugest, and at least one of the last, of his race,—and gave its rich green to the hillsides of what is still the Emerald Island during the latter ages of the Old Red Sandstone, and ere the Carboniferous period had yet begun. The *Cyclopterus Hibernicus*, as shown both by the Prestonhaugh specimen and those of Ireland, was a bipinnate fern of very considerable size,—probably a tree fern. Its pinnæ, opposite in the lower part of the frond, are alternate in the upper; while its leaflets, which are of a sub-rhomboidal form, and so closely ranged as to impinge on each other, are at least generally alternate in their arrangement throughout. Among living plants it seems most nearly represented

by a South American species,—*Didymoclœna pulcherrima,*—one of
the smaller tree ferns. The leaves of this graceful species are
bipinnate, like those of the fossil; and the pinnæ (thickly set with
simple alternately arranged leaflets) are opposite in the lower part
of the frond, and alternate in the upper. Widely as they are
separated in time, the recent South American Didymoclœna and
the Old Red Sandstone Cyclopterus, that passed into extinction
ere the times of the Coal, might be ranged together, so far at least
as appears from their forms, as kindred species. It were very
desirable that we had a good monograph of the Irish Old Red
plants, the contemporaries of the latter, as the completest and best
preserved representatives of the Middle Palæozoic flora yet found.
Sir Roderick Murchison has figured a single pinnæ of this
Cyclopterus in his recently published "Siluria;" and Sir Charles
Lyell, both that and one of its contemporary Lepidodendra, in the
last edition of his "Elements." These interesting fragments,
however, serve but to excite our curiosity for more. When urging
Professor Edward Forbes on the subject, ere parting from him for,
alas! what proved to be the last time, he intimated an intention of
soon taking it up; but I fear his purposed monograph represents
only one of many works, important to science, which his untimely
death has arrested for mayhap long years to come.

In the uppermost beds of the Upper Old Red formation in
Scotland, which are usually of a pale or light-yellow colour, the
vegetable remains again become strongly carbonaceous, but their
state of preservation continues bad,—too bad to admit of the
determination of either species or genera; and not until we rise a
very little beyond the system do we find the remains of a flora
either rich or well preserved. But very remarkable is the change
which at this stage at once occurs. We pass at a single stride from
great poverty to great wealth. The suddenness of the change seems
suited to remind one of that experienced by the voyager,
when,—after traversing for many days some wide expanse of
ocean, unvaried save by its banks of floating sea-weed, or where,
occasionally and at wide intervals, he picks up some leaf-bearing
bough, or marks some fragment of drift-weed go floating past,—he
enters at length the sheltered lagoon of some coral island, and sees

all around the deep green of a tropical vegetation descending in tangled luxuriance to the water's edge,—tall, erect ferns, and creeping lycopodiaceæ, and the pandanus, with its ærial roots and its screwlike clusters of narrow leaves, and, high over all, tall palms, with their huge pinnate fronds, and their curiously aggregated groupes of massive fruit. And yet the more meagre vegetation of the earlier time is not without its special interest. The land-plants of the Old Red Sandstone seem to compose, all over the world, the most ancient of the terrestrial floras. It was held only a few years ago, that the Silurians of the United States had their plants allied to the Lepidodendron. But the group in which these occur has since been transferred from the Upper Silurian to the Old Red System; and we find it expressly stated by Professor H. D. Rogers, in his valuable contribution to the "Physical Atlas" (second edition, 1856), that "the Cadent [or Lower Old Red] strata are the oldest American formations in which remains of a true terrestrial vegetation have yet been discovered." It has been shown, too, by Sir Roderick Murchison, that the supposed Silurian plants of Oporto are in reality Carboniferous, and owe their apparent position to a reverse folding of the strata. I have already referred to the solitary spore-cases of the Ludlow Rocks; and beneath these rocks, says Sir Roderick (1854), "no remains of plants have been discovered which are recognisably of terrestrial origin." Scanty, too, as the terrestrial flora of the Old Red Sandstone everywhere is, we find it exhibiting very definitely the leading Palæozoic features. Its prevailing plants are the ferns and their apparent allies. It has in our own country, as has been just shown, its ferns, its lepidodendra, its striated plants allied to the calamites, and its decided araucarite; in America, in the Cadent series, it had its "plants allied to ferns and lepidodendra;" and in the Devonian basin of Sabero in Spain, its characteristic organisms are, a lepidodendron (*L. Chemungensis*), and a very peculiar fern (*Sphenopteris laxus*).* But while in its main features it resembled the succeeding flora of the

* "Though the coal of Sabero is *apparently* included in Devonian rocks," says Sir Roderick Murchison, "M. Casiano de Prado thinks that

Carboniferous period, it seems in all its forms to have been specifically distinct. It was the independent flora of an earlier creation than that to which we owe the coal. For the meagreness of the paper in which I have attempted to describe it as it occurs in Scotland, I have but one apology to offer. My lecture contains but little; but then, such is the scantiness of the materials on which I had to work, that it could not have contained much: if, according to the dramatist, the "amount be beggarly," it is because the "boxes are empty." Partly, apparently, from the circumstance that the organisms of this flora were ill suited for preservation in the rocks, and partly because, judging from what appears, the most ancient lands of the globe were widely scattered and of narrow extent, this oldest of the floras is everywhere the most meagre.

this appearance may be due to inverted folds of the strata." On the other hand, M. Alcide D'Orbigny regards it as decidedly Old Red; and certainly its Sphenopteris and Lepidodendron bear much more the aspect of Devonian than of Carboniferous plants.

LECTURE TWELFTH.

ON THE LESS KNOWN FOSSIL FLORAS OF SCOTLAND.

PART II.

In the noble flora of the Coal Measures much still remains to be done in Scotland. Our Lower Carboniferous rocks are of immense development; the Limestones of Burdiehouse, with their numerous terrestrial plants, occur many hundred feet beneath our Mountain Limestones; and our list of vegetable species peculiar to these lower deposits is still very incomplete. Even in those higher Carboniferous rocks with which the many coal workings of the country have rendered us comparatively familiar, there appears to be still a good deal of the new and the unknown to repay the labour of future exploration. It was only last year that Mr Gourlay* of this city (Glasgow) added to our fossil flora a new Volkmannia from the coal-field of Carluke; and I detected very recently in a neighbouring locality (the Airdrie coalfield), though in but an indifferent state of keeping, what seems to be a new and very peculiar fern. It presents at first sight more the appearance of a Cycadaceous frond than any other vegetable organism of the Carboniferous age which I have yet seen. From a mid stem there proceed at right angles, and in alternate order, a series of sessile, lanceolate, acute leaflets, nearly two inches in length by about an eighth part of an inch in breadth, and about three lines apart.

* Now, alas! no more. In Mr Gourlay the energy and shrewd business habits of the accomplished merchant were added to an enlightened zeal for general science, and no inconsiderable knowledge in both the geologic and botanic provinces. The marked success, in several respects, of the brilliant meeting of the British Association which held in Glasgow in September 1855 was owing in no small measure to the indefatigable exertions and well-calculated arrangements of Mr Gourlay.

Fig. 125.

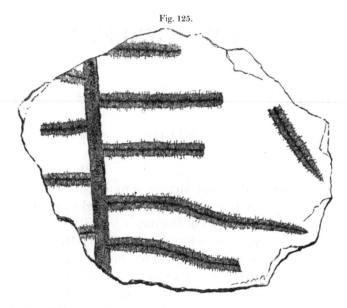

Each is furnished with a slender midrib; and, what seems a singular, though not entirely unique, feature in a fern, their edges are densely hirsute, and bristle with thick, short hair, nearly as stiff as prickles. The venation is not distinctly preserved; but enough remains to show that it must have been peculiar,—apparently radiating outwards from a series of centres ranged along the midrib. Nay, the apparent hairs seem to be but prolongations of the nerves carried beyond the edges of the leaflets. There is a Stigmaria, too, on the table, very ornate in its sculpture, of which I have now found three specimens in a quarry of the Lower Coal Measures near Portobello, that has still to be figured and described. In this richlyornamented Stigmaria the characteristic

Fig. 126.

STIGMARIA.

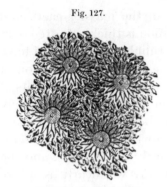

Fig. 127.

THE SAME ~NAT. SIZE.

areolæ present the ordinary aspect. Each, however, forms the centre of a sculptured star, consisting of from eighteen to twenty rays, or rather the centre of a sculptured flower of the composite order, resembling a meadow daisy or sea-aster. The minute petals,—if we are to accept the latter comparison,—are of an irregularly lenticular form, generally entire, but in some instances ranged in two, or even three, concentric lines round the depressed centre of the areolæ; while the interspaces outside are occupied by numerous fretted markings, resembling broken fragments of petals, which, though less regularly ranged than the others, are effective in imparting a richly ornate aspect to the whole.

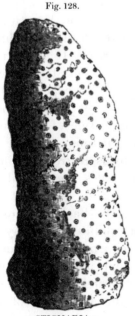

Fig. 128.

STIGMARIA.

Ever since the appearance, in 1846, of Mr Binney's paper on the relations of stigmaria to sigillaria as roots and stem, I have been looking for distinguishing specific marks among the former; and, failing for a time to find any, I concluded that, though the stems of the sigillarian genus were variously sculptured, their roots might in all the species have been the same. The present rich specimen does seem, however, to bear the specific stamp; and, from the peculiar character of the termination of another specimen on the table, I am inclined to hold that the stigmaria may have borne the appearance rather of underground stems than of proper roots. This specimen suddenly terminates, at a thickness of two and a half inches, in a

rounded point, abrupt as that of one of the massier cacti; and
every part of the blunt sudden termination is thickly fretted over
with the characteristic areolæ. The slim tubular rootlets must have
stuck out on every side from the obtuse rounded termination of
this underground stem, as we see, on a small scale, the leaflets of
our larger club-mosses sticking out from what are comparatively
the scarce less abrupt terminations of their creeping stems and
branches. In at least certain stages of growth the sub-aerial stems
of Lepidodendron also terminated abruptly (see fig. 24); and the
only terminal point of Ulodendron I ever saw was nearly as obtuse
as that of Stigmaria.

I have been long desirous of acquainting myself with the true
character of this latter plant (Ulodendron), but hitherto my
labours have not been very successful. A specimen of *Ulodendron
minus*, however, now on the table, which I disinterred several
years ago from out a bed of ferruginous shale in the Water of Leith,
a little above the village of Colinton, exhibits several peculiarities
which, so far as I know, have not yet been described. Though
rather less than ten inches in length by about three inches in
breadth, it exhibits no fewer than seven of those round, beautifully
sculptured scars, ranged rectilinearly along the trunk, by which
this ancient genus is so remarkably characterized. It is covered
with small, sharply relieved, obovate scales, most of them
furnished with an apparent midrib, and with their edges slightly
turned up; from which peculiarities, and their great beauty, they
seem suited to remind the architect of that style of sculpture
adopted by Palladio from his master Vitruvius, when, in
ornamenting the Corinthian and composite torus, he fretted it into
closely imbricated obovate leaves. These scales are ranged in
elegant curves, not unlike those ornamental curves,—a feat of the
turning-lathe,—which one sees roughening the backs of ladies'
watches of French manufacture. My fossil exhibited, as it lay in
the rock, what I never saw in any other specimen,—a true branch
sticking out at an acute angle from the stem, and fretted with
scales of a peculiar form, which in one little corner appear also on
the main stem, but which differ so considerably from those of the
obovate, apparently imbricated type, that, if found on a separate

specimen, they might be held to indicate difference of species. It has been shown by Messrs Lindley and Hutton, on the evidence of one of the specimens figured in the "Fossil Flora," that the line of circular scars so remarkable in this genus, and which is held to be the impressions made by a rectilinear range of almost sessile cones, existed in duplicate on each stem,—a row occurring on two of the sides of the plant directly opposite each other. The branch in my specimen struck off from one of the intermediate sides at right angles with the cones. We already know that these were ranged in one plane; nor, if the branches were ranged in one plane also,—certainly the disposition of branch which would consort best with such a disposition of cone,—would the arrangement be without example in the vegetable kingdom as it even now exists. "Our host," says the late Captain Basil Hall, in his brief description of the island of Java, "carried us to see a singular tree, which had been brought from Madagascar, called familiarly the *Traveller's Friend*, Urania being, I believe, its botanic name. We found it to differ from most other trees in having all its branches in one plane, like the sticks of a fan or the feathers of a peacock's tail." I may further mention, that the specimen which showed me the abrupt cactus-like terminations of Ulodendron repeated the evidence of Messrs Lindley and Hutton's specimen regarding the arrangement of the cone scars on opposite sides, and showed also that these scars ascended to within little more than an inch of the top of the plant.

As there are cases in which the *position* of a fossil plant may add, from its bearing on geologic history, a threefold interest to the fossil itself, regarded simply as an organism, I may be permitted to refer to a circumstance already recorded, that there was a well-marked Bechera detected about two years ago by Dr Macbean of Edinburgh, an accomplished naturalist and careful observer, in a thin argillaceous stratum, interposed, in the Queen's Park, between a bed of columnar basalt and a bed of trap-tuff, in the side of the eminence occupied atop by the ruins of St Anthony's Chapel. The stratified bed in which it occurs seems, from its texture and colour, to be composed mainly of trappean materials, but deposited and arranged in water; and abounds in carbonaceous markings, usually in so imperfect a state of keeping that, though long known to some of the Edinburgh geologists, not a single species, or even genus, were they able to determine. All that could be said was, that they seemed fucoidal, and might of course belong to any age. The Bechera, however, shows that the deposit is one of the Lower Coal Measures. There was found associated with it a tooth of a Carboniferous Holoptychius, whose evidence bore out the same conclusion; and both fossils derive an importance from the light which they throw on the age of the bed of tuff which underlies the stratum in which they occur. At least this trap-rock must be as old as the fossiliferous layer which rests upon it, or rather, as shown by its underlying position, a little older: it must be a trap of the earlier Carboniferous period. Further, it must have been, not injected among the strata, but poured out over the surface,—in all probability covered at the time by water; and there must have formed over it, ere another overflow of trap took place, a thin sedimentary bed charged with fragments of the plants of the period, and visited, when in the course of deposition, by some of its fishes.

Even among the vegetable organisms of our Coal Measures, already partially described and figured, much remains to be accomplished in the way of restoration. Portions of *Sphenopteris bifida*, for instance, a fern of the Lower Carboniferous rocks, have been repeatedly figured; but a beautiful specimen on the table, which exhibits what seems to be the complete frond of the plant, will give, I doubt not, fresh ideas respecting the general framework, if I may so speak, of this skeleton fern, to even those best acquainted with the figures; and an elaborate restoration of its contemporary, *Sphenopteris affinis* (see frontispiece) which I completed from a fine series of specimens in my collection, will be new, as a whole, to those most familiar with this commonest of the Burdiehouse fossils.

From comparisons instituted between minute portions of this Sphenopteris and a recent fern, it has been held considerably to resemble a Davallia of the West Indies; whereas it will be seen from the entire frond, that it was characterized by very striking peculiarities, exemplified, say some of our higher botanical

Fig. 129.

SPHENOPTERIS BIFIDA.
(*Burdiehouse.*)

authorities, to whom I have submitted my restoration, by no fern that now lives. The frond of *Davallia Canariensis*, though unlike in its venation, greatly resembles in general outline one of the larger pinnæ of *Sphenopteris affinis*; but these pinnæ form only a small part of the entire frond of this Sphenopteris. It was furnished with a stout leafless rachis, or leaf-stalk, exceedingly similar in form to that of our common brake (*Pteris aquilina*). So completely, indeed, did it exhibit the same club-like, slightly-bent termination, the same gradual diminution in thickness, and the same smooth surface, that one accustomed to see this part of the bracken used as a thatch can scarce doubt that the stipes of Sphenopteris would have served the purpose equally well; nay, that were it still in existence to be so employed, a roof thatched with it, on which the pinnæ and leaflets were concealed, and only the club-like stems exposed, row above row, in the style of the fern-thatcher, could not be distinguished, so far as form and size went, from a roof thatched with brake. High above the club-like termination of the rachis the stem divided into two parts, each of which, a little higher up, also divided into two; these in turn, in at least the larger fronds, also bifurcated; and this law of bifurcation,—a marked, mayhap unique, peculiarity in a fern,—regulated all the larger divisions of the frond, though its smaller pinnæ and leaflets were alternate. It was a further peculiarity of the plant that, unlike the brake, it threw off, ere the main divisions of its rachis took place, two pinnæ placed in the alternate order, and of comparatively small size. The frond of *Sphenopteris bifida* was of a more simple form than that of its larger cogener, and not a little resembled a living fern of New Zealand, *Cœnopteris vivipara*. It was tripinnate; its secondary stems were placed directly opposite on the midrib, but its tertiary ones in the alternate arrangement; and its leaflets, which were also alternate, were as rectilinear and slim as mere veins, or as the thread-like leaflets of asparagus. Like the fronds of Cœnopteris when not in seed, it must have presented the appearance of the mere macerated framework of a fern. I need scarce remark that, independently of the scientific interest which must attach to restorations of these early plants, they speak powerfully to the imagination, and supply it with materials from which to construct the vanished landscapes of the Carboniferous ages. From one such restored fern as the two now submitted to the Association, it is not difficult to pass in fancy to the dank slopes of the ancient land of the Lower Coal Measures, when they waved as thickly with graceful Sphenopteres as our existing hill-sides with the common brake, and when every breeze that rustled through the old forests bent in mimic waves their slim flexible stems and light and graceful foliage.

In 1844, when Professor Nicol, of Marischal College, Aberdeen, appended to his interesting "Guide to the Geology of Scotland," a list of the Scottish fossils known at the time, he enumerated only two vegetable species of the Scotch Oolitic system,—*Equisetum columnare* and *Pinites* or *Peuce Eiggensis;* the former one of the early discoveries of our distinguished President, Sir Roderick Murchison; the latter, of the late Mr William Nicol of Edinburgh. Chiefly from researches in the Lias of Eathie, near Cromarty, and in the Oolites of Sutherland and the Hebrides, I have been enabled to increase the list from two to rather more than fifty species,—not a great number certainly, regarded as the sole representatives of a flora; and yet it may be deemed comparatively not a very small one by such as may remember, that in 1837, when Dr Buckland published the second edition of his "Bridgewater Treatise," Adolphe Brogniart had enumerated only seventy species of plants as occurring in all the Secondary formations of Europe, from the Chalk to the Trias inclusive. In a paper such as the present I can of course do little more than just indicate a few of the more striking features of this Scottish flora of the middle Secondary ages. Like that of the period of the true Coal, it had its numerous coniferous trees. As shown by the fossil woods of Helmsdale and Eigg, old Oolitic Scotland, like the Scotland of three centuries ago, must have had its mighty forests of pine;* and in one respect these trees seem to have more nearly resembled

---

* Trees must have been very abundant in what is now Scotland in these Secondary ages. Trunks of the common Scotch fir are of scarce more frequent occurrence in our mosses than the trunks of somewhat resembling trees among the shales of the Lower Oolite of Helmsdale. On examining in that neighbourhood, about ten years since, a huge heap of materials which had been collected along the sea-shore for burning into lime in a temporary kiln, I found that more than three fourths of the whole consisted of fragments of coniferous wood washed out of the shale beds by the surf, and the remainder of a massive Isastrea. And only two years ago, after many kilnfuls had been gathered and burnt, his Grace the Duke of Argyll found that fossil-wood could still be collected by cart-loads along the shore of Helmsdale. The same woods also occur at Port Gower, Kintradwell, Shandwick, and Eathie. In the island of Eigg, too, in

those of the recent pine-forests of our country than the trees of the coniferous forests of the remote Carboniferous era. For while we scarce ever find a cone associated with the coniferous woods of the Coal Measures,—Lindley and Hutton never saw but one from all the English coal-fields, and Mr Alexander Bryson of Edinburgh, only one from all the coal-fields of Scotland,—tree-cones of at least four different species, more probably of five, are not rare in our Scottish deposits of the Lias and Oolite. It seems not improbable that in the Carboniferous genera Pinites, Pitus, and Anabathra, which approach but remotely to aught that now exists, the place of the ligneous scaly cone may have been taken, as in the junipers and the yews, by a perishable berry; while the Pines and Araucarians of the Oolite were, like their cogeners in recent times, in reality coniferous, *i.e.* cone-bearing trees. It is another characteristic of these Secondary conifers, that while the woods of the Palæozoic periods exhibit often, like those of the tropics, none of the dense concentric lines of annual growth which mark the reign of winter, these annual lines are scarce less strongly impressed on the Oolitic woods than on those of Norway or of our own country in the present day. In some of the fossil-trees these yearly rings are of great breadth; they seem to have sprung up in the rich soil of sheltered hollows and plains, and to have increased in diameter from half an inch to three quarters of an inch yearly; while in other trees of the same species the yearly zones of growth are singularly narrow,—in some instances little more than half a line in thickness. Rooted on some exposed hill-side, in a shallow and meagre soil, they increased their diameter during the twelvemonth little more than a line in the severer seasons, and

an Oolite deposit, locked up in trap, and whose stratigraphical relations cannot in consequence be exactly traced, great fragments of *Pinites Eiggensis* are so abundant, that, armed with a mattock, I have dug out of the rock in a few minutes, specimens enough to supply a dozen of museums. In short, judging from its fossiliferous remains, it seems not improbable that old Oolitic Scotland was as densely covered with coniferous trees as the Scotland of Roman times, when the great Caledonian forest stretched northwards from the wall of Antoninus to the farthest Thule.

little more than an eighth part of an inch even when the seasons were most favourable. Further, whether the rings be large or small, we ordinarily find them occurring in the same specimens in groupes of larger and smaller. In one of my Helmsdale specimens, indicative generally of rapid growth, there are four contiguous annual rings, which measure in all an inch and two twelfths across, while the four contiguous rings immediately beside them measure only half an inch. "If at the present day," says a distinguished fossil-botanist, "a warm and moist summer produces a broader annual layer than a cold and dry one, and if fossil plants exhibit such appearances as we refer in recent plants to a diversity of summers, then it is reasonable to suppose that a similar diversity formerly prevailed." The same reasoning is of course as applicable to *groupes* of annual layers as to *single* annual layers; and may we not venture to infer from the almost invariable occurrence of such groupes in the woods of this ancient system, that that ill-understood law of the weather which gives us in irregular succession groupes of colder and warmer seasons, and whose operation, as Bacon tells us, was first remarked in the provinces of the Netherlands, was as certainly in existence during the ages of the Oolite as at the present time?

Twigs which exhibit the foliage of these ancient conifers seem to be less rare in our Scotch deposits than in those of England of the same age. My collection contains fossil sprigs, with the slim needle-like leaves attached, of what seem to be from six to seven different species; and it is worthy of notice, that they resemble in the group rather the coniferæ of the southern than those of the northern hemisphere. One sprig in my collection seems scarcely distinguishable from that of the recent *Altinga excelsa*; another, from that of the recent *Altinga Cunninghami*. Lindley and Hutton figure in their fossil flora a minute branch of *Dacrydium cupressinum*, in order to show how nearly the twigs of a large tree, from fifty to a hundred feet high, may resemble some of the "fossils referrible to Lycopodiaceæ." More than one of the Oolitic twigs in my collection are of a resembling character, and may have belonged either to cone-bearing trees or to clubmosses. Respecting, however, the real character of at least one of the specimens,—a

Fig. 130.

CONIFERS?

minute branch from the Lias of Eathie, with the leaflets attached,—there can be no mistake. The thicker part of the stem is in such a state of keeping, that it presents to the microscope, in a sliced preparation, the internal structure, and exhibits, as in recent coniferous twigs of a year's growth, a central pith, a single ring of reticulated tissue arranged in lines that radiate outwards, and a thin layer of enveloping bark. Nothing, then, can be more certain than that this ancient twig, which must be accepted as

Fig. 131.

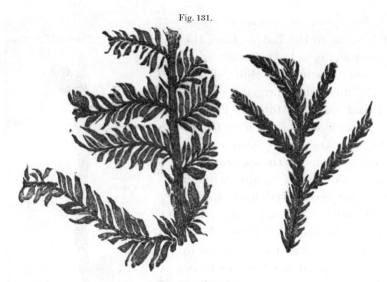

CONIFER TWIGS.

representative of the foliage of whole forests of the Secondary ages in Scotland, formed part of a conifer of the Lias; and the foliage of several of the other twigs, its contemporaries, though I have failed to demonstrate their true character in the same way, bear a scarce less coniferous aspect. The cones of the period, from the circumstance that they are locked up in a hard limestone that clings closely around their scales, and from the further circumstance that the semi-calcareous lignite into which they are resolved is softer and less tenacious than the enclosing matrix, present, when laid open, not their outer surfaces, but mere sections of their interior; and give, in consequence, save in their general proportions and outline, but few specific marks by which to distinguish them. We see, however, in some cases in these sections what would be otherwise unseen,—the flat naked seeds lying embedded in their hollow receptacles between the scales, and in as perfect a state of keeping as the seeds of recent pines that had ripened only a twelvemonth ago. Had not the vitality of seeds its limits in time, like life of all other kinds, one might commit these perfect fossil germs to the soil, in the hope of seeing the old extinct forests called, through their agency, a second time into existence.

Of three apparent species of cones which occur in the Eathie Lias, the smallest seems to have resembled in size and appearance that of the Scotch fir; the largest, which consisted from bottom to top, as seen in section, of from nine to ten scales, appears to have been more in the proportions of the oblong oval cones of the spruce family; while a cone of intermediate length, but of considerably greater breadth, assumed the rounded form of the cones of the cedar. I have found in the same deposit what seems to be the sprig of a conifer, with four apparently embryo cones attached to it in the alternate order. These

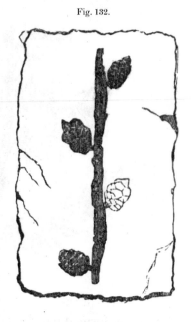

Fig. 132.

are rather more sessile than the young cones of the larch; but the aspect of the whole is that of a larch twig in early summer, when the minute and tender cones, possessed of all the beauty of flowers, first appear along its sides.

Among conifers of the Pine and Araucarian type we mark the first appearance in this System, in at least Scotland, of the genus Thuja. One of the Helmsdale plants of this genus closely resembles the common Arbor Vitæ (*Thuja occidentalis*) of our gardens and shrubberies. It exhibits the same numerous slim, thick-clustered branchlets, covered over by the same minute, sessile, scale-like leaves; and so entirely reminds one of the recent Thuja, that it seems difficult to conceive of it as the member of a flora so ancient as that of the Oolite. But not a few of the Oolitic plants in Scotland bear this modern aspect. The great development of its Cycadaceæ—an order unknown in our Coal Measures,—also forms a prominent feature of the Oolitic flora. One of the first known genera of this curious order,—the genus Pterophyllum,—appears in the Trias. It distinctively marks the commencement of the Secondary flora, and intimates that the once great Palæozoic flora,

Fig. 133.

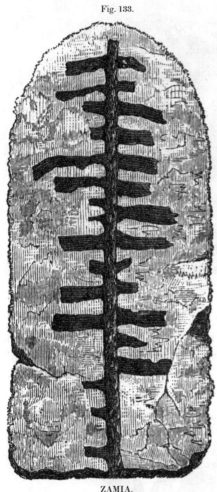

ZAMIA.

after gradually waning throughout the Permian ages, and becoming extinct at their close, had been succeeded by a vegetation altogether new. At least one of the Helmsdale forms of this family is identical with a Yorkshire species already named and figured,—*Zamia pectinata*: a well-marked Zamia which occurs in the Lias of Eathie appears to be new. Its pinnate leaves were furnished with a strong woody midrib, so well preserved in the rock, that it yields its internal structure to the microscope. The ribbon-like pinnæ or leaflets were rectilinear, retaining their full breadth until they united to the stem at right angles, but set somewhat awry; and, like several of the recent Zamiæ, they were striped longitudinally with cord-like lines. (Fig. 133.) Even the mode of decay of this Zamia, as shown by the abrupt termination of its leaflets, exactly resembled that of its existing cogeners. (Fig. 134.) The withered points of the pinnæ of recent Zamiæ drop off as if clipped across with a pair of scissors; and in fossil fronds of this Zamia of the Lias we find exactly the same clipped-like appearance. (Fig. 135.) Another Scotch Zamia (fig. 136), which

Fig. 134.

ZAMIA.

occurs in the Lower Oolite of Helmsdale, resembles the Eathie one
in the breadth of its leaflets, but they are not wholly so rectilinear,
diminishing slightly towards their base of attachment; they are

Fig. 135.

Fig. 136.

ranged, too, along the stem or midrib, not at a right angle, but at an acute one; the line of attachment is not set awry, but on the general plane of the leaf; and the midrib itself is considerably less massive and round. A third species from the same locality bears a general resemblance to the latter; but the leaflets are narrower at the base, and, as the print indicates (fig. 136), so differently attached to the stem, that from the pressure in the rock most of them have become detached; while yet a fourth species (fig. 137) very closely resembles a Zamia of the Scarborough Oolite,—*Z. lanceolata*. The leaflets, however, contract much more suddenly from their greatest breadth than those of *lanceolata*, into a pseudo-footstalk; and the contraction takes place not almost equally on both sides, as in that species, but almost exclusively on the upper side. And so, provisionally at least, this Helmsdale Zamia may be regarded as specifically new.

With the leaves of the Eathie Zamia we find, in this northern outlier of the Lias, cones of a peculiar form, which, like the leaves themselves, are still unfigured and undescribed, and some of which

Fig. 137.

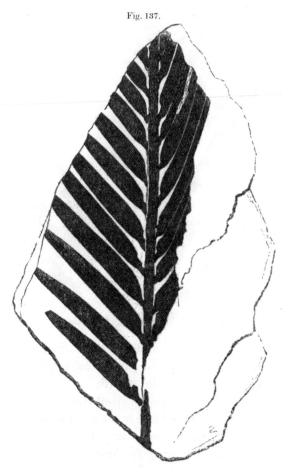

could scarce have belonged to any coniferous tree. In one of these (fig. 138), the ligneous bracts or scales, narrow and long, and gradually tapering till they assume nearly the awl-shaped form, cluster out thick from the base and middle portions of the cone, and, like the involucral appendages of the hazel-nut, or the sepals of the yet unfolded rose-bud, sweep gracefully upwards to the top, where they present at their margins minute denticulations. In another species the bracts are broader, thinner, and more leaf-like: they rise, too, more from the base of the cone, and less from its middle portions; so that the whole must have resembled an

Fig. 138.

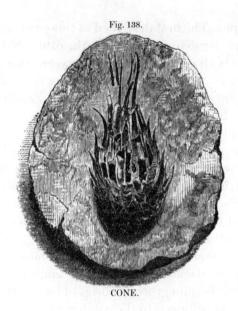

CONE.

enormous bud, with strong woody scales, some of which extended

Fig. 139.

from base to apex. The first described of these two species seems to have been more decidedly a *cone* than the other; but it is probable that they were both connecting links between such leathern seed-bearing flowers as we find developed in *Cycas revoluta,* and such seed-bearing cones as we find exemplified in *Zamia pungens.* The bud-like cone, however, does not seem to have been that of a Cycadaceous plant, as it occupied evidently not a terminal position on the plant that bore it, like the cones of Zamia or the flowers of Cycas, but a lateral one, like the lateral flowers of some of the Cactus tribe. Another class of vegetable forms, of occasional occurrence in the Helmsdale beds, seems intermediate between the Cycadaceæ and the ferns; at least, so near is the approach to the ordinary fern outline, while retaining the stiff ligneous character of Zamia, that it is scarce less difficult to determine to which of the two orders of plants such organisms belonged, than to decide whether some of the slim graceful sprigs of foliage that occur in the rocks beside them belonged to the conifers or the club-mosses. And I am informed by Sir Charles Lyell, that (as some of the existing conifers bear a foliage scarce distinguishable from that of Lycopodiaceæ), so a recently dis-covered Zamia is furnished with fronds that scarce differ from those of a fern. Even *Zamia pectinata* may, as Sternberg remarks, have been a fern. Lindley and Hutton place it merely provisionally among the Cycadaceæ, in deference to the judgment of Adolphe Brogniart, and point out its resemblance to *Polypodium pectinatum*; and a small Helmsdale frond which I have placed beside it bears the impress of a character scarce less equivocal. The flora of the Oolite was peculiarly a flora of intermediate forms.

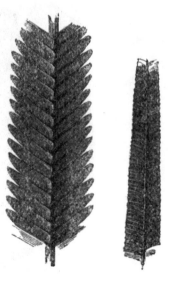

Fig. 140.

We recognise another char-acteristic of our Oolitic flora in its simple-leaved fronds, in some of the species not a little resembling those of the recent Scolopendrium, or Hart's-Tongue fern,—a form regarded by Adolphe Brogniart as peculiarly characteristic of his third period of vegetation. These simple ferns are, in the

Fig. 141.

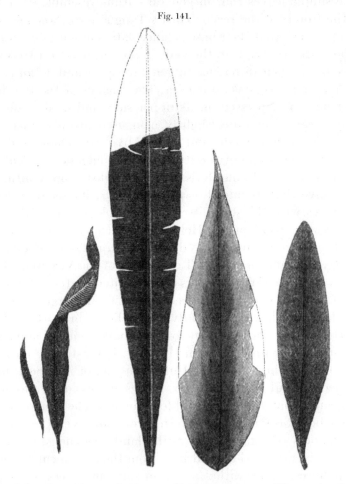

Helmsdale deposits, of three distinct types. There is first a lanceolate leaf, from two and a half to three inches in length, of not unfrequent occurrence, which may have formed, however, only one of the four leaflets, united by their pseudo-footstalks, which compose the frond of Glossopteris,—a distinctive Oolitic genus.

There is next a simple ovate lanceolate leaf, from four to five and a half inches in length, which in form and venation, and all save its *thrice* greater size, not a little resembles the leaflets of a Coal Measure neuropteris,—*N. acuminata*. And, in the third place, there are the simple leaves that in general outline resemble, as I have said, the fronds of the recent Hart's-Tongue fern (*Scolopendrium vulgare*), except that their base is lanceolate, not cordate. Of these last there are two kinds in the beds, representative of two several species, or, as their difference in general aspect and detail is very great, mayhap two several genera. The smaller of the two has a slender midrib, depressed on its upper side, and flanked on each side by a row of minute, slightly elongated protuberances, but elevated on the under side, and flanked by rows of small but well-marked grooves, that curve outwards to the edges of the leaf. The larger resemble a Tæniopteris of the English and Continental Oolites, save that its midrib is more massive, its venation less at right angles with the stem, its base more elongated, and its size much greater. Some of the Helmsdale specimens are of gigantic proportions. From, however, a description and figure of a plant of evidently the same genus,—a Tæniopteris of the Virginian Oolite, given by Professor W. B. Rogers of the United States,—I find that some of the American fronds are larger still. My largest leaf from Helmsdale must have been nearly five inches in breadth; and if its proportions were those of some of the smaller ones of apparently the same species from the same locality, it must have measured about thirty inches in length. But fragments of American leaves have been found more than six inches in breadth, and whose length cannot have fallen short of forty inches. The Tæniopteris, as its name bears, is regarded as a fern. From, however, the leathern-like thickness of some of the Sutherland specimens,—from the great massiveness of their midrib,—from the rectilinear simplicity of their fibres,—and, withal, from, in some instances, their great size,—I am much disposed to believe that in our Scotch, mayhap also in the American species, it may have been the frond of some simple-leaved Cycas or Zamia. But the point is one which it must be left for the future satisfactorily to settle; though provisionally I may be permitted to regard these leaves as belonging to some

Fig. 142.

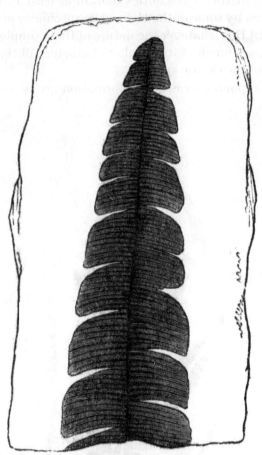

Cycadaceous plant, whose fronds, in their venation and form, resembled the simple fronds of Scolopendrium, just as the leaves of some of its congeners resembled the fronds of the pinnate ferns.

I have already referred to the close resemblance which certain Cycadaceous genera bear to certain of the fern family. In at least two species of Pterophyllum,—*P. comptum* and *P. minus*,—the divisions of the leaflets seem little else than accidental rents in a simple frond; in *P. Nelsoni* they are apparently *nothing* more; and similar divisions, evidently, however, the effect of accident, and less rounded at their extremities than in at least *P. comptum*, we find exhibited by some of the Helmsdale specimens of Tæniopteris. (See fig. 142.) But whatever the nature of these simple fronds, they seem to impart much of its peculiar character, all the world over, to the flora of the Oolitic ages.

The compound ferns of the formation are numerous, and at

Fig. 143.

PECOPTERIS OBTUSIFOLIA.

least proportionally a considerable part of them seem identical in species with those of the Oolite of England. (See fig. 143.) Among these there occur *Pecopteris Whitbiensis, Pecopteris obtusifolia, Pecopteris insignis,*—all well-marked English species; with several others. It has, besides, its apparent ferns, that seem to be new—(fig. 144)—that are at least not figured in any of the fossil floras to which I have access,—(fig. 145),—such as a well-defined Pachypteris, with leaflets broader and rounder than the typical *P. lanceolata*, and a much stouter midrib; a minute Sphenopteris too, and what seems to be a Phlebopteris, somewhat resembling *P.*

Fig. 144.

Fig. 145.

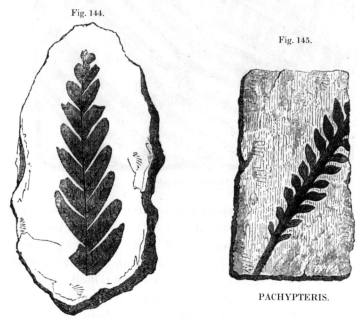

PACHYPTERIS.

propinqua, but greatly more massive in its general proportions. The equisetaceæ we find represented in the Brora deposits by *Equisetum columnare,*—a plant the broken remains of which occur in great abundance, and which, as was remarked by our President many years ago, in his paper on the Sutherlandshire Oolite, must have entered largely into the composition of the bed of lignite known as the Brora Coal. We find associated with it what seems to be the last of the Calamites,—*Calamites arenaceus,*—a name, however, which seems to have been bestowed both on this Oolitic plant and a resembling Carboniferous species. The deposit has also its Lycopodites, though, from their resemblance in foliage to the

Fig. 146.

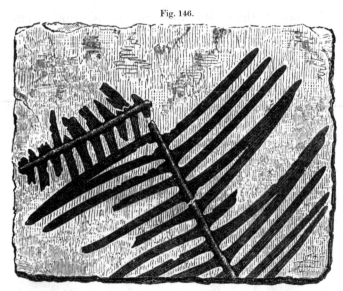

PHLEBOPTERIS.

conifers, there exists that difficulty in drawing the line between them to which I have already adverted. One of these, however, so exactly resembles a lycopodite of both the Virginian and Yorkshire Oolite,—*L. uncifolius,*—that I cannot avoid regarding it as specifically identical; and it seems more than doubtful whether the stem which I have placed among the conifers is not a lycopodite also. It exhibits not only the general outline of the true club-moss, but, like the fossil club-mosses too, it wants that degree of ligniferous body in the rock which the coniferous fossils almost always possess. Yet another of the organisms of the deposit seems to have been either a lycopodite or a fern. Its leaflets are exceedingly minute, and set alternately on a stem slender as a hair,—circumstances in which it resembles some of the tiny lycopodites of the tropics, such as *Lycopodium apodium.* I must mention, however, that the larger plant of the same beds which I have placed beside it, and which resembles it so closely that my engraver finds it difficult to indicate any other difference between them than that of size, appears to be a true fern, not a lycopodium. To yet another vegetable organism of the system,—an organism

Fig. 147.

which must be regarded, if I do not mistake its character, as at once very interesting and extraordinary, occurring as it does so low in the scale, and bearing an antiquity so high,—I shall advert, after a preliminary remark on a general characteristic of the flora to which it belongs, but to which it seems to furnish a striking exception.

From the disappearance of many of those anomalous types of the Coal Measures which so puzzle the botanist, and the extensive introduction of types that still exist, we can better conceive of the general features and relations of the flora of the Oolite than of those of the earlier floras. And yet the general result at which we arrive may be found not without its bearing on the older vegetations also. Throughout almost all the families of this Oolitic flora there seems to have run a curious bond of relationship, which, like those ties which bound together some of the old clans of our country, united them, high and low, into one great sept, and conferred upon them a certain wonderful unity of character and appearance. Let us assume the ferns as our central group. Though less abundant than in the earlier creation of the Carboniferous system, they seem to have occupied, judging from their remains, very considerable space in the Oolitic vegetation; and with the ferns there were associated in great abundance the two prevailing families of the Pterides,—Equiseta and Lycopodia,—plants which, in most of our modern treatises on the ferns proper, take their place as the fern allies. (See fig. 148.) Let us place these along two of the sides of a pentagon,—the Lycopodia on the right side of the ferns, the Equiseta on the left; farther, let us occupy the two remaining sides of the figure by the Coniferæ and the Cycadaceæ,—placing the Coniferæ on the side next the Lycopodia, and the Cycadaceæ, as the last added key-stone of the erection, between these and the

Fig. 148.

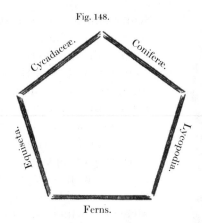

Ferns.

Equiseta. And now, let us consider how very curious the links are which give a wonderful unity to the whole. We still find great difficulty in distinguishing between the foliage of some of even the existing club-mosses and the Conifers; and the ancient Lepidodendra are very generally recognised as of a type intermediate between the two. Similar intermediate types, exemplified by extinct families, united the Conifers and the ferns. The analogy of *Kirchneria* with the *Thinnfeldia*, says Dr Braun, is very remarkable, notwithstanding that the former is a fern, and that the latter is ranked among Conifers. The points of resemblance borne by the Conifers to the huge Equiseta of the Oolitic period seem to have been equally striking. The pores which traverse longitudinally the channelled grooves by which the stems of our recent Equiseta are so delicately fluted, are said considerably more to resemble the discs of pines and araucarians than ordinary stomata. Mr Francis does not hesitate to say, in his work on British Ferns, that the relation of this special family to the Coniferæ is so strong, both in external and internal structure, that it is not without some hesitation he places them among the fern allies; and it has been ascertained by Mr Dawes, in his researches regarding the calamite, that in its internal structure this apparent representative of Equiseta in the earlier ages of the world united "a network of quadrangular tissue similar to that of Coniferæ to other quadrangular cells arranged in perpendicular

Fig. 149.

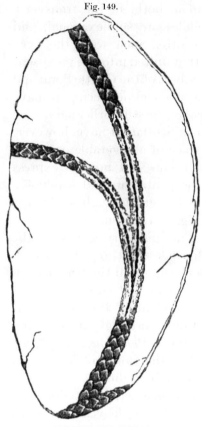

IMBRICATED STEM.
(*Helmsdale.*)

series," like the cells of plants of a humbler order. The relations of
the Cycadacean order to ferns on the one hand, and to the
Coniferæ on the other, are equally well marked. As in the ferns, the
venation of its fronds is circinate, or scroll-like,—they have in
several respects a resembling structure,—in at least one recent
species they have a nearly identical form; and fronds of this fern-
like type seem to have been comparatively common during the
times of the Oolite. On the other hand, the Cycadaceæ manifest
close relations to the Conifers. Both have their seeds originally
naked; both are cone-bearing; both possess discs on the sides of

Fig. 150.

their cellules; and in both, in the transverse section, these cellules are subhexagonal, and radiate from a centre. Such were the very curious relations that united into one great sept the prevailing members of the Oolitic flora; and similar bonds of connection seem to have existed in the floras of the still earlier ages.

In the Oolite of Scotland I have, however, at length found trace of a vegetable organism that *seems* to have lain, if I may so express myself, outside the pentagon, and was not a member of any of the great families which it comprised. (See fig. 151.) I succeeded about four years ago in disinterring from the limestone of Helmsdale what *appears* to be a true dicotyledonous leaf, with the fragment of another leaf, which I at first supposed might have belonged to a plant of the same great class, but which I now find might have been a portion of a fern. When *Phlebopteris Phillipsii* was first detected in the Oolite of Yorkshire, Lindley and Hutton, regarding it as dicoty-ledonous, originated their term Dictyophillum as a general one for all such leaves. But it has since been assigned to a greatly lower order,—the ferns; and Sir Charles Lyell has kindly shown me that an exotic fern of the present day exhibits exactly such a reticulated style of venation as my Helmsdale fragment. (See fig. 152.) The other leaf, however, though also fragmentary, and but indifferently

(*Helmsdale.*)

preserved, seems to be decidedly marked by the dicotyledonous character; and so I continue to regard it, provisionally at least, as one of the first precursors in Scotland of our great forest-trees, and of so many of our flowering and fruit-bearing plants, and as apparently occupying the same relative place in advance of its contemporaries as that occupied by the conifer of the Old Red

Fig. 151.

Sandstone in advance of the ferns and Lycopodiaceæ with which I found it associated. In the arrangement of its larger veins the better preserved Oolitic leaf somewhat resembles that of the buckthorn; but its state of keeping is such that it has failed to leave its exterior outline in the stone.

One or two general remarks, in conclusion, on the Oolite flora of Scotland may be permitted me by the Association. In its aspect as a whole it greatly resembles the Oolite flora of Virginia, though separated in space from the locality in which the latter occurs by a distance of nearly four thousand miles. There are several species of plants common to both, such as *Equisetum columnare, Calamites arenaceus, Pecopteris Whitbiensis, Lycopodites uncifolius,* and apparently *Tæniopteris magnifolia*; both, too, manifest the great abundance in which they were developed of old by the beds of coal into which their remains have been converted. The coal of the Virginia Oolite has been profitably wrought for many years: it is stated by Sir Charles Lyell, who carefully examined the deposit, and has given us the results of his observations in his second series of Travels in the United States, that the annual quantity taken

Fig. 152.

from the Oolitic pits by Philadelphia alone amounted to ten thousand tons; and though, on the other hand, the Sutherlandshire deposit has never been very profitably wrought, it has been at least wrought more extensively than any other in the British Oolite. The seam of Brora, varying from three feet three to three feet eight inches in thickness, furnished, says Sir Roderick Murchison, between the years 1814 and 1826, no less than seventy thousand tons of coal. Such is its extent, too, that nearly thirty miles from the pit's mouth (in Ross-shire under the Northern Sutor) I have found it still existing, though in diminished proportions, as a decided coal-seam, which it must have taken no small amount of vegetable matter to form. And almost on the other side of the world, nearly five thousand miles from the Sutherland beds, and more than eight thousand miles from the Carolina ones, the same Oolitic flora again appears, associated with beds of coal. At Nagpur in Central India the Oolitic Sandstones abound in simple fronded ferns, such as Tæniopteris and Glossopteris, and has its Zamites, its coniferous leaves, and its equisetaceæ.

Compared with existing floras, that of our Scottish Oolite seems to have most nearly resembled the flora of New Zealand,—a flora remarkable for the great abundance of its ferns, and its vast forests of coniferous trees, that retain at all seasons their coverings of acicular spiky leaves. It is to this flora that *Dacrydium cupressinum*,—so like a club-moss in its foliage,—belongs; and *Podocarpus ferrugineus*,—a tree which more closely resembles in its foliage the Eathie conifer, save that its spiky leaves are somewhat narrower and longer than any other with which I am acquainted. About two thirds of the plants which cover the plains, or rise on the hill-sides of that country, are cryptogamic, consisting mainly of ferns and their allies; and it is a curious circumstance,—which was, however, not without precedent in the merely physical conditions of the Oolitic flora of Scotland,—that so shallow is the soil even where its greatest forests have sprung up, and so immediately does the rock lie below, that the central axes of the trees do not elongate downwards into a tap, but throw out horizontally on every side a thick network of roots, which rises so high over the surface as to render walking through the woods a difficult and very fatiguing exercise. The flora of the Oolite, like that of New Zealand, seems to have been in large part cryptogamic, consisting of ferns and the allied horsetail and club-moss families. Its forests seem to have contained only cone-bearing trees; at least among the many thousand specimens of its fossil woods which have been examined, no tissue of the true dicotyledonous character has yet been found; and, with the

exception of the leaves just described, all those yet found in the
System which could have belonged to true trees are of the acicular
form common to the Coniferæ, and show in their dense ligneous
structure that they were persistent, not deciduous. Nor is there
evidence wanting that many of the Coniferæ of the period grew in
so shallow a soil, that their tap-roots were flattened and bent
backwards, and they were left to derive their sole support, like the
trees of the New Zealand forests, from such of their roots as shot
out horizontally. We even know the nature of the rock upon which
they rested. As shown by fragments still locked up among the
interstices of their petrified roots, it was an Old Red flagstone
similar to that of Caithness in the neighbourhood of Wick and
Thurso, and containing the same fossil remains. In the water-
rolled pebbles of the Conglomerate of Helmsdale and Port
Gower,—pebbles encrusted by Oolitic corals, and enclosed in a
calcareous paste, containing Oolitic belemnites and astreæ,—I
have found the well-marked fishes and fucoids of the Old Red
Sandstone. As shown by the appearance of the rounded masses in
which these lay, they must have presented as ancient an
appearance in the times of the Lower Oolite as they do now; and
the glimpse which they lent of so remote an antiquity, through the
medium of an antiquity which, save for the comparison which they
furnished the means of instituting, might be well deemed
superlatively remote, I have felt singularly awe-inspiring and
impressive. Macaulay anticipates a time when the traveller from
some distant land shall take his stand on a broken arch of London
Bridge to survey the ruins of St Paul's. In disinterring from amid
the antique remains of the Oolite the immensely more antique
remains of the Old Red Sandstone, I have felt as such a traveller
would feel if, on setting himself to dig among the scattered heaps
for memorials of the ruined city, he had fallen on what had been
once the Assyrian Gallery of the British Museum, and had found
mingling with the antiquities of perished London the greatly older
and more venerable antiquities of Nineveh or of Babylon. The land
of the Oolite in this northern locality must have been covered by a
soil which,—except that, from a lack of the boulder clays, it must
have been poorer and shallower,—must have not a little resembled

that of the lower plains of Cromarty, Caithness, and Eastern Ross.
And on this Palæozoic platform, long exposed, as the Oolitic
Conglomerates abundantly testify, to denuding and disintegrating
agencies,—a platform beaten by the surf where it descended to the
sea level, and washed in the interior by rivers, with here a tall hill
or abrupt precipice, and there a flat plain or sluggish
morass,—there grew vast forests of cone-bearing trees, tangled
thickets of gigantic equisetaceæ, numerous forms of Cycas and
Zamia, and wide rolling seas of fern, amid whose open spaces club-
mosses of extinct tribes sent forth their long creeping stems, spiky
and dry, and thickly mottled with pseudospore-bearing catkins.

The curtain drops over this ancient flora of the Oolite in
Scotland; and when, long after, there is a corner of the thick
enveloping screen withdrawn, and we catch a partial glimpse of
one of the old Tertiary forests of our country, all is new. Trees of
the high dicotyledonous class, allied to the plane and the
buckthorn, prevail in the landscape, intermingled, however, with
dingy funereal yews; and the ferns and equisetæ that rise in the
darker openings of the wood approach to the existing type. And
yet, though *eons* of the past eternity have elapsed since we looked
out upon Cycas and Zamia, and the last of the Calamites, the time
is still early, and long ages must lapse ere man shall arise out of the
dust, to keep and to dress fields waving with the productions of yet
another and different flora, and to busy himself with all the labour
which he taketh under the sun. Our country, in this Tertiary time,
has still its great outbursts of molten matter, that bury in fiery
deluges, many feet in depth, and many square miles in extent, the
debris of wide tracts of woodland and marsh; and the basaltic
columns still form in its great lava-bed; and ever and anon as the
volcanic agencies awake, clouds of ashes darken the heavens, and
cover up the landscape as if with the accumulated drifts of a
protracted snow-storm. Who shall declare what, throughout these
long ages, the history of creation has been? We see at wide
intervals the mere fragments of successive floras; but know not
how what seem the blank interspaces were filled, or how, as
extinction overtook in succession one tribe of existences after
another, and species, like individuals, yielded to the great law of

death, yet other species were brought to the birth and ushered upon the scene, and the chain of being was maintained unbroken. We see only detached bits of that green web which has covered our earth ever since the dry land first appeared; but the web itself seems to have been continuous throughout all time; though ever, as breadth after breadth issued from the creative loom, the pattern has altered, and the sculpturesque and graceful forms that illustrated its first beginnings and its middle spaces have yielded to flowers of richer colour and blow, and fruits of fairer shade and outline; and for gigantic club-mosses stretching forth their hirsute arms, goodly trees of the Lord have expanded their great boughs; and for the barren fern and the calamite, clustering in thickets beside the waters, or spreading on flowerless hill-slopes, luxuriant orchards have yielded their ruddy flush, and rich harvests their golden gleam.

THE END.